AFGANTSY

Also by Rodric Braithwaite

Across the Moscow River (2002)
Moscow 1941 (2006)

AFGANTSY

THE RUSSIANS IN AFGHANISTAN 1979–89

RODRIC BRAITHWAITE

P

PROFILE BOOKS

First published in Great Britain in 2011 by
Profile Books Ltd
3a Exmouth House
Pine Street
Exmouth Market
London ECIR OJH
www.profilebooks.com

1 3 5 7 9 10 8 6 4 2

Typeset in Garamond by MacGuru Ltd
info@macguru.org.uk

Printed and bound in Great Britain by
Clays, Bungay, Suffolk

A CIP catalogue record for this book is available from the British Library.

ISBN 978 1 84668 054 0
eISBN 978 1 84765 327 7

The paper this book is printed on is certified by the © 1996 Forest Stewardship Council A.C. (FSC). It is ancient-forest friendly. The printer holds FSC chain of custody SGS-COC-2061.

FSC
Mixed Sources
Product group from well-managed
forests and other controlled sources
Cert no. SGS-COC-2061
www.fsc.org
© 1996 Forest Stewardship Council

As she lay dying Jill said to me, with all her customary firmness, that I was not even to think of following her until I had finished this book. It is dedicated to her courageous and generous spirit.

CONTENTS

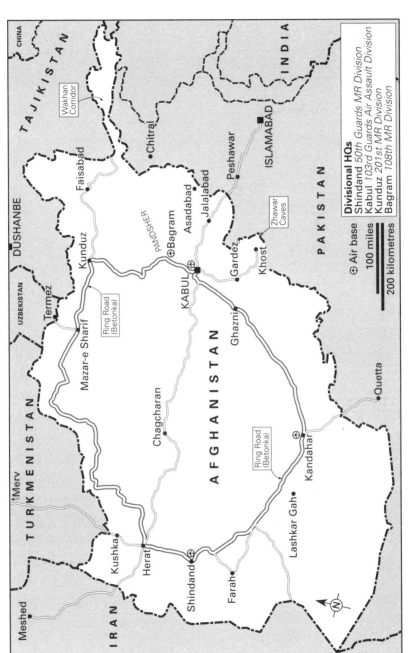

Map 1: Afghanistan, 1979–89

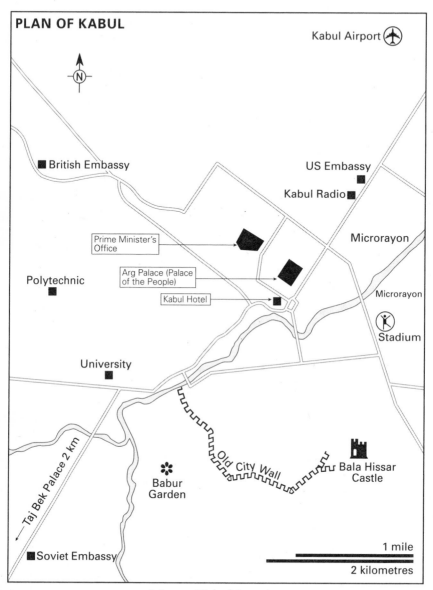

Map 2: Kabul in 1980

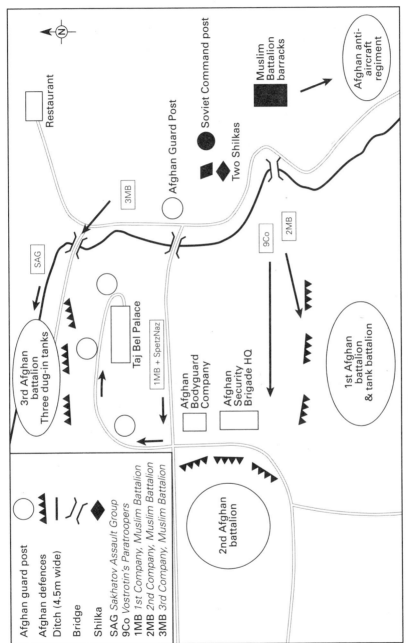

N

Restaurant

3rd Afghan battalion
Three dug-in tanks

SAG

3MB

Afghan Guard Post

Soviet Command post

Two Shilkas

Muslim Battalion barracks

Afghan anti-aircraft regiment

Taj Bel Palace

1MB + SpetzNaz

Afghan Bodyguard Company

Afghan Security Brigade HQ

9Co

2MB

1st Afghan battalion & tank battalion

2nd Afghan battalion

Afghan guard post

Afghan defences

Ditch (4.5m wide)

Bridge

Shilka

SAG *Sakhatov Assault Group*
9Co *Vostrotin's Paratroopers*
1MB *1st Company, Muslim Battalion*
2MB *2nd Company, Muslim Battalion*
3MB *3rd Company, Muslim Battalion*

Map 3: Storming the Palace

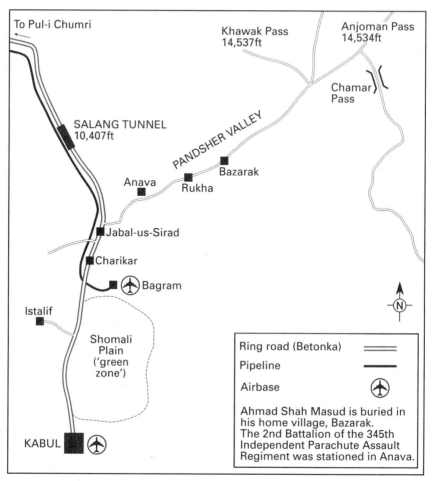

Map 4: The Pandsher Valley

AUTHOR'S NOTE

Afganets (plural: *Afgantsy*): An inhabitant of Afghanistan; a hot sand-laden south-west wind; a veteran of the Soviet war.

It was the Soviet government which sent the soldiers into Afghanistan in 1979, but it was following in the tradition of the Russian governments which preceded it. Policy was directed from the Russian capital, Moscow. The majority of those who fought in Afghanistan were Russians. I have tried to use the words 'Soviet' and 'Russian' in a way that makes these subtle distinctions reasonably plain, and to ensure that the non-Russians in Afghanistan are given their historical due. But I have doubtless been inconsistent from time to time.

I have not adopted any of the standard scholarly systems of transliteration. My system attempts to be simple, phonetic, and as easy as may be for the non-Russian speaker (Russian speakers will be able to work out the original spelling for themselves). The sounds should be spoken as written. Some sounds which do not exist in English are represented thus:

'kh', as in Khrushchev, sounds like 'ch' in 'loch';
'zh', as in Zhukov, sounds like 'ge' in 'rouge'.

An 'e' at the beginning of a Russian word is usually pronounced 'ye'. Thus 'Yeltsin' not 'Eltsin'; but 'Mount Elbruz' not 'Mount Yelbruz' (because in Russian the 'E' in this case is a different letter).

I have used the English versions of names where these are more familiar: 'Moscow' not 'Moskva'; 'Peter' not 'Pyotr'; 'Alexander' not 'Aleksandr'. I have preferred to end Russian surnames in '-ski'. I prefer, inconsistently, 'Mikhail' to 'Michael'.

I have used the names of cities, streets, and other places as they were known at the time of the action.

For Afghan names I have used whatever seemed to be both common usage in English and simple to pronounce.

The index contains short descriptions of people, and of foreign and technical words, in the hope that this will be of help to the reader.

AFGANTSY

PROLOGUE

The young men went off to the war with enthusiasm – because they had never been in a battle.

Thucydides[1]

Of course, the private soldier's field of vision is much more limited than that of his general. On the other hand, it is of vital importance to the latter to gloss over his mistakes, and draw attention only to those things which will add to his reputation. The private soldier has no such feeling. It is only to the officers of high rank engaged that a battle can bring glory and renown. To the army of common soldiers, who do the actual fighting, and risk mutilation and death, there is no reward except the consciousness of duty bravely performed.

Private Warren Olney, who fought in the Union army at the
Battle of Shiloh, 1862[2]

By no means everything that happened to me during the two years I was in Afghanistan is set down here. Some things I did not want to describe. We Afgantsy talk among ourselves about things which those who were not in Afghanistan may not understand, or will understand in the wrong way.

Vitali Krivenko[3]

The explosion of violence which erupted in Herat in March 1979 was beyond anything that had happened since the bloody Communist coup a year earlier. Resistance to the Communists was already spreading throughout the country. But this was a full-scale revolt in a provincial capital, one of Afghanistan's most important cities, an ancient centre of Islamic learning, music, art, and poetry. Power fell entirely into the hand of the insurgents, and it was a week before Afghan government forces finally regained control after the spilling of much blood.

The Communists had promised much: 'Our aim was no less than to give an example to all the backward countries of the world of how to jump from feudalism straight to a prosperous, just society … Our choice was not between doing things democratically or not. Unless we did them, nobody else would … [Our] very first proclamation declared that food and shelter are the basic needs and rights of a human being … Our programme was clear: land to the peasants, food for the hungry, free education for all. We knew that the mullahs in the villages would scheme against us, so we issued our decrees swiftly so that the masses could see where their real interests lay … For the first time in Afghanistan's history women were to be given the right to education … We told them that they owned their bodies, they could marry whom they liked, they shouldn't have to live shut up in houses like pets.'

But the Communists knew that such ideas would not be welcome to the pious and conservative people of Afghanistan, and they were not prepared to wait. They had expected resistance and acted ruthlessly to put it down: '[I]t was not the time to put on kid gloves. First and foremost we had to hold on to power. The alternative was to be liquidated and for Afghanistan to revert to darkness.'[4] So they started a massive reign of terror: landowners, mullahs, dissident officers, professional people, even members of the Communist Party itself, were arrested, tortured, and shot in large numbers. When their friends in Moscow protested, they replied that what had worked for Stalin would work for them too.

There are various accounts of what triggered off the violence in Herat. Sher Ahmad Maladani was there at the time and later commanded a local band of mujahedin – Muslim fighters against the Communists and the Russians. He said that the peasants in an outlying village, incensed by a decision of the local Communists to force their daughters to school, rose up, killed the Communists, killed the girls for good measure, and marched on the city.[5] Others said that the rising took place on orders from émigrés in Pakistan, who had planned for a countrywide rebellion. Some said that the rising was led by mutinous soldiers from the 17th Division, the local Afghan army garrison. Still others said it was stirred up by agents from Iran.

Whatever the basis for these stories, the peasants of the neighbouring villages gathered at their mosques on the morning of Thursday, 15 March, and moved towards the city carrying religious slogans and brandishing ancient rifles, knives, and other improvised weapons, destroying the symbols of Communism and the state as they marched. They were rapidly joined by the people of Herat itself. The mob flooded down the pine-tree avenues that led to the city, past the great citadel and the four ancient minarets in the north-western corner, through the Maliki Gate, and into the new suburbs to the north and east where the provincial governor's office was situated. They stormed the prison, sacked and torched banks, post offices, newspaper offices, and government buildings, and looted the bazaars. They tore down the red flags and the portraits of the Communist leaders. They beat people not wearing traditional Muslim clothes. Party officials, including the governor himself, were hunted down and killed.[6] So were some of the Soviet advisers who were working in the city and were unable to make their escape. By noon most of the city was in rebel hands. That evening there was dancing in the bazaars.[7]

In the months and years that followed, the story of what happened in Herat on those March days grew mightily in the telling, fanned by the reports of courageous but uncritical Western journalists who had no way of checking what they were told. The mutilated bodies of a hundred Soviet advisers, their wives and children, were said to have been paraded through the streets. It was confidently asserted that Soviet long-range bombers had pounded the city for two days. Up to twenty thousand people were said to have died in the rebellion and its aftermath.

As so often during the Soviet war in Afghanistan, facts were hard to establish, and hard to distinguish from myth-making. Most of the figures about the Herat rising have been much exaggerated. But whatever the truth of the matter, the immediate reaction of the Communist government in Kabul was to panic, and to ask Moscow to send military forces to put the rising down. The Soviet Politburo debated the question for four whole days and then came to a very sensible conclusion. They would not send troops, though they would supply the Afghan government with additional military and economic aid. As the Soviet Prime Minister, Alexei Kosygin (1904–80), told the Afghan President, Nur Mohamed Taraki (1913–79), 'If we sent in our troops, the situation in your country would not improve. On the contrary, it would get worse. Our troops would have to struggle not only with an external aggressor, but with a part of your own people. And people do not forgive that kind of thing.'

In the event, the Afghan government was able to put down the Herat rising on its own. But a slow-burning fuse had been lit. Unrest and armed resistance continued to spread throughout the country. Infighting within the Communist Party grew increasingly bloody, until it culminated in September with Taraki's murder by the Prime Minister, Hafizullah Amin (1929–79).

For the Russians this was the last straw. Driven step by step, mostly against their will, they tried to get a grip. Their decisions were bedevilled by ignorance, ideological prejudice, muddled thinking, inadequate intelligence, divided counsel, and the sheer pressure of events. Needless to say, the experts who actually knew about Afghanistan – and there were many of them in the Soviet Union in those days – were neither consulted nor informed.

In December 1979 Soviet troops poured into Afghanistan. Soviet special forces seized key objectives in Kabul, stormed Amin's palace, and killed him. The intentions of the Soviet government were modest: they aimed to secure the main towns and the roads, stabilise the government, train up the Afghan army and police, and withdraw within six months or a year. Instead they found themselves in a bloody war from which it took them nine years and fifty-two days to extricate themselves.

The Afgantsy, the soldiers who did the actual fighting, came from all parts of the Soviet Union: from Russia, Ukraine, Belarus, Central Asia, the Caucasus, the Baltic States. Despite the great differences between them, most thought of themselves as Soviet citizens. That changed towards the end, as the Soviet Union began to disintegrate, and men who had been comrades in arms found themselves living in different and sometimes hostile countries. Many took years to find their feet again in civilian life. Some never did.

None shook free of the memories of their common war.

PART I
THE ROAD TO KABUL

The country is extremely well adapted to a passive resistance. Its mountainous nature and the proud and freedom-loving character of its people, combined with the lack of adequate roads, makes it very difficult to conquer and even harder to hold.

General A. Snesarev, 1921[1]

– ONE –

PARADISE LOST

It took the Russians two hundred and fifty years to get to Kabul. The British started later, but got there sooner.

Both were driven by the same imperial logic. The Russian Foreign Minister, Prince Gorchakov (1789–1883), set it out in December 1864: 'The position of Russia in Central Asia is that of all civilised states which are brought into contact with half-savage nomad populations possessing no fixed social organisation. In such cases it always happens that the more civilised state is forced, in the interests of the security of its frontiers and its commercial relations, to exercise a certain ascendancy over those whose turbulent and unsettled character makes them undesirable neighbours.' In their turn these newly pacified regions had to be protected from the depredations of the lawless tribes beyond them. The Russian government therefore had to choose between bringing civilisation to those suffering under barbarian rule and abandoning its frontiers to anarchy and bloodshed. 'Such has been the fate of every country which has found itself in a similar position.' Britain and the other colonial powers, as well as Russia, had been 'irresistibly forced, less by ambition than by imperious necessity, into this onward march'. The greatest difficulty, Gorchakov rightly concluded, lay in deciding where to stop.[1]

Gorchakov's defence of Russian policy was of course self-serving, though his analysis was plausible. The Russians soon resumed their southward movement. This provoked a hypocritical outrage among other imperial powers engaged in much the same pursuit in other parts of the world. The British, in particular, were incensed: in the last part of the nineteenth century they created the romantic myth of the 'Great Game', brilliantly fuelled by Rudyard Kipling in *Kim*, in which gallant British officers rode into the Himalayan mountains and the desert lands to their north, and risked their lives to frustrate the knavish tricks of sinister Russian agents seeking to subvert the Indian jewel in the Imperial British Crown.

Afghanistan in the Modern Era

Afghanistan, the country on which the Russians and the British had both set their eye, is one of the oldest-inhabited places in the world, a crossroads between the Central Asian empires to the north, the Indian subcontinent to the south, Persia to the west, and China to the east. Alexander the Great ruled there briefly. Buddhist and Persian empires followed, until all were swept aside by Genghis Khan (*c.* 1162–1227) and Tamberlane (1336–1405) in the thirteenth and fourteenth centuries. Babur (1483–1530), a descendant of both men, established the Mogul empire in the sixteenth century. Delhi was its capital, but he chose to be buried in Kabul. Despite successive wars, 'the bulk of Afghanistan's cultural heritage remains intact (albeit under threat): it is still one of the greatest cultural storehouses of all Asia'.[2]

The people of Afghanistan are divided by race into Pushtuns, Tajiks, Uzbeks, Hazaras and other lesser ethnic groupings. Each of these is subdivided into clans defined often by the accidents of geography, as so often in mountainous regions. And each clan is further divided into often mutually hostile families. All are ruled by an ethic of fierce pride, martial valour, honour, and hospitality, mediated by the institution of the blood feud. At all levels, from the local to the central, politics and loyalties are defined by conflicts and deals between these groups, and even between individual families. There is thus little sense of a national entity on which to build a functioning unitary state.

Most Afghans are Sunni Muslims. The Pushtuns make up

two-fifths of the population and their language, Pushtu, is one of the two official languages of the country. Most of them live in the southern part of the country, and in neighbouring Pakistan on the other side of the 'Durand Line', the artificial frontier drawn by the British at the end of the nineteenth century. But substantial numbers live in the north, where they were settled at the end of the nineteenth century to reinforce Kabul's control over the non-Pushtun inhabitants. The Pushtuns used to consider themselves, and were considered by outsiders, to be the true Afghans. Some still do, which is not well taken by the rest.

The next largest groupings – the Tajiks (27 per cent), who live in the north and west, and the Uzbeks (9 per cent), who live in the north – are related to the peoples across the border in what used to be Soviet Tajikistan and Uzbekistan. Many Tajiks and Uzbeks fled into Afghanistan when the Bolsheviks were imposing their regime in Central Asia in the 1920s and 1930s. The Tajiks speak Dari, the Afghan form of Persian, the second official language.

The Hazaras (9 per cent) live in the central mountains and are said to be descended from the Mongols. They are Shias, and the rest of the country despises them as infidels. They are often found in menial positions and they have often been persecuted. But when occasion calls, they too are effective warriors.

Afghanistan's modern history was shaped by three remarkable rulers: Ahmad Shah Abdali (*c.* 1722–73), Dost Mohamed (1793–1863), and Abdur Rahman (*c* 1840–1901). They and their successors have always had to tackle four main tasks. The first has been to preserve a semblance of national unity, despite ethnic divisions, local lawlessness and violence, the arrogance of provincial satraps, and the determination of most Afghans to preserve their independent way of life whatever the plans and intentions of the government in Kabul. Any Afghan government has to try to negotiate a compromise where it can, and to suppress dissent and rebellion – often by the most ruthless means – where it cannot. Only the most exceptional rulers have succeeded.

The second task has been to preserve the independence of the state from the depredations of outside powers. Afghan foreign policy has usually combined a precarious neutrality with a willingness to distance itself from one predatory rival in return for a guarantee of security and a large bribe from the other. This policy has often failed, and Afghanistan has often been successfully invaded. But invaders have always found it even harder than its own native rulers to manage the country. Sooner or later they have preferred to cut their losses and pull out, and that has always been Afghanistan's ultimate defence.

In the twentieth century Afghanistan's rulers set themselves a third and equally difficult task: to modernise their country – its army, its communications, its economy, its governmental apparatus, its educational system. Most have tried to do something about the subordinate status of women. But reform has always come up, and often been shattered, against the conservatism of the people and their religious and traditional local rulers. Reform in Afghanistan has been a matter of two steps forward and one – sometimes two or even three – steps back.

The fourth task of any Afghan ruler, and the precondition for tackling the first three, has been to remain alive. Afghanistan's rulers have succeeded one another with bewildering rapidity, often for very short periods. Between 1842 and 1995 seven of them fell victim at an accelerating pace to family feud, palace coup, mob violence, or outside intervention. Between 1878 and 2001 four more were forced into exile. Others prudently abdicated while the going was good.

Ahmad Shah Abdali was a Pushtun who was elected king in 1747 by a *loya jirga* (consultative assembly) at Kandahar. In a flamboyant and symbolic gesture, he is said to have shown himself to the people dressed in the Cloak of the Prophet, which was reverently kept in its own mosque in the city. The state of Afghanistan, within roughly its present border, takes its beginning from that event.

By the time Ahmad Shah died in 1772, he had reconciled the turbulent Pushtun tribes, subdued most of present-day Afghanistan, extended his empire to Delhi and into Persia, and earned the name of Father of his People. Under his successors, however, many of these achievements were undone. The Pushtun tribes resumed their quarrels and the empire crumbled. In 1775 Ahmad Shah's son moved the capital from Kandahar to Kabul, where it remained. His grandson Shah Shujah (1785–1842), signed Afghanistan's first treaty with a foreign power in

1809, when he and the British agreed to support one another in the event of aggression by the Persians or the French. Shah Shujah was deposed a few weeks later. He fled to India, was brought back to Kabul in the baggage train of a British army during the First Anglo-Afghan War, and was murdered when the British cut their losses and left.

Dost Mohamed, who first came to power in 1823, was deposed by the British in favour of Shah Shujah, but returned to power after the British departed, and successfully ruled the country for the next nineteen years. For most of this time he was on good terms with the British. But after his death in 1863, the country collapsed back into civil war.

A battle lost in that war left Abdur Rahman Khan without an army and without funds. He was forced to seek exile under the protection of the Russians in Tashkent, where he remained for eleven years. He emerged as ruler of Afghanistan in 1880 in the wake of the Second Anglo-Afghan War. Grim, sardonic, barely literate but highly intelligent, he was determined to fit his country for survival in the modern world. His brutal methods of government earned him the name of 'The Iron Amir'. His power, like that of many of his successors, was fortified by a ruthless and omnipresent secret police. His methods worked. He set up the rudiments of a modern state bureaucracy, modernised and financed his army with the help of the British, and struck a skilful balance between them and the Russians.

Abdur Rahman's successors attempted to push Afghanistan further along the path of modernisation. His son Habibullah (1872–1919) was assassinated in 1919 and succeeded by Amanullah (1892–1960), who took advantage of British weakness at the end of the Great War to invade India. The British bombed Kabul and Jalalabad and drove the invaders back. Neither side had much stomach for the war, and it fizzled out after a month. The British ceased both their subsidies and their control of Afghan foreign policy. Amanullah promptly opened a fruitful relationship with the new Bolshevik government in Moscow – the first foreign government to do so.

He then embarked on an ambitious programme of reform in imitation of the secularising reforms of Atatürk in Turkey. He established a Council of Ministers, promulgated a constitution, decreed a series of administrative, economic and social reforms, and unveiled his queen. His plans for the emancipation of women, a minimum age for marriage, and compulsory education for all angered religious conservatives and provoked a brief rebellion. Tribesmen burned down the royal palace in Jalalabad and marched on Kabul. In 1929 Amanullah fled into exile in Italy.

Nadir Shah (1883–1933), a distant cousin of Amanullah, seized the throne, reimposed order, but allowed his troops to sack Kabul because he had no money to pay them. He built the first road from Kabul over the Salang Pass to the north and continued a cautious programme of reform until he was assassinated in 1933.

His son Zahir Shah (1914–2007) reigned from 1933 to 1973. This was the longest period of stability in Afghanistan's recent history, and people now look back on it as a golden age. Reform continued. A parliament was elected in 1949, and a more independent press began to attack the ruling oligarchy and the conservative religious leaders.

In 1953 Zahir Shah appointed his cousin Daud (1909–78) as prime minister. Daud was a political conservative but an economic and social reformer. For the next ten years he exercised a commanding influence on the King. He built factories, irrigation systems, aerodromes and roads with assistance from the USSR, the USA, and the German Federal Republic. He modernised the Afghan army with Soviet weapons, equipment, and training.

In 1963 Zahir Shah got rid of Daud to appease conservatives infuriated by his flirtations with the left and the Soviets. But the King continued with the policy of reform. He introduced a form of constitutional monarchy with freedom of speech, allowed political parties, gave women the vote, and guaranteed primary education for girls and boys. Women were allowed to attend the university and foreign women taught there. Ariana Airlines employed unveiled women as hostesses and receptionists, there were women announcers on Kabul Radio, and a woman was sent as a delegate to the United Nations.

During all these years, the educational system was systematically developed, at least in the capital city. Habibia College, a high school modelled on an elite Muslim school in British India, was set up in

Kabul in 1904. Amanullah sent many of its students to study in France and elsewhere in Europe. A School of Medicine was inaugurated in 1932, followed by faculties of Law, Science, Agriculture, Education, and Engineering, which were combined into a university in 1947. Most of the textbooks and much of the teaching were in English, French, or German. A faculty of Theology was founded in 1951 linked to the Islamic University of Al-Azhar in Cairo. In 1967 the Soviet Union helped establish a Polytechnic Institute staffed largely by Russians. Under Zahir Shah's tolerant regime student organisations were set up in Kabul and Kandahar.

Daud rapidly expanded the state school system. Between 1950 and 1978 numbers increased by ten times at primary schools, twenty-one times at secondary schools, and forty-five times at universities. But the economy was not developing fast enough to provide employment for the growing numbers of graduates. Many could find jobs only in the rapidly expanding government bureaucracy. Salaries, already miserable, lost half their real value in the 1960s and 1970s. The good news – though not for conservatives – was that about 10 per cent of this expanded bureaucracy were women.

The American scholar Louis Dupree called Kabul University 'a perfect breeding ground for political discontent'. It was in the universities that Afghanistan's first political movements were created. A Communist Party, the People's Democratic Party of Afghanistan, was set up in 1965 by Nur Mohamed Taraki, Babrak Karmal (1929–96), and Hafizullah Amin, all of whom were to play a major role in the run-up to the Soviet invasion. A number of students who were later to become prominent in the anti-Communist and anti-Soviet struggle also fledged their political wings there: Rabbani (1940–), Hekmatyar (1947–), Abdul Rasul Sayyaf (1946–), and Ahmad Shah Masud (1953–2001) all studied together in Kabul University. Students rioted in 1968 against conservative attempts to limit the education of women. In 1969 there were further riots, and some deaths, when high school students protested against the school management. The university was briefly closed.

Social and political dissatisfaction increased with the return of young Afghans who had been sent abroad for technical or military training. Between 1956 and 1978 nearly seven thousand Afghan students attended Soviet academic and technical institutions. An agreement with the Soviets in 1955 provided for military training in the Soviet Union: about a hundred young men went to the Soviet Union and Czechoslovakia every year.[3]

All these institutional changes, admirable as they were in principle, had little support among the Afghan people. The number of educated and reform-minded Afghans grew in Kabul and some of the other towns. But they had very little influence in the villages, which remained under the sway of tribal leaders, landlords, and mullahs. Time and again reform and the emancipation of women by liberals in the cities fell foul of the religious conservatism of the villages and the mountains. And when push came to shove, it was the views of the countryside that prevailed and derailed the best efforts of the reformers.

Imperial Russia Moves South

From the eighteenth century onwards new predators began to circle round the struggling Afghan state. Once the Russians had secured their western frontiers against their European neighbours, and their eastern and southern frontiers against the nomads and the Tatars, the logic of empire – the search for security and the search for trade – led them into the forests of Siberia and into the vast and underpopulated southern steppes and deserts.[4]

Their expansion was not unopposed. They clashed with the Turkish and Persian empires, and soon came to see the less sophisticated states of Central Asia as a threat, an opportunity, and a barrier to any ambitions they had towards Afghanistan and the riches of India beyond.

Peter the Great's imagination was fired by reports of gold to be found along the Amu Darya, the river which was eventually to become the boundary between Afghanistan and Russia. The local ruler, the Khan of Khiva, was said to be willing to become Peter's vassal in exchange for Russian protection from his rebellious subjects. Peter ordered Alexander Bekovich, a captain in the Life Guards and a converted Muslim prince from the North Caucasus, to find out more. He gave Bekovich a force of over six thousand men – horse, foot, guns, and a clutch of merchants – to build fortresses along the Amu Darya, to persuade the Khan of Khiva to help find the gold, and to open the trading route to India. Bekovich reached Khiva in the summer of 1717. After an initial welcome, the Khan treacherously slaughtered him and his men, stuffed his head with straw, and sent it to the Khan of Bukhara. A few years later, in 1728, the Russians collided for the first time with the Afghans, when their troops encountered an Afghan army which had invaded Persia. The Russians prevailed.[5]

By the middle of the century the Russians became aware that they were facing another adversary, one whose imperial ambitions matched their own. In Peter's day, the British in India had been mere tradesmen. But the Russians began to take them more seriously as the East India Company consolidated its position after the Battle of Plassey in 1757, annexing native Indian states by force, imposing its hegemony on nominally independent Indian rulers, and driving out its French, Dutch, and Portuguese rivals.

Over the coming decades, anxious to get revenge for their defeats in India, the French proposed to the Russians a number of ill-considered schemes for the invasion of India through Persia or Afghanistan.[6] In 1791 a French adviser to Catherine the Great suggested that she send her troops to march on India via Bukhara and Khiva, 'announcing as they advanced that they had come to restore Muslim rule under the Moguls to its former glory [and thus] foment mass uprisings against the British within India as word of their coming spread'.[7] Catherine's confidant and former lover, Potemkin, dissuaded her from pursuing this hare-brained scheme.

Another Franco-Russian scheme emerged in 1801. Even though their two countries were still technically at war, the Russian emperor Paul I proposed to Napoleon that they should mount a joint attack on India. Without waiting for an answer, Paul ordered General Orlov, the commander of the Don Cossacks, to take thirteen regiments 'by one or all of three routes through Bukhara and Khiva to the English possessions in India which lie beyond the River Indus'. Orlov could take the riches of India as his reward. Worryingly, Paul added, 'My maps go only as far as Khiva and the Amu Darya. Beyond that it is up to you to get information about the English possessions and the Indian peoples who are subject to them.'

Orlov set out in the depths of winter, with over twenty thousand men. In the first month his force, hungry and ill-provided, lost a fifth of its horses and an uncertain number of men. He had not even left imperial territory before he was ordered to turn back after Paul was assassinated on 11 March, strangled by his ministers with the conniv-ance of his son and (so Russians believe) the active complicity of the British Ambassador.[8]

Hare-brained schemes continued to be bandied around by hotheads in St Petersburg for some decades. But sober opinion agreed with General von Bennigsen, the Baltic German aristocrat who commanded the Russian army in 1807. The British, he argued, had created a Euro-pean-style military system in India funded by local taxpayers. This army, 'formed on the same lines as our European regiments, commanded by English officers, and excellently armed, manoeuvres with the precision of our grenadiers'. In the past Asiatic cavalry armies had invaded India over its north-west frontier and conquered the subcon-tinent, but these had no chance against the Anglo-Indian infantry and artillery. Meanwhile no rival European army could reach the subcon-tinent because the British dominated the sea routes and the logistical problems of getting a European-style army across Persia or Afghanistan were insurmountable. Having himself campaigned in northern Persia, Bennigsen spoke with authority.[9]

But as the nineteenth century advanced, the Russians became increasingly suspicious of the predatory intentions of the British in northern India. British merchants were competing with increasing success in Central Asian markets. British agents were popping up all over Central Asia. All this, the Russians considered, was directly contrary to their own legitimate interests. So they began to prepare more systematically for a renewed move south.

This time there was no question of despatching troops without maps on the basis of rumour. The main agency for conducting relations with Russia's neighbours in Central Asia and for collecting intelli-gence about them was the Frontier Commission based in Orenburg in Siberia. From 1825 to 1845 the Commission was headed by General Grigori Fedorovich Gens (1787–1845), a distinguished Orientalist and scholar. In 1834 Gens sent one of his young officers, a naturalised

Frenchman called Pierre Desmaisons, disguised as a mullah, to discover what he could about the Emirate of Bukhara. The following year he sent Jan Witkiewicz (1798–1839) on a more substantial mission. Witkiewicz (known in Russian as Ivan Viktorovich Vitkevich) came from Polish Lithuania, then part of the Russian empire. He had been conscripted into the army and exiled to Orenburg at the age of sixteen for participating in an anti-Tsarist underground organisation. A gifted linguist, he was noticed by his superiors, promoted, and appointed to the Frontier Commission.

Unlike Desmaisons, Witkiewicz made no attempt to pretend he was not a Russian officer and travelled in full uniform. He learned to his dismay that a British officer, Alexander Burnes (1805–41), had got to Kabul before him. But he remained there for four months, attempting to negotiate a trade agreement with the Emir Dost Mohamed, and returned to Orenburg with an Afghan emissary carrying a request from the Emir for Russian financial and diplomatic support against British interference in Afghanistan.

The Governor of Orenburg, General Perovski, welcomed the proposal, arguing to his superiors that if the British succeeded in establishing themselves in Kabul 'it would be only a step for the British to reach Bukhara; Central Asia would be subjected to their influence, our Asian trade would be ruined, they might arm … our Asian neighbours against us, and supply them with powder, weapons and money'.[10] The Russian government agreed and sent Witkiewicz back to Kabul bearing gifts, and with secret instructions to collect intelligence. He arrived in Kabul to find that Alexander Burnes had once again beaten him to it. But Burnes's negotiating position was fatally undermined when the Governor General of India, Lord Auckland (1784–1849), sent an arrogant and ill-judged ultimatum to Dost Mohamed, threatening that if he allied himself with the Russians or anyone else, he would be forcibly deposed.

Not surprisingly, Dost Mohamed received Witkiewicz with every mark of favour. Witkiewicz offered a Russian alliance and a guarantee of Afghanistan's independence and territorial integrity. But on his return to St Petersburg, the offer was repudiated by the Tsar's government, perhaps in order not to provoke the British. Witkiewicz committed suicide, and the documents he brought back with him disappeared. The background to this bizarre turn of events has not been satisfactorily explained.[11]

By now British spies and agents were moving ever further northwards, penetrating deep into Central Asia, into Bukhara, Khiva, Kokand, places of particular interest to Russia for more than a hundred years. The government in St Petersburg agreed with General Perovski that the valuable trade through Central Asia could only be protected by force of arms.

In 1839, as the First Anglo-Afghan War was getting into its stride, General Petrovski was sent to bring the Khan of Khiva to heel. His force consisted of three battalions of infantry and three regiments of Cossacks, together with twenty guns and ten thousand camels. The force was well supplied and the winter season had been deliberately chosen to avoid the heat of the desert. Unfortunately the winter turned unusually savage, the temperature fell below thirty degrees centigrade, and men and camels melted away. The last remnants of the expedition got back to Orenburg in June 1840.

But the Russians did not give up. Military defeat following the Anglo-French invasion of the Crimea (1853–6) had clipped their wings in Europe, so they turned their energies to the east and the south. In 1854 the Faculty of Oriental Languages was set up at St Petersburg University, marking the beginning of a distinguished tradition of Oriental studies in Russia. Rumours and agents' reports now told of British plans to advance from Persia or through Afghanistan to the Caspian Sea and beyond. In 1857 Prince Baryatinski, commanding the Russian forces in the Caucasus, warned that 'the British are preparing in detail for war, and will attack from two directions: from the Persian Gulf in the south and from the east through Afghanistan ... The appearance of the British flag on the Caspian Sea would be a mortal blow not only to our influence in the east, not only to our external trade, but to the political independence of the empire.' Schemes were once again bandied around among Russian officials for an incursion into India; they were not taken up.[12] A more sober paper, 'On the Possibility of Unfriendly Clashes between Russia and England in Central Asia', by two senior staff officers, sensibly concluded that the British would hardly risk their armies so far from the oceans they commanded. They might, however, seek to inflict political damage through 'secret intrigues in our Muslim provinces and among the Caucasian mountaineers' and interfere in the affairs of 'our neighbouring regions'. The authors went on to reject categorically any idea of an Indian campaign: the flanking route through Herat was too difficult to supply and the direct route through Afghanistan could too easily be fortified against an invading Russian army. For the time being the Russian attitude should be purely defensive. These conclusions, which were in part conditioned by the need not to provoke Britain without good cause in the aftermath of defeat in the Crimean War, were strongly endorsed by the Foreign Minister, Gorchakov.[13]

A defensive policy did not exclude – indeed, in the eyes of some soldiers and policymakers it explicitly justified – a further move south for the protection of trade and the exclusion of the British. After 1857 the Russians, and in particular the well-informed Asiatic Department of the Foreign Ministry, stepped up their collection of intelligence on the region through agents, scientific expeditions, and diplomatic missions. One of the most important was led by Nikolai Ignatiev, an ambitious young officer who had been military attaché in London. On his return, he became head of the Asiatic Department. He was on good terms with the hawkish War Minister, Dmitri Milyutin, and like him he believed that Foreign Minister Gorchakov was insufficiently robust in his promotion of Russian interests. His influence in favour of an active Russian policy in the east was to grow substantially over the decades.[14]

In the light of all this new intelligence, one confidential analysis after another argued that the British were aiming at establishing control over Central Asia and driving out the Russian trade; and that it was essential for the Russians to pre-empt them. Whether the British ever had any such intention is not so important. The belief affected and distorted policymaking in St Petersburg and Orenburg, just as policymaking in London and Delhi was affected and distorted by the belief that the Russians intended to come through Afghanistan into India. Paranoia affected judgement in all four cities.

And so the Russians concluded that their interests in Central

Asia could not be finally secured by diplomacy alone. In the years that followed they annexed or took into their protection all the independent states of Central Asia, city by city: Tashkent in 1865, Samarkand in 1868, Khiva in 1873 and the remaining lands east of the Caspian Sea in 1881–5.

The Russian colonial regime which was then installed was, in the view of one recent British historian, less burdensome than the British regime in India: the Russian were more corrupt and less efficient; the British taxed more heavily and were more prone to impose their will through violence.[15] The most notorious event in the Russian record in Central Asia – General Skobelev's massacre of the garrison and people of Geok Tepe in 1881 – pales by comparison with the slaughter inflicted by the British in India after the Rising (or Mutiny) in 1857.

Things changed after the First World War. The British began to prepare – reluctantly – to depart from India, and to leave workable institutions behind them. It was a comparatively peaceful withdrawal, though the British cannot escape responsibility for the horrors of Partition in 1947. In Central Asia the Soviets, according to their very different lights, also tried to create modern social and economic institutions. But hundreds of thousands of people died and many more fled the forcible imposition of a ruthless new regime and a collectivised agriculture. In 1991, four decades after the British, the Russians abandoned their empire as they too ran out of imperial steam.

Imperial Britain Moves North

The British, deploying the same arguments as the Russians, and using the same tactics of armed force, diplomacy, guile, bribery, deceit, and treachery, were meanwhile continuing their advance towards the north. They too wished to promote their trade and the security of their imperial frontiers. They too concluded that mere diplomacy was insufficient, and they too swept aside the obstacles to their forward march with considerable violence. By 1801 they were on their way to taking over the whole of northern India, and they had reached the border with Afghanistan. They soon began to nibble away at the Afghan border territories; particularly painful for the Afghans was the loss of Peshawar, which the British first handed to their Sikh ally Ranjit Singh

(1780–1839) and then took for themselves when they annexed the Sikh territories in 1849.

Hitherto the British had worried about a possible French invasion backed by the Persians. With the final defeat of Napoleon, they concluded that the main threat to their expanding Indian empire now came from the Russians. They argued among themselves about whether this threat was best countered by bribing the Afghan rulers to keep the Russians at bay or by imposing their own representative in Kabul, by force if necessary, and exercising a direct control, as they had done in India.

The war party prevailed on two occasions. Before the First Anglo-Afghan War (1838–42) the British manufactured the evidence they needed to justify their overthrow of the Afghan ruler, Dost Mohamed, doctoring and publishing the reports they received from their agents in Kabul to represent him as determinedly anti-British.[16] They launched the Second Anglo-Afghan War (1878–80) with a brutality almost as cynical, though this time without resorting to forgery. The murders of their representatives in Kabul, Alexander Burnes in 1841 and Louis Cavagnari in 1879, were both the consequence of British bullying and the final British excuse for war.

The British advance was opposed not only by the Afghan army, which they could deal with, but also by a widespread insurgency, which they had not expected and to which they could find no satisfactory answer. They suffered some spectacular reverses: the destruction in 1842 of an entire army and the defeat of part of the Kandahar garrison at Maiwand in June 1880. Both wars nevertheless technically ended in a British military victory followed by a salutary revenge. In the autumn of 1842 a British 'Army of Retribution' hanged the city's notables in the centre of Kabul and burned the seventeenth-century bazaar, 'one of the great crossroads of Central Asia where one could buy silk and paper from China in the north; spices, pearls and exotic wood from India in the east; glass, pottery, silver and wine from Persia and Turkey in the west, and slaves bought from both directions … flames were said to have still filled the sky two days later when the troops left'.[17] Among the other villages and towns they also destroyed with fire and the sword were the beautiful village of Istalif, famous for its pottery, and the provincial capital of Charikar, where a company of Gurkhas had been wiped out the previous year. A British officer who was there wrote to his mother, 'I returned home to breakfast disgusted with myself, the world, and above all, with my cruel profession. In fact we are nothing but licensed assassins.' [18] The devastation of Kabul in 1879 was less extensive, though the British did dismantle part of the city's Bala Hissar fortress and hanged forty-nine Afghans on a gallows set up in the ruins of Cavagnari's residence for their alleged part in his murder. [19]

But these were pyrrhic triumphs, and the British eventually realised that they could not achieve their original ambition of adding Afghanistan to the Indian empire. Nor could they sustain their own candidate in Kabul: they had to accept the reinstatement of Dost Mohamed after the First Anglo-Afghan War and the installation of the untried and possibly pro-Russian Abdur Rahman after the Second. At a high cost in blood and treasure, the British did achieve their most important objective: to keep Afghanistan out of the orbit of Russia and within that of India. By means of bribes, threats, and guarantees of support against their neighbours, they were able to persuade Afghanistan's rulers to remain – reluctantly perhaps – on their side. They remained responsible for Afghanistan's foreign policy for eight decades, until the agreement which ended the brief Third Anglo-Afghan War in 1919.

This relative success did not relieve the British of their exaggerated fear of the Russian threat. Charles Marvin, a correspondent from the *Newcastle Daily Chronicle*, interviewed many senior Russian generals and officials in the late 1880s. He complained that 'Most of the English writers on Central Asia are personally unacquainted with Russia, and have no knowledge of the Russian language ... they know nothing of the Russian aspect of the problem, except what they derive from the exaggerated and distorted intelligence appearing in the newspapers.' The language used by some British politicians was as intemperate, and as lacking in a sense of the logistical realities, as any used by the Russian hotheads. Concerned that the Russians might seize Constantinople in the course of their war against the Turks, Disraeli (1804–81) wrote to Queen Victoria on 22 June 1877 that 'in such a case Russia must be attacked from Asia, that troops should be sent to the Persian Gulf, and that the Empress of India should order her armies to clear Central Asia of the Muscovites, and drive them into the Caspian. We have a good instrument in Lord Lytton [1831–91; Viceroy of India, 1876–80], and indeed he was placed there with that view.' [20] But the more sensible British officials realised that it would be hard for a modern army to maintain itself through the treacherous mountain passes and deserts of Central Asia. A more realistic danger was that foreign meddling could spark off an uncontrollable revolt among the Indians themselves: the British still remembered the Indian Rising of 1857 and its bloody suppression.

Herat became their key strategic concern. Controlled sometimes by the Persians, at others by the Afghans, Herat was, in the eyes of British officials, 'the Gateway to India', through which Alexander, Genghis Khan and the first Mogul emperor Babur had all passed on their way south. The British feared the Russians might be next. Twice the British and the Russians came close to war over the control of Herat. In 1837 the Russians supported a Persian move on the city. The siege lasted for four months and was conducted, according to a contemporary historian, 'in a spirit of unsparing hatred and savage inhumanity'.[21] It was lifted when British forces were deployed in the Persian Gulf to intimidate the Shah.

In 1885 a crisis over the remote oasis of Pandjeh, which lies on the Amu Darya river between Merv and Herat, also nearly led to a war. The Afghans maintained that Pandjeh – which was called Kushka by the Russians and is now Serhetabat in Turkestan – belonged to them. The Russians nevertheless took Pandjeh, with considerable loss of Afghan life. The British warned that any further advance towards Herat would mean war. On British advice, the Afghan defenders of Herat demolished several of the glorious buildings of the fifteenth century in order to provide a clear field of fire. In the event the Russians never attacked and the crisis fizzled out, thanks primarily to the good sense of Abdur Rahman.

Anglo-Russian rivalry in the high mountains to the east of Afghanistan continued into the 1890s, with armed skirmishes continuing there between the Russians and the Afghans as late as 1894.[22] But as tensions in Europe grew with the rise of Germany, both sides decided it made more sense to curb their territorial ambitions in Asia. An Anglo-Russian Boundary Commission agreed that the frontier between Afghanistan and the Russian empire should lie along the Amu Darya. As a buffer between India and Russia the British insisted in 1891 that Abdur Rahman should accept sovereignty over the Wakhan Corridor, a thin sliver of land – in places less than ten miles wide – high up on the borders of China, Afghanistan, and the Russian empire. Both these borders were strategically important during the Soviet war.

But the boundary which carried the most burdensome implications for Afghanistan's future international and strategic position was the Durand Line, the artificial frontier drawn in 1893 by a senior British official of the Indian government. This drove straight through the middle of the Pushtun tribal areas in the borderland between the Punjab and southern Afghanistan. Successive Afghan governments resented the loss of territories, including Peshawar, which they regarded as rightfully theirs: Afghanistan was the only country to vote against the admission of Pakistan to the United Nations when it became independent in 1947. Prime Minister, later President, Daud backed the cause of 'Pushtunistan', which called for the recovery of the Pushtun lands on the Pakistan side of the Durand Line. The Pakistanis retaliated by doing all they could to destabilise and control their smaller neighbour. The hostility between the two countries was to have a most negative effect on Afghanistan's affairs into the twenty-first century.

The local people took no notice of the Durand Line except when they were compelled: they feuded, smuggled, traded, and fought indifferently on both sides of the border. The British attempted to control the border in the 1920s and the 1930s by a policy of 'butcher and bolt', with punitive raids against errant tribesmen, including the destruction of their villages from the air. Soviet attempts to seal the border during the war of 1979–89 were almost a total failure.

The Soviet Union Becomes Afghanistan's Best Friend

In August 1907 Russia and Britain reached an agreement to regulate their affairs in Persia, Afghanistan, and Tibet. The Russians took advantage of this more relaxed state of affairs to improve their knowledge of the country. General Andrei Snesarev, a professor at the Academy of the

General Staff, spent much of his life studying and travelling in Central Asia, and ruminating on the significance of Afghanistan in the wider geopolitics of the area. He concluded that Afghanistan was a military nightmare for a foreign invader, that it could not justify the resources needed to dominate it, but that it was indeed, as some of his British predecessors had believed, the gateway to India. His book about the geographical, ethnic, cultural, and military aspects of Afghanistan was published in 1921. It rapidly faded from the public consciousness after he was arrested in 1930, sentenced to be shot, released, and then died at home in 1937. But it was republished after the Soviets withdrew from Afghanistan in 1989, and Snesarev has since become something of a cult figure among Russians interested in the country.

As soon as the British relinquished their control of Afghan foreign policy, Amanullah signed a Treaty of Friendship with the infant Soviet Union in 1921, under which the Russians agreed to give Afghanistan financial support, to build a telegraph line between Moscow and Kabul, and to supply military specialists, weapons, and aircraft. A Non-Aggression Treaty followed in 1926. In 1928 the first regular air route was opened between Moscow and Kabul, and Soviet consulates were set up in Herat and Mazar-i Sharif.

By the 1930s the Soviet Union was Afghanistan's most important commercial and political partner. There were occasional irritations. Fugitives from the Soviet Union's Central Asian republics regularly sought refuge in Afghanistan, followed by detachments of the Red Army in hot pursuit. In the spring of 1929 the Russians invaded Afghanistan in an attempt to restore Amanullah Khan to his tottering throne. Stalin sent about a thousand men, disguised in Afghan uniform and commanded by the former Soviet military attaché in Kabul, General Vitali Primakov (1897–1937), who was himself disguised as a Turkish officer. The Russians captured Mazar-i Sharif, Balkh and other places after heavy fighting. But they rapidly lost the sympathy of the local people and Stalin recalled the force when he heard that Amanullah had fled into exile. In 1937 Primakov was shot, yet another victim of Stalin's purges. But on the whole Russia's relations with Afghanistan flourished well enough.

In the years immediately before the Second World War, the

Germans tried with some success to increase their influence in Afghanistan through economic assistance and military training – the Presidential Guard was still wearing German helmets at the time of the
Soviet invasion. During the war itself, Zahir Shah steered a skilful path
between the British and the Russians, who found themselves cooperating with one another to frustrate German intrigues. In 1943 Zahir Shah
expelled German agents operating in Afghanistan who had been identified by the intelligence agencies of the two wartime allies.[23]

Zahir Shah and his prime minister, Daud, were equally skilful
at playing off East and West against one another as the Cold War
developed. In 1953 John Foster Dulles, the American Secretary of State,
came up with the idea of a 'Northern Tier' of Muslim states in the
Middle East, including Afghanistan, which would act as a barrier to
Soviet Communism. He tried but failed to get Afghanistan to join the
Baghdad Pact when it was set up in 1955. President Eisenhower visited
Kabul in 1959. The Americans constructed the concrete highway which
linked Herat to Kabul via Kandahar, and promoted a number of educational and economic schemes, including a major irrigation project in
Helmand province. The Americans' interest in Afghanistan waned in
the 1960s as they were increasingly distracted by their growing involvement in Vietnam.

Even so, the Americans did not give up. The Secretary of State,
Henry Kissinger (1923–), visited Kabul in 1974 and 1976, and with the
rapid decline of British influence after 1945, it was fear of American
rather than British meddling that became endemic in Soviet thinking
about Afghanistan. Nikita Khrushchev (1894–1970), the First Party
Secretary of the Soviet Union, visited Kabul in 1955 and concluded
that the Americans were doing all they could to draw Afghanistan into
the American camp, because they intended to set up military bases
there.[24] Such beliefs played a part in the Soviet government's decision
to intervene in Afghanistan in 1979.

After Khrushchev's visit the Soviets announced a $100 million
development loan,[25] and thereafter continued to provide loans, grants,
training, and technical and military assistance. They also developed
their links with the small but fractious Afghan Communist Party, the
People's Democratic Party of Afghanistan (PDPA). The PDPA quickly

split into two viciously rival factions: Parcham (Banner), which had its main support in the cities, and Khalq (People), which drew its main support from the countryside. Throughout the 1970s the Russians devoted much energy to trying to dissuade these two factions from destroying one another. They were to have little success and the feud was to poison Afghan politics for the next twenty years.

The violent events which were now to convulse Afghanistan's domestic politics presented the Russians with great opportunities and even greater headaches.

Daud had been waiting in the wings since Zahir Shah had sacked him in 1963. In July 1973, while Zahir was on holiday in Italy, Daud deposed him in a bloodless coup, supported by leading members of the PDPA and a group of Communist officers whose names will crop again in this story: Kadyr, Watanjar, and Gulabzoi. Those of Zahir's relatives who were still in Kabul – one of the princesses was halfway through her wedding – were bundled unceremoniously out of the country. The Soviet Union recognised the new regime two days later. Despite their connections with the Communists, the Russians claim, reasonably convincingly, that they had no part in Daud's coup.

Zahir Shah's constitution prohibited members of the royal family from holding a government ministry. So Daud abolished the monarchy and declared himself President and Prime Minister. He denounced the previous decade as a period of 'false democracy' and promised 'revolutionary reforms'. His new government contained members of the PDPA.

More forceful than Zahir, Daud ruled with a rod of iron. The freedom of the parties and the students was curtailed. A former prime minister died mysteriously in prison. There were hundreds of arrests and five political executions, the first in more than forty years. In 1977 Daud pushed through a new constitution which turned Afghanistan into a presidential one-party state, in which only his own party, the National Revolutionary Party, was allowed to operate.

Soon Daud's spies started to tell him that the Muslim youth organisations and extreme factions among the Communists were plotting his overthrow. He began to move against both. Moscow did its best to get the Communists to support Daud, and warned Daud against pushing his repressions too far. Neither the Communists nor Daud took much notice.

In the summer of 1975 Hekmatyar and other Afghan Muslim leaders, backed by the Pakistani prime minister, Zulfikar Bhutto, launched a series of risings, which were easily suppressed by the government. The leaders were executed, imprisoned, or fled to Pakistan, where they were taken under the wing of the Pakistani Intelligence Service. Many of the survivors – Rabbani, Hekmatyar, Ahmad Shah Masud – had studied together at Kabul University. They later played a major role in the struggle against the Russians. This did not stop them manoeuvring and occasionally fighting viciously against one another, a conflict which broke out with such violence after the Russians left Afghanistan in 1989 that it practically destroyed the country and persuaded the war-weary people that anything – in this case the Taliban, the radical young Islamic fundamentalists who emerged in the early 1990s – would be preferable to a peculiarly murderous civil war.

Daud's main aims were to build up the internal power of the state at home and its international position abroad. The instrument of both was the army, which he took great pains to strengthen. The Americans refused to help him, so he reinforced the previous practice of seeking arms and training from the Russians. Thousands of Afghan officers and military specialists studied in establishments scattered across some seventy Soviet cities.

But Daud was well aware that a small country should try not to rely too heavily on any one source of outside assistance: he is reputed to have said that his aim was to light his American cigarette with a Russian match.[26] He strengthened his relations with the Shah of Iran, who offered him $2 billion on easy terms. The Saudis said they would help him only if he reduced his links with the Soviet Union. He increased his surveillance on the leftist parties, closed several of their publishing houses, purged leftist officials from the government, and released from prison some of the conservative politicians who had languished there since the coup of 1973. Outbreaks of armed opposition from the right, not always distinguishable from banditry, nevertheless occurred in several provinces.

Meanwhile the Soviets continued to increase their support for

Daud. Afghan-Soviet trade trebled. There were many more high-level exchanges between Kabul and Moscow. Nikita Khrushchev visited Afghanistan again in 1960, his successor Leonid Brezhnev (1906–82) in 1964. The Treaty of Neutrality and Non-Aggression was renewed for another ten years.

In April 1977 Daud visited Moscow, where he signed a twelve-year agreement for the development of bilateral Soviet–Afghan economic and trade relations. But his meeting with Brezhnev ended in a row. Brezhnev told him to stop leaning towards the West and said he should expel the numerous Western advisers in Afghanistan. Daud stormed out, saying that he was the President of an independent country and would part with his foreign advisers only when he himself decided they were no longer necessary.

He now began to look for ways out of his dependence on the Soviet Union. The US Secretary of State, Cyrus Vance, met Daud in Vienna in October 1977 and invited him to visit the United States. The Americans began to increase their credits and grants to Afghanistan. In January 1978 the US Embassy in Kabul reported that the relationship with Afghanistan was excellent. Daud had accepted Vance's invitation. Finance for the US military training programme had been doubled to offset – at least in part – Soviet assistance to the Soviet armed forces. And the Afghan government was cooperating, so the embassy said, in the struggle against narcotics.

This rising trend was reversed by the Communist coup of 1978, which brought to power a government determined to turn Afghanistan into a modern socialist state in a matter of years using the techniques perfected by Stalin in Russia and Pol Pot in Cambodia.

Paradise Lost

By the 1970s Afghanistan had many of the rudiments of a modern state. It was reasonably secure, and you could travel and picnic and see the sights with comparatively little risk. Foreigners who lived in Kabul in the last days before the Communists took over – diplomats, scholars, businessmen, engineers, teachers, aid workers, hippies – later looked back on that time as a golden age. So did many of the very thin crust of the Afghan middle class who lived in Kabul and some of the big cities.

In the 1970s much of old Kabul still stood, a rabbit warren of streets, bazaars, and mosques, still dominated by the great fortress of Bala Hissar, a place, the Emperor Babur said more than four hundred years earlier, with 'the most pleasing climate in the world ... within a day's ride it is possible to reach a place where the snow never falls. But within two hours one can go where the snows never melt.'[27]

In the centre of the city was the imposing Arg, the fortified palace build by Abdur Rahman, the scene of one violent turn in Afghan politics after another. Amanullah, Abdur Rahman's grandson, commissioned European architects to build him a monumental new capital, a vast palace, the Dar-ul Aman, on the south-western edge of the city; and a summer resort in Paghman, a village in the nearby hills, complete with Swiss chalets, a theatre, an Arc de Triomphe, a golf course, and a racecourse for elephants. Across the road from the Dar-ul Aman palace stood the Kabul museum, which was opened in 1924 and contained one of the richest collections of Central Asia art and artefacts in the world: flint tools forty thousand years old from Badakhshan, a massive gold hoard from Bagram, glass from Alexandria, Graeco-Roman statuary, ivory panels from India, Islamic and pre-Islamic artefacts from Afghanistan itself, one of the largest coin collections in the world, and more than two thousand rare books. A grandiose British Embassy, built in the 1920s as a symbol of British power, lay on the northern edge of the city. An equally large Soviet Embassy lay in the south-west on the road to the Dar-ul Aman.

'Kabul', said a guidebook sponsored by the Afghan Tourist Bureau, 'is a fast-growing city where tall modern buildings nuzzle against bustling bazaars and wide avenues fill with brilliant flowing turbans, gayly [sic] striped chapans, mini-skirted school girls, a multitude of handsome faces and streams of whizzing traffic.'[28]

Those were the days when Kabul was on the Hippie Trail and thousands of romantic, adventurous, and often improvident young people poured along the road from Iran through Herat and Kabul to India, driving battered vehicles which regularly broke down and had to be repaired by ingenious local mechanics, seeking enlightenment, drugs, and sex, living on nothing and sometimes dying on the way.

But behind that fragile façade lay the real Afghanistan, a land of devout and simple Muslims, where disputes between individuals, or families, or clans and tribes, were still settled in the old violent way, where women were still subject to the absolute authority of their menfolk, where the writ of the government in Kabul barely ran, and where the idea of national rather than family or local loyalty was barely formed.

Andrew Abram travelled to Kabul in 1975 and described what he saw: 'Plane loads of young American and European tourists with their carefully shampooed waist length hair, wearing "ethnic" Afghan costume (which I haven't yet seen any Afghans wearing), custom made Afghan boots, sequinned waistcoats, and custom made leather money pouches on each custom made leather belt. All looking pretty much identical and wandering around Chicken Street [the tourist shopping bazaar] looking for expensive souvenirs to show Mom and Pop at the country club before they jet off to their next sanitised travel experience. In the evening they return to their hippie style hotels to eat Western food from an extensive Western, misspelled, menu and smoke Hashish supplied by the smiling management … What a wasted opportunity to see how another culture lives. If they were to take a walk past the miles of export carpet shops and camel burger stalls they would reach the old city on the banks of the Kabul River and see part of the real Afghanistan. The old part of the city, which extends half way up the sides of the surrounding hills, is just like Herat, bazaars and filth, teeming with people. Shops selling anything and everything, factories making shoes and buckets from old car tyres, stalls with real, and good, Afghan food at low prices.' [29]

The hippies departed with the arrival of the Soviets in 1979. But apart from the influx of foreign soldiers and some incidental damage during the fighting, life in Kabul continued comparatively unchanged in many ways. 'Even at that time,' one woman wrote, 'we still went to school. Women worked as professors and doctors and in government. We went for picnics and parties, wore jeans and short skirts and I thought I would go to university like my mother and work for my living.' [30] Jonathan Steele, a British journalist who was there at the time, later wrote, 'In 1981, Kabul's two campuses thronged with women students, as well as men. Most went around without even a headscarf. Hundreds went off to Soviet universities to study engineering, agronomy and medicine. The banqueting hall of the Kabul hotel pulsated most nights to the excitement of wedding parties. The markets thrived. Caravans of painted lorries rolled up from Pakistan, bringing Japanese TV sets, video recorders, cameras and music centres. The Russians did nothing to stop this vibrant private enterprise.'[31]

A few months after the Russians left, one journalist reported that Kabul, 'although still a city at war, had almost a festive air. It was June, the wedding month, flowers and blossoms perfuming the air, the Kabul River swollen with molten snows, and I had sat in the sunshine licking ice-creams in the University café with lively young women in high heels, some with dyed blonde hair, one even wearing a T-shirt proclaiming "I'm not with this idiot" tightly pulled across her large breasts. At the apartment of a bureaucrat I had met, I had danced at a party where a well-known singer called Wajiha had strummed at her guitar in between puffs of her cigarette. The only real signs of war, apart from the large number of men – and women – in uniform and the drone of planes, had been the dawn queues at the bakers as people waited for the daily rations of five pieces of *nan* per family and the music and ideological commentary blaring from the loudspeakers hung in trees around the city which bizarrely sometimes included work-out classes and the theme from *Love Story*.'[32]

But by then paradise was already doomed. Kabul was reduced to ruins by the civil war which broke out after the Russian departure and the old life was swept away by the arrival of the Taliban, which brought the civil war to an end. The palaces and the hotels were destroyed, the museum looted, music, dancing, and women's education all brought to nothing.

TWO

THE TRAGEDY
BEGINS

On 27 April 1978 President Daud was bloodily overthrown by the
Afghan Communists, the innocuous-sounding People's Democratic Party of Afghanistan. The victors called it the 'April Revolution',
the beginning of a new age which would transform their country.
More than a decade later Russians were still arguing whether it had
been a proper revolution or only a coup. But General Lyakhovski, the
chronicler of the war that followed in which he himself served for five
years, had a starker name. For him the April coup was the beginning
of tragedy not only for Afghanistan, but for the Soviet Union as well.[1]

Several accounts maintain that the PDPA leaders were closely
linked to the Soviet KGB from the start and that most of them were
directly under Soviet control.[2] But reliable evidence that the Russians
were behind the coup is lacking. Vladimir Kryuchkov was in charge of
the KGB's external operations at the time and was a leading figure in
the formulation of Soviet policy on Afghanistan until he was arrested
after the unsuccessful coup in 1991 against President Gorbachev (1931–);
he claimed that the KGB had nothing to do with it.[3] Kryuchkov was
perhaps not the most obviously reliable witness, but other Russians in
some position to know back him up.

Whatever the truth – and until the KGB archives are opened

nothing can be said for certain – the Afghan Communists were a growing nightmare for the Russians almost from the beginning. Though they had only fifteen hundred members in 1968,[4] the Russians could not ignore them. They proclaimed their devotion to Marxism and their loyalty to the Soviet Union, and they should have been a great asset inside the complicated politics of Afghanistan. But their political views were crude and unsophisticated. Their Marxist theories, which they propounded at length in writing and on the tribune, had little application in a country which lacked the theoretically essential attribute of an urban proletariat and was about as far from a classical revolutionary situation as it was possible to be. Their solution was to sweep theory aside. They concentrated instead on the seizure and exercise of power.

Even worse, almost from the beginning the party was riven, sometimes murderously, by the feud between its two wings, Parcham and Khalq.

Parcham was made up mainly of urban intellectuals. It was led by Babrak Karmal, a Pushtun and the son of an army general. Karmal studied law at Kabul University and was imprisoned for several years for his part in student politics. He later worked in the ministries of Education and Planning. He helped found the PDPA in 1965 and later became a member of parliament. The Russian military, who kept profiles of the Afghan leaders, said of Karmal that he was 'emotional, inclined to abstraction to the detriment of concrete analysis. He has little knowledge of or interest in economic matters. He speaks English fluently and knows some German.'[5]

Khalq drew its supporters from the countryside and the Pushtun tribes. Its leaders were Nur Mohamed Taraki and Hafizullah Amin. Taraki learned English while working as a clerk in Bombay as a young man and studied political economy at Kabul University. Amin also studied at Kabul University, spent some time at Columbia University in New York as a postgraduate, and on his return worked as a teacher.

There was some theoretical basis for the division between the factions. Both believed in the goal of a socialist Afghanistan. But the adherents of Parcham thought that Afghanistan was not yet ripe for socialism. That target would have to be achieved gradually, in alliance at least at first with other nationalist and progressive forces. Khalq thought, on the contrary, that the urgent task was to seize power by force. Thereafter socialism could be imposed on Afghanistan in short order, using the methods that Stalin and Mao had applied so successfully in their own backward countries.

Each faction set up its own organisation to work among the military. In 1974 Colonel Kadyr, who had played a significant role in getting rid of the King the previous year and was a firm supporter of Khalq, set up a secret United Front of Afghan Communists within the army, where Khalq became a significant covert force.

Because the Soviet government valued its relationship with the Daud government, the Ambassador and the Chief Soviet Military Adviser were instructed to have no dealings with the PDPA leaders. Relations with them were conducted instead through the KGB representative in Kabul. In January 1974 he was instructed to see Taraki and Karmal separately, and express the Soviet government's 'deep alarm' about the continuing mutual fighting between the leadership of Parcham and Khalq. This, he was told to say, only played into the hands of domestic and foreign enemies. The PDPA should instead 'combine their efforts at giving comprehensive aid to the republican regime' of President Daud.[6]

Daud himself was worried about the intrigues of the PDPA within the army and the bureaucracy. In April 1977 he told the Russians that he was concerned 'about information given him by security agencies of plans supposedly hatched by leftist forces to remove him from power. He stepped up the arrest of activists on left and right, who were incarcerated in the notorious Pul-i Charkhi prison on the eastern outskirts of Kabul. This had been built by Germans according to a Czech design. It was in the form of a 'snowdrop': there were eight blocks radiating out like spokes from the centre. The ends of the spokes were joined in a circle by a stone wall. There were guard towers where the spokes joined the wall. From the air the prison looked like the wheel of a wagon. The roofs of the spokes were covered with copper sheeting, which glowed in the evening light with a bloody colour. The prison was guarded by a battalion of three hundred soldiers and four tanks. Executions were carried out in a small square in the central part of the prison; the victims were shot lying face down on the ground, so there were no traces of bullets on the walls. Built to hold five thousand prisoners, by the time of the Soviet invasion it was holding at least twelve thousand.[7]

Under continued Russian pressure, the two factions of the PDPA eventually agreed to reunite. In July 1977 they met in Jalalabad, their first joint meeting in ten years. They elected a new Central Committee and Politburo, and appointed Taraki as their General Secretary and Babrak Karmal as Taraki's deputy. But the candidacy of the other leading Khalq leader, Amin, was contested. Some of his opponents accused him of having had links with the CIA while he was studying in New York. He replied that he was short of money at the time and that he had merely been stringing the CIA along. The Russians got hold of a transcript of the meeting.[8] They made much of the accusation when they decided to move against Amin two years later.

Daud's worries were perfectly justified. By now the PDPA were indeed plotting a coup: Colonel Kadyr was one of the main advocates. On 17 April Mir Akbar Khaibar, a leading ideologist from Parcham, was murdered in suspicious circumstances – some said by the government, others that it was a provocation by Amin. Either way, this was the trigger. Khaibar's funeral became the occasion for a massive demonstration by tens of thousands of people. The demonstration was roughly put down by the police. Daud ordered the arrest of a number of leaders of the PDPA. Taraki, Karmal, and others were taken in on the night of 25 April. Amin avoided arrest for long enough to pass the signal for a coup to his people in the army through Mohamed Gulabzoi, a young air-force lieutenant who figured largely in the politics leading up to the Soviet invasion and for many years thereafter.

The Communists Take Power

The Khalqists in the army acted the next day. The first to move was the 4th Tank Brigade, which was stationed by the Pul-i Charkhi prison. The brigade was commanded by an officer fiercely loyal to Daud. But the Chief of Staff, Mohamed Rafi, and two of the battalion commanders, Mohamed Aslam Watanjar and Shirjan Masduriar, were key members of the PDPA and central to the plot. Watanjar persuaded his commander that in view of the unrest in the city his ten tanks should be armed, so that they could go to support Daud if necessary.

At about midday the first column of tanks arrived outside the Arg, the presidential palace in the centre of the city. It was constructed like a fortress and guarded by two thousand soldiers with tanks. Watanjar ordered the first shell to be fired at the palace at twelve o'clock exactly. Daud was holding a cabinet meeting. He told his ministers to save their lives and leave. The ministers of Defence and Internal Affairs slipped out the back to organise resistance. But troops loyal to the Khalq were already seizing key points throughout the city and by evening the 4th Brigade had been joined by commando units. Troops loyal to Daud were neutralised, the arrested PDPA leaders were liberated, and aircraft from the base at Bagram began bombing the palace.

The large Soviet Embassy on the southern edge of the city was caught in the crossfire. The women and children were safely shepherded into the cellars, even though bullets were already flying around the embassy compound, where one anti-tank shell hit a tree. But no one was hurt.[9]

That evening a group of commandos broke into the palace and demanded that Daud lay down his arms. Daud shot and wounded their commander. In the ensuing firefight – or, according to some reports, cold-bloodedly after the fight was over – Daud and all the members of his family were killed. The Minister of Defence was killed when the division he was leading into the city to oppose the insurgents was dive-bombed. After a good deal of further fighting elsewhere in Kabul, resistance had ceased by the following morning. Power passed to the PDPA at the cost of forty-three dead among the military and others among the civilian population. One of those wounded was Mohamed Gulabzoi. It was the bloodiest so far of the twentieth-century changes of power in Afghanistan.

Though the Soviets have been accused of standing behind the coup, it is not clear how much if anything they knew about it. Despite their worries about Daud's flirtations with the West, the Soviets' policy of friendship with the Afghan government currently in power had paid off in the past, and there was no particular reason to assume that it could not be satisfactorily managed in the future. The coup came like a bolt from the blue to Soviet officials in Kabul, including the KGB representative. The PDPA leaders had neither informed nor consulted them, since they believed that their plans would not be approved by Moscow.[10] Brezhnev's diplomatic adviser, Andrei Aleksandrov-Agentov, later claimed later that Brezhnev had learned of the coup through foreign press reports. General Gorelov, the Chief Soviet Military Adviser, said that the first he knew of the coup was when he came into his Kabul office that morning, heard shooting, and rang the Soviet adviser with the 4th Tank Brigade to ask what was going on.[11] Others say that the KGB had been working with people in the PDPA to bring about a coup, but had assumed it would not take place until August. It may be that, once again, the Soviet right hand did not know what the left hand was up to. In the end it did not matter much. Once the coup had taken place, the Soviet government had little choice but to give the new Communist government their full support.

The new leaders immediately set up a Revolutionary Council as the supreme political organ of the new Democratic Republic of Afghanistan. Taraki was named Head of State and Prime Minister, Karmal became his deputy, and Amin the Minister of Foreign Affairs. Watanjar, Rafi, and Kadyr were all given government posts. Although the portfolios were evenly distributed between Khalq and Parcham, Amin retained his influential links in the army.

On 9 May the new government issued a radical programme of social, political, and economic reform. 'The Main Outlines of the Revolutionary Tasks' proclaimed the eradication of illiteracy; equality for women; an end to ethnic discrimination; a larger role for the state in the national economy; and the abolition of 'feudal and pre-feudal relationships' – code for the power of landowners, traditional leaders, and mullahs, especially in the countryside. As for Islam, when Kryuchkov visited Kabul on a fact-finding mission in July 1978, the new President, Taraki, told him to come back in a year, by which time the mosques would be empty.[12] It was all a measure of how far out of touch the new regime was with the realities of their own country.

A woman was appointed to a top political position for the first time in modern Afghan history. Anakhita Ratebzad (1930–), a doctor by training, was one of four women members of the Afghan parliament in 1965, a founding member of the PDPA, and a member of Parcham. Her first husband had been Zahir Shah's personal physician. Now she was the partner of Babrak Karmal. In the *Kabul Times* on 28 May, immediately after the coup, she stated firmly, 'Privileges which women, by right, must have are equal education, job security, health services, and free time to rear a healthy generation for building the future of the country …' Educating and enlightening women are now the subject of close government attention.' A striking person in her own right, she succeeded in charming some of the most senior Soviet officials in Kabul, and they took care to remain on good terms with her as long as Karmal was in power.

The Soviet authorities were distinctly uneasy about what had happened. The Soviet Ambassador, Alexander Puzanov, attempted at the end of May to draw the threads together in a letter to Moscow. He argued that the failed politics of the Daud regime had led to 'an abrupt sharpening of the contradictions between the Daud regime and its class supporters and the fundamental interests of the working masses, the voice of which is the PDPA'. The actions of the PDPA had been 'met with approval by the popular masses'. This crude piece of Marxist analysis was characteristic of much of Moscow's thinking about a country where it was almost totally inapplicable, a cast of thought which underlay some of the Russians' later policy mistakes.

Puzanov nevertheless conceded that the continuing friction between Khalq and Parcham was already undermining the effectiveness of the new regime. This was a crucial weakness, and he and his specialist party advisers had told the new leadership that they must eliminate their differences. This, he admitted, had not yet happened. Nevertheless, he optimistically concluded that the overall situation was stabilising as the government took measures against the domestic reaction.[13]

His optimism was misplaced. The new government's programme was a mixture of typical Communist nostrums and some admirable aspirations. The new men had little or no practical experience in government. Whatever attractions the programme might have had in theory, it was not thought through and the people, especially in the villages, where most Afghans lived, were almost entirely unprepared for it. The promotion of women's liberation and education for girls, laudable as it was in principle, came up against the same fiercely conservative prejudices which had plagued Afghanistan's reforming kings.

Revolts against the new regime began straight away, in both the towns and the villages. The countryside began to slip out of control.

The new government was nothing if not determined, however, and when persuasion failed it used ruthless measures of repression. It targeted not only known members of the opposition but also local leaders and mullahs who had committed no crime. Several generals, two former prime ministers, and others who had been close to Daud – up to forty in all – were executed immediately. Nine months after the coup, ninety-seven men from the influential Mojadedi clan were executed. The Islamists who had been imprisoned by Daud in the Pul-i Charkhi prison in Kabul were executed in June 1979.[14]

In their fanaticism, and in their belief that a deeply conservative and proudly independent country could be forced into modernity at the point of a gun, the Afghan Communists resembled the Pol Pot regime. Unlike in Cambodia, however, in Afghanistan the people were not prepared to be treated in this way by their government. Previous rulers, such as Abdur Rahman, had imposed their authority through-out the country – more or less – by the most brutal methods. But they could make a plausible claim to be good Muslims, after a fashion. The Afghan Communists made the fatal mistake of underestimating the power of Islam and its hold on the people.

The Soviet Leaders Devise a Policy

The shocking news of the Herat rising on 15 March 1979 reached the embassy in Kabul and the Soviet leadership in Moscow in a fragmen-tary form, and was further confused by the self-interested accounts they were fed by the Afghan authorities. Valeri Ivanov, a senior Soviet economic advisor in Kabul, spent most of that day trying to get through to the Soviet experts in Herat. He managed to speak to the boss of the twenty-five Soviet construction workers there, a Georgian whose name was something like Magradze. The telephone kept on breaking down, but Ivanov could get a clear enough idea of what was happening. The mob was on the rampage, armed with pikes, staves, and knives. They were out for blood and, as they got closer, Magradze kept repeating, 'Help us!'

There was little enough that Ivanov could do. But the men and their families were rescued by the senior Soviet military adviser in Kabul, Stanislav Katichev, and Shah Navaz Tanai, an Afghan officer who later became Minister of Defence. They sent an Afghan special forces unit with an old T-34 tank, a lorry, and a bus to evacuate the specialists and their families. The tank broke down on the way to the airport. By then, however, the crowd had been left behind and the refugees were flown to Kabul, wearing only what they stood up in. They were housed in the embassy school until they could be sent home. Ivanov's wife, Galina, helped collect clothes for them.[15]

Not everyone was so lucky. A Soviet wool buyer called Yuri Bogdanov lived with his pregnant wife, Alevtina, in a villa. When the crowd attacked, Bogdanov threw his wife over the wall to his Afghan neighbours. She broke her leg, but was hidden by the Afghans and survived. Bogdanov was butchered. A military adviser with the 17th Afghan Division, Major Nikolai Bizyukov, was also torn to pieces when part of the division mutinied. A Soviet oil expert was killed by a stray bullet when he went out into the street to see what was going on. Although the Western press and some Western historians continued to maintain that up to a hundred Soviet citizens were massacred, the total number of Soviet casualties in Herat seems to have been no more than three. They appear to have had no influence on the decisions which the Soviet government then took.[16]

On hearing the news of the rising Andrei Gromyko (1909–89), the elderly Soviet Foreign Minister (he was seventy and had been in the job since 1957), telephoned Amin to find out what was going on. Amin claimed that the situation in Afghanistan was normal, that the army was in control, and that all the governors were loyal. Soviet help would be useful, he said, but the regime was in no danger. Gromyko found his 'Olympian calm' irritating. A mere three hours later, the chargé d'affaires in Kabul and the Chief Soviet Military Adviser, General Gorelov, rang through with a quite different and much less optimistic picture. The government forces in Herat, they said, had evidently collapsed or gone over to the rebels, who were now said to be backed by thousands of Muslim fanatics, and by saboteurs and terrorists trained and armed by the Pakistanis, the Iranians, the Chinese, and the Americans.

The Politburo met on 17 March. Neither the Soviet Union nor

its elderly leadership were in a good shape to cope with the crisis that was now thrust upon them. By the 1970s the Soviet Union was already decaying from within. Its institutions were essentially the same as those which Stalin had forged, but they were ill-adapted to an increasingly complex world. Perceptive observers, even inside the Soviet government, could see the extent of the decline only too clearly. But few people drew any far-reaching conclusions. In 1979 the Soviet Union looked to the West as though it would remain a serious military and ideological threat for a long time to come.

The leaders were gloomy, cautious, and hampered by the fact that they had little idea what was actually happening. The main opinions were voiced by Gromyko, by the Prime Minister, Aleksei Kosygin, by the Defence Minister, Dmitri Ustinov (1908–84), and by the Chairman of the KGB, Yuri Andropov (1914–84). These were all able men. But they were of Gromyko's generation, they too had begun their careers under Stalin, and their thinking was still locked in the orthodox Marxist-Leninist stereotypes of the day. They were not to be looked to for innovative solutions.

Leonid Brezhnev, the General Secretary of the Soviet Communist Party, did not join in the initial discussions, although several of the participants consulted him individually. He had been in power for fifteen years and more. His health was already failing, and towards the end he became a figure of fun, in private of course, to the wits of the Moscow intelligentsia. But whatever the state of his health in the last year or two of his life, at this stage he still retained his authority and his word was in the end decisive.

For four long days the leaders worried away at some almost intractable problems. What was the real Soviet interest in Afghanistan? What could the Russians do about the deviousness, brutality, and incompetence of their Communist allies in Kabul? How should they react to Kabul's increasingly desperate pleas for Soviet troops to help put down the insurgency?

And all the time they had in their minds the Cold War background which in so many ways underlay and distorted the policymaking process in Moscow, just as it did in the capitals of the West. Brezhnev had hoped that détente, the relaxation of tension with the West, would figure as one of the great achievements in his historical legacy. Things had started well enough. The Helsinki Treaty of 1975 seemed to offer a way of reducing tension and regulating the East–West relationship in Europe. The SALT II negotiations for further limitations on US and Soviet stocks of intercontinental ballistic missiles were moving towards completion. But then things had started to go wrong. The likelihood that the Senate would ratify SALT II was receding. The row over the deployment by the Russians of SS-20 medium-range missiles in Europe was growing, as the Americans sought with increasing success to persuade their European allies to allow the matching deployment of their Pershing II missiles.

More pertinently, the Americans would surely not take lying down their humiliation in Iran, where their close ally the Shah had been ousted. Might they not see Afghanistan as some kind of substitute for Iran as a base from which to threaten the Soviet Union? Might they not move into Afghanistan if the Soviets moved out? They had sent a carrier battle group into the western Indian Ocean, ostensibly in case of more trouble in Iran; but might the ships not be equally useful to further American intentions in Afghanistan as well? The Russians did not of course know that the Americans had been considering how to support the Afghan rebellion against the Communists even before the Herat rising. But the logic of the Cold War meant they were in any case bound to react to American moves on their sensitive southern border, just as the Americans had been bound to react when the Russians put offensive missiles in Cuba. The Russians could no more abandon Afghanistan than the Americans had felt able to abandon Vietnam in the 1950s and 1960s. These painful parallels did not make it any easier for the Russian leaders to reach decisions in a situation which risked ending badly whatever they did.

The men in the Politburo were in no doubt that the Soviet Union would have to stick with Afghanistan come what may. The two countries had been close for sixty years and it would be a major blow to Soviet policy if Afghanistan was now lost. The trouble was that, as they started their discussions on that March day, they still had little idea what was happening on the ground. The Afghan leaders were not being frank about the true state of affairs, complained Kosygin. He demanded that

Ambassador Puzanov should be sacked, and suggested that Ustinov or General Ogarkov, the Chief of Staff, should go to Kabul immediately to discover exactly what was happening.

Ustinov sidestepped the proposal. Amin, he said, had abandoned his earlier optimism and was now demanding that the Soviet Union should save the regime. But why had it come to that? Most of the soldiers in the Afghan army were devout Muslims and that was why they were deserting to the rebels. Why had the Afghan government not taken sufficient account of the religious factor earlier?

Andropov added a devastatingly bleak analysis. The main problem was the weakness of the Afghan leadership. They were still busy shooting their opponents and then had the cheek to argue that in Lenin's day the Soviets had also shot people. They had no idea what forces they could rely on. They had failed to explain their position either to the army or to the people at large. It was perfectly clear that Afghanistan was not ripe for socialism: religion was a tremendous force, the peasants were almost completely illiterate, the economy was backward. Lenin had set out the necessary elements of a revolutionary situation. None were present in Afghanistan. Tanks could not solve what was essentially a political problem. If the revolution in Afghanistan could only be sustained with Soviet bayonets, that was a route down which the Soviet Union should not go.

Gromyko was beginning to boil over. The lack of seriousness with which the Afghan leaders treated complicated matters was like something out of a detective story. The mood of the Afghan army was still unclear. Suppose the Afghan army came out against the legitimate government and against any forces the Soviet Union might send in? Then, as he delicately put it, 'the situation would become extremely complex'. Even if the Afghan army remained neutral, the Soviet forces would have to occupy the country. The impact on Soviet foreign policy would be disastrous. Everything the Soviet Union had done in recent years to reduce international tension and promote arms control would be undermined. It would be a splendid present for the Chinese. All the non-aligned countries would come out against the Soviet Union. The hoped-for meeting between Brezhnev and President Carter (1924–) and the forthcoming visit of the French President, Giscard d'Estaing, would be put in question. And all the Soviet Union would get in exchange was Afghanistan, with its inadequate and unpopular government, its backward economy, and its insignificant weight in international affairs.

Moreover, Gromyko confessed, the legal basis for any Soviet military intervention was shaky. Under the UN Charter, a country could ask for external assistance if it had been the victim of aggression. But there had been no such aggression. What was going on was an internal struggle, a fight within the revolution, of one group of the population against another.

Andropov weighed in forcefully. If Soviet forces went in, they would find themselves fighting against the people, suppressing the people, firing upon the people. The Soviet Union would look like aggressors. That was unacceptable. Kosygin and Ustinov agreed. Ustinov went on to report that the Soviet military were already doing some prudent contingency planning. Two divisions were being formed in the Turkestan Military District and another in the Central Asian Military District. Three regiments could be sent into Afghanistan at short notice. The 105th Airborne Division and a regiment of motorised infantry could be sent at twenty-four hours' notice. Ustinov asked for permission to deploy troops to the Afghan frontier and carry out tactical exercises there to underline that Soviet forces were at high readiness. He was, he nevertheless reassured his listeners, as much against the idea of sending troops into Afghanistan as everyone else. Anyway, the Afghans had ten divisions of troops, and that should be quite enough to deal with the rebels.

As for the Afghans' demand for Soviet troops, the more the Soviet leaders thought about it, the less they liked it. No one had entirely ruled it out. But when they put the arguments to Brezhnev, he made it clear that he was opposed to intervention, remarking sourly that the Afghan army was falling to bits and that the Afghans expected the Soviets to fight their war for them. You

And so the final conclusion was that the Soviet Union should send military supplies and some small units to 'assist the Afghan army to overcome its difficulties'. Five hundred specialists from the Ministry of Defence and the KGB would reinforce the five hundred and fifty who were already in Afghanistan. The Russians would supply 100,000 tons of grain, increase the price paid for Afghan gas, and waive interest payments on existing loans. They would protest to the Pakistani government about its interference in Afghanistan's internal affairs. Two divisions should go down to the border. But no Soviet troops should be sent to Afghanistan itself.[17]

The next day Kosygin rang Taraki to tell him of the Politburo's conclusions. By now the initial complacency of the Afghan leaders had given way to panic. Five thousand men of the Herat garrison, said Taraki, had gone over to the rebels with their weapons, ammunition, and supplies. The government forces now numbered only five hundred men, who were defending themselves at Herat airfield. If Soviet troops and weapons were not forthcoming, Herat would fall within twenty-four hours, and the rebels would march on Kandahar and on Kabul itself.

Naively arguing from Marxist first principles, Kosygin suggested that the government should arm the workers, the petty bourgeoisie, and the white-collar workers in Herat. They should emulate the Iranians, who had thrown out the Americans with no outside help. Could the Afghan government not raise, say, fifty thousand students, peasants, and workers in Kabul, and arm them with additional weapons supplied by Moscow?

Taraki pointed out drily that there were very few workers even in Kabul. The rest were under the influence of Islamic propaganda, which denounced the government as heathen. The Afghan army simply did not have enough trained crews to man more tanks and aircraft, even if the Soviets supplied them. He suggested that the Soviets place Afghan markings on their own tanks and aircraft, man them with Central Asian soldiers who could speak Afghan languages, airlift them to Kabul, and advance from there on Herat. Kosygin said the subterfuge would become known immediately; the Politburo would have to discuss all this. Taraki responded that, while the Politburo talked, Herat would fall.

Taraki was summoned to Moscow for talks and arrived on Monday 20 March. That morning Afghan government forces recaptured

Herat, so the immediate pressure was off. His first meeting was with Kosygin, Ustinov, Gromyko, and Ponomarev, the long-standing head of the International Department of the Central Committee. Kosygin emphasised the deep, continuing, and unconditional nature of the relationship between the Soviet Union and Afghanistan. But the Afghan government should not give the impression that it could only solve its problems by calling in Soviet troops. That would undermine its authority in the eyes of the people, spoil relations between Afghanistan and neighbouring countries, and injure the country's international prestige. If Soviet soldiers came to Afghanistan, they would find themselves fighting Afghans, and the Afghan people would never forgive them. The Vietnamese had defended their country against the Americans and the Chinese without relying on foreign soldiers; Afghanistan could do the same. The Russians would help by providing military supplies and massive political support against the country's foreign enemies: Pakistan, Iran, China, and the United States.

Taraki agreed that politics were key. He claimed – against the evidence – that the mass of the people supported the government and its reforms. But this had incensed the reactionaries in Iran and Pakistan, who had accused the Kabul government of betraying Islam, and had stirred up a campaign of subversion against it.

What the Afghan army needed urgently, said Taraki, was armoured helicopters, armoured vehicles, communications equipment, and the people to operate and maintain them. Ustinov replied that the Russians would supply twelve helicopters. But they would not supply pilots and crews. Kosygin pointed out that the Vietnamese had managed to operate the equipment they received on their own. Unfortunately, countered Taraki, many of the Soviet-trained officers were politically unreliable: 'Muslim brothers' or Chinese sympathisers.

That, said Kosygin, was something Taraki would have to sort out for himself. He gave Taraki a word of friendly advice: the Afghan government should broaden its political base. In a coded reference to the massive shootings and torture which had so exercised the Politburo, he added, 'In Stalin's time, many of our officers were put in jail. And when the war broke out, Stalin was forced to send them to the front. These people showed themselves to be true heroes. Many of them rose to high rank. We are not interfering in your internal affairs, but we want to express our opinion regarding the necessity of behaving solicitously toward cadres.'

Taraki did not pick up this point, but concluded sourly that it looked as if the Russians would give his government every assistance, short of a guarantee against aggression. If an armed invasion of Afghanistan took place, Kosygin countered, a completely different situation would arise. He then hurried Taraki off to his meeting with Brezhnev.[18]

Brezhnev described that meeting to his colleagues two days later. Taraki had arrived in Moscow 'in a somewhat excited condition, but during the discussion he gradually cheered up and towards the end he behaved calmly and sensibly'. Brezhnev had told him firmly that the government must broaden its political base and stop shooting people. He had emphasised yet again that in the present circumstances the Soviets would send no troops. So far, the Politburo agreed, so good.[19]

On 1 April Gromyko, Andropov, Ustinov and Ponomarev submitted a policy document. For the most part it simply summarised the arguments and conclusions which had already been adopted. Although it was overlaid with a heavy dose of orthodox Marxist jargon, the analysis was sober and realistic enough. The problem, it said, was primarily political. Afghanistan had not been ripe for a full-blown socialist revolution in the first place. The leaders of the new regime were not up to their tasks. They were inexperienced and prone to excess. They were bloodily divided among themselves; they had alienated the Islamic clergy, the party, the army, and the administration by their ruthless repression of real and imagined dissent; and they had pressed ahead too fast with half-baked socialist reforms which had backfired among the very people they were supposed to benefit. They should now broaden their political base: they should allow religious freedom except to those who worked against the government; they should observe the rule of law even when suppressing subversion; they should draw up a constitution to strengthen democratic rights and regulate the activities of the state organs. These thoughts remained a consistent part of Soviet policy. Gorbachev picked them up in 1985, and the last Communist leader of Afghanistan, Najibullah (1947–96), tried to implement them with the

Policy of National Reconciliation which he launched in January 1987. By then it was too late.

The paper recommended that the Soviets should continue to supply military weapons and equipment, and train the Afghan army and security organs to use them properly. They should help the Afghans to develop a viable economy. But the government should remain firm in its refusal to send Soviet military units to Afghanistan – even if there were further unrest in Afghanistan, which could not be ruled out.

This was not a bad policy as far as it went. But it came under increasing pressure throughout the summer of 1979. The Kabul government entirely failed to mend its ways. Internecine strife festered on within the PDPA, and arbitrary arrests and executions continued on a massive scale. In June Taraki and Amin moved decisively against Parcham, a number of whose leaders were sent into honourable exile as ambassadors: Nur to Washington, Wakil to London, Anakhita Ratebzad to Belgrade, Najibullah to Tehran. Lesser figures such as Keshtmand, Rafi, and Kadyr were arrested, tortured, and sentenced to death, though the sentences were commuted to imprisonment when the Soviets protested.[20]

And though there was nothing on the scale of the Herat rising, unrest continued to spread throughout the country. At the end of April, Afghan soldiers loyal to the government massacred hundreds of men in the village of Kerala in Kunar province following guerrilla attacks in the area. Unconvincing rumours said that the soldiers were under the command of Soviet advisers in Afghan uniform. On 9 May there were massive risings in six provinces, including the province of Kabul. On 23 June there was a rising for the first time in the capital. Several thousand people demonstrated against the regime, many from the minority group of Hazaras armed with knives, rifles, and machine guns. On 20 July rebels attempted to occupy Gardez, the capital of the province of Paktia: two Soviet advisers were killed. On 5 August, a commando battalion mutinied at Bala Hissar, the ancient fortress on the outskirts of Kabul. The rebels were stopped in their tracks by forces loyal to the government.[21] On 11 August a government infantry division suffered heavy losses when it was attacked; some of the survivors went over to the rebels.

These rebellions were put down more or less successfully by government forces. But by midsummer the government controlled perhaps
no more than half the country.[22]

Taraki had barely got back to Kabul after his meeting with the Politburo
in March before the stream of requests from the Afghan government
started up again: requests for attack helicopters, requests for fighting
vehicles, requests for guns and ammunition. These all fell within the
limits of agreed policy and the Soviets did their best to meet them.

But other requests certainly did not. The Afghans began yet again
to plead with the Soviet government to send its own troops, disguised if
necessary in Afghan uniforms. On 14 April they asked for up to twenty
helicopters with crews. On 16 June they asked for armoured troops to
guard government buildings and the airports at Bagram and Shindand.
On 11 July they asked for Soviet special forces battalions to come to
Kabul. On 19 July they asked for a couple of divisions. The requests
continued and multiplied throughout August.[23]

During these months the Soviet military were divided. Some senior
officers were opposed to intervention. But others, including Ustinov,
were not. In the circumstances the general staff did what general staffs
do: they made plans, they raised troops, they began training appropriate to the conditions that the troops would face if they were ever sent to
Afghanistan, and they started to deploy resources to the border. In May
General Bogdanov, a senior staff officer, tried his hand at a plan for the
introduction of Soviet forces into Afghanistan. He concluded that six
divisions would be needed. A colleague who saw his plan advised him
to lock it away: 'Otherwise we'll be accused of violating the sovereignty
of a neighbouring state.' The plan was brought out of the safe at the
beginning of December. But instead of six divisions, the Russians at
first sent three, then later added one more.[24]

The first troops had already arrived. In February 1979 the American
Ambassador, Adolph Dubs, was kidnapped by terrorists, imprisoned in
a Kabul hotel, and killed in a botched attempt by government forces
to release him. The Russians sent KGB protection squads to Kabul to
protect their own senior officials there.[25]

Following the Politburo's decisions in April, elements of the

5th Guards Motor-rifle Division and the 108th Motor-rifle Division began moving towards the Afghan frontier under the guise of training exercises. General Yepishev, the Chief of the Main Political Administration of the Soviet Defence Ministry, who had helped prepare the Soviet invasion of Czechoslovakia in 1968, visited Kabul to give advice and promise military supplies. Taraki and Amin again asked for Soviet troops and were again turned down. The numbers of Soviet transport aircraft flying in and out of Bagram sharply increased. Soviet military and civilian advisers continued to pour into Afghanistan. Rumours persisted that Soviet servicemen were flying helicopters and operating tanks on combat missions. Soviet frontier troops were increasingly involved in clashes with rebel groups along the Afghan border.[26]

Another military delegation followed in August under General Pavlovski, who had commanded the force which invaded Czechoslovakia. Pavlovski's main task was to review the state of the Afghan army and its operation against the rebels, and to make recommendations to Amin. On the eve of his departure Pavlovski asked Defence Minister Ustinov if it was planned to introduce Soviet forces into Afghanistan. 'In no circumstances!' the minister answered categorically.[27] Pavlovski remained in Kabul until 22 October and was a close witness of the events which led to the overthrow of Taraki by Amin.

Many of the Afghan requests for troops came through the Soviet representatives in Kabul – the ambassador, Puzanov; the Chief Soviet Military Adviser, Gorelov; and the KGB representative, Ivanov. As often happens, the people on the spot were sometimes more sympathetic to their clients' predicament than to the views of their principals, and often supported the Afghan requests, or at least forwarded them without comment. Within a week of Yepishev's visit, Amin asked Gorelov to forward a request for helicopters with crews. Ogarkov, the Chief of Staff, minuted on Gorelov's report: 'That should not be done.' The Politburo agreed, and Gorelov was told to remind the Afghans of the reasons why the request had been turned down. When Pavlovski arrived, Amin asked him if the Russians could send a division to Kabul. It would not be expected to take part in combat, but it would free an Afghan division to tackle the rebels on the ground. This request, too, was turned down. A month later Gorelov, Puzanov, and Ivanov came up with an idea of their own. The Soviets should set up a military training centre near Kabul on the lines of the one they had in Cuba – a somewhat disingenuous proposal, since everyone knew that the 'training centre' in Cuba consisted of a brigade of combat troops.[28]

Military Preparations

For its part the Soviet Ministry of Defence had already quietly begun to take measures directly related to the possibility of combat in Afghanistan. In April 1979 its Main Intelligence Directorate (Glavnoe Razvedyvatelnoe Upravlenie, or GRU) ordered the creation of a special battalion, based in Tashkent in Turkmenistan, to consist of Tajik, Uzbek, and Turkmen soldiers from the Central Asian republics who spoke the same languages as the people on the other side of the Afghan frontier. Major Khalbaev was appointed to command the battalion and given two months to complete its formation.

The unit, soon to be known as the 'Muslim Battalion', consisted of some five hundred men selected from across the Soviet Union. The main requirement was that they should know the relevant languages and be in good physical shape. Each was expected to have two specialities: radio operator and mortar specialist; medical orderly and driver, and so on. The battalion was equipped with two mobile anti-aircraft guns, known as Shilkas, which could also fire at ground targets. These were manned by Slavs, since no Central Asian specialists were available.[29]

The KGB now set up two small detachments of SpetsNaz (special purpose) forces, drawn from the force later known as the *Alfa* group. This was originally set up by Andropov in July 1974 to deal with terrorism and the release of hostages, taking the British SAS among others as its model. Its members were all officers, selected for their fitness and intelligence.

The first detachment of forty men was code-named *Zenit*. It was sent to Kabul under the command of Colonel Grigori Boyarinov, who had fought in the Second World War and since 1961 had lectured on low-intensity warfare at the KGB Academy. At first *Zenit* was housed in the school of the Soviet Embassy in Kabul. Its immediate task was to protect the embassy itself and the senior members of the Soviet community. At Amin's request, the group also provided training in counterterrorism for its Afghan opposite numbers.

Boyarinov's group returned to Moscow in September. But it was replaced by a similar group, known as *Zenit-2*, under Colonel Polyakov. Polyakov and his officers systematically reconnoitred and mapped the main Afghan administrative and military buildings in Kabul: invaluable intelligence when the time came for the forcible takeover of Kabul in December.

In June Ustinov sent an air assault battalion to protect Soviet transport aircraft and their crews based in Bagram, and if necessary to cover the evacuation of Soviet advisers in an emergency. The troops were to travel as 'technical advisers' under the command of Colonel Vasili Lomakin, and their officers were to wear sergeants' insignia of rank to disguise the provenance and structure of the unit. The paratroopers flew to Bagram early in July.[30] The movement was picked up by the Americans, who concluded that the soldiers were indeed intended to protect Bagram and that the Russians had no intention of committing them to combat elsewhere in Afghanistan.[31]

Thus by the late summer of 1979 several of the military units that were to play a significant role in the first days of the Soviet intervention in Afghanistan were already in place. The denouement was now to be driven forward at ever greater speed by dramatic political events in Kabul itself. Step by step, with great reluctance, strongly suspecting that it would be a mistake, the Russians slithered towards a military intervention because they could not think of a better alternative.

THREE

THE DECISION TO
INTERVENE

Now there began a period of plotting and counterplotting. Throughout the summer and autumn Taraki and Amin pursued their separate and contradictory intrigues, which ended in mutual betrayal and tragedy. The Soviet role in all this is still shrouded in ambiguity, and even those who were involved disagree about who was responsible for what. But whatever the truth, Soviet agencies were by now deeply involved in the domestic politics of Afghanistan, which they never fully understood and were never able effectively to shape to their own ends.[1]

As the domestic situation worsened throughout Afghanistan, and violent resistance to the Communist regime continued to spread, the confrontation within the ruling Khalq faction began to turn nasty. Amin gathered ever more power to himself. By the beginning of the summer, he held the key positions in the party and the state. He was a member of the Politburo and a secretary of the Central Committee. He was Prime Minister and Deputy Chairman of the Supreme Council of National Defence. He was putting his relatives and trusties into key positions in the army and the security organs. He had manoeuvred his son-in-law Colonel Yakub into the post of Chief of the General Staff. And he was doing all he could to undermine the position of his nominal superior, President Taraki, openly accusing him in the Politburo of dereliction of duty.

On 28 July Amin demoted several members of the cabinet whom he regarded as obstacles to his ambition, including the Minister of Defence, Colonel Watanjar, and the Minister of Internal Affairs, Major Mazduryar. He took over the Defence Ministry himself, and began to post officers and units which he distrusted away from the capital.

A group – Amin later christened it the 'Gang of Four' – now began to form in opposition to Amin. It consisted of Watanjar, Mazduryar, the previous head of the security service, Asadulla Sarwari, and the Minister of Communications, Gulabzoi. All were former military officers who had been involved in the coups against the King in 1973 and against Daud in 1978. They appealed to Taraki for support, but it was not forthcoming. Amin complained to Taraki about them, accusing them of spreading false rumours about him and trying to discredit him with foreigners. The head of the security police AGSA, Ahmad Akbari, who was also Amin's cousin, told him at the end of August that Taraki was preparing a terrorist act against him.

It was at this point, on 1 September, that the KGB submitted a memorandum to the Central Committee, with some thoughts on what might be done. The Amin–Taraki government, the analysts said, was losing its authority. The Afghan people were becoming increasingly hostile to the Soviet Union. Taraki and Amin were ignoring advice from Soviet representatives to broaden the political and social base of the regime. They still believed that their domestic problems could be solved by military force and the massive use of terror. Amin was the chief driving force behind this policy, so a way should be found of removing him from power. This seems to have been the first time that the idea of removing Amin was formally articulated at the highest levels of the Soviet government.

Taraki, the memorandum continued, should be persuaded to set up a democratic coalition government. The PDPA – including Parchamists currently excluded from office – should retain the leading role. But 'patriotic' clergy, representatives of national minorities, and the intelligentsia should also be brought in. People who had been unjustly imprisoned should be released, including representatives of the Parcham faction. Meanwhile an alternative PDPA government should be prepared and held in reserve; Babrak Karmal, who was still in exile, should be brought into the planning process. This was essentially the plan that was implemented in December.

The Crisis Explodes

From now on the Politburo's Committee on Afghanistan – Gromyko, Andropov, Ustinov, and Ponomarev – became the chief policymaking body for Afghan affairs. It met regularly, often with Soviet representatives brought in from Kabul. The pace of decision-making was greatly accelerated.[2] Analyses and recommendations prepared by the Foreign Ministry, the KGB, the Ministry of Defence, and the International Department of the Central Committee were put to the Committee, who passed their recommendations on to the Politburo for decision. Needless to say, the arrangements for coordination between departments, like their counterparts in other governments, were fine in theory, but did not work so well in practice. Departments remained at loggerheads, while the careful but sometimes conflicting analyses and recommendations put forward by cautious officials were often ignored or set aside by leaders who had their own ideas.

The KGB had long experience of dealing with Afghanistan, many covert contacts there, and its own ideas of how things should be handled: it was in many ways the lead department. It had invested much of its capital in the Parcham faction, and tended to reflect their views, even though these were a comparatively small proportion of the membership of the PDPA – fifteen hundred out of fifteen thousand.

The rest of the membership was from Khalq. That was also the faction to which most of the Communist officers in the army belonged, men whom Amin had made a special effort to cultivate.[3] The result was a growing contradiction between the views of the KGB, who came to favour intervention and the replacement of Amin by their man, the Parcham leader Babrak Karmal, and the views of the Soviet military, who were prepared to live with Amin because they believed that the main thing was to retain the support of the Khalq officers in the army, many of whom had been trained in the Soviet Union and had good professional relations with their Soviet military colleagues. These disagreements were exacerbated by poor personal relations between senior KGB and army officers, and by rivalries between the KGB and the army's own intelligence organisation, the GRU.

All this had an increasingly negative effect on the formulation and execution of policy, including the decision to invade Afghanistan in the first place, and the management of policy in the nine years after the invasion took place. Afghan government leaders naturally took advantage of these differences to play one faction off against the other.

Artem Borovik, who was one of the first journalists to tell the Soviet public what was actually going on, concluded, 'One of our problems in Afghanistan, it seemed to me, was that the Soviet Union never had a central office in charge of the various delegations of its super-ministries: the KGB, MID [Ministry of Foreign Affairs], MVD [Ministry of Internal Affairs], and Ministry of Defence. The chiefs of these groups acted autonomously, often sending contradictory information to Moscow and often receiving conflicting orders in return. The four offices should have been consolidated under the leadership of the Soviet ambassador. But there were so many different Soviet ambassadors that none of them had enough time to become thoroughly familiar with the state of affairs in Kabul. There was Tabeev, then Mozhayev, then Yegorychev, then Vorontsov – all within a two-year period. Of these four men, only Vorontsov was a professional diplomat with extensive experience in Central Asia. While the rest had enjoyed successful careers within the Party apparatus, they had no background in Central Asia affairs.'[4]

Such dysfunction was not unique to the Soviet effort in Afghanistan. Fifteen years earlier the US mission in Saigon in 1966 had been in equal disarray, the consequence of a rapid build-up, pressure from above, frequent changes of staff, personal frustration, poor leadership, and fatigue. The Americans had landed themselves with an open-ended commitment which, as one American official said at the time, could 'lure us unwillingly and unwittingly into a strange sort of "revolutionary colonialism" – our ends are "revolutionary", our means quasi-colonial'.[5] Much the same could have been said of the US-led coalition in Kabul forty years later.

The crisis now exploded. Taraki was due to fly to Havana for a meeting of the Heads of the Non-Aligned Movement. The KGB warned him not to leave Kabul at this time, since Amin might move in his absence. He ignored them and departed on 1 September. His delegation was almost wholly composed of men with confidential links to Amin, notably Major Tarun, Taraki's personal adjutant, who played an equivocal – and for himself fatal – role in the events of the next two weeks.

In Taraki's absence relations between Amin and the Gang of Four deteriorated still further. The four men stopped sleeping at home to avoid arrest, and began to circulate leaflets calling for opposition to Amin and the restoration of unity between the party's two warring factions. Sarwari telephoned Taraki in Havana to warn him that Amin was preparing to take power.

On his way back from Havana Taraki stopped in Moscow on 10 September to meet Brezhnev and Gromyko. Brezhnev spoke in grave terms about the situation in the Afghan leadership, 'which is causing particular concern not only to your Soviet comrades, but also, according to information we have, to the members of the PDPA ... [T]he concentration of excessive power in the hands of others, even your closest aides, could be dangerous for the fate of the revolution. It can hardly be expedient for one person to occupy an exclusive position in the leadership of the country, the armed forces, and the organs of state security.' Brezhnev clearly had Amin in mind; but if it was a hint that Moscow would support the removal of Amin, Taraki did not pick it up.[6] Instead he asked once again for direct military support, and once again the request was rejected. He also met Babrak Karmal, who had been brought by the KGB to Moscow. The two men discussed ways of restoring party unity and getting rid of Amin. News of this meeting apparently leaked to Amin, perhaps through Major Tarun.

That evening, at his lodging on the Lenin Hills overlooking Moscow, Taraki met Alexander Petrov, a KGB officer who had previously worked in Afghanistan. Petrov warned him that Amin was plotting against him. Taraki replied, 'Don't worry. Tell the Soviet leadership that for the time being I am in complete control of the situation, and that nothing happens without my knowing about it.'[7] He repeated this optimistic assurance to Brezhnev as he left Moscow for the onward flight to Kabul.

The Russians were by no means so sure. That same night, Colonel Kolesnik (a code name adopted for the purpose of this operation: his real name was Kozlov), the GRU staff officer who was later to plan and direct the storming of Amin's palace in Kabul, briefed Major Khalbaev, the commander of the Muslim Battalion, to join his men in Tashkent and prepare them to fly to Kabul to protect Taraki. He showed Khalbaev a picture of Taraki and said, 'The order to protect that man comes straight from Brezhnev himself. If he dies, then you and your battalion had better not come back alive.' The men of the Muslim Battalion were ordered to hand in all their documents and don Afghan uniform, ready to move at a moment's notice. But Andropov was already considering various covert ways of removing Amin, including kidnapping him and taking him to the Soviet Union. He persuaded Brezhnev and Taraki that the Muslim Battalion should stay where it was, at least for the time being.

On 11 September Taraki flew back to Kabul. Amin had already begun to take his own measures. Taraki's aircraft was made to circle over Kabul for a whole hour while Colonel Yakub, the Chief of the General Staff, completely revised the security arrangements to ensure that they were under the control of Amin's men.[8] As soon as he had landed, Taraki demanded that Amin tell him what had happened to the four ministers, the Gang of Four. 'Don't worry, they're all safe and well,' replied Amin. The two men then drove together to the Central Committee in town, where Taraki reported on his trip to Havana.

The next morning the row over the four ministers continued. Amin claimed that the four men had been behind an attempt to assassinate him while Taraki was away. They should be sacked and punished. Taraki asked Amin to accept their apologies, then reinstate them. Amin retorted that if the ministers did not go he would refuse to follow any of Taraki's further instructions.

Meanwhile the four ousted ministers were operating out of the presidential palace, Abdur Rahman's Arg, which the Communists had renamed the House of the People. Watanjar rang round all the commanders of the Kabul garrison to find out which of them was loyal to Taraki. They immediately reported these approaches to Colonel Yakub, who told Amin. Gulabzoi suggested to Taraki that he ask for the Soviet battalion stationed in Bagram to be sent to Kabul to guard him. Taraki told him that was unnecessary. The quarrel had been settled. In any case it was inappropriate for him to hide behind Soviet bayonets.[9] Gulabzoi told him that there had been a shoot-out that morning at the Ministry of Security when Amin's men had come to arrest Sarwari. Two people had been killed. Gulabzoi again asked Taraki to act. Again Taraki calmed him down, saying all was going according to plan. Tarun faithfully reported these goings-on to Amin.

By now the Russians were getting far more deeply involved, though this brought them no greater influence on events. On the evening of 13 September the four ousted ministers came to the Soviet Embassy. In the name of Taraki they asked for Soviet help to arrest Amin. Less than two hours later, Tarun rang from the palace to say that Amin had arrived there. He and Taraki were both asking the Russians to join them.

The Russians judged that the situation had become critical. 'The possibility that H [Hafizullah] Amin might order the military units loyal to him to take up arms against Taraki,' they later telegraphed to Moscow, 'could not be excluded. Both groups were trying to enlist our support. For our part we were sticking firmly to the line that the situation in the leadership must be normalised along party lines, i.e. collectively. At the same time we were trying to restrain both groups from acting in haste and without thinking.'[10]

Hoping they might calm things down, Puzanov and his three senior colleagues went to the palace. Taraki and Amin were waiting for them. The Russians read out another appeal for unity from Brezhnev. Taraki welcomed the appeal in fulsome terms. Amin followed suit, asserting in even more sycophantic language that he was honoured to serve under Taraki: if service to Taraki and the revolution required his own death, he would be happy to make the sacrifice.[11] The four Russians left, satisfied by the appearance of reconciliation.

Later they heard (and reported to Moscow – incorrectly) that Amin and Taraki had reached some agreement. They did not know the details. But they congratulated themselves that their visit, and the appeal from Comrade Brezhnev, had calmed things down: 'Amin did not resort to extreme actions, as he was convinced that the Soviet side would not support any actions which might aggravate the situation in the Afghan leadership and work against the unity of the PDPA.'[12] This massive misjudgement was a measure of how far the Soviet representatives were out of touch with what was actually going on.

The following morning Puzanov and his three senior colleagues called on Taraki once again. At last Taraki spoke openly about his difficulties with Amin. Dmitri Ryurikov, a Soviet diplomat acting as Puzanov's executive assistant and interpreter, recorded the conversation in the diary he was keeping for his ambassador.

'I noticed long ago,' Taraki told the Russians, 'that Amin has the tendency to concentrate power in his own hands but I did not attach any particular significance to this. However, recently this tendency has become dangerous.' He went on to complain about Amin's refusal to accept criticism, the way he was building up his own public position, the authoritarian way he treated his ministers, and the way he had placed his relatives in key government and party posts. 'One family is ruling the country just as it was in the times of the King and Daud.'

Reversing the assurances he had given to Brezhnev, Taraki now confessed that he had had doubts about Amin even before he left for Havana. Since his return Sarwari had informed him of three separate conspiracies launched by Amin, who had aborted them once he realised that they had been uncovered.

He went on to tell the Russians that his talks with Amin the previous day had not (as they had thought) resulted in agreement. Amin had again demanded that the four ministers be sacked. Taraki had accused Amin of persecuting them and forcing them into hiding. He, Taraki, was the commander-in-chief of the armed forces, and Amin must obey his orders. Amin had smiled and said that, on the contrary, it was he who commanded the troops. Now, said Taraki, open conflict could not be ruled out. He was prepared to go on working with Amin, but only if Amin abandoned his present policies of repression.

The Russians suggested that Amin be invited to join the discussions, and Taraki telephoned him accordingly. As they were waiting, the KGB representative, General Boris Ivanov, remarked that there were persistent rumours of a plot to kill Amin when he got to the palace. Taraki pooh-poohed the idea.

Taraki's aide Tarun then went out to meet Amin. A few minutes later, there was a burst of automatic fire on the other side of the door. Gorelov went to the window and saw Amin running towards his car. There was blood on the sleeve of his shirt.

Ryurikov was sent out to see what had happened. Tarun was lying halfway down the stairs. He had bullet wounds in his head and chest. A sub-machine gun was lying on the floor. There was still gun smoke in the stairwell. Taraki's wife was there too: she had come out of the bedroom to see what was going on.

Taraki's bodyguard came in and reported with a crisp military salute that, when Amin had begun to walk up the staircase, Tarun had told Taraki's guards to leave and threatened them with his pistol. When they refused he fired at one of them and they killed him immediately.

Taraki then rang Amin to tell him that what had happened was the result of a misunderstanding with the guards. But after he put the receiver down he told the Russians that it had been a deliberate provocation. He agreed that the Russians should go to see Amin straight away.

All the Afghans involved in the shoot-out on the staircase died then or soon afterwards. None of the Russians actually saw what happened. This has left room for two alternative explanations. The first is that it was a put-up job by Amin designed to give him the excuse to arrest Taraki. The second is that there really was an attempt to get rid of Amin that went wrong. Ryurikov later inclined to the former view: assassination was not Taraki's style, whereas Amin came from a family which was notorious for the bloody way in which it conducted its feuds and its political intrigues.[13]

Amin himself fled to the Ministry of Defence, and ordered his troops to surround the Palace, disarm the guard, and arrest Taraki. Two hours later Kabul Radio announced that Taraki and the four ministers had been relieved of their posts. That night many of Taraki's people were arrested and some were shot, including the two guards who had opened fire on Amin. Taraki told his wife that Amin would not touch him: the Soviet comrades would not allow Amin to make a fool of himself. But the couple were soon taken under guard to a room in a smaller building within the palace complex. The room had not been used for some time and was thick with dust. Taraki comforted his wife: 'Everything will be all right. I know this room. Soldiers used to be quartered here. Now it's our turn.' She immediately set to work to clean it up.[14] Later she was taken to a separate building. The rest of Taraki's family and his personal staff were moved from the presidential palace to the Pul-i Charkhi prison a couple of days after Amin took power.

That evening the Soviet officials called on Amin to express their regret at the shooting and their deep sympathy at the death of Tarun, whom they 'had known to be a true friend of the Soviet Union'. Amin then gave his version of the story and concluded, 'I am convinced that it was me whom they wanted to kill. More than a hundred shots have been fired at me before this. Now you can see for yourselves what Taraki wanted. I knew that an attempt on my life was being planned and was ready for this when I met Taraki at the airport on his return from Havana. Today Taraki wanted to kill me. He clearly did not plan to do this in the presence of Soviet comrades, but he must have forgotten to cancel his orders and his people began to shoot.'

The Russians again expressed their regret, emphasised the need for restraint, and repeated Brezhnev's call for unity: a split in the Party would be ruinous for the Afghan revolution. Amin said that the revolution could survive without him, provided it had Soviet support. But the reality was that the army would now obey only him, not Taraki; an attempt the previous day by Watanjar to bring the army over to Taraki had failed. Amin had nevertheless sacked the commanders of the 4th and 15th Armoured Brigades as a precaution.

The Central Committee would now meet to relieve Taraki of his posts, said Amin, though he claimed that he personally was against that. The Russians replied that the Soviet leaders firmly believed that Taraki should remain as head of state and that Amin should keep his current posts. They would not understand it if Amin stripped Taraki of his position.

Amin said that he himself was ready enough to take Soviet advice. But things had gone too far. Blood had been spilled (he showed them the stains on his shirt). His comrades in the army were angrily demanding vengeance. The Russians forcefully reiterated their view that unity must be preserved within the leadership and between Taraki and Amin. They appealed to Amin to prevent the demonstrations against Taraki which were planned for the following day.

Throughout that night the soldiers of the Soviet parachute battalion in Bagram sat in their aircraft with their weapons, awaiting the order to fly to Kabul to rescue Taraki. Neither the paratroopers nor the Muslim Battalion ever received the order to move. Amin had meanwhile given instructions that any aircraft landing or taking off from the airfield should be shot down.[15] Early on the following day, 15 September, Moscow ordered the special forces soldiers from *Zenit* to stand by for an operation against Amin. They assembled in the courtyard of the embassy, where they were briefed in detail. At about eleven o'clock the embassy security officer, Colonel Bakhturin, put them on fifteen minutes' notice to move. But they too were never ordered to act: the Russians had sensibly decided that the balance of forces in Kabul was overwhelmingly against them.[16]

The four went into hiding. Mazduryar found his own refuge. Watanjar, Gulabzoi, and Sarwari took themselves to the villa of one of their KGB contacts. The officer's wife found them in the sitting room when she came home from work. Colonel Bogdanov, the head of the KGB office in Kabul, had them taken to a KGB safe house on his own responsibility and then phoned Moscow to ask what he should do next. To his relief Moscow endorsed what he had done. The three men were dressed in SpetsNaz uniform, and they were put to live on the second floor of the villa.

The Party Plenum and the Revolutionary Council of the PDPA met on 16 September in a building surrounded by tanks and soldiers. The office of the Soviet Military Adviser was in the same building; the Soviet officers could hear the cheers as the meeting passed the resolutions expelling Taraki and the four ministers from the party, and electing Amin to the posts previously held by Taraki, the General Secretaryship of the party and the Chairmanship of the Revolutionary Council.[17] The public was told that Taraki had asked to be relieved of his posts on grounds of ill-health and that Amin had been elected to succeed him. In a public broadcast the following day Amin attacked the excesses of the secret police and promised that the rule of law would prevail in future. He did not once mention Taraki. When he told the story later, Ambassador Puzanov said bitterly, 'Amin made fools of us all.'[18]

The day after the shoot-out, 15 September, the Soviet Politburo met in Moscow to consider what to do. They had before them a memorandum prepared by Gromyko, Ustinov, and the KGB. This described the course of events in Kabul reasonably accurately. Taraki had failed to act decisively. Amin had ruthlessly exploited the situation. Now all the organs of power were in his hands. The pleas of the Soviet Politburo had been ignored.

Gromyko recommended that the Soviet government accept the accomplished fact and deal with Amin, while seeking to dissuade him from punishing Taraki and his associates. Soviet officials and military advisers should continue with their duties as before, but should not get involved in any of Amin's repressive measures. Supplies of arms to Amin's government should be somewhat reduced, except for spare parts and ammunition needed for operations against the insurgents. Public statements by the Soviet government should be purely factual and avoid all comment.

The Politburo agreed with these proposals and Gromyko cabled appropriate instructions to Kabul.[19] The Russians were not, however, prepared to take their reverse entirely lying down. Their first move, on 18 September, was to mount Operation *Raduga* (Rainbow) to rescue the three Afghan ministers who had taken refuge with the KGB in Kabul. Two aircraft – an Il-76 and a An-12 – flew into Bagram, carrying a lorry with three boxes inside it, and a make-up artist whose job was to make the three men look like the photographs in the Soviet passports prepared for them. Colonel Bogdanov was put in charge of the operation.

Lieutenant Valeri Kurilov, of the *Zenit* group, described what happened: 'We prepared three containers at our Moscow base at Balashikha: three wooden boxes, like the ones used for transporting arms. We put mattresses on the bottom and bored holes in the top and sides so that the ministers would not suffocate.

'Once the boxes had been delivered to Bagram airport, we took them in a covered lorry with local number plates to the villa where the ministers were hidden. We blocked the entrance to the villa with a bus while the ministers crawled into the boxes, each with a weapon and a water bottle. Then we nailed down the lids.

'We dragged the boxes – now much heavier than before – to the lorry and piled cardboard boxes on top of them. Our boys, some in civilian clothes, sat in the back of the covered lorry. Each had a sub-machine gun, a pistol, grenades, and a double supply of ammunition.

'We'd taken care to provide backup: two other vehicles were travel-ling with us, a Zhiguli and a UAZ, with seven of our boys on board. There were six men in the bus and another six in the lorry. If anything had happened, we would have reacted and taken down a pile of people. But that was the last thing we needed. Our task was to get to Bagram without incident and load the three boxes on to the aeroplane …

'At the checkpoint on the way out of Kabul the Afghans tried to inspect our vehicles. We got ready for a fight. Our commander, Dolmatov, told us not to shoot unless he gave the order. A tall young officer with a carefully trimmed moustache spoke to the driver in our lorry and then tried to open the canvas cover. Although the interpreter told him that there was nothing there except boxes with the personal belongings of the Soviet specialists, the officer tried to climb in. At that point Dolmatov's heavy boot came down on his hand and the officer looked up to see Dolmatov's Kalashnikov pointing straight at his head. The officer backed down and the convoy was allowed to proceed. We travelled the seventy kilometres to Bagram without further incident.

'A huge Aeroflot transport plane was waiting for us. A guard of SpetsNaz was set up around it, the ramp was lowered, and the lorry drove straight into the belly of the aircraft. After take-off I took out my bayonet and levered off the tops of the boxes. All three men were alive and well, but bathed in sweat.'

The three men were then smuggled through to Bulgaria, where they went into hiding in a villa on the Black Sea. To put the Afghans off the scent, the KGB spread the rumour that they had sought sanctuary in Iran. Gulabzoi later maintained that he had never left Afghani-stan and never travelled in a box. But the Russian participants in the operation all insisted that he did.[20]

By now the Soviet government was getting increasingly worried by KGB reports that Amin was turning towards the Americans. These suspicions were not idle. On 27 September Amin told Bruce Amstutz, the American chargé d'affaires, that he hoped for an improvement in relations. His new Foreign Minister, Shah Wali, said much the same to David Newsom, the US Under Secretary of State, in New York. Amstutz reported to Washington on 30 September that a senior official in the Afghan Foreign Ministry had expressed interest in improving relations with the US government.[21]

Amin's people were also beginning to criticise the Soviet Union directly. On 6 October, at a meeting of socialist ambassadors to which the Soviet Ambassador was not invited, Shah Wali openly accused the Soviet Union, and Ambassador Puzanov in particular, of involvement in the attempted assassination of Amin on 14 September. Wali claimed that Puzanov had assured Amin on the telephone that he could come to Taraki's office safely, and pointed out that Puzanov had been there throughout the shooting.

Moscow was infuriated by the accusation. Three days later Puzanov and his colleagues conveyed the Soviet government's protest to Amin. His reaction, they later reported, was 'brash and provocative. He sometimes contained his fury with difficulty.' For most of the meeting he barely allowed the Russians to get a word in edgeways. Wali, he shouted, had merely repeated what Amin had told him to say. The interpreter who had translated Puzanov's remarks could confirm his version of events. So could the Afghan officials who had been in his office at the time.

The Russians insisted that they had not telephoned until after the shooting, when they had asked Amin if they might call on him. He calmed down and spoke in a more conciliatory manner: he evidently did not want to ruin his relationship with the Russians entirely. But he absolutely refused to put out a public retraction of his story, or to accept that his memory might have been confused by the shock of events. A retraction, he said, would be interpreted in the party and in the country as a sign that he had succumbed to Soviet pressure.

As the Russians left he made a partial apology: 'Maybe I have been speaking too loudly and too quickly during our conversation but, you know, I was brought up in the mountains and that is how we speak in the mountains.'

In private Amin was unreconciled. In his own entourage, in the most colourful language, he repeatedly accused Puzanov of lying to him directly: 'I do not wish to meet him or talk to him. It is difficult to understand how such a liar and tactless person has been ambassador here for so long.' All this was reported back to the Russians.[22]

The Death of Taraki

By the time the Soviet representatives had that meeting with Amin on 9 October, Taraki was already dead, though Amin did not see fit to tell them as much. He had been murdered, in an intrigue worthy of Shakespeare's *Richard III*. A key role was played by the commander of the Presidential Guard, Major Jandad, who had studied in the Soviet Union and spoke reasonable Russian. Although his task was to protect the President, he was by now closely associated with Amin.

On the evening of 8 October Jandad summoned three of his people to his office: Lieutenant Ekbal, the head of counter-intelligence in the Presidential Guard, Captain Vadud, its communications officer and Lieutenant Ruzi, the head of its political department.

Jandad said, 'There's trouble brewing.' Ekbal thought that he was talking about some imperialist plot. Instead, Jandad went on, 'The Central Committee and the Revolutionary Council have decided that Nur Mohamed Taraki is to be executed. You have been entrusted with the task of carrying out this order.' Ekbal replied, 'As far as I know, the orders of the Central Committee and the Revolutionary Council are given in writing. I think that we need the appropriate document before we carry out this order.' Jandad said, 'Don't be stupid. What do you mean, you need a document? The Central Committee Plenum expelled him from the Revolutionary Council and the Central Committee. He's as good as dead already. There's nothing secret about the decision.' Ekbal and Vadud mentioned a rumour that Taraki was to be sent to the Soviet Union. Jandad said the Russians had refused to receive him. The two men objected that if Taraki had committed a crime, then the facts should have been broadcast over the radio. Jandad assured them that there would be a broadcast in due course. 'But the party has its secrets which are none of your business. Do what you've been ordered to do.' He then sent Ekbal out to buy nine yards of white cotton cloth for a shroud.

Yakub ordered that Taraki was to be buried next to his brother. Ekbal and Ruzi found the grave with some difficulty, made the necessary preparations, and then joined Vadud in the palace.

Taraki was in his dressing gown when the three men came for him. Ruzi said, 'We've come to take you to another place.' Taraki gave him some money and jewellery to pass on to his wife. Ruzi told him to leave his belongings behind – they would be returned to him in due course.

The party went downstairs to another small room, in which there was a dilapidated bed. Taraki handed over his party card and his watch, which he asked should be given to Amin. Ruzi told Ekbal to bind Taraki's hands with a sheet and ordered Taraki to lie down on the bed. Taraki did so without protest. Ruzi put his hand over Taraki's mouth and told Vadud to bind his legs while Ekbal sat on them. Ruzi then covered Taraki's head with a pillow and when he removed it Taraki was dead. The whole business lasted fifteen minutes. Not bothering with the cotton shroud, they rolled Taraki's body in a blanket and took him in their Land Rover to the cemetery, where they buried him. They were in tears when they reported back to Jandad.[23]

Later that evening it was officially announced that Taraki had died of 'a brief and serious illness'.[24]

The Mood Shifts in Moscow

The murder of Taraki was the crucial turning point in the Soviet decision-making process. Brezhnev took the news particularly badly. He had promised to protect Taraki. 'What a bastard, Amin, to murder the man with whom he made the revolution … Who will now believe my promises, if my promises of protection are shown to be no more than empty words?'[25] Andropov, mortified by his department's failure to keep control of events, was now determined to get rid of Amin and install a more malleable Afghan leader.

But the debacle was not merely a personal matter. Though much is confused about these events, one thing is not. Despite the numerous Soviet advisers attached to Afghan military and civilian organisations, despite all the economic, military, and political assistance they had given, the Soviet government in Moscow and its representatives in Kabul had been powerless to influence events in Kabul, and had been left looking impotent. Their man Taraki had been outmanoeuvred and had paid with his life. Soviet influence in Kabul was now practically non-existent. Amin, the victor in the power struggle, was mishandling the domestic situation in Afghanistan with disastrous brutality. It was a challenge that the Soviets could hardly leave unanswered. One of the driving forces in Soviet policymaking over the next three months was a determination to recover from humiliation and reassert control over events.

The mood in Moscow now shifted towards the possibility of replacing Amin, if necessary through armed intervention. The contingency arrangements that had been made earlier in the year began to be looked at more urgently. The Chief Soviet Military Adviser in Kabul, General Gorelov, was called back to Moscow for discussions in September and again in October to meet his military superiors, Ogarkov and Ustinov, and also to meet Andropov, Gromyko, and Ponomarev. On the second visit Gorelov was accompanied by General Vasili Zaplatin, who since 1978 had been adviser to the head of the Political Department of the Afghan army. Asked about Amin, Gorelov described him as a man of strong will, a very hard worker, an exceptional organiser, and a self-proclaimed friend of the Soviet Union. He was, it was true, cunning, deceitful, and ruthlessly repressive. But both he and Zaplatin believed that Amin was nevertheless someone whom the Russians ought to be able to work with. Asked about the Afghan army, Gorelov said that it could deal with the rebels, even though it was not up to modern standards. Asked whether the Afghan army would fight the Soviet army he replied, 'Never' – correctly as it turned out. But it was only later that he realised the purpose of the question.

Inevitably Moscow now looked for scapegoats to blame for the collapse of its policies. The obvious candidates were the Soviet representatives in Kabul. In the course of November, Gorelov was replaced by Lieutenant General Magometov and the Chief Interior Ministry Adviser, General Veselkov, was replaced by General Kosogovski. Ambassador Puzanov's usefulness was in any case at an end, given the hostility that Amin now bore towards him. He was recalled to Moscow 'in accordance with his oft-repeated requests' and pensioned

off. Although he was a senior Party member, with a distinguished diplomatic career behind him, and had spent seven years in Afghanistan
– longer than any other Soviet ambassador before or after – no one in
authority bothered to debrief him or ask his opinion. He was replaced
by Fikryat Tabeev, the first secretary of the Tatarstan Party Committee,
who arrived in Kabul on 26 November. He had been posted in such a
hurry that he was almost wholly ignorant of the situation in Afghanistan: he was not even aware that the Afghan Communist Party was split
into two factions. He spent his first days in Kabul planning for a visit
by Amin to Moscow. Nobody warned him that Moscow was already
thinking of a different way of dealing with Amin. Amin himself was
still smarting over Puzanov, that 'Parchamist' as he called him, and said
to Tabeev at one of their first meetings, 'I hope you've drawn the right
conclusion from the fate of your predecessor.'

General Zaplatin was not recalled until 10 December, as the final
decisions were being taken. Once again he told Ogarkov and Ustinov
that the Afghan army was up to the job. Amin, he said, had given not
the slightest sign of wavering in his loyalty to the Soviet Union. Ustinov
said irritably, 'You people in Kabul keep on coming up with differing
assessments. But we here have to take decisions.' There was no mention
of sending in the troops, though Ogarkov did mutter something about
the possibility of military action. Zaplatin said roundly that he saw no
need for any such thing.[26]

And so those senior Soviet officials who had doubts about the use
of military force were sidelined or ignored. Only the KGB representatives in Kabul seem to have argued consistently in favour of getting
rid of Amin. When the crisis peaked, the senior Soviet officials in the
Afghan capital were men with little or no experience of the country.

The Decision

The situation in Afghanistan continued to deteriorate. In an attempt
to place the blame for the excesses on his predecessor, Amin published
in November an official list of twelve thousand people who had been
liquidated since the coup in April 1978. But he nevertheless stepped up
his own use of terror against his opponents. He kept a portrait of Stalin
on his desk and brushed off Soviet remonstrations with the remark,

'Comrade Stalin showed us how to build socialism in a backward country: it's painful to begin with, but afterwards everything turns out just fine.' According to one foreign scholar, in the period between the Communist coup and the Soviet invasion twenty-seven thousand people may have been executed in the Pul-i Charkhi prison alone. After the invasion, mass graves were discovered at Herat and Bamyan. Other estimates put the number of people killed in the course of 1979 at fifty thousand or more. Many Afghans sought refuge in exile in Pakistan or Iran. As usual there can be no certainty about the figures.[27]

Despite the repressions, the unrest continued. In mid-October there were mutinies in the 7th Infantry Division, which was based on the outskirts of Kabul. Amin used regular forces and air strikes to discipline tribes that failed to obey his commands. The measures were insufficient. Amin controlled only 20 per cent of the country, and the proportion was steadily shrinking.

The Soviet leadership was still wavering over the decision to mount a major military action. Nothing had happened to alter their basic assessment, now eight months old, that the involvement of Soviet troops in Afghanistan would have damaging consequences for Soviet interests. But events were now accelerating beyond their control and preparations for a forceful change of government in Kabul began to take concrete form.

At the beginning of November the KGB brought Babrak Karmal and other potential members of an alternative Afghan government to Moscow.

The first military deployment directly connected with a possible operation against Amin was not authorised until 6 December. On that day the Politburo endorsed a proposal by Andropov and Ogarkov to despatch a detachment of five hundred men to Kabul, without any attempt to disguise their membership of the Soviet armed forces. After all, Amin had repeatedly pressed for the Russians to send a motor-rifle battalion to protect his residence.

On 8 December Brezhnev met Andropov, Gromyko, Suslov (1902–82), and Ustinov to discuss the situation at length, and to weigh the pros and cons of introducing Soviet forces. No record of this meeting has yet surfaced.

On 10 December Ustinov called Ogarkov into his office and told him that the Politburo had taken the preliminary decision to send troops into Afghanistan on a temporary basis. He ordered Ogarkov to devise a plan to deploy 75–80,000 troops. Ogarkov was surprised and angered. He was against sending any troops, because it made no sense. A force of seventy-five thousand was too small to do the job anyway. Ustinov ticked him off sharply. Ogarkov's job was not to teach the Politburo its business but to carry out its orders.

Ogarkov was called into Brezhnev's office later the same day. Andropov, Gromyko, and Ustinov were already there. Ogarkov reiterated his arguments: the Afghan problem had to be settled by political means; the Afghans had never tolerated the presence of foreigners on their soil; the Soviet troops would probably be drawn into military operations whether they liked it or not. His arguments fell on deaf ears, though he was assured that the executive decision to send the soldiers had not yet been taken.

That evening Ustinov told a meeting of senior officials in the Ministry of Defence that a decision to use force in Afghanistan would be taken shortly. From then onwards he issued a stream of verbal directives which the general staff converted into written orders.[28] The forces on the Afghan frontier were mobilised, and parachute and other elite units were sent to Turkestan from their bases all round the country.

The crucial meeting of the Politburo took place on 12 December. Those present included Brezhnev, Suslov, Andropov, Ustinov, and Gromyko. Others were also present, though the story has got around that they were excluded.[29] The meeting had before it a note from Andropov which said that following the murder of Taraki the situation in the party, the army, and the government apparatus had become more acute as a result of the mass repressions carried out by Amin.

Andropov made particular play with the stories of Amin's increasing contacts with the West. There was evidence, he said, that Amin had had contacts with the CIA, who may have recruited him while he was studying in the United States in the 1960s. The CIA were attempting to set up a 'New Great Ottoman Empire' to embrace also the southern republics of the Soviet Union. Soviet anti-aircraft defences were inadequate to defend targets in the southern republics, such as the cosmodrome in Baikonur, if the Americans installed missiles in Afghanistan. Afghanistan's uranium resources might become available to the Iranians and Pakistanis. The Pakistanis might successfully attempt to detach the southern provinces of Afghanistan. If Amin were indeed to shift Afghanistan's foreign policy decisively towards the West, it would be a serious setback to the long-standing Soviet aim – which went back to Khrushchev and beyond – of keeping Afghanistan orderly and friendly as a buffer on the southern border of the Soviet Union. Meanwhile anti-Soviet sentiment in Afghanistan was on the increase. Babrak Karmal and other Afghan exiles were asking the Soviets to help change the political situation in Afghanistan, if necessary by force of arms. The Soviet Union should act decisively to replace Amin and shore up the regime.

These arguments were not entirely specious. In 1979 CIA experts looked at the possibility of moving to Afghanistan the electronic intelligence facilities in Iran that had been closed down by Khomeini.[30] At the beginning of November American diplomats had been taken hostage in Tehran, and US policy had become more unpredictable. Soviet fears about the impact of events in Afghanistan on the security of Central Soviet Asia turned out retrospectively to have some justification when first the mujahedin and then the Taliban began to operate in Tajikistan and Uzbekistan alongside the Islamist opposition.[31]

Western and even Russian historians have tended to argue that the Russians were being paranoid, or that they were inventing reasons to justify their invasion. There may have been an element of that. But in the overwrought atmosphere of the Cold War each side was prone to exaggerate the threat from the other, and to engage in worst-case analysis – so much safer than simply hoping for the best. Later commentators have made much of the coincidence that NATO's decision to deploy Pershing II missiles in Europe was taken on the same day as the Politburo took its fateful decision on Afghanistan. Given the complex and confused way in which decisions are taken by most governments, it is unlikely that the news would have had much effect on the Politburo, even if it had reached them in time.

Whether Amin was ever recruited or even contacted by the CIA is unclear, and perhaps a red herring. Early in 1979 Ambassador Dubs had asked his CIA station chief whether it was true that Amin was a CIA agent and had been assured that he was not.[32] The Russians knew that Amin had met with Amstutz, the acting head of the US Embassy after Dubs's assassination, five times since February 1979. They had been unable to discover what had passed between the two men. But it would have been natural for Amin to follow the example of Daud and reinsure with both sides.

It may be, as some Americans have since maintained, that the Americans had no designs on Afghanistan of the kind the Russians attributed to them. But the Russians could not be sure of that at the time. So it was probably inevitable that they should now plan for the worst case: a significant strengthening of their enemy's position right on their southern border.

Andropov, backed by Ustinov, argued that these considerations were sufficient to justify a military intervention. He went on to note that there were already two Soviet battalions in Kabul. That should be enough for a successful operation: a grossly optimistic judgement with which the Soviet military strongly disagreed. But it would be wise, said Andropov, to have additional forces stationed close to the border, to be used, for example, against rebel groups.[33]

The meeting decided unanimously to send in the troops. No proper official note was kept. Instead Chernenko recorded the decision in a brief handwritten document coyly entitled 'The Situation in "A"'. It read:

1. Approve the considerations and measures set out by Comrades Andropov Yu V, Ustinov D F, and Gromyko A A. Authorise them to make minor modifications to these measures in the course of their execution. Questions which need to be decided by the Central Committee should be brought to the Politburo in good time. Comrades Andropov Yu V, Ustinov D F, and Gromyko A A are charged with the execution of these measures.

2. Instruct Comrades Andropov Yu V, Ustinov D F, and Gromyko A A to keep the members of the Politburo informed as these measures are being implemented.[34]

The only one of the inner circle of decision-makers who has left a personal account was Gromyko. In his memoirs he wrote: 'This bloody act [the murder of Taraki] produced a shocking impression on the Soviet leadership. Brezhnev was particularly upset by the murder. It was in that context that the decision was finally taken to introduce a limited contingent of Soviet forces into Afghanistan.

'After the decision was taken, I looked into Brezhnev's office and said, "Should we go for a formal governmental decision to send in the troops?" Brezhnev did not answer at first. He reached for the telephone: "Mikhail Andreevich, will you look in? We need to talk."'

Mikhail Suslov, the Politburo's influential chief ideologist, came into Brezhnev's office.

'Brezhnev told him of our conversation. He added, "In the circumstances we need to take a rapid decision, either to ignore the Afghan request for help, or to save the people's power and act in accordance with the Soviet–Afghan Agreement."

'Suslov said, "We have an agreement with Afghanistan, and we should fulfil our obligations under it quickly, now we have already taken our decision. We can discuss it in the Central Committee later."

'During the working sessions before the final decision was taken to invade, the Chief of the General Staff, Marshal Ogarkov, expressed the view that units of the Afghan army might resist. At first it was considered that our forces would simply help local inhabitants defend themselves against armed groups from outside the country, and assist the population with supplies of food and essentials such as fuel, cloth, soap, and so on.

'We wanted neither to increase the size of our contingent nor to get involved in serious military operations. And indeed our forces were for the most part garrisoned in the cities.'[35]

The Russians had foreseen all the disadvantages of forceful intervention – bloody involvement in a ferocious civil war, a huge expenditure of blood and treasure, and international pariahdom. They had worried that military intervention in Afghanistan would seriously affect East–West relations. By the end of 1979 this last was no longer such a consideration. Kryuchkov spelled out the background at a highly critical session of the Congress of People's Deputies in late 1989.[36] Détente had been unravelling and the arms race had been accelerating again, he then said. The US Senate had balked at the ratification of the SALT II treaty on the limitation of strategic nuclear weapons, a key element in the building of trust between the two superpowers. The Americans were developing a whole panoply of new weapons – the B-1 bomber and the new MX missile among them – and enforcing their strategic embargo against the Soviet Union with increasing rigour. Kryuchkov admitted that some of these American moves were in response to moves made by the Soviet side. But to the Russians it looked as if the Americans were trying to undermine the principle of strategic parity which for some years had provided a fairly stable framework for the superpower confrontation. The Russians calculated that they had little more to lose.

And after the death of Taraki their options were in any case progressively reduced. Their decision to intervene in Afghanistan, couched in the language of self-defence and aid to a friendly country, was certainly a grave error of policy. But it was not irrational, and by the time the final decisions were taken in December 1979 it had become all but inevitable. The idea that it was no more than an irresponsible move taken in secret by a small clique of gerontocrats – an idea convenient to all the other members of the Politburo of the day, and to all the innumerable civilian, military, and intelligence officials involved in Afghan affairs – does not stand up.

In any case, the consensus-building mechanisms of Soviet power were still working adequately enough. A special Party Plenum was held in June 1980, at which Gromyko delivered a rousing defence of Soviet policy in Afghanistan. The policy was endorsed by all those present. Edward Shevardnadze (1927–), Gorbachev's future Foreign Minister, was warmly applauded when he said, 'The whole world knows that the Soviet Union and its leader do not abandon their friends to their fate, that its words are always followed by deeds.'[37]

FOUR

THE STORMING OF
THE PALACE

Surprisingly, Amin appears to have had no suspicion that the tide in Moscow had turned against him. Right up to the very last minute he continued to ask Moscow to send troops to help him cope with the spreading opposition to his rule.

Practical preparations for his forceful overthrow had already begun even before the final political decision was taken in Moscow. A crack reconnaissance company was sent to reinforce the 345th Guards Independent Parachute Assault Regiment already in Bagram. Another small detachment from *Zenit*, disguised as technical troops under the command of Colonel Golubev, arrived in Bagram and was attached to the Muslim Battalion. There were now 130 *Zenit* troops in Afghanistan. The contingent in Kabul was housed in three villas rented by the Soviet Embassy in Kabul.

On 4 December General Kirpichenko, a senior KGB officer, and a group of officers of the Airborne Forces headed by General Guskov, were sent to Kabul to plan for the removal of Amin. On 11 December Guskov issued a preliminary directive for the seizure of *Dub* (Oak) – the code name for the Arg Palace where Amin was now in residence. The operation was to be carried out by the *Zenit* troops and a company of the Muslim Battalion. The Russians had no plan of the building, and all they knew of the arrangements for defending it was that the Presidential Guard consisted of up to two thousand men. Smaller squads were to seize the radio and television building, the security service building, and other objectives in Kabul.

At this stage the plan was that the Parchamists led by Karmal should mount a coup against Amin and that Soviet support should be provided by no more than the forces that were already available. Babrak Karmal, accompanied by Anakhita Ratebzad, was secretly flown into Bagram to join Watanjar, Gulabzoi, and Sarwari, who had been brought there a few days earlier. The new arrivals were housed in inadequately heated dugouts and badly fed on kasha, supplemented by cheese, sausages, and canned food bought by their escorts before they left Moscow.

On Thursday, 13 December, the Soviet commanders were briefed on their objectives. They were told that the local people would welcome them and would rise up against Amin, and the soldiers were told to show them every friendliness. Those stationed in Bagram were ordered to stand by to move to Kabul.[1]

Yevgeni Kiselev, a military interpreter who later became a well-known TV presenter, was on duty in Kabul that night. There were two other duty officers: a colonel and a junior lieutenant. At about seven o'clock the Chief of Staff to General Magometov, the new Chief Soviet Military Adviser, came to the duty officer's room for a private talk with the colonel. Afterwards the colonel, puzzled and anxious, told Kiselev and his colleague to go round the homes of all the senior military advisers – about three dozen of them – and tell them to assemble at the headquarters by nine o'clock to await orders. The orders never came, and the officers were allowed to go home. A few days later a young KGB officer told Kiselev that there had been a plan for a coup, but that it had been called off at the last minute.[2]

What had happened was that General Magometov and other senior Soviet representatives had discovered what was going on. They were appalled. They had not been consulted about the KGB plan. It was worthless, they told Moscow, and could not be carried out with the limited forces available. Without more military muscle, the plan might well fail, and the Soviet position in Afghanistan would be seriously compromised.

The operation was therefore postponed until a bigger force could be put together. Disagreement flared among the Soviet military and the politicians in Moscow about how large a force was needed. In 1968 the Soviet Union had deployed eighteen divisions, backed by eight Warsaw Pact divisions – some five hundred thousand men – to invade Czechoslovakia, a country with a much more forgiving terrain and no tradition of armed resistance to foreigners; a country moreover where, unlike Afghanistan, there was not already a civil war in progress.[3] The government and the KGB initially believed that the job could be done with some 35–40,000 soldiers. The generals naturally wanted more. During the planning phase, under pressure from General Magometov in Kabul and others, the number was increased, and the force which crossed the frontier at the end of December consisted of some eighty thousand soldiers.[4] Even this was nothing like the number that the soldiers believed would be necessary: Russian military experts later calculated that they would have needed between thirty and thirty-five divisions to stabilise the situation in Afghanistan, close the frontiers, secure the cities, road networks, and passes, and eliminate the possibility of armed resistance.[5]

The 40th Army Moves in

As the pace of preparations accelerated, an 'Operational Group of the Ministry of Defence of the USSR' was established on 14 December under Marshal Sergei Sokolov, the First Deputy Minister of Defence, a man already over seventy, tall, with a big bass voice and a calm, fatherly manner.[6] It began work in Termez, the last town on the Soviet side of the Afghan border, but before long moved to Kabul, where it remained. The group set up a new army, the 40th, in the Turkestan Military District, under General Tukharinov, who had arrived in September as the district's deputy commander. Since its objectives, its size, and the amount of time it spent in Afghanistan were all intended to be limited, the force was publicly referred to as 'The Limited Contingent of Soviet Forces in Afghanistan' (Ogranichenny Kontingent Sovietskikh Voisk v Afganistane, or OKSVA). This bland name was retained throughout the war for propaganda purposes, sneered at by foreign and domestic critics of the war, and is still often used even today.

The chain of military command which was thus created was riddled with contradictions. The 40th Army operated inside Afghanistan, but was formally subordinated to the Commander of the Turkmenistan Military District in Tashkent, who was himself responsible to the Chief of Staff in Moscow. Much of the military planning for operations within Afghanistan was done by the staffs of these three organisations. But the most senior officer in Afghanistan was the head of the Operational Group of the Ministry of Defence, and he too could and did take on himself the responsibility for managing operations, communicating directly with Moscow without taking too much notice of Tashkent. In addition there was the Chief Soviet Military Adviser to the Afghan government, who headed the large numbers of Soviet military advisers attached to the Afghan army, was responsible for coordinating the operations of that army with those of the 40th Army, and believed that he too had a responsibility for operational management. All this further added to the confusion which already surrounded the Soviet handling of policy in Afghanistan because of the divided counsels in Moscow and among the various Soviet representatives in Kabul. Forceful personalities – Gorbachev; General Varennikov (1923–2009), as head of the Ministry of Defence's Operational Group the most senior general in Afghanistan from 1984 to 1989; Yuli Vorontsov, the ambassador in the last months of the Soviet military presence – could knock heads together from time to time. But the problems caused by these tortured and contradictory arrangements never entirely went away and they compounded the difficulties which already existed because of the long-standing rivalry between the army and the KGB.

Thanks to some heroic feats of improvisation, the 40th Army was more or less ready to move by the end of 24 December. In his directive to the commanders, Ustinov justified the action as follows: 'In view of the political and military situation in the Middle East the latest appeal by the government of Afghanistan has been considered positively. It has been decided to introduce a few contingents of Soviet forces, deployed in the southern regions of the country, on the territory of the Democratic Republic of Afghanistan in order to provide international help to the friendly Afghan people, and also to create favourable conditions for the prevention of possible anti-Afghan actions on the part of neighbouring states…'[7] This was to remain the Soviet government's official justification for the war.

At midday on 25 December Ustinov issued the formal order to move: 'The state frontier of the Democratic Republic of Afghanistan is to be crossed on the ground and in the air by forces of the 40th Army and the Air Force at 1500 hrs on 25 December (Moscow time)'.[8] The Soviet intervention had begun.

What is surprising is not that there was a good deal of chaos, which of course there was; but that the formidable administrative and logistical difficulties were overcome, and the army deployed into Afghanistan on time. Indeed the Soviet general staff had always been very good at moving and supplying very large armies in very difficult situations. The methods were often crude in the extreme. They could cause great hardship to the soldiers themselves. But they had worked in the Second World War. In Afghanistan, despite the last-minute improvisations and the formidable obstacles of terrain and climate, they worked again, though some of the soldiers went hungry because the system had hiccuped.[9]

The main route for the invasion was the great road which runs around the periphery of Afghanistan, avoiding the mountains and linking the country's great cities, from Balkh, destroyed by Genghis Khan in 1220, through Mazar-i Sharif, with its great shrine devoted to Ali, the cousin and brother-in-law of the Prophet, and onwards anti-clockwise to Herat, Kandahar, and Kabul. This was part of the Silk Road, the road along which trade and armies passed for thousands of years, along which the British feared the Russians – or the Persians, or the French – would burst into their Indian empire. In those days the eastern arc of the circle did not exist; until a new road was built by Nadir Shah over the Salang Pass in the early 1930s, there was no proper road through the mountains of the Hindu Kush from Kabul to Mazar-i Sharif. In the 1950s the Americans and the Russians competed to modernise the road. The Americans built the southern stretch from Kabul to Kandahar, and the Russians built the rest. It became a road along which you could drive cars, lorries, and if necessary tanks. The Soviet soldiers called it the *betonka*, from the Russian word for concrete.

The plan was that the 5th Guards Motor-rifle Division would enter Afghanistan along the western route through Herat and Shindand. The 108th Motor-rifle Division would cross the Amu Darya at Termez. The 103rd Guards Air Assault Division and the remaining battalions of the 345th Guards Independent Parachute Assault Regiment would fly into Kabul and Bagram. The three divisions would be accompanied by the 860th Independent Motor-rifle Regiment, the 56th Guards Independent Airborne Assault Brigade, and a number of other units. In the course of the next six weeks they would be joined by another motor-rifle division, the 201st, and further smaller units.[10] The troops would secure the highway and garrison the main administrative centres along it. Tabeev, the Soviet Ambassador, had already informed Amin that the troops were coming. To ensure that their movements were properly coordinated, the commander of the 40th Army, General Tukharinov, met the commander of the operational division of the Afghan general staff, General Babadzhan, to discuss the details at Kunduz, the first Afghan town on the road from Termez.

The move began during the night of 24 to 25 December, when Soviet aircraft landed practically non-stop at Kabul and Bagram airports, carrying the soldiers of the 103rd Guards Air Assault Division from Vitebsk and the 345th Guards Independent Parachute Assault Regiment. Seven thousand seven hundred men, nine hundred items of military equipment, and over a thousand tons of supplies were flown to Kabul in the course of the next forty-eight hours. One aircraft – an Il-76 under the command of Captain Golovin carrying thirty-seven paratroopers – was lost when it crashed into a mountain and exploded as it was making its approach to Kabul airport. The British Embassy had observers at the airport. They were surprised that no attempt was made to disguise what was going on. The airport remained open for ordinary traffic and the British saw six helicopters with Soviet markings there.[11]

On the following afternoon the troops in Tajikistan began to cross the bridge which sappers had built with some difficulty across the fast-flowing and tricky Amu Darya. The soldiers were told that they were going to support the ordinary Afghan people against the counter-revolution, and that they had to get there before the Americans did. Although some conscripts were disgruntled because their demobilisation had been postponed, most of the soldiers were excited at the prospect of adventure. Though the mission was supposed to be peaceful, one battalion was told by its political officer that they would go through Afghanistan with fire and the sword, and the battalion commander added, 'If a single shot is fired at you, you should open up with everything you have got.' Marshal Sokolov, the head of the Operational Group of the Ministry of Defence then still stationed in Termez, came to see the soldiers off as they marched away to the tears of women and the sound of military music.[12]

The fourth battalion of the 56th Guards Independent Airborne Assault Brigade was sent ahead to secure the strategically indispensable Salang Pass, which lay on the route to the troops' final destinations.[13] Among them was a conscript sergeant, Sergei Morozov. He and his comrades found that there was no fighting to be done and the only casualties were two men wounded by accident. They lived in buildings without windows originally put up for the workers who had built the road over the Salang Pass. It was very cold at that height in midwinter, but the soldiers had brought their own stoves with them and scrounged the fuel from passing convoys. They had little else to do.[14]

Next came the 108th Motor-rifle Division under the command of Colonel Valeri Mironov. The division's officers had already flown across the frontier in helicopters to reconnoitre the route.[15] After a nasty moment when the column got stuck in the Salang Tunnel,[16] the division reached its position outside Kabul on the morning of 28 December. It was at first welcomed by the local population. The relationship deteriorated sharply when it became clear that the soldiers had come to stay. There was a nasty incident at the beginning of February, when a patrol was ambushed outside Kabul and an officer and eleven soldiers – all reservists – were killed. But on the whole these early months were the calmest the division was to experience during the whole of its time in Afghanistan.

The division got a new Chief of Staff, Colonel Boris Gromov, in the middle of January. He was not best pleased: it was a sideways move, when he had hoped for promotion. In Tashkent, where he stopped on his way down, officers were already saying that there would be a real fight in Afghanistan, though attacks on Soviet troops had barely started.

He continued to Kabul in a hospital plane, embarrassed because he was wearing the uniform of a peacetime colonel when all the other officers were in their wartime gear. In Kabul he had to sleep in the freezing aircraft because there was no other accommodation. The next day the plane would not take off because its wheels were frozen to the runway.[17]

Planning a Coup

The tangled situation inside Afghanistan itself was still evolving. On 20 December Amin moved from the Arg, the presidential palace in the centre of Kabul, to the Taj Bek Palace.[18] This had previously housed the headquarters of the Central Army Corps. It was situated on the south-west outskirts of the city and Amin may have thought that it would be more easily defensible. Some of the specialists from the Soviet KGB who advised Amin on his security arrangements were stationed inside the palace itself.

The palace was very solidly constructed: its walls were capable of withstanding artillery. Its defences had been carefully and intelligently organised. All the approach roads except one had been mined, and heavy machine guns and artillery were sited to cover the single open road. The inside of the palace was protected by Amin's personal bodyguard, consisting of his relatives and people he particularly trusted. They wore a special uniform which distinguished them from other Afghan soldiers: forage caps with white piping, white belts and holsters, and white cuffs on their sleeves.

A second line of defence consisted of seven posts, each manned by four sentries armed with a machine gun, a mortar, and automatic rifles. They were relieved every two hours. The external ring of the defences encircling the palace was manned by the Presidential Guard: three battalions of motorised infantry and one tank battalion, around 2,500 men in all. On one of the commanding heights three T-54 tanks were dug in and these could fire directly on the area around the palace with their cannon and machine guns. In addition, not far off there was an anti-aircraft regiment, armed with twelve 100mm anti-aircraft guns and sixteen anti-aircraft multiple machine guns; and also a construction battalion of about a thousand men. In Kabul itself there were two divisions and a tank brigade of the Afghan army.[19]

This was a powerful force for the Russians to contend with. Even with the reinforcements they were now bringing in, the forceful destruction by the Russians of Amin and his regime would be a daring military operation, in which the Soviet forces would be heavily outnumbered by well-armed opponents.

Amin and the Taj Bek Palace were the main target. But to secure Kabul as a whole the Russians also needed to control the General Staff building, the Radio and Television Centre, the telegraph building, the Ministry of Internal Affairs, the headquarters of the Gendarmerie (Tsarandoi), the headquarters of the Afghan Central Army Corps in the Arg Palace, and the Military Counter-intelligence building. These presented more tractable military problems than the Taj Bek, but would still require substantial forces and careful timing.[20]

On 18 December Kryuchkov sent General Yuri Drozdov, head of the KGB's Directorate of Illegal Intelligence, a war veteran, an accomplished linguist, and formerly an illegal agent in West Germany, to Afghanistan to consult with the KGB officers on the spot, see what was going on, and report back.[21] Drozdov told his alarmed wife that he was off for a few days, then left early the following morning with Colonel Kolesnik of the GRU, who was briefly back in Moscow. Drozdov's assistant took with him a briefcase for the KGB officer who was to meet them on arrival. The briefcase contained a recording of the speech that Babrak Karmal would broadcast once Amin had been overthrown. The party left it by accident at Bagram after they landed. Luckily it was safely recovered the next day.

That same day, the Muslim Battalion was moved from Bagram to Kabul and stationed on the outskirts of the city, less than a mile from the Taj Bek Palace, in an unfinished building with no glass in the windows. It was bitterly cold and the temperature went down to minus twenty degrees. The soldiers filled the gaps in the windows with waterproof capes, installed wood stoves, and erected bunk beds. The Afghans gave the Soviet soldiers woollen blankets made from camel hair and food was available in the local bazaar.

On 21 December Magometov summoned Kolesnik and Khalbaev, the commander of the Muslim Battalion, and ordered them to draw up a plan for the defence of the Taj Bek Palace in cooperation with Amin's

Presidential Guard. He told them nothing of any more dramatic plans. Kolesnik and Khalbaev accordingly went to call on Major Jandad, the commander of Amin's Guard. They quickly agreed on where the companies of the Muslim Battalion were to be placed and on the construction of a bridge across an irrigation ditch which formed an obstacle on the approaches to Taj Bek. Jandad gave the Russians a small Japanese radio so that they could communicate directly. The two Soviet officers reconnoitred the approach routes to the palace and the positions of the Afghan units surrounding it, and began drawing up their plans.

Soviet troops continued to arrive in Kabul, including another special forces detachment, code-named *Grom*. This consisted of another thirty men from *Alfa*, the KGB's anti-terror force, put together at one day's notice under the command of Major Mikhail Romanov. The men told their families that they were going for winter training to Yaroslavl, north of Moscow, and would therefore miss the New Year celebrations. They had no idea that they were about to be involved in some real fighting. As they were getting ready to leave Moscow in Andropov's personal Tu-134, someone photographed them boarding the plane; he was forced to expose his film.

On arrival in Kabul, they were briefly accommodated in the embassy before moving up to join the soldiers of the Muslim Battalion near the Taj Bek Palace. Here they zeroed in their weapons and were given Afghan uniforms – too small for many of them. They sewed pockets on their uniforms to take extra grenades and magazines; and on their sleeves they sewed white armbands as a recognition signal.

But the scenario for the deployment of Soviet troops in Kabul was about to change drastically. On 23 December Kolesnik and Khalbaev went to the embassy to explain their plan for defending the palace to General Magometov and General Ivanov. Out of the blue Ivanov suggested that they should consider an alternative plan, not to defend the palace, but to seize it by force. For that purpose Kolesnik would be given the two special forces groups *Grom* and *Zenit*, a company of the Muslim Battalion, and a company of paratroopers from the 345th Guards Independent Parachute Assault Regiment at Bagram commanded by Senior Lieutenant Vostrotin. Three members of the Gang of Four, Watanjar, Gulabzoi, and Sarwari, would take part in the assault to make it appear that it was not wholly a Soviet operation.[22]

Given the number of the Afghan troops defending the palace, even this enlarged contingent could hardly hope to prevail by force alone. Surprise and deception would be needed as well. Kolesnik and his colleagues spent the whole night planning. He reported back to Magometov the following morning that the success of the mission could only be assured if the whole of the Muslim Battalion was employed.

Kolesnik's plan was approved, with the additional forces he had requested. He was appointed to command the operation, which was code-named *Storm 333*. The plan was for two Shilka mobile anti-aircraft guns to bombard the palace. Vostrotin's paratroopers and two companies of the Muslim Battalion would prevent reinforcements from coming to the aid of the defenders. An anti-tank platoon under Captain Satarov would take out the three Afghan tanks guarding the palace. One company of the Muslim Battalion and the special forces groups *Zenit* and *Grom* would then mount the assault on the palace itself. The operation was originally planned for 25 December, but was postponed until 27 December.

At General Ivanov's request, Colonel Boyarinov was attached to the operation at the last minute to coordinate the actions of the two KGB groups. He had only returned to Kabul the previous day and was not yet familiar with either the situation or the people.[23]

To lull the suspicions of the Afghan guards, the Russian troops around the palace spent their time manoeuvring around their positions, firing flares, and starting up their vehicles. When the flares went off for the first time, the Afghans were naturally suspicious. They illuminated the Soviet positions with searchlights and Major Jandad came to find out what was going on. The Russians explained that they were simply engaged in normal training. The flares were intended to light up the approaches to the palace to guard against surprise attack. The vehicles' engines had to be kept running so that they did not freeze up. The Afghans' suspicions were eventually assuaged, though they complained that the noise of the engines was keeping Amin awake. These deceptive manoeuvres continued throughout the next three days.

On 26 December the officers of the Muslim Battalion invited their colleagues from the Presidential Guard to a party. The cooks prepared the pilaff, and the KGB provided the vodka, cognac, caviar, and other delicacies. Fifteen Afghan officers attended, including Major Jandad, the Guard commander, and Lieutenant Ruzi, who had murdered Taraki on his orders. Many toasts were drunk to Soviet–Afghan friendship. The Soviet waiters carefully served generous portions of vodka to the Afghans, but only water to the Russians. In a remarkable fit of indiscretion, Ruzi told one of the Russians that Taraki had been suffocated on Amin's orders. Jandad had the man taken away, telling the Russians that he was drunk and talking rubbish. The evening passed off without further incident.

The Russians still did not have good information about the internal layout of the palace. The next day therefore – the day planned for the actual assault – Drozdov persuaded the chief KGB adviser to Amin's personal guard, Yuri Kutepov, to take him, Kolesnik, and Khalbaev to look round. Drozdov was able to draw a sketch plan of each storey of the building. The Russians asked Jandad if his KGB advisers might take that evening off to attend a birthday party in honour of one of the Soviet officers. He agreed – which probably saved their lives.

Major Romanov and Major Semenov, the commanders of *Grom* and *Zenit*, set out separately to familiarise themselves with the terrain over which they would have to lead their men. Their expedition ended in farce and almost frustrated the whole operation. Not far from the palace was a smart restaurant much frequented by Afghan officers, from which there was a first-class view of Taj Bek, the approaches to it, and its defensive arrangements. It was closed, but they found the owner and told him that they were looking for somewhere to celebrate New Year's Eve with their officers. After observing what they needed, the two officers set off for their base. But on the way they were detained at an Afghan security post. The Afghan soldiers found their documents unconvincing and attempted to disarm them. After four hours and the consumption of a great deal of tea, they managed to persuade the Afghans to let them go. But for a moment it had looked as if their men might have had to go into action without their commanders.

Despite all these comings and goings, those Afghans who survived the assault said later that they had not believed that the Soviets were preparing an assault.

To facilitate the seizure of the palace and the other objectives in the centre of Kabul, and paralyse any Afghan response, the Russians planned to sabotage the government communications system. All the main cables ran through a single conduit just outside the communications centre in the middle of Kabul. The conduit was covered with a heavy slab of concrete. Specialists from *Zenit* reconnoitred the surroundings and laid their explosive charges. The sound of the explosion itself would be the signal to begin the assault.

Drozdov and Kolesnik gathered their commanders for a briefing on the second floor of the barracks where the Muslim Battalion was based. They told them that Amin had betrayed the April Revolution. Thousands of innocent people had been killed on his orders. He was in contact with the CIA. He therefore had to be eliminated.

Each group was then given its specific mission, its call signs, and its recognition signals. Each soldier handed in his personal documents for security reasons and was given the traditional hundred grams of vodka, and some sausage and bread. Most were too keyed up to eat.

No one questioned the orders. But some of the more perceptive – or cynical – wondered why, if Amin had gone over to the Americans, he had invited Soviet rather than American forces to protect him. Some said that the plan was crazy: they would all be killed. Boyarinov was still not entirely familiar with the operational plans and he was visibly nervous.[24] Almost none of the others had ever been in action. Some drank vodka to calm their nerves, others took valerian, but it did not help. Some left their cumbersome flak jackets behind so that they could move more freely.

Poison

The KGB had hankered after an alternative to the use of military force: assassination. Attempts had been made, but they had been abortive. KGB snipers had planned to kill Amin on his way to work, but they were frustrated when the Afghans changed their security measures. On 13 December the KGB tried to poison Amin with doctored Pepsi-Cola. Amin was unaffected.[25] His nephew Asadullah, the head of the counter-intelligence service, did fall ill. He was sent to Moscow with what the doctors thought was serious hepatitis. There he was arrested and imprisoned in the prison of Matrosskaya Tishina. The Russians returned him to Kabul after the overthrow of Amin. He was interrogated, tortured, and executed.

The KGB did not abandon their attempts to get rid of Amin quietly right up to the very last minute. Hours before the assault was due to begin, Amin organised a lunch party for members of his Politburo, ministers, and their families, in order to show them his splendid new palace and to celebrate the return from Moscow of Politburo member Panjshiri. Amin was in a state of euphoria. He told his colleagues that the Soviets were at last sending troops to support him. They had accepted his version of the death of Taraki and the change in the country's leadership. Panjshiri's visit had further strengthened the relationship. 'Soviet divisions are already on their way here,' he boasted. 'Paratroopers are landing in Kabul. Everything is going very well. I am always on the telephone with Comrade Gromyko and we are working together on the line to take with the outside world.'[26]

But in the course of the meal Amin and several of the guests lost consciousness. Jandad telephoned the Central Military Hospital and the Soviet Embassy polyclinic to get help. The food was sent for analysis and the Afghan cooks were arrested.

It so happened that a delegation of senior Soviet military doctors led by Colonel Alekseev was in Kabul at the time. Colonel Alekseev and Colonel Kuznechkov, a doctor from the embassy's polyclinic, had been invited to the palace among other things to attend to Amin's daughter, who had just had a baby.[27] They arrived at about two o'clock in the afternoon, accompanied by a woman doctor and a nurse from Kabul. They were subjected to an unusually rigorous search when they arrived, and understood why when they saw people sitting and lying in the vestibule, on the stairs, and in the rooms. Those who had recovered consciousness were doubled up in pain. They had evidently been poisoned, allegedly by a long-standing KGB agent, Mikhail Talybov, who had been infiltrated into Amin's entourage as a cook. Kryuchkov subsequently maintained that the substance administered was no more than a powerful sleeping draught. If so, they seem to have got the dose wrong.[28]

The Soviet doctors were summoned to Amin. He was dressed only in his underpants, with his jaw hanging and his eyes rolling. He was in a deep coma and his pulse was very weak. He looked as if he were dying. The doctors immediately set to work to save him and by six o'clock they had succeeded. When he opened his eyes, he asked, 'What happened? Was it an accident, or was it sabotage?'

Alexander Shkirando, who had been working as a Soviet military interpreter in Afghanistan since September 1978, was also at the palace that day. He too ate whatever it was that had been used to poison Amin and his colleagues. He was taken severely ill, spent six weeks in an Afghan military hospital, and was then evacuated to hospital in Moscow. He did not go back to the military, but returned on many occasions to Afghanistan as a journalist.[29]

The doctors realised that something very odd was going on, so they sent the nurse and the woman doctor back to Kabul, out of harm's way. They did not know, of course, that they had frustrated a plan to simplify the whole Soviet military operation by putting Amin out of action before it began.

The Storm

Jandad was greatly disturbed by the incident. He posted additional guards inside and outside the palace and put the Afghan tank brigade on alert.

The time for the assault was altered several times during the day. But at about 6 p.m. Magometov ordered Kolesnik to begin the operation as soon as possible, without waiting for the explosion that was to destroy the communications centre. Twenty minutes later an assault group under Captain Satarov quietly moved out to neutralise the three entrenched Afghan tanks commanding the approaches to the palace. The men covered the last part of the approach on foot through snow up to their waists. The Afghan sentries were rapidly killed by snipers. The tank crews were in their barracks, too far away to get to their vehicles, and the tanks were soon secured.

Now two red rockets were fired to signal the beginning of the assault. It was by then about 7.15 p.m. The palace was fully illuminated inside and out, and the Afghans were sweeping the surroundings with their searchlights. The Soviet Shilka anti-aircraft guns opened fire. The palace walls were so solid that most of the shells simply bounced off, scattering splinters of granite but causing little serious damage.

The 1st company of the Muslim Battalion then moved forward in their armoured fighting vehicles. The KGB special forces groups under the command of Boyarinov travelled with them. They had orders to take no prisoners, and not to stop to aid wounded comrades: their task was to secure the building whatever the odds.

Almost as soon as they started, one of the BMPs (infantry fighting vehicles) from the Muslim Battalion stopped. The driver had lost his nerve, jumped out of the vehicle, and fled. He returned almost immediately: things were even more frightening outside the vehicle.[30] The vehicles crashed through the first barrier, crushing the Afghan sentry. They continued under heavy fire, and for the first time the crews heard the unfamiliar, almost unreal, sound of bullets rattling against the armour of their vehicles. They fired back with everything they had and soon the gun smoke inside the vehicles made it almost impossible for the crews to breathe. The safety glass in the vehicles was shot out. A vehicle was hit and caught fire; some of the crew were wounded when they bailed out. One man slipped as he jumped and his legs were crushed under the vehicle. Another vehicle fell off the bridge which the Russians had constructed across the irrigation ditch and the crew were trapped inside. Their commander called for help by radio, and in doing so managed to block the radio link, paralysing the communications of the whole battalion.

The assault force drove as near as they could to the palace walls, disembarked, and threw themselves at the doors and windows of the ground floor. Confusion was increasing by the minute. Unified command had broken down and the soldiers were having to act in small groups on their own initiative. They were pinned down by fire from the defenders of the palace which the artillery had failed to neutralise. There was a moment of panic, and they froze for perhaps five minutes. Then a Shilka destroyed the machine gun which had been firing down from one of the palace windows, and the men picked themselves up and moved forward with their assault ladders.

They burst into the palace in ones and twos. Boyarinov was among them. The entrance hall was brightly lit, and the defenders were shooting and lobbing grenades from the first-floor gallery. The Russians shot out all the light bulbs they could, but some remained burning. They fought their way up the staircase and began to clear the rooms on the first floor with automatic fire and grenades. They heard the crying of women and children. One woman was calling out for Amin. A grenade cut the power supply and the remaining lights went out. Many Russians had already been wounded, including Boyarinov.

The Russians' distinctive white armbands were by now barely visible under a layer of grime and soot. To make matters worse, Amin's personal guards were also wearing white armbands. But in the excitement, the Russians were swearing horribly, using the choicest works in the Russian lexicon; and it was this that enabled them to identify one another in the darkness. It also meant that the defenders, many of whom had trained in the Soviet airborne school in Ryazan, now realised for the first time that they were fighting Soviet troops, not Afghan mutineers as they had thought. They began to surrender, and despite the order not to take prisoners, most of them were spared.

'Suddenly the shooting stopped,' one *Zenit* officer remembered. 'I reported to General Drozdov by radio that the palace had been taken, that there were many dead and wounded, and that the main thing was ended.'[31]

During the fighting, Colonel Alekseev and Colonel Kuznechkov, the two Soviet doctors, had hidden as best they could in the ballroom. There they caught sight of Amin, walking painfully along the corridor in white shorts and a T-shirt, illuminated by the fires that had broken out, covered with tubes and holding up his arms to which the bottles of medical solution were still attached, 'looking like grenades'. Alekseev left his shelter and removed the tubes and the bottles, pressing the veins with his fingers to stem the blood. He then took Amin to the bar. A child emerged from one of the side doors, crying and rubbing his eyes with his fists. It was Amin's five-year-old son. Amin and the small boy both sat down by the wall.

Amin still not realise what was happening. He told his adjutant to telephone the Soviet military advisers: 'The Soviets will help.' The adjutant said that it was the Soviets who were doing the firing. Amin threw an ashtray at him in a fury and accused him of lying. But after he himself had tried and failed to get through to the Chief of the Afghan General Staff he quietly muttered, 'I guessed it. It's all true.'[32]

There are various accounts of how he died. Possibly he was killed deliberately, possibly he was caught by a random burst of fire. One story is that he was killed by Gulabzoi, who had been given that specific task.[33] When the gun smoke cleared, his body was lying by the bar. His small son had been fatally wounded in the chest.[34] His daughter was wounded in the leg. Watanjar and Gulabzoi certified that he was dead. The men from *Grom* left, their boots squelching as they walked across the blood-soaked carpets. Later that night Amin's body was rolled up in a carpet and taken out to be buried in a secret grave.

The battle had lasted forty-three minutes from start to finish, apart from some brutal skirmishes with elements of the Presidential Guard stationed nearby, who were rapidly dealt with. Five members of the Muslim Battalion and the 9th Company of paratroopers were killed and some thirty-five suffered serious wounds.[35] The KGB special forces groups also lost five dead. Among them was Colonel Boyarinov, who was killed by friendly fire right at the end of the battle. He seems to have been cut down by Soviet soldiers who had orders to shoot anyone who emerged from the palace before it was properly secured.[36]

Colonel Kuznechkov, the military doctor who had helped to cure Amin of his poisoning, was also dead, killed by a burst of bullets fired into the ballroom. When his colleague, Colonel Alekseev, tried to load his body on one of the BMPs, he was roughly told by the crew that they were taking only the wounded, not the dead. But Alekseev managed to persuade them to take the colonel nevertheless.

The victorious Soviets took a hundred and fifty prisoners from Amin's personal guard. They did not count the dead. Perhaps two hundred and fifty of the Afghans guarding the palace had been killed by their erstwhile Soviet comrades in arms.

The Soviet soldiers who had been wounded during the storming of the palace were taken to the polyclinic at the nearby Soviet Embassy. Galina Ivanov, the wife of the economic adviser Valeri Ivanov, had of course known nothing of what was happening until a terrible sound of shooting broke out down the road and vehicles started bringing in the dead and wounded. One of the vehicles was shot up by the embassy guards, who also had no idea what was going on.

All the embassy doctors lived in one of the *microrayons*, the Soviet-built suburbs on the other side of town, and were unable to get to the embassy. Galina had taken courses in nursing while she was at university and she was called in to help. She worked from 8 a.m. until 11 p.m. Apart from Galina, the only other helpers available were the embassy dentist, a woman who had been a nurse in the Second World War, and a couple of other women. There was another medically qualified person around: the wife of one of the Orientalist advisers. She was a neurosurgeon, but when she saw what was going on she spun on her heels and walked off.

First the little team sorted out the living from the dead. Then the dentist had to use his barely relevant skills to operate as best he could, while Galina and the others bound up the wounds. Galina found it an absolutely horrible experience. When she went back to Moscow soon afterwards she could not understand how people could walk around the streets as if nothing had happened.[37]

Meanwhile the Russians, triggered by the explosion at the communications centre, had moved with brutal speed and carefully focused violence to take over their other objectives in the city.

The most important and difficult target was the General Staff building. Fourteen special forces troops, accompanied by Abdul Wakil, a future foreign minister of Afghanistan, were assigned to deal with it. A deception plan was devised to ease the odds. That evening General Kostenko, the Soviet adviser to Colonel Yakub, the Chief of Staff, took a number of Soviet officers to pay a formal call, including General Ryabchenko, the commander of the newly arrived 103rd Guards Air Assault Division. They discussed questions of mutual interest with the unsuspecting Yakub, a powerful man who had trained in the Ryazan Airborne School and spoke good Russian. Ryabchenko had no difficulty in behaving naturally, since he knew nothing of what was about to take place. Meanwhile other Soviet special forces officers were spreading through the building, handing out cigarettes and chatting to the Afghan officers working there. When the explosion went off, they burst into Yakub's office. Yakub fled to another room after a scuffle in which his assistant was killed, but then surrendered and was tied up and placed under guard. Ryabchenko, taken wholly by surprise, sat immobile throughout. Kostenko was nearly killed by the Soviet troops.

The fighting lasted an hour. As it died away, Abdul Wakil appeared in Yakub's office. He talked in Pushtu to the general for a long time, and then shot him. Twenty Afghans were killed. A hundred were taken prisoner, and as they so heavily outnumbered the attackers, they were herded into a large room and tied up with electric cable.

There was an unpleasant moment when a company of Soviet paratroopers, who had arrived forty minutes late, advanced on the General Staff building in armoured personnel carriers and opened up a heavy fire, forcing the *Zenit* troops inside to take cover as tracer bullets flew across the room glowing like red fireflies. Order was restored and the paratroopers helped to secure the building.

The Russians needed the Radio and Television Centre to broadcast Karmal's appeal to the people at the earliest moment. They reconnoitred it very carefully throughout 27 December, some of them posing as automation experts to get inside the building. In the assault seven Afghans were killed, twenty-nine wounded, and over a hundred taken prisoner. One Soviet soldier received a minor wound.

No one was killed on either side in the telegraph building, and the defenders in the Central Army Headquarters and the Military Counter-Intelligence building surrendered without a fight. There was no serious resistance at the Interior Ministry building either, though one Russian soldier was wounded and subsequently died. The attackers had orders to arrest the Interior Minister, S. Payman, but he had fled in his underwear and sought refuge with his Soviet advisers.

By the morning the firing had more or less died down. But not quite. As they drove into town in their Mercedes, the senior officers who had directed the attack on the palace were fired on by a nervous and trigger-happy young paratrooper. The bullets hit the car but not the occupants. A colonel jumped out and gave the soldier a sharp clip round the ear. General Drozdov asked the young lieutenant in charge, 'Was that your soldier? Thank you for not teaching him to shoot straight.'[38]

Once the fighting in the Taj Bek Palace had stopped, Colonel Kolesnik set up his command post there. The victorious Soviet soldiers were dropping with fatigue. Since it was possible that Afghan troops in the area might try to retake the palace, they set up a perimeter defence, their nerves still at full stretch. When they heard rustling in the lift shaft, they assumed that Amin's people were launching a counter-attack through the passages which led into the palace from outside. They sprang to arms, fired their automatic weapons, and hurled grenades.

It was the palace cat.[39]

– FIVE –

AFTERMATH

The inhabitants of Kabul paid little attention to what happened during that dramatic night. They were too used to shooting in the capital and most slept quietly. When they woke up the next day, Afghanistan had a new government, and the small boys were back selling cigarettes around the ruined government communications conduit as if nothing had happened.

Once the city had been secured, Kabul Radio broadcast Babrak Karmal's pre-recorded appeal to the peoples of Afghanistan. 'Today the torture machine of Amin has been smashed,' he announced, 'his accomplices – the primitive executioners, usurpers and murderers of tens of thousands of our fellow countrymen – fathers, mothers, sisters, brothers, sons and daughters, children and old people...'

Karmal himself was not in the studio: he had remained in Bagram under the protection of the KGB. On the evening of 27 December – before the fighting was over – Andropov came through on the telephone 'to congratulate him on the victory of the second stage of the revolution' and on his 'appointment' as chairman of the Revolutionary Committee of the Democratic Republic of Afghanistan, an appointment which had not yet been endorsed by any formal Afghan body. The next morning Karmal travelled to Kabul in a column of armoured fighting vehicles, supported by three tanks, and lived for the first few days with his KGB protection team in a guest villa on the outskirts of Kabul. On 1 January a telegram arrived from Brezhnev and Kosygin congratulating him on the occasion of his 'election' to the highest state and party posts.[1]

The gates of the Kabul prisons were thrown open and thousands of prisoners now poured out into the streets. One of them was Dr Lutfullah Latif, a Parchamist who had worked in the Health Ministry. He had been arrested in November 1978, interrogated and tortured for ten days, then sent to Pul-i Charkhi. Three days before the Soviet coup, he and the other prisoners could see and hear the Soviet aircraft landing non-stop at the airport. Then one evening there was firing for half an hour, followed by silence. The door to the prison block was broken down, some Afghan and Russian officers appeared, took the guards prisoner and then left again, taking the keys to the cells with them. It took the prisoners a day to force open the locks. There were political meetings going on outside in the prison yard. The prisoners spent the next night in their cells, but the following day buses were sent to take them home. All were freed, whatever their political affiliation.[2]

But that was not the end of the arrests and the repressions. Karmal's people began to settle scores with their political enemies. 'Revolutionary Troikas' arrested people, sentenced them, and executed them on the spot with a bullet in the back of the neck. Amin's guards were among the first victims. The commanders of units which had remained loyal to Amin were arrested, and the prisons were soon full again. The Russians protested. Karmal replied, 'As long as you keep my hands bound and do not let me deal with the Khalq faction there will be no unity in the PDPA and the government cannot become strong ... They tortured and killed us. They still hate us! They are the enemies of the party!'[3]

Taraki's wife had been imprisoned in Pul-i Charkhi in a separate small building surrounded by a wall and barbed wire. Now her place was taken by the women from Amin's family (the men had all been killed). They operated on Amin's eldest daughter – the one who had been wounded when the palace was stormed – and then incarcerated her in the prison with her new baby. Najibullah released the women twelve years after their arrest, two years after the official end of the Soviet war in Afghanistan, on the eve of the final collapse of his regime.[4]

The large number of Soviet civilians living in Kabul had, of course, no idea of what was going on. Even the new Soviet Ambassador, Fikryat Tabeev, had not been warned what was to happen. He was taken entirely by surprise when the communications conduit exploded and the lights in the embassy went out. His wife was furious that her husband had been left – literally – in the dark.[5] He called General Kirpichenko for clarification. Kirpichenko replied that he was too busy to talk just then, but would report in the morning.

Andrei Greshnov, a military interpreter with the 4th Afghan Tank Brigade, had stolen a small fir tree in preparation for the New Year, set it up in his apartment in the new *microrayon*, and decorated it with baubles looted from the officers' mess. On the wall he wrote 'Happy New Year 1980'. When he looked in on his old apartment nine years later, the inscription was still there. For several days he had heard the aeroplanes flying into Bagram, taking off and landing in a continual distant roar. Like everyone else, he had assumed that these were the aircraft bringing the regiment which the Soviet government had promised to send to defend Amin. In fact they were bringing in not a regiment but the whole 103rd Guards Air Assault Division, as well as the remaining paratroopers from the 345th Guards Independent Parachute Assault Regiment.

After he had finished work on the evening of 27 December, Greshnov took a bottle of Aist vodka round to his Azerbaijani friend Mamed Aliev, who lived in the old *microrayon*. Aliev had a splendid Japanese television with a built-in radio, which he had acquired in town in exchange for a pistol which was surplus to his requirements. They turned on the radio. Something odd was happening. Several stations were on air, all calling themselves 'Radio Kabul'. One, broadcasting in Pushtu, was denouncing the enemies of Amin and the April Revolution. Another, broadcasting in Dari and barely audible through the jammers, claimed that power was passing into the 'hands of the healthy forces in the party'.

Greshnov and Aliev were frying potatoes and arguing about how much salt to put on them when the firing started. The street outside was lit up as if it were daytime. They rushed out on to the balcony – and rushed straight back in again as tracer bullets whistled around them. Tanks started firing further off.

Greshnov set out for home; the Soviet military advisers would be looking for him to interpret. But as he ducked out of the door, he was gripped by a huge figure in an anorak, armed with a foreign-looking machine gun. He stuttered in Dari that he had to go to work to help defend the regime against counter-revolutionary treachery. 'Work's over for today, laddie,' was the quiet reply in pure Russian. 'Thank your mother that you were born with fair hair, otherwise you'd have been shot outright. Go back where you came from.' It was a long time before Aliev opened the door in response to his frantic banging: he was terrified that he would be shot because he looked like an Afghan. The two men spent the night watching through the window as soldiers and civilians were rounded up and taken away, Soviet armoured vehicles clattered around the streets and disorganised firing echoed throughout the city.

Greshnov got home early the following morning. Where there had been a flowerbed on the roundabout outside his house, there was now an anti-tank gun, its barrel trained on his apartment block. The wives of some of the Soviet advisers were giving home-made food to the Soviet soldiers. Out on the street he met Latif, a driver from the 4th Afghan Tank Brigade, who told him, 'Our tanks were destroyed outside the TV station. No one survived.' Greshnov swore loudly and asked, 'Who did that?' Then he realised he was being stupid: it was of course the Russians who had done it. It took him some time to sort out his loyalties, and when Latif told him that one Afghan tank had knocked out a Soviet armoured personnel carrier before it was destroyed he was briefly delighted.[6]

Alexander Sukhoparov had been an adviser to the PDPA since August 1979. He too could not understand what was happening during the night. He had to get his news from the BBC and other foreign radio stations. On the morning of 28 December Soviet paratroopers arrived to protect the hotel where he was staying. They were in a state of high excitement, but they too had no good idea of what had happened or of why they were there. They asked Sukhoparov about Afghan customs, about the layout of the town, about the attitude of the people to their arrival. It was a cold sunny day and people were wandering the streets, congratulating one another that Amin had been overthrown.

'They greeted our soldiers warmly,' Sukhoparov wrote later, 'gave them flowers, and called them friends and liberators.'[7]

Nikolai Zakharov, a Komsomol official, had arrived in May 1979 to help the Afghans create a Communist youth organisation. He was at the airport on 25 December and saw military vehicles being unloaded from a transport aircraft and soldiers mustering alongside.

'They're ours,' cried Zakharov's interpreter, Abramov.

'You're off your head,' Zakharov said dismissively. 'How would our soldiers have got here?'

'They really are ours,' said the interpreter. 'Look at the red stars on their fur hats.'

Three days later Zakharov wrote up his diary: 'Last night, 27 December, at about 18.30, there was an outbreak of automatic and artillery fire which grew until it reached a maximum at 19.30. The sound of gunfire came from the airport, from the House of the People, and at times very close from the nearby residential area.' And then he solemnly transcribed the official justification for the overthrow of Amin.[8]

It had been a remarkably daring, successful, and – considering the circumstances – cheap affair. Twenty-nine Soviet soldiers had been killed in action, forty-four in accidents (including the paratroopers who were killed when their transport plane crashed into the mountains as it was coming in to land in Kabul), and seventy-four wounded. Afghan military losses were of course higher: about three hundred dead. There were no civilian casualties because the Russians had not used aircraft to soften up their targets. Almost exactly ten years later, in December 1989, the Americans invaded Panama to oust General Noriega. The military casualties suffered by both sides were similar to those suffered in Kabul. But because the Americans used aircraft, there were also civilian casualties, the number of which remains a matter of controversy.[9]

The operation seemed to have been politically successful as well. An oppressive ruler had been removed and one agreeable to the Soviets had been installed. Dmitri Ryurikov and his colleagues in the Soviet Embassy were sent out to canvass opinion. All reported that their Afghan contacts were pleased Amin had gone. But some had added,

'We are glad to see you. But you will be very well advised to leave again as soon as you can.'[10] As they fanned out through Afghanistan, the Soviet troops heard much the same thing: their arrival was welcomed, sometimes with flowers; but they too were reminded that their early departure would be even more welcome.

Protesters and Doubters

But back in the Soviet Union the first few protests were voiced almost immediately. A handful of dissenters – Yelena Bonner, the wife of Andrei Sakharov, and others – issued a statement on 29 January 1980. They entirely rejected the official version of events and the contention of the authorities that the Soviet people wholeheartedly supported their action. 'There is a war in Afghanistan, Afghans are dying and our own boys are dying too, the children and grandchildren of those who survived the Second World War and those who did not return from it.' They appealed to those who remembered the earlier war, those who remembered Vietnam, people of goodwill everywhere, to demand that the Soviet troops be withdrawn in accordance with the resolution which had just received overwhelming support at an emergency meeting of the UN General Assembly.

Andrei Sakharov, the Nobel Prize winner who had helped develop the Soviet hydrogen bomb, also demanded the withdrawal of Soviet troops and their replacement by UN or neutral Muslim forces. He called for the widest possible boycott of the Olympic Games, which were shortly due to be held in Moscow, and castigated the militaristic thinking which had led first to the invasion of Czechoslovakia and now to the invasion of Afghanistan.[11] He was exiled to the provincial city of Gorky (Nizhni Novgorod) for his pains. That summer, Tatiana Goricheva and Natalya Malachuskaya were expelled from the Soviet Union for appealing to conscripts to go to prison rather than serve in Afghanistan.[12]

Even inside the official machine, some were filled from the very beginning with a sense of foreboding, not only for the fate of the Soviet intervention in Afghanistan, but for the fate of the Soviet Union itself. On 20 January Academician Oleg Bogomolov of the Institute of the Economy of the World Socialist System, one of Moscow's most prestigious think tanks, sent a stinging analysis to the Central Committee and to Andropov, the head of the KGB. The paper was entitled 'Some Ideas about Foreign Policy Results of the 1970s (Theses)' and it contained a substantial section on the consequences of the Afghan adventure. It pointed out that the rebels could now appeal to the Afghan people to fight the foreign infidels as well as the godless Communists in Kabul. The USSR had got itself involved in yet another confrontation, this time on its volatile southern flank. Aid to the rebels from the Americans, the Arabs, and the Chinese was increasing. The Soviet Union's influence on the Non-Aligned Movement had already suffered. Détente and arms control had been blocked. Even some of the Warsaw Pact countries seemed unhappy. The invasion might even help to reconcile the USA and Iran, despite the crisis in which the two countries were now locked.[13]

All these disadvantages had, of course, been pointed out in the policy discussions which preceded the decision to invade. The paper was too late to influence events and produced no reaction from those to whom it had been addressed. But at least the authors were not punished.

The Moscow Institute of Oriental Studies had carried on the distinguished academic tradition of the Russian Orientalists of the nineteenth and earlier twentieth centuries. Their Afghanistan department was strongly staffed with scholars who covered every aspect of the country's political, economic, and social life. Many of the linguists were called up at the beginning of the war to serve as interpreters and specialist advisers. There was no way of hiding what was going on from the staff of the institute, where opinion was almost entirely against the war. But the politicians did not listen to them either.[14]

The British Foreign Office presented a Soviet Deputy Foreign Minister who visited them in January 1980 with a historical account of British failures in Afghanistan. He said, 'This time it will be different,' as people usually do when they set out to repeat the mistakes of their predecessors.[15]

Many well-placed officials inside the government machine were appalled. Anatoli Chernyaev, an official in the International Department of the Central Committee Secretariat, described in his diary on

30 December how the rest of the world had universally condemned the Soviet action. The Soviet Union's claims to be promoting détente lay in ruins. 'Who needed that? The Afghan people? Amin might well have turned the place into a second Cambodia. But was it merely out of a sense of revolutionary philanthropy and charity that we have taken a step that will be classed in world opinion with Finland in 1939 and Czechoslovakia in 1968? The argument that we had to act to defend our frontiers is laughable … I don't think there has ever been a time in the history of Russia, not even under Stalin, when such an important step was decided in such a small circle, without any hint of the slightest consultation, advice, discussion, consideration.' A few weeks later, as he tried to work out how and why the decision had been taken, he concluded, 'In a word – the very existence of the state, not only its prestige, is at stake because the whole system and the mechanisms of power have decayed, because of the psychological decay of the supreme leader, and the advanced years of the other leaders whose average age is seventy-five. And there is absolutely no way out.' Speculation about who was behind the decision to invade was spreading among officials in Moscow. Chernyaev drew what he thought was the obvious conclusion: the KGB had exploited Brezhnev's incapacity in order to launch this 'crime'.[16]

Early in the New Year Anatoli Adamishin, an up-and-coming official in the Foreign Ministry, wrote even more strongly in his own diary: 'A few days ago we moved our troops into Afghanistan. What an exceptionally ill-considered decision! What are they thinking about? It's clear that they are showing one another how tough they are. OK, let's show our muscle. In reality it is an act of weakness, of despair. To hell with Afghanistan. Why on earth should we get mixed up in a completely lost situation? We are wasting our moral capital, others will stop trusting us entirely. We have not been in such a mess since the Crimean War in the last century: everyone is against us, and our allies are weak and unreliable. If they are incapable of running their own country, then we will not succeed in teaching them anything with our economy in tatters, our inability to manage our political affairs or to organise anything properly and so on. What's more, we seem to be getting mixed up in a civil war, even though it is being fed from abroad. Did we learn nothing from Vietnam? Why should we try to play the role of a universal saviour, when we need to work out properly what we want in our own external and internal affairs. The terrible thing is that this is not what concerns our leaders. Their concern is to hold on to power, to engage in domestic manoeuvres, to demonstrate their high ideological principles, which incidentally we no longer understand ourselves ... The action in Afghanistan is the quintessence of our internal affairs. The economic disorganisation, the fear of the Central Asian republics, the approaching Congress, the habit of deciding problems by force, the ideological dogmatism – what sort of a socialist revolution is that, what sort of revolutionaries are these? There is the same obscurity everywhere. What sort of help can we give them? We were better off with the King [Zahir Shah]: at least he listened to us.'[17]

The Outside World Reacts

The Americans had of course been keeping close track of what the Russians were up to in Afghanistan. Their most reliable resource was satellite intelligence, which enabled them to follow the changes in Soviet military dispositions. But they were painfully aware that they had very little idea of what lay behind the Soviet moves. On 17 September 1978 Thomas Thomson, the President's assistant for national security, sent his boss, Zbigniew Brzezinski, a memorandum entitled 'What are the Soviets doing in Afghanistan'. His answer was blunt: 'Simply, we don't know'.[18] The Americans correctly concluded after the Herat rising that the Russians would be unlikely to send their army to support an unpopular Afghan government.[19] By the autumn they still judged that the forces the Russians were now assembling were sufficient only to protect Soviet citizens, not to subdue the country. They nevertheless began to make contingency plans in case the Russians did invade after all.[20] Later the analysts were blamed for not having predicted the invasion earlier. The CIA's own post-mortem showed that what had gone wrong was quite simple: the Russians themselves had been uncertain until the last minute if, when, or in what numbers to invade, and so there was no basis on which an earlier assessment could sensibly have been made.

With far less intelligence capacity than the Americans, the British were also keeping track of events. The murder of Taraki, they thought, did raise the possibility that the Soviets might move into Afghanistan. One British official wondered towards the end of November 1979, perhaps presciently, 'Wouldn't we be better off with a socialist regime rather than a reactionary Islamic type that is giving us problems elsewhere?'[21]

After the invasion had taken place, most British and American analysts tended to agree that the Soviets had undertaken it with reluctance, in order to prevent the crumbling of their position in a country which was within their legitimate sphere of influence. Both before and after the invasion, British analysts specifically rejected the idea – popular in the press at the time – that the Russians were after a warm-water port in the Indian Ocean. And indeed no serious evidence has yet emerged, beyond a couple of remarks reported in one Soviet military memoir, that the Soviet invasion was intended as a first step towards securing a warm-water port or – another theme of Western propaganda – towards incorporating Afghanistan into the Soviet Union.[22]

Both themes were, however, to form a telling element in the all-out campaign of public denunciation which was now unleashed by the Americans and the British. The Soviets, they said, had violated international law with their brutal and unprovoked surprise attack on a very small neighbour. The claim that the Soviet forces had been invited in was a transparent fiction, just as it had been before the invasion of Czechoslovakia. It was another example of the Soviet Union's insatiable imperial appetite, of their claim that the so-called 'Brezhnev Doctrine' gave them the right to keep countries in their bloc by force.

The outrage was genuinely felt, but there was also an element of posturing. The Americans were still smarting over their humiliation at the hands of the Iranians, who had just taken American diplomats hostage in Tehran. President Carter was determined to show his mettle and remarked to an aide, 'Because of the way that I've handled Iran, they think I don't have the guts to do anything. You're going to be amazed at how tough I'm going to be.'[23] He publicly denounced the Soviets on 28 December, told his cabinet that the invasion was 'the greatest threat to world peace since the Second World War' (ignoring the much more dangerous crises around Cuba and Berlin in Khrushchev's day), called for a world boycott of the forthcoming Moscow Olympic Games, and imposed economic sanctions. The British Prime Minister, Mrs Thatcher (1925–), enthusiastically followed suit.[24] On 23 January, in his annual State of the Union Address, the President accused the Soviet Union of deliberately moving to threaten Western oil supplies and said, 'Let our position be absolutely clear: An attempt by any outside force to gain control of the Persian Gulf region will be regarded as an assault on the vital interests of the United States of America, and such an assault will be repelled by any means necessary, including military force.' [25] This uncompromising language, which soon became known as the 'Carter Doctrine', was at least as bad as anything the Soviet leaders had contemplated when they were weighing up the arguments for intervention. All hopes of salvaging détente were dead.

Just as the critics in Moscow had predicted, the non-aligned nations were in uproar. On 14 January 104 countries supported an American resolution in the UN condemning the invasion. A similar resolution was introduced annually, and support for it grew every year.[26]

Support for the Olympics boycott was more lukewarm. British athletes refused to do what Mrs Thatcher told them, and only China, Japan, the German Federal Republic, and Canada joined the United States in a full boycott. Carter had to buy off American grain producers to compensate them for losing the Soviet market. The Americans' allies were just as reluctant to support sanctions if their own commercial interests were affected. There was in any case no way that the Soviets could have bowed to the Olympic boycott and the economic sanctions. Soviet policy towards Afghanistan was unaffected.

The Americans and the British turned instead to more practical measures. On 26 December, the day after the Russians crossed the frontier, Zbigniew Brzezinski, President Carter's National Security Advisor, told him that the Russians were on the verge of achieving their age-old goal, access to the Indian Ocean: the moment, perhaps, at which this myth was born. Brzezinski judged that Afghanistan was unlikely to become the Soviet Vietnam, because unlike the Vietnamese the Afghan rebels were badly organised and led, had no organised army, no central government, and negligible outside support. But the comparison with Vietnam was to colour American thinking for the next nine years, as it coloured the thinking of the Russians. Ways should be found, said Brzezinski, to make the Soviets pay.[27]

It was not as if the Americans had so far been idle. Even before the Herat rising in March 1979, well before there had been any question of Soviet troops entering Afghanistan, the CIA had put forward proposals for helping the growing anti-Communist rebellion. President Carter decided at the end of March that the Soviet presence in Afghanistan must be reversed. American officials were already drawing the parallel with Vietnam. In the summer Carter authorised the CIA to spend $500,000 on helping the Afghan rebels. Brzezinski later claimed that this was not a deliberate move to provoke the Soviets to intervene, but that 'we knowingly increased the probability that they would'.[28]

The Saudis and the Chinese looked as if they too would help. But the Pakistani role would be crucial. The Americans were in a dilemma. They were pressing the Pakistanis to rein in their nuclear weapons programme, but the pressures needed to bend the Pakistanis to their will were incompatible with seeking their aid on Afghanistan. Brzezinski persuaded the President to swallow his scruples and give the Afghan project priority over non-proliferation. Within weeks of the invasion, the US covert agencies were meeting their British, French, and German counterparts to discuss practical ways of supporting the mujahedin.

American assistance to the mujahedin was at first comparatively modest. President Reagan (1911–2004) had now taken over from Carter, and his new CIA director, William Casey, a religious man, believed that Christianity and Islam could combine against the godless Soviets. Charlie Wilson, the Congressman who mustered support for the mujahedin, said, 'There were 58,000 dead in Vietnam, and we owe the Russians one.'[29] Casey redefined the objective. The aim should not be to make the Russians bleed, but to drive them out of Afghanistan altogether. The American programme expanded massively. After 1985 the American deliveries of arms multiplied by a factor of ten. The Pakistanis funnelled most of this stuff to the more radical groups. By the time the project ceased at the end of 1991, the Americans had given

Top: Gorbachev, the last president of the Soviet Union, with Najibullah, the last Communist president of Afghanistan.

Bottom: Eduard Shevardnadze, the Soviet Foreign Minister, signs the Geneva Agreements. He said, 'It was hard for me to realise that I was the Foreign Minister who had signed what was certainly not an agreement about a victory. There aren't many examples of that in Russian or Soviet history. And I couldn't stop thinking about the people we had trained up, pushed into a revolution, and were now abandoning to face a mortal foe alone.'

2. Afghans and Russians

Top: Nur Mohamed Taraki. A founder of the Afghan Communist Party and first Communist president of Afghanistan, his murder in October 1979 on the orders of his comrade Hafizullah Amin was probably the immediate trigger for the Soviet invasion.

Bottom: Leonid Brezhnev, the elderly Soviet leader, greets Babrak Karmal, whom the Russians installed as leader in Kabul after Soviet special forces had stormed Amin's palace and killed him.

Afghan women

Top: Communist activists. The position of women was significantly improved by the Communists – at least in the big cities.

Bottom: Students at the Kabul Polytechnic Institute which was largely built by the Russians in 1967. During the war it had a Soviet rector and many Russian staff.

4. Soldiers

Clockwise from top left: Igor Morozov, KGB special forces officer and one of the most distinguished 'bards'. Sergeant Alexander Gergel of the 860th Independent Motor-rifle Regiment; Nikolai Bystrov, a private soldier, was captured by the mujahedin outside Bagram, converted to Islam, became a bodyguard to Masud, went back to live in Russia with his Afghan wife, but regularly returned to Afghanistan in search of the bodies of men missing in action; Lieutenant Alexander Kartsev served in the 108th Motor-rifle Division outside Kabul and gave simple medicine to the local villagers – a useful way of picking up intelligence.

Top: The elite troops – parachutists, reconnaissance units and special forces, went into action looking like the crew of a pirate ship.

Bottom: But when the time came for them to be demobilised, the *dembels* cleaned up their dress uniforms, got presents for their families and girls, and had their pictures taken.

6. The 86oth Independent Motor-rifle Regiment off duty

Top: The medical team – note the tents in the background.

Bottom: Two weddings.

8. The withdrawal

Summer 1988. Soviet troops withdraw from Jalalabad towards Kabul, through th mountains where the British Army of the Indus was slaughtered in 1842. Perfect countr for an ambush: but this time the soldiers were escorted by battle helicopters.

assistance to the rebels of up to $9 billion, supplemented by very large sums from the Saudis.[30]

The mujahedin cause began to move out of the executive branch, win patrons in Congress in both parties, and become a major issue in US domestic politics. This made it harder for the American government to negotiate flexibly with the Russians when the time came, established even the least reputable of the mujahedin leaders as heroes, and helped to blind the Americans to the nature of the forces they had helped to unleash.[31]

The Russians knew, of course, that Soviet military deployments were readily visible to Western spy satellites and other intelligence gatherers. Years later the Soviet generals asked themselves why the Americans had made no comment, made no protest, and issued no meaningful warnings. They concluded that the Americans deliberately planned to entrap the Russians in a quagmire.[32] It is not much of an excuse. The Americans did warn the Russians on several occasions before the invasion that they could not be indifferent to what the Russians got up to in Afghanistan. And if there was an American trap, the Russians should have had more sense than to fall into it.

The Heroes Go Home

For the men who had captured the Taj Bek Palace none of this mattered too much. They knew that they had taken part in a remarkable feat of arms. But it had been a very confused business, and in later years many of the participants found it hard to remember exactly what had happened. 'Much has been wiped from my memory,' remarked Vladimir Grishin of the Muslim Battalion. 'When veterans of the Great Patriotic War talk, I am surprised at how well they can remember. I have switched off several episodes. Some of it remained there in my memory: for example, for several months I could sense the smell of flesh and blood.'[33] A survivor later remembered that the fight on the staircase was just like the storming of the Berlin Reichstag in April 1945, one of the most celebrated moments of the Second World War. Another was surprised when he revisited the ruined palace some years later how narrow the staircase was: he remembered it being as broad as the Odessa Steps in the film of *The Battleship Potemkin*. One of them wondered whether the deception that had been practised on the Afghan defenders – ostensibly their comrades in arms – had not amounted to outright treachery. He consoled himself with the thought that the Russian soldiers had had no choice but to win, and that victory could have been achieved no other way.

These men were later to be treated as heroes who had turned a glorious page of Russian military history. But for the time being the authorities in Moscow were determined that the details of the assault on the palace should remain secret, and so they did for nearly ten years. The men were sworn to absolute silence, their heroism was recognised with an absolute minimum of pomp, and no concessions were made in matters of discipline. Lieutenant Vostrotin and his 9th Company of the 345th Guards Independent Parachute Assault Regiment did not rejoin their unit in Bagram until New Year's Eve. They used the time to good effect, collecting bits and pieces lying around the palace: German helmets worn by Amin's palace guard, television sets, ghetto blasters, pistols, carpets, and a sewing machine. They loaded them on a lorry and took them off to Bagram to improve the limited amenities of their camp. Alas, their regimental commander, Colonel Nikolai Serdyukov, chose – probably with justification under military law – to regard their actions as looting. The soldiers were relieved of their prizes, Vostrotin was threatened with court martial, and his action cost him both the medal and the promotion he had hoped for.[34]

On 4 January the men from *Grom* and *Zenit* were loaded into a slow turboprop plane and flew – endlessly, it seemed – until they finally reached Dushanbe, the capital of Tajikistan. They had no documents of any kind and no money. At the airport they were met by a colonel of the frontier guards, who had heard nothing of their arrival. There was a bad moment until they convinced him who they were. The wounded were then sent to hospital in Tashkent. The rest went on to Moscow. Here they were received with honour, but told that they were in no circumstances to talk about what they had done, and made to sign a secrecy agreement. The secrecy was such that medals – not as many as the men had hoped for – were handed out in hugger-mugger. Colonel Boyarinov, who had been killed by friendly fire, was posthumously made a Hero of the Soviet Union. Kryuchkov went in secret to his Moscow apartment to give the medal personally to his wife and son.[35]

The men were then sent off for two weeks to a sanatorium in the countryside, where they were treated for stress. Some dealt with their stress in the traditional way, by drowning their nightmares in vodka. Leonid Gumenny found the adjustment hard: 'I was tormented by terrible insomnia. I slept no more than two hours a night. My dreams were in colour, and before I could even get off to sleep I could smell shit, gunpowder, and blood – the smell of death. I was only able to get myself back together – more or less – six months later, after treatment in a sanatorium in Sochi.'

The men of the Muslim Battalion flew home on 9 January. Before taking off they too were relieved by the military policemen of the KGB of all the souvenirs they had picked up after the battle – ornamental daggers, a couple of pistols, a transistor radio and a tape recorder. A rumour later circulated that the soldiers had brought home jewellery looted from the palace. But they had no more than their personal weapons and no documents with them at all. They knew that they had done something remarkable. But they also knew that their government was determined that the way Amin had been set aside should remain shrouded in the deepest secrecy. One young officer even believed that their aircraft might be shot down before they got home, to ensure that the evidence was destroyed. It was a bizarre and irrational thought: a sign of the strain they had been under, but a sign perhaps also of the way they saw the state which they had been prepared to serve so loyally.[36]

PART II

THE DISASTERS
OF WAR

We tried to teach the Afghans how to build a new society, knowing
that we ourselves had failed to do so ... Our army was given tasks
which it was in no position to fulfil, since no regular army can
possibly solve the problems of a territory in revolt.

Ivan Chernobrovkin[1]

THE 40TH ARMY GOES TO WAR

The creation and deployment of the 40th Army may have been a triumph of improvisation. But there were many serious shortcomings, which might not have mattered so much if the army had been able to leave, as it had originally hoped, without much fighting and after little more than a year. But as the soldiers settled in, the weaknesses became painfully apparent: inadequate accommodation, lack of spare clothing for the troops, tasteless and unwholesome food, and primitive sanitary arrangements. Funds allocated to put things right were never forthcoming. The near collapse of the army's health system which resulted was more damaging in its way than the effects of enemy action.

At first the new army consisted mainly of understrength units from the military districts bordering on Afghanistan. These cadre units were manned only by a core of officers and warrant officers (*praporshchiki*), and had to be brought up to strength with local reservists: more than fifty thousand of them – officers, sergeants, and soldiers. Many were Uzbeks and Tajiks, though contrary to what many Western observers believed the soldiers from Central Asia fought well enough against their Afghan co-religionists. About eight thousand vehicles and other equipment were commandeered from local factories and farms. Even the local taxis were pressed into service to move the soldiers forward.[1]

Responsibility for managing the mobilisation fell on the Central Asian Military District, with its headquarters in Alma Ata, and on the Turkestan Military District, with its headquarters in Tashkent.[2] The two military districts had never attempted anything on this scale before, and the local authorities, the directors of factories and farms, the Voenkomats (recruiting offices), and the military units themselves were all unprepared for the task. In the interests of security they were told that the mobilisation was only an exercise, and so their main concern was to show how quickly they were capable of bringing units up to strength, regardless of quality. There was a serious shortage of specialists (drivers for the armoured vehicles, gunners, and so on), because the local reservists, like most Central Asian soldiers, had served in construction or motor-rifle units, where they had been unable to acquire the necessary specialist skills. Many reservists could not be found, because their names and addresses had not been properly recorded. Others produced false medical certificates or hid themselves so that they could not be served with their call-up papers. Many of the reserve officers were students: they had never actually served in the army and had no practical military skills, because they had received their training in the military faculties of their universities.

By spring 1980 the 40th Army had been brought up to a strength of about 81,000 men, of which 62,000 thousand were in front-line units, equipped with six hundred tanks, fifteen hundred infantry fighting vehicles, nearly three hundred armoured personnel carriers, nine hundred artillery pieces, and five hundred fixed-wing aircraft and helicopters. The motley collection of civilian vehicles was soon sent back to their owners, and the reservists were replaced by professional officers and conscripts. The presence of these soldiers in Afghanistan was regulated by a bilateral agreement between the two governments, which set out the facilities which would be provided to the Soviet troops, the sixteen cities where they would be stationed, and the five airports from which their aircraft would operate.[3]

The 40th Army eventually consisted of three motor-rifle divisions, an air-assault division, four independent motor-rifle regiments (brigades), two independent air-assault regiments (brigades), two special forces brigades, communications, intelligence, rear and repair units, and – uniquely – its own aviation corps of fighter bombers, helicopters, and transport planes, units for aircraft repair and airfield defence. At its maximum it mustered 109,000 men and women, supplemented by KGB frontier troops and specialised troops from the Ministry of the Interior. (See Annex 2, 'Order of Battle of the 40th Army', page 342.)

The Task

The task before the 40th Army and its commanders as they swept into Afghanistan may have seemed simple, clear, and limited. The Russians had intervened to put an end to the vicious feuding within the PDPA, and to force a radical change in the extreme and brutally counterproductive policies of the Communist government. The aim was not to take over or occupy the country. It was to secure the towns and the roads between them, and to withdraw as soon as the Afghan government and its armed forces were in a state to take over the responsibility for themselves.

This may have looked like a strategy, but it turned out to be little more than an impractical aspiration. The Russians understood well enough that the problems of Afghanistan could only be solved by political means: Andropov had after all argued right at the beginning that the regime could not be sustained with Soviet bayonets. But they also hoped that the Afghan people would in the end welcome the benefits they promised to bring: stable government, law and order, health, agricultural reform, development, education for women as well as men.

They discovered instead that most Afghans preferred their own ways, and were not going to change them at the behest of a bunch of godless foreigners and home-grown infidels. The Russians did not, and could not, address this fundamental strategic issue. The vicious civil war which greeted them had started well before they arrived and continued for seven years after they left, until it ended with the victory of the Taliban in 1996. It was a war in which loyalties were fluid and divided. Individuals and whole groups switched sides in both directions, or negotiated with one another for a ceasefire or a trade deal when the opportunity arose. Fighting and bloodshed erupted within each of the Afghan parties to the war as leaders and groupings struggled for advantage. The Russians found themselves fighting the worst kind of war, a war against an insurgency which they had not expected and for which they were not equipped or trained. All sides behaved with great brutality. There were executions, torture, and the indiscriminate destruction of civilians, their villages, and their livelihood on all sides. Like others who had entered Afghanistan before and since, the Russians were appalled at the violence and effectiveness of the opposition which faced them almost immediately and which made a mockery of their hopes.

One day, both the Russians and the Afghans knew, the Soviets would go home. The Afghans would have to go on living in the country and with one another, long after the last Russian had left. Even those Afghans who supported the Kabul government and acquiesced in the Soviet presence, or perhaps even welcomed it, had always to calculate where they would find themselves once the Soviets had departed.

And there was another fundamental weakness in the strategic thinking of the Soviet government. They had underestimated – maybe they had not even considered – the eventual unwillingness of their own people to sustain a long and apparently pointless war in a far-off country. They were never of course faced by the massive popular movement in America which opposed the war in Vietnam. But a growing disillusion inside and outside government sapped the will of the leadership to continue a war that was brutal, costly, and pointless.

These two misjudgements were sufficient to nullify the military successes of the 40th Army.

The Commanders
The 40th Army had seven commanders during its existence: Yuri Tukharinov, Boris Tkach, Viktor Yermakov, Leonid Generalov, Igor Rodionov, Viktor Dubynin, and Boris Gromov. Between 1975 and 1991 another eleven generals served as advisers to the Afghan armed forces. A number of these men, appalled by the humiliations inflicted on their army and their country, played a significant part in the politics surrounding the collapse of the Soviet Union and the emergence of the new Russia.

These men were sophisticated professionals. They had attended the Academy of the General Staff. They had managed major military formations, run military districts inside the Soviet Union, and commanded armies outside it. In 1979 they still enjoyed the reflected glory of the victory over the Germans in 1945. They were paid more than other public servants except the KGB. They shared with the political leadership the basic objective of maintaining strategic parity with the United States, and the politicians were content that they should have the first claim on the country's economic resources, provided they kept out of politics. Like professional officers elsewhere, they had been drilled during their training with a strong sense of military honour, duty, and patriotism. They were devoted to the glories of Russian military history. They kept themselves apart from civilian life, but they were quite sure that civilians should not be allowed to meddle in any aspect of military affairs. Even the Defence Minister, Dmitri Ustinov, did not in their eyes quite fit the bill. Despite his long connection with the military, he was a Party bureaucrat, not a professional officer.

Some of these generals had seen action as junior officers in the Second World War. Many of them had served and a significant number had died in the Far East, the Middle East and Africa, where the Soviet Union had given active military support to Communist allies, to 'progressive' governments in the Third World, or to peoples seeking independence from their former colonial masters.[4]

The generals had successfully deployed seventeen divisions into Hungary in 1956; and eighteen divisions, backed by eight Warsaw Pact divisions, into Czechoslovakia in 1968. Eighty-seven officers and 633 soldiers died in the operations against the Hungarian rebels. There was no fighting in Czechoslovakia, and only one officer and eleven other ranks were killed there. As an exercise in logistics, these were formidable achievements. But they were not the real thing. Unlike many of their American counterparts, the Soviet generals had no recent experience of managing large numbers of troops in battle. And they did not have the equipment, the training, the doctrine, or the experience to fight a counter-insurgency war in the mountains of Afghanistan.

Although four Soviet generals perished in the fighting,[5] the brunt was borne by colonels, majors, and captains, by young lieutenants, and of course by the ordinary soldier. Only a small proportion, less than 10 per cent, of the officers of the motor-rifle forces, the backbone of the army, went to Afghanistan. The rest were spread across the Soviet Union or Eastern Europe, ready for a major war with NATO while keeping a careful eye on the Chinese.

Most Soviet officers genuinely believed in their professional duty to carry out the orders of their government. Even had they known about them, they would not have regarded the doubts which assailed the Soviet leadership as any of their business. At least to start with, they believed that they were indeed in Afghanistan to protect it from outside interference and domestic rebellion. Even as disillusion grew towards the end, some idealism remained. Anatoli Yermolin went to Afghanistan as a young lieutenant in 1987 and was in no doubt about the value of Soviet intervention. The doubts came later, when he returned home and became a liberal politician in the post-Communist Russian parliament.[6]

By the time they arrived in Afghanistan, young men who had been through the Soviet officer schools were mostly reasonably well trained, or at least equipped to absorb the indispensable lessons they could only learn on the battlefield.

Specialists were given extra training. After finishing at the Academy, Alexander Kartsev was sent off for a year's further training in intelligence. By then the GRU had decided that they needed better local intelligence in Afghanistan. Technical means of gaining intelligence were proving inadequate. Aerial intelligence arrived too late. Radio listening stations did not work well in the mountains. They recorded a huge number of significant conversations on to ancient tape recorders, but there were not enough qualified interpreters to process the material. One solution, the GRU decided, was to imitate the French charity Médecins Sans Frontières and give selected intelligence officers basic medical skills. They would be welcomed in the villages, where they ought to be able to pick up much useful information.

And so for two months Kartsev was trained by professors of medicine from Moscow, and learned the 'Short Russian–Dari Phrasebook' by heart. He was then sent off to a camp in Turkmenistan, where he learned mountaineering, shooting, mountain driving, and a bit more about the local languages. Then, after being issued with a Soviet passport and enjoying the unsympathetic attentions of the Soviet customs officials at Tashkent airport, he was posted to the 180th Motor-rifle Regiment in Kabul and served in Afghanistan from 1986 to 1988.

He was assigned to a small post west of Bagram. Here he was involved in the raids, ambushes, and house-to-house searches which were the bread-and-butter tasks of such units. In addition he used his medical skills to gain the confidence of the headmen in the nearby village, or *kishlak*, and provide the villagers with simple medical services which were otherwise unavailable to them. Using this as cover, he was able to pick up local intelligence, and maintain a secure link with 'Shafi', an Afghan agent who had studied in Oxford and Japan. Kartsev guessed that 'Shafi' was acting as a go-between for Ahmad Shah Masud, the mujahedin commander in the Pandsher Valley. From 'Shafi' Kartsev acquired an intense interest in Eastern medicine, and after he left the army he turned the knowledge he had acquired in Afghanistan to good use, setting up his own massage practice in Moscow.[7]

What Kind of a War?

Like other counter-insurgency wars, the campaign in Afghanistan was not a war of set-piece battles and great offensives, of victories, defeats, and headlong retreat, and there was no front line. In such a war, there was little scope for generalship in the normal sense of the word. Nor was it a war which lent itself to easy narrative. It was not that the generals were still fighting the Second World War, though there was an element of that too. They had thought long and hard about the conditions of modern warfare, and they believed that they had made the necessary adjustments to fight such a war and win. Their mistake was to assume that if the army was well prepared to fight a major war, it could without too much adaptation successfully fight minor wars as well. The Americans had thought the same at the beginning of the Vietnam War. They had adapted their tactics, but never cracked the problem. Even though they had that example before them, the Soviet commanders had not worked out in advance how to deal with small, lightly equipped, and highly mobile groups of strongly motivated men moving across difficult terrain with which they were intimately acquainted. Until they had gained experience the officers and men of the 40th Army were not very good at this kind of war. And even though many of them adapted well enough, they were in the end no more successful than the Americans at defeating their elusive enemy.

The country in which the 40th Army now found itself could not have been more different from the European plains for which the Soviet army had trained. It might have been specially designed for the conduct of guerrilla warfare, for mountain skirmishes, ambushes along road and tracks, punitive expeditions, occasional massive operations by thousands of Afghan and Soviet soldiers to relieve a beleaguered garrison or smoke out a rebel base, mujahedin raids on Soviet and Afghan government outposts, brief fights around villages or on the outskirts of towns, destruction, retaliation, and great brutality.

The mountains which cover four-fifths of Afghanistan sweep from the Pamirs in the east, where Tajikistan, India, Pakistan, and China join, almost to the frontier with Iran beyond Herat in the west. They divide the country from north to south, and the people into different and often hostile groupings who speak different languages, have different cultures, and for much of history had different religions as well. They are pierced by valleys and defiles, which are negotiable by people on foot: local farmers and shepherds, merchants, smugglers, travellers, tourists, hippies, and guerrilla fighters with their caravans of weapons. Proper roads are a luxury; until the twentieth century there were little more than tracks, passable enough by men and pack animals, but not at all friendly to wheeled traffic.

These mountains are hard enough to fight in at the best of times. The locals know all the paths and tracks, often cutting along the sides of precipitous mountains, easy to ambush, easy to defend, hard to find. But it is worse than that. At sixteen thousand feet, where some of the fighting took place, you can be incapacitated by altitude sickness until you become acclimatised. If you are wounded it can take as many as six of your comrades to get you down to help, often under fire.

Here even quite small numbers of determined men can hold their own against a powerful enemy column. You occupy the overlooking heights, block the front and rear of the column, and then destroy your enemy at leisure. This is what happened to the British 'Army of the Indus' in January 1842 on the road east from Kabul through Jalalabad to the Khyber Pass. More than a hundred years later the mujahedin would man the heights overlooking the route of the slow-moving Soviet columns, with their cumbersome lorries and their escorting tanks and personnel carriers. They would knock out the first and last vehicles with a mine or a rocket, and then systematically destroy the remainder.

But if the guerrilla tactic was simple, so was the answer, at least in theory. The British learned to adopt 'a form of tactics then new to military science in Asia, namely the picketing of flank hills to protect a column on the march through the defiles of a mountainous terrain … [T]he Afridis [Pushtuns] still remember the occasion; it was only when [General] Pollock adopted, as they say, their own tactics, and applied them to the movements of his troops, that he became successful.'[8] The Russians adopted the same broad tactic as they fought their convoys through the mountain passes and along the desert roads, sending special forces and paratroopers by forced march or by helicopter to occupy the heights before the mujahedin could get there and to block off their line of retreat.

Most Afghans live neither in the mountains nor in the ancient cities, but in *kishlaks* in the ribbon of low land which fringes the north of the country, swings southward past Herat and then round towards the east, through the desert, until it reaches the mountains again at Kandahar. This sliver of land constitutes about 15 per cent of the total area of the country. But only 6 per cent is actually farmed: livestock, wheat and cotton, fruit, nuts, melons, raisins, and of course poppies.[9]

Patches of lush green punctuate the arid landscape, a 'flowering, fertile plain', as the Soviet writer Alexander Prokhanov described it, 'where settlements built of golden mud bricks spread out among the gardens and vineyards, where cool water filled the hand-made wells, where the young rice showed green in tiny, carefully cultivated fields, where flowering poppy and yellow sunflower flamed and burned'.[10] Two decades later a journalist with the British soldiers in the southern province of Helmand went so far as to say, 'The narrow strip of fertile meadows, irrigation ditches and mud-bricked compounds lining the

Helmand river suggest a tranquillity unmolested by time. It can feel like Tuscany.'[11]

The villages themselves tend to conform to a common pattern. The streets are narrow and the houses have flat roofs, with walls presenting a blank face to the outside world. They are built of mud brick; they age rapidly and it is often hard to tell how old they are. If they collapse, or are destroyed by bombing, the buildings soon melt back into the soil from which they sprang, as if they had never been. If you go there today the ravages of the war are hard to trace.

Alexander Kartsev described a typical village near his guard post: 'The *kishlak* was not at all large, about ten fortified buildings and a few others built of mud bricks. The fortified buildings are striking both by their size and by their purpose. For the people of Kalashakhi the fortified buildings are ordinary dwellings, just like any other. They differ from the crowded and dirty Afghan cities completely ... Walls up to six metres high, made of mud brick. More than a metre thick. Even a shell from a tank will not always pierce a wall like that. Watchtowers at the corners of the fortification two or three storeys high. On the inner side of the wall one- or two-storey dwellings of unfired brick, usually set out in the form of the [Cyrillic] letter 'П'. There are no buildings on the northern side. That is the coldest wall, uneconomic to heat in winter. Fuel is very hard to get here. Only one room has anything like a fireplace. People use *kizyaki* for fuel – dried and concentrated cow or camel dung. Only the richest can afford to use wood for heating.

'On the ground floor you usually find the kitchen, and a kind of living room for eating and receiving guests where the floor is covered with matting or sometimes with carpets. A few other rooms are joined to the guest room: people live here in the summer, because the mud brick walls keep out the exhausting heat.

'On the first floor are the rooms where people sleep and live in the winter. These are usually situated immediately above the kitchen, where there is an open stove for the preparation of food. There is no chimney. Instead a number of small holes in all the internal walls distribute the warm air through the rooms. The houses are like a large and living organism. It is not surprising that the Afghans are so warmly attached to them. In the far corner of the fortress is an enclosure for the cattle. Not far from the kitchen is a large well, called a *kyariz* ... The fortress covers an area of not less than 400 square metres. It is inhabited, usually, by only one family.'[12]

The Soviet soldiers – and the British soldiers who came after them – called the cultivated land around the villages the 'green zone', the *zelenka* in Russian. Despite its beguiling appearance, the green zone was in many ways an even worse place to fight than the mountains. The farmland and vineyards were irrigated with water from springs and rivers, distributed through a delicate and complicated system of surface ditches and underground tunnels punctuated by vertical shafts. Lounging along the roadside there were always men in shirts and long Afghan robes, in turbans and local headgear, armed to the teeth; and there was no way that the soldiers could tell whether they were part of the local self-defence organisation, or mujahedin waiting for a juicy target – or both.[13]

These villages, into which guerrilla fighters could infiltrate, catch their enemies unawares, and then disappear back down the tunnels to evade retaliation, where every house and road might be booby-trapped, where peaceful civilians could suddenly become concealed enemies, were a nightmare for the Russian soldiers. In one incident a reconnaissance battalion incautiously entered a village in the green zone. They emerged two hours later, having lost twenty-five dead and forty-eight wounded. Such incidents were almost always the avoidable result of stupid and undisciplined behaviour.[14]

Although the fighting was messy, piecemeal and confused, the main objective of each side was simple enough: to stifle the supply routes of the other. The Russians brought in all their fuel, their equipment, their ammunition, and much of their food by lorry from the Soviet Union. The mujahedin got most of their weapons, ammunition, and other military supplies over the mountains from Pakistan.

Because it was a battle for roads and tracks and mountain pathways, both the Russians and the rebels used mines in very large numbers and with little discrimination. But in an asymmetrical war mines, booby traps, and roadside bombs are the preferred weapon of the weaker side, and can have a devastating effect on the morale of the stronger, as the Americans discovered in Vietnam. The rebels' mines came from a wide variety of sources – America, Britain, Italy, China – and they also improvised their own. The largest mines could destroy a tank or an infantry fighting vehicle. The smallest could blow off a foot. The Russians used flail tanks to clear the roads. Sappers used trained dogs, probed for mines by hand – it was no good using a metal detector because the mujahedin often used plastic mines – and defused them, as columns and raiding parties followed at a snail's pace. As they said, a sapper only ever makes one mistake.

For their part the Russians set mines in a protective belt round their own positions, and along routes and mountain tracks used by the rebels. In principle they kept proper maps of the places where they had sown their mines. In practice maps were inaccurate, got lost, or were never made in the first place, and so the Russians were sometimes blown up on their own mines. The rebels did not bother to make maps.

It was not for nothing that the Russians called it a 'war of mines': Afghanistan remains littered with mines sown by all parties both to the Soviet war and to the civil war which followed. There are still casualties as old mines are set off by children playing and by peasants working their fields.

The mujahedin avoided pitched battles and struck from ambush where they had the advantage. Occasionally they went further, attacked garrisons and airbases, and tried towards the end of the war to capture towns. But the Soviet convoys went on running, the main roads remained open, and no town of any consequence fell to the mujahedin while the Russians were still in Afghanistan.

For their part the Russians raided villages suspected of harbouring rebels, struck into the mountains to destroy their bases and disperse their men, mounted counter-ambushes, and mined the routes along which the mujahedin moved. Their operations were supported by transport and battle helicopters, by artillery, by fighter bombers under the command of the 40th Army, and by long-range bombers from the Soviet Union. Quite junior officers – lieutenants and captains in charge of guard posts – could call down artillery support if they needed it. The inevitable result was a heavy loss of life and property among the civilian population.

But to confront the mujahedin and their unorthodox methods of fighting effectively, special skills and special tactics and special troops were needed, troops that could operate in the mountains to ambush and counter-ambush the guerrilla bands, and to cut the routes taken by their caravans. Although the ordinary motor-rifle units took regular part in such operations, the main brunt of the fighting inevitably fell on the elite special and parachute units, and on the reconnaissance battalions and companies in the motor-rifle divisions and regiments. These troops fought very effectively, both in the high mountains and in the green zone. They made up some 20 per cent of the total strength of the 40th Army: according to some calculations, of the 133 battalions in the 40th Army, only fifty-one took part regularly in operations. The rest spent much of their time in their garrisons or escorting convoys.[15]

In addition to these regular army units there were a number of special forces teams set up by the GRU, the KGB, and the Ministry of the Interior. Of these the GRU special forces teams were the most substantial. A 'special forces group' was set up in 1985 which eventually consisted of two brigades, each of eight battalions, an independent company, an independent reconnaissance battalion, four regimental reconnaissance companies, nine reconnaissance platoons, and thirteen other units, a total of three thousand men in all. The 15th Brigade was stationed in Jalalabad and the 22nd Brigade in Asadabad in Kunar province on the Pakistani border. The 22nd Brigade was pulled out in the summer of 1988 as the 40th Army began its withdrawal. The 15th Brigade remained behind to cover the final stage of the withdrawal in February 1989.[16]

The main purpose of the GRU special forces units was to block the supply routes of the mujahedin through the mountains. They acquired a formidable reputation as they became increasingly well trained and equipped to fight their elusive enemy. Enduring extreme heat and cold in the harsh Afghan climate, suffering from altitude sickness in the high mountains, backed by helicopters and attack aircraft, they ambushed the guerrillas or were ambushed in their turn, and they did what they could to stop the caravans with military supplies streaming in from CIA and Pakistani bases across the frontier. They achieved some impressive results: in one action in May 1987 they destroyed a large caravan, killed

187 mujahedin, and captured a considerable amount of equipment and ammunition. But in spite of all their efforts, and those of the other elite troops, they succeeded in intercepting barely 15–20 per cent of the mujahedin caravans.[17] No more than the mujahedin did they succeed in their prime purpose: to block their enemies' supply routes.

The Problem of Intelligence

The KGB and MVD (Interior Ministry) teams were much smaller, and their prime job was to gather intelligence – to build networks of agents among the mujahedin, to study the tribal and clan relationships in their area of operations, and to discover the whereabouts of mujahedin bases, supply routes, and arms dumps. They were also given the task of hunting down and capturing – dead or alive – foreign advisers attached to the mujahedin; persuading mujahedin commanders to bring their bands over to the government side; and sowing dissension between bands so that they fought one another instead of the Russians – the tactic adopted by Rudyard Kipling's hero on the Khyber Pass in the last chapter of *Stalky & Co.*[18] Of course the Afghans were playing a similar game, and fed the Russians with false information to provoke operations against their own personal or tribal enemies.

The KGB's teams formed part of an organisation called *Kaskad*, which Andropov set up in the summer of 1980.[19] It consisted of about a thousand KGB special forces officers, stationed in eight different places throughout Afghanistan. They were not permitted to take part in routine military operations; they were too valuable to lose. The officers called themselves 'Kaskadery', from the French *cascadeur*, a stuntman. *Kaskad* remained in Afghanistan for three years. It was then replaced by a similar group, *Omega*, which itself left Afghanistan after a year. But many individual officers remained, attached to various special forces until the end of the war.

The code name for the Interior Ministry's teams was *Kobalt*. The *Kobalt* officers were mostly from the ministry's criminal investigation department, skilled at manhunting villains across the Soviet Union. Their job was to assist the Afghan secret police, the KhAD (Khadamat-e Etela'at-e Dawlati, the State Information Agency) in tracking down mujahedin leaders. They too were supposed to keep clear of regular military operations. There were twenty-three *Kobalt* teams in Afghanistan, each consisting of up to seven men, with a BTR (armoured personnel carrier) and a radio.[20]

A surprising number of the officers in these small units barely knew the local languages and had to rely on interpreters, often Central Asian soldiers from the nearest Soviet unit. As one of them said, this was inconvenient if you were trying to interrogate a prisoner. Some of them were later withdrawn for two years' intensive language training and then sent back to Afghanistan. The teams were also very thin on the ground. Zabol province shared forty miles of open border with Pakistan, across which passed seven caravan supply routes. Even after 200,000 people had left as refugees, there were still 150,000 living there, divided among seventeen tribes and ethnic groups, mostly Pushtuns. There were 145 mujahedin bands in the province, about two–three thousand men in all. They attacked pro-government *kishlaks*, collected tribute from the locals, mined the Kabul–Kandahar road, and carried out terrorist attacks. The KGB had twenty-eight officers for the whole province. The *Kobalt* team consisted of five officers and three frontier guards. There were only twenty-seven KhAD officers to support them, out of a nominal establishment of just under five hundred. There were eighty Tsarandoi – gendarmes – but they were local men, and their loyalties were suspect.[21]

The problem of intelligence and security bedevilled the 40th Army throughout the war. Their intelligence officers sought the cooperation of local tribal leaders, offering them safety from military operations, paying them subsidies, giving them food, medicine, military advice, and equipment, in exchange for their agreement to prevent ambushes, mines, and the movement of mujahedin caravans within the area they controlled. They successfully recruited agents among the villagers to report on the movements and intentions of the mujahedin. But the local leaders were under equal pressure from the mujahedin and the agreements would break down. The agents were very often illiterate, unable to read maps, and reported gossip as fact. Their handlers had to deal with them face to face, with all the risks that entailed, instead of communicating with them by secret means.[22] Double and triple agents abounded. It was not unknown for rival agencies on the

Russian side – the KGB and the GRU – to employ the same agent unwittingly, paying him twice for the same piece of dubious information. The mujahedin kept their own agents around Soviet bases and along their routes of march, and reported all Soviet troop movements to their principals immediately. Because the Afghan army and police were so heavily penetrated by agents of the mujahedin, the Russians only informed their allies of the objectives of joint operations at the very last minute; or they would issue them with deliberately misleading operational plans, which would be modified only when the operation was already under way. Naturally enough, the Afghans blamed their Russian advisers when things went wrong.

Allies

Fighting alongside the 40th Army were the Afghan government forces. On paper at least these were formidable. At the time of the invasion in 1979, the Afghans had ten divisions, and were armed with modern – if not the most modern – Soviet weapons: aircraft, tanks, and artillery.[23] By the end of the war the army had grown to twelve divisions, and a number of specialised brigades and smaller units. The air force had seven air regiments, with thirty fighters, more than seventy fighter bombers, fifty bombers, seventy-six helicopters, and forty transport aircraft. Many of the officers spoke Russian and had been well trained in the Soviet Union.[24]

But there were serious weaknesses. Units were often reluctant to fight, although they did better if they were backed by Soviet units. Most were well below their nominal strength: an Afghan division might consist of no more than a thousand men, a tenth of what it should have been. The loyalty of the officers was suspect. In what amounted to a continual purge, both Amin and Babrak Karmal systematically moved or got rid of officers whose loyalty they questioned. Many deserted to the mujahedin. Badly paid and barely trained, with little reason to be loyal to Kabul, the soldiers deserted too: most went back to their villages, some to join the rebels. At first whole units defected: two brigades from the 9th Division in Kunar province; three battalions from the 11th Division at Jalalabad in the south; a brigade in Badakhshan in the north-east.

By 1980 the numbers in the army had fallen to 25,000. To stem the haemorrhage, the government lowered the age of conscription; press-ganged reluctant conscripts by force; increased the length of service to three years; and mobilised reservists under thirty-nine. After 1980 few units defected en masse; the number of individual desertions somewhat declined; and overall numbers increased, nominally at least: to 40,000 by 1982 and to 150,000 by the eve of the Soviet withdrawal at the beginning of 1989.[25] The rule of thumb was that if the desertion rate was no more than about 30 per cent a year you were all right. If it went much above that you were in trouble, sixty per cent was bad news.[26]

To maintain the numbers at something like a reasonable level, the 40th Army engaged in so-called 'operative measures in support of the recruitment of volunteers into the People's Army of the Democratic Republic of Afghanistan'. The Russian soldiers loved these operations. You drove instead of marching, there was hardly ever any shooting, you didn't have to go up into the mountains, and the operations took place in comparatively peaceful areas: after all, you could hardly recruit government soldiers in villages that were committed to the mujahedin. Moreover, there were always plenty of fresh fruit and vegetables to be had, livestock to be 'liberated', marijuana to be picked up, a whole month free of routine duty. On these occasions the riflemen were accompanied by a detachment of Tsarandoi and the local 'officer's battalion' of the KhAD, most of whom had been trained in the Soviet Union.

The press gangs went out twice a year, a month after the spring sowing and a month after the autumn harvest. Afghan conscripts had to serve twice: three years in the first instance. Then they got two years' leave. If by then they had not produced a family (and that meant assembling the bride price, which not everyone could do in the time), they would be recalled for another four years.

The 'volunteers' were rounded up in the following fashion. An armoured column would blockade a *kishlak*. The infantry would go in, accompanied by Afghan special forces, and the inhabitants would be collected on the main square in front of the mosque. All men liable to conscription – and some who weren't – would be herded off under guard to the nearest Afghan army barracks. The process would be repeated in another *kishlak* the following day.

At the barracks, men's heads would be shaved (contrary to the religious beliefs of many of them), they would get rudimentary training in the use of their weapons, and they were given severe warnings about what would happen to them if they disobeyed orders. Within six months two-thirds of them had deserted with their weapons, often to the mujahedin. Sometimes they would return: some Afghan soldiers changed sides as many as seven times. By the spring of 1984 the men in the villages had learned to take to the hills for a month in the spring and the autumn. Recruitment rates fell alarmingly, the press gangs met with increased opposition, and the process lost much of its attraction.[27]

An unsurprising consequence was that the Afghan units were unreliable in action: if there were real trouble, the Afghan soldiers would often simply get up and leave the scene. The only Afghan troops that could be relied on were the KhAD: they could expect no quarter if they were captured and so they had nothing to lose.

Most of the Soviet soldiers despised their Afghan allies, and wondered why they fought so badly when the same Afghans fought so well with the mujahedin. But General Kutsenko, who served as an adviser to the Afghan army from September 1984 to September 1987, thought that it had been underestimated: 'By the time I arrived in Afghanistan the Afghan army had been more or less fully reconstructed. Their officers were not bad and they were well armed.' In his view the Afghan military should have been allowed to manage their own affairs. 'The Soviet military served only two years and were then replaced. Few of them learned the customs of the local tribes. But the Afghan commanders had been fighting for five to eight years and they well understood the psychology of their people. Our strategists nevertheless decided that the Soviet and the Afghan forces should fight side by side. The result was endless rows and buck-passing when things went wrong. Soviet officers began to say that if the Afghan forces did not want to fight the mujahedin, why should they be doing so?' Kutsenko, who was also a 'bard', one of many soldiers in the 40th Army who composed songs about the war, wondered, 'Perhaps that was why defeatist songs began to circulate in the period 1984 to 1987, especially among the soldiers.'[28]

The KhAD was brutally efficient. It worked closely with Soviet

KGB advisers and the Soviet military both in Kabul and on the ground. Between 1980 and 1989 about thirty thousand Afghan security officers were trained by the Soviets in Kabul and in Moscow and other Soviet cities, either on short courses of two to six months, or in special institutes for up to two years.[29] Under different names the KhAD continued to operate until the Taliban took Kabul in 1996. It was re-established by President Karzai (1957–) under another name in 2001.

The KhAD succeeded in penetrating the mujahedin inside Afghanistan and their organisations back in Pakistan. But the mujahedin also had substantial success in penetrating the KhAD and the army. In May 1985 the head of the intelligence department of the Afghan General Staff, General Khalil, was arrested with ten of his officers and eight others. He was accused of running a spy network on behalf of Masud, who claimed that no operation had ever been mounted against him without his agents warning him of it in advance.[30]

The Four Phases of the War

The war is usually divided into four distinct phases. The first lasted from December 1979 to February 1980, and covered the initial deployment of the Soviet forces throughout the country.

The original Rules of Engagement permitted the Soviet soldiers only to return fire if attacked, or to liberate Soviet advisers captured by the insurgents. But casualties began to mount from the very start. The first ambush took place soon after the soldiers had arrived. In mid-January an Afghan artillery unit mutinied and its three Soviet advisers were unpleasantly murdered. The Afghans asked the Russians for help. About a hundred Afghans were killed, for the loss of two Soviet soldiers.[31]

A major demonstration broke out in Kabul on 21 February: some three hundred thousand people are said to have come on to the streets, shouting anti-government and anti-Soviet slogans. The demonstrations continued the following day, the largest protest ever seen in the capital provoked, the Russians believed, by agents from outside the country, including an alleged CIA officer, Robert Lee. The demonstrators filled the main roads and the squares, and marched on the Arg, where Karmal was now in residence. Administrative buildings were besieged, the Soviet Embassy was bombarded, and several Soviet citizens were killed. Shops were looted, cars were destroyed, and a major hotel was set on fire. Casualties began to rise among the civilian population. General Tukharinov, the commander of the 40th Army, was ordered to block the main approaches to the city and the demonstrations were brought under control.

But it was a turning point. Moscow ordered the 40th Army to 'begin active operations together with the Afghan army to defeat the detachments of the armed opposition.'[32] The Russians launched their first major operation in Kunar province, on the frontier with Pakistan, in March.[33] Even during this first period the 40th Army lost 245 soldiers, an average of 123 a month.

Soviet columns were already being attacked on the main supply roads from the Soviet Union. In response the Russians set up a system of mutually supporting guard posts (*zastavas*) at regular intervals along the main roads, around the major cities and around airports, observing the movements of the mujahedin, watching over electric power stations and pipelines, escorting convoys, and if necessary calling in an air or artillery strike as backup. There were 862 of them spread throughout the country, manned by over twenty thousand men, a substantial proportion of the 40th Army's strength.

These guard posts where among the most distinctive features of the war. Some were very small – no more than a dozen soldiers. The men in these tiny garrisons might remain there, unrelieved, for as long as eighteen months. Some were perched in inaccessible places, on heights overlooking Afghan villages or supply routes, where they could only be supplied by helicopter. They were regularly attacked: in the eight months between January and August 1987 three *zastava* commanders and seventy-two men were killed; and 283 were wounded.[34] But none of these *zastavas* was ever captured; they survived, not so much by force of arms, which in the long run would have been impossible, but because their little garrisons took care to be on reasonable terms with the people in the surrounding villages.

But life in a *zastava* was a monotonous and exhausting business. Poor food and water, little entertainment apart from the obligatory Lenin room and perhaps a television, and the ever present threat of disease or an enemy attack wore them down morally, physically, and psychologically.[35] They survived, where Western soldiers might not have done perhaps, some of them said, because most of them came from hard lives and cramped quarters back in their own homes in the Soviet Union. The enforced intimacy in a small guard post for months at a time was no worse than the enforced intimacy of life in a communal flat.

General Valentin Varennikov, a veteran of Stalingrad and a ruthless, wilful, and controversial figure, had by now succeeded Sokolov as Head of the Ministry of Defence's Operational Group. He visited one *zastava* perched on the top of a mountain close to Kabul, which was part of the city's outer defences. '[T]he helicopter made one and then another circle above the *zastava* and then cautiously began to lower itself with one wheel of the chassis on to the tiny landing strip, which was about 1.5m by 4m. When the wheel touched the stone, the three of us jumped out and the helicopter flew off...

'The territory of the *zastava* was shaped like an irregular rectangle. On three sides it was surrounded by a solid wall of sandbags brought in by helicopter. There was no fourth wall, because it was here the helicopter would touch down with one "foot" on the land. There were two heavy DShK machine guns at either end of this square, which was about six square metres in area. Steps led down to a little square below. Here there was a 120mm mortar, with a mountain of shells piled up beside it, and a shelter from the weather.

'From the little square, a path ran downwards at about 45°, a set of steps hacked out of the granite rock, on both sides of which was stretched a stout rope instead of banisters. At the bottom there was another little square, about the same size as the one above. Here there was another heavy machine gun and this was where the tiny garrison – 12 men in all – had their living: a place to relax, a kitchen, somewhere to wash and so on, the furniture – chairs, tables, sleeping places – all made out of ammunition boxes.'[36]

The second phase of the war lasted from March 1980 to April 1985. Both sides learned to improve their tactics. After getting a bloody nose in direct confrontations with the Russians, the mujahedin adopted the classic tactics of the guerrilla: hit and run, ambush, booby trap. In the summer of 1980 a band based only four miles from Kabul succeeded in bombarding the headquarters of the 40th Army in Amin's old palace, now repaired after the damage that had been done to it during the fighting in December.[37] With the launching of the first large-scale operation in the Pandsher Valley in April 1980 the Soviet Union stepped deep into the quagmire. Other major operations followed, on a scale which the Soviet army had not experienced since the Second World War. In August the Reconnaissance Battalion of the 201st Motor-rifle Division was ambushed on the border with Tajikistan at Kishim and lost forty-five men. Delegations from the Soviet Union began to arrive to see for themselves what was going on. So did the first concert parties to entertain the troops. It was in this phase that the Soviets suffered most of their casualties: 9,175 killed, an average of 148 a month.

The third phase lasted from May 1985 to the end of 1986. Gorbachev began active negotiations to bring the soldiers home and there was a deliberate effort to reduce casualties in what was becoming an increasingly unpopular war. The Soviet forces sought to confine themselves to air and artillery operations in support of the Afghan forces, although motor-rifle units were primarily used to back up the operations and the fighting morale of their Afghan allies. The special forces – the SpetsNaz and reconnaissance units – concentrated on attempting to prevent supplies of weapons and ammunition reaching the rebels from abroad. But even these support operations could involve very serious and costly fighting: 2,745 soldiers were killed during this period, an average of 137 a month – a decline, but not a substantial one. The Soviet withdrawal began during this third phase, when six Soviet regiments were brought home in the summer of 1986; a net reduction of fifteen thousand troops.[38]

It was in this phase that mujahedin cross-border raids into the Soviet Union instigated by the Pakistanis reached their height. These did little damage. But the Americans worried that they might provoke a disproportionate Soviet response. Indeed when a raiding party penetrated more than twelve miles north of the Amu Darya river and struck a factory with rockets in April 1987, the Soviet Ambassador in Islamabad stormed into the Foreign Ministry to warn that further attacks would have severe consequences, and the raids were called off.[39]

The fourth and final phase of the war began in November 1986 with the installation by the Russians of a new Afghan president, Mohamed Najibullah, to replace Babrak Karmal. With active Russian support, Najibullah launched a Policy of National Reconciliation, which was intended to reach out to moderate non-Communist political and religious leaders, while building up the Afghan army and security forces so that Soviet military support could eventually be dispensed with.

The Soviet forces continued to support the operations of the Afghan army. But the Soviet commanders were now determined to keep their casualties to a minimum and made greater use of long-range bombers flying secret missions from the Soviet Union, missions which for cover purposes were attributed to the Afghan air force. In one incident near the end of the war, a heavy bomb dropped from a long-range bomber landed close to an Afghan military headquarters, and another killed several dozen civilians. Fragments of the bomb were discovered in the wreckage, the Afghans complained, and the Soviets set up a commission of inquiry. But the incident was hushed up and no one was punished. The bombers attempted to suppress mujahedin positions in the areas around Faisabad, Jalalabad and Kandahar which the 40th Army had already abandoned. They ineffectively attacked the mujahedin rocket batteries which were now shelling Kabul with greatly increased frequency. In the very last weeks of the war they bombarded Masud's positions in the Pandsher Valley. The purpose of this so-called Operation *Typhoon* was political rather than military.[40]

But most of the energies of the 40th Army were confined to preparing and then executing their final withdrawal from the country in February 1989. The withdrawal took place in two stages, between May and August 1988 and between November and February 1989. It was accomplished with the same logistical skill that the Russians had shown when they first entered the country. During this period 2,262 soldiers were killed, an average of eighty-seven a month.

The withdrawal was not seriously opposed by the rebels, who by then were much more concerned with jostling for power in the new Afghanistan. The resulting civil war was, at least for Kabul, more destructive than anything that had happened during the Soviet war.[41]

General Lyakhovski, the indefatigable Russian chronicler of the war, paints a devastating picture of the 40th Army's performance. Until the middle of 1980, he says, the troops were hidebound by orthodoxy, sticking close to their armoured vehicles in the valley roads. Later their performance improved, but even so many problems remained unsolved. Units were understrength, and the need to remain alert against mujahedin attacks by day or night led to physical exhaustion and low morale. The soldiers lacked stamina. They were poorly trained. Their personal equipment was inadequate. Junior commanders were careless about security and intelligence, and tactically inept, so that even when they got them at a disadvantage, the rebels were too often able to break out. Lyakhovski's devastating conclusion was that the Soviet Union's comparative failure in Afghanistan, its first war since the Second World War, demonstrated its weakness, robbed it of confidence in its own strength, and dispelled the myth of its military invincibility.[42]

This is not entirely fair. Despite the criticisms levelled against the soldiers of the 40th Army, the best of them became formidable fighting men, respected and feared by their enemy. The troops from the elite parachute and special services units were increasingly well trained and equipped to fight their elusive enemy. Edward Girardet, who spent much time with the mujahedin, reported, 'The special troops are swift, silent and deadly. Swooping down in a single December [1985] raid, they slaughtered 82 guerrillas and wounded 60 more.'[43] A mujahedin commander, Amin Wardak, described the ambush: 'They attacked at night in a narrow gorge. At first, we didn't know we were being shot at because of the silencers. Then our people began falling.'[44]

The 40th Army was unique in its composition. 'Never before in the history of the Soviet armed forces,' said its last commander, General Gromov, 'had an army had its own air force. It was particularly well supplied with special forces units – eight battalions in all, alongside the highly trained air assault and reconnaissance units.'[45] It was unique, too, in the task it was set. Unlike some Western armies, no other Soviet army was ever asked to fight an extended counter-insurgency war in a foreign country. The 40th Army was disbanded as soon as the war was over. It had won all its major battles and never lost a post to the enemy: a record which consoled its commanders. But it was never able to deliver the political success which the leaders of the country had hoped for.

- SEVEN -

THE
NATIONBUILDERS

Even before the troops had crossed the Amu Darya, an army of Soviet advisers had preceded them to try to build 'socialism' there, as other foreigners were later to try to build 'democracy'.

The United States, the Soviet Union, Germany and others all gave aid to Afghanistan before the war. The Russians had the advantage of a direct model on which to base themselves: the Central Asian republics of the Soviet Union, to which in the course of a hundred years of imperial rule they had brought law and order, clean water, health care, universal education for boys and girls, economic development, and for the elite the prospect of glittering prizes in Moscow. This progress was achieved at a very high price: a protracted guerrilla war in the 1920s, perhaps a million dead in the collectivisation of Kazakhstan in the 1930s, widespread corruption, and political repression sometimes even more ruthless than elsewhere in the Soviet Union. Nevertheless one American scholar judged in 1982: 'The Soviet leadership can legitimately claim to have a developmental model that has managed to achieve one of the highest rates of literacy, the best health care system, and the highest general standard of living found anywhere in the Muslim world.'[1] Even though the extreme measures of the 1920s and 1930s could no longer be applied, there seemed few intrinsic reasons why what had worked in Central Asia should not work in Afghanistan too.

Aid Projects

According to Soviet figures, which are neither systematic nor coherent, Soviet aid to Afghanistan between 1954 and 1980 amounted to 1.5 billion roubles. The Russians built power stations, irrigation systems, factories, natural gas wells, and the silo which remained long after the war as one of the sights of Kabul. Many of these were operated with the assistance of Soviet specialists. In addition to army and air-force officers, the Soviets trained labourers, technicians, and engineers – over seventy thousand by 1980, according to Soviet government figures. In 1979 and 1980 the Russians provided 500 million roubles of economic aid to the Afghans: credits, grants, vehicles, fuel, and support for agriculture. In February 1987 they provided 950 million roubles in grant aid, to sweeten the prospect of their eventual withdrawal. Aid to Afghanistan constituted a significant, though not overwhelming, portion of the Soviet aid given to the Third World at this time – estimated at $78 billion between 1982 and 1986. Taken together, aid to the Afghan military and the expenses associated with the Soviet military effort amounted to 1,578.5 million roubles in 1984, 2,623.8 in 1985, 3,197.4 in 1986, and 4,116 in 1987, or roughly $7.5 billion over the four years. By comparison, the entire Soviet military budget as late as 1989 was $128 billion. Similarly, according to Russian government records, Afghanistan's debt to the USSR by October 1991 was 4.7 billion roubles, roughly half of India's, and about a tenth of the total debt owed to the Soviet Union by all developing countries.[2]

Once the war started the Russians made every effort to keep existing projects going, often at considerable risk to the Soviet specialists involved. The major irrigation project outside Jalalabad employed about six thousand people, and consisted of six large state farms, specialising in the production of citrus fruit, vegetable oils, dairy products, and meat. It included a dam and a major canal, a hydroelectric station and a pumping station, a repair works, a wood processing plant, and a jam factory. It was the largest economic project in the country, and was said to be larger than any comparable project anywhere else in the developing world. But it was in a vulnerable place: one hour's drive from Pakistan, close to two Russian brigades and an airbase. The farms came under attack from the mujahedin, who mined the local roads.

B. N. Mikhanov, the chief expert, and his colleagues – there were seventy-eight of them altogether – were professionals, mostly middle-aged and married. They were regularly threatened, and their Afghan fellow workers were sometimes abducted and killed. But they stayed at their posts, and went to work carrying an automatic, a bag of spare ammunition, and hand grenades to defend themselves if necessary. The project survived until after the Russians left, when it was destroyed by the mujahedin in their failed offensive against Jalalabad in the spring of 1989.[3]

Another major project was the Polytechnic Institute in Kabul, which had been completed well before the war began. Alexander Lunin was the chief adviser to the rector, and managed the Soviet teaching staff – more than a hundred of them. In addition to its three faculties – construction, geology, and electro-mechanics – the institute had a pre-paratory department which took in students from poorer families and brought them up to speed in Russian and other subjects. The institute too kept going, despite the threats, the shelling, the booby traps, and the death of colleagues.[4]

How much lasting good all this money did for the Afghan people is not clear. Before the Afghan Communists came to power, Soviet aid was given more or less on its merits. But thereafter it was distorted by the ideologically driven and ultimately futile attempt to build 'socialism'.[5] From the start, many programmes were ill-conceived for local conditions. Many more were ruined in thirty years of fighting. Aid supplies were diverted for private profit or hijacked by the mujahedin.

And all this effort brought the Russians few of the political dividends for which they had hoped. They had almost no influence on the events that led to the murder of Taraki by Amin. They got a closer grip on Amin's successor, Babrak Karmal. But this brought its own problems. The plethora of Soviet advisers, their micromanagement of everyday business, robbed their Afghan opposite numbers of any sense of responsibility and initiative. Why take risks, if the Soviet comrades were willing to take the risks for you? Faced with interference at all levels in the military as well as the civilian bureaucracy, the Afghans often simply shrugged their shoulders and let the Russians take the strain. Najibullah, who was President of Afghanistan after 1986, described a typical meeting of the Afghan council of ministers: 'We sit down at the table. Each minister comes with his own [Soviet] adviser. The meeting begins, the discussion becomes heated, and gradually the advisers come closer and closer to the table, so accordingly our people move away, and eventually only the advisers are left at the table.'[6]

The Advisers

Many of the Soviet advisers genuinely believed in their mission to help the local people and were wholeheartedly enthusiastic about it. The youth adviser and journalist Vladimir Snegirev exulted on his arrival, 'It may be that we have had the good fortune to witness one of the most brilliant and tragic revolutions of the end of the century.' He was present in March 1982 at the celebrations for the Afghan New Year in the Kabul stadium. 'There is a striking contrast,' he noted, 'which is only possible here: many of the women on the terraces conceal their faces under the chador – a primitive, medieval superstition; but parachutists are landing in the stadium and they are women too, who grew up in this country. The chador and the parachute. You don't have to be a prophet to foretell the victory of the parachute.'

For the next months and years Snegirev and many others like him found themselves wrestling with the problem of why this essentially democratic and well-intentioned revolution was so bitterly opposed by so many of the Afghan people. More than twenty years later – after the Afghan civil war, the reign of the Taliban, and the American invasion – Snegirev ruefully recognised how naive he had been: he himself had been living in a decaying Orwellian regime without a future. 'But the dreams remained: 'Liberty, Equality, Fraternity. Social justice. Down with the oppressors of the working class!' … After all, our own country was huge, and still seemed powerful. Yes, everyone was equally poor, but there was no terrible poverty, and there was a giant industry, canals, hydroelectric stations. Were it not for our sclerotic leadership, people like Brezhnev, everything would work out differently. That's what I thought, that's what many people my age thought. When we arrived in Afghanistan, even before we had had time to look round, we began to do what we had prepared ourselves to do for the whole of our previous lives … [H]ere [in Afghanistan] it was as if time had gone backwards

... But now a power had arisen in this land which wanted to drag the people from out of their superstition, to give children the chance to go to school, peasants the possibility to plough their fields with tractors instead of oxen, women the opportunity to see the world directly, instead of through the eye slits of the chador. Was that not a revolution? The battle of the future against a past already condemned? And I was part of it.'[7]

The number of advisers and aid workers increased throughout the summer of 1979 – Party advisers, military advisers, technical advisers, advisers on youth affairs from the Komsomol, trade union advisers despite the absence of an Afghan working class, advisers from the Soviet Ministry of Shipping even though the rivers in Afghanistan were barely navigable.[8] There were advisers in all the ministries, in the factories, in the transport companies, banks, and educational institutions. The number of advisers in the Foreign and Internal Affairs ministries probably ran into the hundreds.[9] Before the war began Soviet experts in Afghanistan were not well paid, even by comparison with experts from other Socialist countries, who might get as much as $1,000 a month. But after the invasion their pay went up, to about $700 a month, significantly more than they would have received back home. The bonus was known, with grim humour, as 'coffin money'.[10]

Many of the people who went were well-qualified specialists. Others were enthusiastic amateurs. Many came voluntarily, because they were idealists, or because they wanted adventure, or because that was the only way they could get abroad, or because they thought they could better themselves. Of course, many other people who ended up as advisers in Afghanistan, perhaps the majority, had little choice in the matter. The military and Party political specialists were simply ordered to go. Others were invited to volunteer, which most of them did more or less willingly: it would have been a bad career move to refuse.

There were some sixteen to eighteen hundred Soviet military advisers in Afghanistan by the end of 1980. Sixty to eighty of them were generals. There were three or four officers attached to each Afghan army battalion, four or five in each regiment, eleven or twelve in each division, with interpreters to match.[11] They wore Afghan army uniform and were better paid than officers in the 40th Army. Advisers could put together the money for a car in one year, and for the down payment on a cooperative apartment back home in two, something that would take very much longer for an officer on Soviet pay scales. Not surprisingly the regular Soviet military hated the military advisers – the word was not exaggerated, according to Valeri Shiryaev, who served as a military interpreter with an Afghan division. Some Soviet units had notices on the entrance to their bases: 'No dogs or advisers admitted'.

The attitude of the regular officers changed when it became clear that working with the Afghan army could be very dangerous. Two generals died in action: General Vlasov, and Lieutenant General Shkidchenko, whose helicopter went down while he was directing an Afghan army operation in Khost in January 1982. One in three of the advisers serving in Shiryaev's division died in 1983–4. Even so, there were cases when Soviet units refused to make space on their helicopters for the evacuation of wounded advisers, saying that since they worked for the Afghans, it was for the Afghans to evacuate them.[12]

The Party advisers were the most numerous among the civilians. In 1983 the Central Committee of the PDPA had eighty Soviet advisers supported by fifty interpreters. They were intimately involved in the workings of party and government, often writing speeches for senior Afghans, which were then translated into Pushtu or Dari for the politicians to read out.[13] These people had no specialised training for their mission beyond a one-week induction course. It seems to have been assumed that the ideological orthodoxies that were supposed to work in the Soviet Union would work just as well in Afghanistan. In practice they worked just as badly, or even worse. Many Party advisers were of poor calibre, especially in the early years, when Afghanistan was regarded as a convenient dumping place for people who were not making the grade back in the Soviet Union. With some honourable exceptions very few of them had any knowledge or understanding of the country and simply attempted to apply to Afghanistan the tired political and organisational formulas which were already failing in the Soviet Union.

The idea of sending Soviet youth advisers to Afghanistan was mooted soon after the April 1978 coup. Between May 1979 and November 1988 about a hundred and fifty officials from the Young Communist League of the Soviet Union, the Komsomol, served in Afghanistan as advisers. Their task was to set up a youth movement in the *kishlaks* as well as in the towns.[14] All were volunteers, at least in principle. They were recruited from all over the Soviet Union. They would get a phone call from out of the blue: 'It's been suggested that you be recommended for a trip "across the river"' (the accepted euphemism),[15] to work with the Democratic Organisation of the Youth of Afghanistan (DOMA). They would get a six-week crash course in the history, culture, traditions, and languages of Afghanistan. They would then be sent off, initially to Kabul.

The Komsomol advisers were organised into teams to work with children and adolescents, on ideological and international affairs, on publishing, and in the provinces. But initially they concentrated on providing the DOMA with all the proper trappings: a Central Committee, a Secretariat, and departments for organisation, political work with the masses, military-patriotic affairs, work with the 'young pioneers', international affairs, financial, and general administrative affairs. They set up committees in the provinces and opened the Central Palace of the Pioneers in 1981 in the presence of Karmal's partner Anakhita Ratebzad. They distributed ten thousand translations of Nikolai Ostrovski's Socialist realist classic about Stalin's first Five Year Plan, *How The Steel Was Tempered*, no doubt to the complete mystification of the lucky recipients. By the time the youth advisers were withdrawn at the end of 1988, they claimed that the DOMA had 220,000 members – a figure padded, a sceptic might think, by some serious double counting.

Nikolai Zakharov was one of the first to arrive. He landed at Kabul airport in the middle of a firefight and whatever illusions he may have had about his mission were soon dispelled. It was quite clear that his new Afghan colleagues were determined to work in their own way. He noted in his diary that Abdurrahman, a deputy leader of the DOMA, said after a drink too many, 'In order to achieve total victory we will permit no internal attempts at opposition, even if we have to wade through blood.'[16] The young people the DOMA was working with were unpromising material, heavily influenced by Islamic, Maoist, and nationalistic thinking. The advisers did not have the finance to carry through their ideas. Neither the Afghan authorities not the people back in the Soviet Union took much notice of their recommendations. Methods which might have worked in the Soviet Union were quite inappropriate in Afghanistan. As early as December 1981 one adviser ruefully recognised, 'Copying the Komsomol system of personnel management takes no account of the real circumstances. Even though an instruction has been issued to that effect, there is no unified system of personnel in the country, and one reason for that is that it is not viable.'[17] Not surprisingly, most of their efforts were in vain.

Of course, most of the advisers needed interpreters. Some were recruited from Tajikistan and Uzbekistan, where the people spoke languages similar to those in Afghanistan. Others came from the elite academic institutions of Moscow and Leningrad, where the study of Afghanistan, its history, its peoples, its languages, and its culture, could stand comparison with any in the world.

In June 1979 Yevgeni Kiselev was preparing for his final exams in the Oriental Department of Moscow State University. Soviet Union students were normally posted on graduation to jobs picked for them by the authorities. Kiselev was expecting to work for the news agency TASS in Kabul. Instead he was summoned out of the blue to a meeting in the Dean's office. Here he and a couple of other fellow students met two men in civilian clothes who told them that all postings had been cancelled. All that year's graduates in Persian and Pushtu were being sent to Afghanistan as interpreters. They were then interviewed by two colonels – polished, refined, polite, typical staff officers – who reminded them that as students they were liable to military service. They were therefore being taken into the army. On 12 July they were flown to Kabul and assigned to Afghan units to work alongside the Soviet military advisers. They wore Afghan military uniform and, like the advisers, were paid more than Soviet officers of the equivalent rank. Kiselev and five others were put to live in a three-bedroomed flat in a new *microrayon* which was barely finished and was still inadequately equipped. The rooms in the apartments had cement floors, and there were no mattresses, pillows, or sheets on the metal bed frames. Kiselev managed to track down some blankets and mattresses in the town. He and his colleagues had to improvise their own furniture.[18]

Another new arrival was Andrei Greshnov. He hoped to complete his studies in Kabul, but he had not yet passed the exam on the History of the Communist Party, an essential qualification for any foreign trip. He just scraped through, and was sent on his way after a short course at the Institute of African and Asian Studies on how to comport himself as a Soviet citizen abroad. But instead of continuing his studies as he had hoped, he was brutally told that he was going to be an interpreter with the Afghan army. If he refused, he would be excluded from the university. Two weeks later, without having taken his final exams, he too was on the aeroplane to Kabul. He discovered as soon as he landed that the Farsi he had learned at university had little in common with the Dari spoken on the Kabul streets: he could not understand what the airport workers were saying. He was assigned to the same apartment as Kiselev.[19]

The Women

Women went to Afghanistan during the war for various reasons. If they were in the military they were simply posted, whether they liked it or not. By the 1980s women made up just over 1.5 per cent of the total numbers in the Soviet armed forces.[20] Unlike the women who fought in the Second World War as bomber and fighter crews, as tank commanders, as snipers, these women served on the headquarters staff as archivists, cipher clerks, and interpreters, at the logistics base in Pul-i Khumri and in Kabul, or in the military hospitals and front-line medical units as doctors and nurses. Female civilian contract workers began to arrive in 1984 and worked in offices, in regimental libraries, as secretaries, in military stores and laundries, in Voentorg (the network of military shops). The commander of the 66th Independent Motor-rifle Brigade in Jalalabad even managed to get hold of a typist who could double up as a hairdresser.[21]

The volunteers had mixed motives. Doctors and nurses went to work in the military hospitals and forward medical stations out of a sense of professional commitment and duty. Some tended the wounded under fire, as their predecessors had done in the Second World War, and dealt with the most horrible wounds within days of arriving in Afghanistan.[22] Some went for personal reasons: because their private lives had failed or because they badly needed the extra money. In Afghanistan they were fed regularly and for nothing, and they received a double salary.[23] Some went out of a spirit of adventure: service as a civilian employee with Soviet forces abroad was one of the few ways a single woman with no connections could travel. Unlike the women in the military, the civilians could always break their contracts if they did not like what they found in Afghanistan: within a week they could be back in the Soviet Union.

Lena Maltseva went from a genuine sense of idealism and adventure, to make her own contribution to the help her country was giving the Afghan people. She was nineteen, a student at the Medical Institute in Taganrog. In 1983 she wrote to *Komsomolskaya Pravda* that the girls at her school as well as the boys wanted to test themselves, to harden themselves. 'And what's more, we all wanted to prepare ourselves to defend the Motherland – I'm sorry for the bombastic language, but I can't express it in any other way … Why do I want to go now? Well, it may sound stupid, but I'm afraid I won't get [to Afghanistan] in time. It's now so difficult there, with an undeclared war in progress. What's more, one day I will be a teacher. But honestly, I'm not yet ready for that. One can only teach when one has had some experience of life … Surely I could be useful there? (Bombast again, but what else can I say?) I want to help the people of that country, and our Soviet people who are already there.'[24]

The female volunteers, like the conscripts, were processed through their local Voenkomat. Many hoped to go to Germany, but there were few vacancies there and the officers in the Voenkomats needed to make up the quota for Afghanistan. So they persuaded or bullied the women to go there instead.

Though the women did not fight, they did from time to time come under fire. Forty-eight civilian employees and four *praporshchiki* died during the war, some as a result of enemy action, some in accidents, some from illness.[25] A total of 1,350 women received state awards for their service.[26] Two of the three women who were killed when an AN-12 was shot down over Kabul airport on 29 November 1986 were on the way to their first posting in Jalalabad. One had been recruited in the Soviet Union sixteen days earlier; the other only six days before.[27]

Like the soldiers, the women were first sent to a transit camp in Kabul until their final destination was decided. Some enterprising women got so bored with waiting that they took matters into their own hands. The twenty-year-old Svetlana Rykova hitched a flight from Kabul to Kandahar, then persuaded a helicopter pilot to take her to Shindand, the great airbase in western Afghanistan. There she was offered a job in the officers' mess. She refused it and held out until a vacancy opened as assistant to the director of financial services. She served in Afghanistan from April 1984 to February 1986.

Tatiana Kuzmina was a single mother in her early thirties. She served in Jalalabad first as a nurse, but then managed to wangle a job in a BAPO (Boevoi Agitatsionno-Propagandistski Otryad), a Military Agitation Propaganda Detachment. Tatiana was the only woman in this unit, which delivered food, medicine, and propaganda to the mountain villages around Jalalabad, put on concerts, and helped the sick and the mothers with their new babies. While she was out on a mission with the detachment on the eve of her final return to the Soviet Union, she was drowned in a mountain river. It was two weeks before her body was found.[28]

Lilya, a highly qualified typist on the staff of one of the military districts back in the Soviet Union, was not paid enough to take her through to the end of the month and she made up the difference by collecting bottles for salvage. She could not afford adequate clothing for the winter. But in the 40th Army she was warm and well fed, beyond what she had believed possible.[29]

Many women did get married, often while they were still in Afghanistan, whether that was their original intention or not. One said, 'All of us women are lonely and frustrated in some way. Try to live on 120 roubles a month, as I do, especially if you want to dress decently and have an interesting holiday once a year. "They only go over there to find themselves a husband," people often say. Well, what's wrong with that? Why deny it? I'm 32 years old and I'm alone.'[30] Marriages could only be formally registered with the Soviet authorities in Kabul. A young couple from the 66th Independent Motor-rifle Brigade in Jalalabad were killed by rocket grenade fire on the road to the airport shortly after they had left the garrison. Natasha Glushak and her fiancé, an officer from the brigade's communications company, managed to get to Kabul and register their marriage. Instead of flying back, they returned aboard a BTR. Just as it was arriving at Jalalabad, it was blown up by a remotely detonated mine. Only the upper half of Natasha's body was recovered.[31]

The women were far outnumbered by the men, whose attitude to them was mixed. Colonel Antonenko, who commanded the 860th Independent Motor-rifle Regiment, said, 'There were forty-four women in the regiment: nurses, laboratory assistants in the water purification station, waitresses, cooks, a canteen manager, shop assistants. We had no store of blood. When the regiment came out of battle, if we had wounded, the women would occasionally give their own blood. That really happened ... Our women were wonderful and worthy of the highest praise.'[32]

There was no dispute about the role of the nurses and doctors. One nurse remembered when soldiers brought in a wounded man, but wouldn't leave, saying, 'We don't need anything, girls, can we just sit by you for a bit?' Another remembered how one young boy, whose friend had been blown to pieces, couldn't stop talking to her about it.[33] A telephone operator in a Kabul hotel who visited a mountain outpost where the men often saw no one for months at a time was asked by the commander, 'Miss, would you take off your cap? I haven't seen a woman for a whole year.' All the soldiers came out of the trenches just to look at her hair. 'Here, back home,' one nurse later remarked, 'they've got their mums and sisters and wives. They don't need us now – but over there they told us things you wouldn't normally tell anybody.'[34]

After he left the Central Hospital for Infectious Diseases in Kabul, where he had been treated for a mixture of typhus, cholera, and hepatitis, one young officer started an affair with the nurse who had looked after him. His envious fellow officers told him maliciously that she was a witch. She drew portraits of her lovers and hung them on the wall of her room. His three predecessors had all been killed in action. Now she began to draw him too. He was half gripped by the superstition. But she never finished the drawing and he was only wounded, not killed. 'We soldiers were very superstitious while the war was going on,' he later said ruefully. He lost touch with his nurse after leaving Afghanistan. But he always preserved the warmest memory of her.[35]

At the end of the day the nurses got little official recognition for what they had done. Alexander Khoroshavin, who served in the 860th Independent Motor-rifle Regiment in Faisabad, discovered to his disgust twenty years after the war that Ludmila Mikheeva, who had been a nurse with the regiment in 1983–5, was not entitled to any of the benefits which even the most unprepossessing veteran received for his service in Afghanistan.[36]

The women were too often subjected to unbearable pressure from men prepared to use threats as well as blandishments. Many of the veterans talked of them with distasteful contempt. They called them *chekistki*, implying that they sold themselves for *cheki*, cheques, the special currency used by the Soviets in Afghanistan. Some conceded that women who went to Afghanistan as nurses and doctors may have done so for the best of reasons. But few of them had a good word for the others, the secretaries, the librarians, the storekeepers, or the laundrywomen. These they accused of going to Afghanistan solely in search of men and money.

The women themselves always resented the slander. They resorted to a variety of defensive tactics. Some accepted one protector in order to keep the others off.[37] Many Second World War generals, such as Rokossovski and Zhukov, had 'Field Service Wives' (PPZh – Pokhodno-Polevaya Zhena), who travelled with them from post to post. Now the institution was revived: it is portrayed with compassion by Andrei Dyshev in his novel *PPZh*, about a volunteer nurse, Gulya Karimova, and her lover Captain Gerasimov.[38]

Valeri Shiryaev, the military interpreter, thought that all this represented the social reality inside Russia itself: many of the men came from the provinces and regarded women as prey or as something to be knocked about. But at least in Afghanistan the Party representatives sensibly did not try to interfere with people's relationships as they would have done back home. There were inevitable tensions: 'The smaller the garrison, the fewer the women, and the greater the competition, which sometimes led to fights, duels, suicide, and the search for death in battle.'[39]

Not all the Soviet women in Afghanistan came there in the service of the Soviet state. Some came as the wives of Afghans, often students, whom they had met at home. Galina Margoeva was the wife of the engineer Haji Hussein. She and her husband remained in Kabul through all the changes in regime, through the horrors of the civil war and the depredations of the Taliban, living in their apartment in the *microrayon* by the housing construction combine near the airport. Tania was the wife of Nigmatulla, an Afghan officer who had trained in the Soviet Union and married her despite the opposition of her family and his own superiors. Their first child was born in Minsk. After five years he was posted first to Kabul, then to Kandahar and then to Herat. He continued to serve despite the changes of regime: he was the political officer of a division under Najibullah, a brigade under the mujahedin, and a division again under the Taliban. Tania was with him throughout. She wore the veil, learned Farsi, but remained an atheist. When Nigmatulla's three brothers were killed, she took the nine orphans into her family and brought them up with her own children.[40]

Life and Death in Kabul

In Kabul there was a curfew after eight o'clock, you could not safely walk in a large part of the city, and there was always shooting at night. Although the city was heavily garrisoned and its streets were continually patrolled by troops, police, and armoured vehicles, the mujahedin occasionally mounted attacks inside Kabul itself. In January 1981 they got close enough to the villa of the Chief Soviet Military Adviser in the embassy quarter to attack it with rocket-propelled grenades. The same day they attacked – unsuccessfully – a key electric power station some twenty-five miles outside Kabul. The following day a large cinema and the Soviet bookshop were blown up. In the next few days there were more than two hundred terrorist attacks in other major cities.[41] In 1983 a bomb under the table in Kabul University dining room killed nine Soviets, including a woman professor.[42]

People always carried their personal weapons and every apartment block had an armed guard. Nevertheless the capital was thought to be safe enough for senior officials and military advisers to bring their wives and families to live with them. Their standard of living was often higher than it would have been at home. Most lived in the *microrayon*, the pay was good, parcels and letters arrived regularly. The children were

educated in the embassy school: it had to work in three shifts to accommodate them all, and even so it was overcrowded. You could watch the
latest Soviet films in the embassy or the Soviet House of Culture.

The range in the embassy shop was limited, and the wives could
buy only the goods that matched their husbands' rank. So they spent
much of their time shopping in the local market in the old *microrayon*,
the *parvanistka*, a Russification of the words *parva nist* – 'not to worry'.
Here they could find Western consumer goods and clothes which none
of them had ever seen back home, some of it sent by Western aid
agencies to relieve the Afghan poor. They bargained ruthlessly for second-hand jeans, jackets, and dresses, despite threats from the authorities to send them straight back to the Soviet Union if they persisted in
shopping. Needless to say, the threats had no effect.[43]

As the security situation deteriorated, greater constraints were
placed upon the Soviet women in Afghanistan. In Jalalabad, after a
number had been killed, women were not allowed to go on the streets
without an armed escort. By 1986 they were not allowed to go without
escort even into the centre of major cities such as Kabul. But the
temptations of the Afghan bazaars, with their rich variety of Western
consumer goods and designer clothes, were too great for some to resist.
The more daring or irresponsible of them found their way to the bazaars
despite the obstacles. Some hoped that if they kept their mouths shut
while they were walking through the bazaars they would be mistaken
for Western missionaries whom – they optimistically believed – the
mujahedin would leave unharmed.[44]

The advisers were never specially targeted by the mujahedin. But
there were casualties nevertheless. Evgeni Okhrimiuk was a geologist
who was posted to Afghanistan in 1976, when he was already sixty-
three years old; at that time geologists were among the few Soviet
advisers then working there. Okhrimiuk was put in charge of the team
searching for natural resources, especially natural gas. Once the war
started, and work in the outlying provinces became too difficult, he
and his colleagues worked in the neighbourhood of Kabul, looking for
water and building materials.

On 18 August 1981 Okhrimiuk left his apartment in the *microrayon*
in his official car with his usual driver to go to his office about a mile

away. He never arrived. The Russians later learned what had happened. Okhrimiuk agreed to let his driver give a lift to a couple of relatives. It was a put-up job. The two men took Okhrimiuk prisoner, so that he could be exchanged for the brother of one of the local guerrilla commanders, who had been captured by the Afghan army. Okhrimiuk wrote to his people that his captors had taken him on foot for five days to a hiding place in the high mountains, and asked for a helicopter to pick him up once the exchange had been agreed. Unfortunately the commander's brother had already been shot. There were protracted negotiations about a ransom. They petered out. After Okhrimiuk had spent a year in captivity, the French Communist paper *L'Humanité* reported that he had been executed. His wife asked for a memorial to be erected in a Moscow cemetery. The authorities refused permission.[45]

Aleksei and Marina Muratov first went to Afghanistan in 1970, above all because they needed the money. In Moscow they both worked as junior scientific assistants in the university, they had two sons, and they had to rely on help from Aleksei's parents to get by. In Kabul Aleksei lectured in the polytechnic and Marina worked as a secretary. They liked the country and the people, and they remained there for three years.

Then the war came. 'We understood from the beginning,' said Marina later, 'that the invasion was a crime. And when we returned to Afghanistan in the autumn of 1981, we continually felt ashamed: ashamed for our country which had sent its soldiers there to kill and be killed.' This time both Aleksei and Marina taught in the Polytechnic Institute. Marina helped prepare Afghan students who were going to study in the Soviet Union.

They got used to the wartime conditions – continual shooting, breakdowns in the supply of electricity, sleeping with an automatic rifle under the bed – and the difficulties of life in the Soviet community, where you could be sent home for stepping even an inch out of line, and where their immediate superior disliked the Afghans and drank a lot too much.

The movements of the advisers and their families who lived at the Polytechnic Institute were strictly controlled. Alarms were signalled by the firing of a rocket, three long bursts from an automatic rifle, and by repeated banging on a length of rail outside the guardroom. Those who were assigned to the local defence force took up their positions; the rest took shelter. All lights in the apartments had to be turned out. The all clear was signalled by separate blows on the rail, by word of mouth, and by radio. The radios in the apartments had to be left on all the time.

The polytechnic regularly came under fire, and the inhabitants had to keep their eyes out for bombs and booby traps hidden under tables and in corners. Marina once picked up an explosive device disguised as an electric torch, but luckily it did not go off. She rarely saw any bloodshed, though she was there when a member of the embassy was shot down outside a shop after collecting his son from school. The boy sat by his body for forty minutes before he was picked up.

Towards the end of their third year in Afghanistan Aleksei and Marina went shopping. On their way out of the polytechnic she noticed one of the young Afghan guards looking at her oddly. She thought he must be under the influence of drugs. As they were returning to the polytechnic she fell over; it was only later that she realised the man had shot her. Aleksei was lying just behind her. He was dying. Marina subsequently had ten operations to save her leg. Her Afghan students visited her every day; one brought his father from the northern city of Mazar-i Sharif to pray for her.[46]

Life and Death in the Provinces

Work in the provinces was more difficult than in Kabul and more dangerous too. The advisers had to travel across roads that were regularly mined. One group of Komsomol advisers from Kabul was ambushed and a woman was killed. In Herat the advisers were in principle only allowed to travel in armoured vehicles. But often there would be none available, so they had to travel in ordinary vehicles. And though the armour might protect you from bullets, it would not save you from a roadside mine. Herat did have one advantage, however. If you ran out of vodka, you could send a special messenger to get some from Kushka, the major logistics base, only three hours away by road.[47]

As well as being dangerous, the work in the regions was depressing. In Logar province the advisers discovered that not one village supported the Kabul regime. Only 2.5 per cent of the children there were going to school.[48] From 1984 to 1986 Alexander Yuriev was in Kandahar: he had volunteered to go there when his predecessor, Grisha Semchenko, had been badly wounded. He described the state of the city in his diary: 'Kandahar is a very beautiful town. But half of it has been destroyed, whole streets and blocks are in ruins, and the surviving buildings are pitted with scars from shell splinters and bullets. It is very dangerous to drive around: the rebels are firing from the green zone outside the city, and mount ambushes inside the city itself. Everyone goes around with their guns at the ready. What makes it worse is that we control only two of the city's six administrative regions. The other four are controlled by the rebels, and the road along which we have to travel goes through the middle of them.'[49]

Yuriev wrote home cheerfully enough: 'Everything is fine with me. I live in a villa outside town, which was built by the Americans. Our working day is quite short – from 8–9 a.m. to 2 p.m. We sometimes get two or three days off in the week.' These bland words were not inaccurate, but they concealed the reality. The villa had indeed been built by Americans constructing the local airport. But the water supply had broken down, and there was neither lighting nor heating. The place was bombarded several times a day. 'During the bombardments, you made sure there were two walls between you and the street. You lay on the floor in your flak jacket and helmet, and hoped that there wouldn't be a direct hit on the ceiling.' It was several miles from the villa to the Kandahar headquarters of the local committee of the DOMA, where Yuriev worked. The road was always heavily mined: every week someone got blown up on it. Every morning a flail tank cleared the mines, Soviet soldiers were posted along the road, and it was safe to travel. Then the soldiers were withdrawn and the road was back in the hands of the rebels. So Yuriev had to get home again by two o'clock. If serious fighting was going on, it was better not to leave the house at all; those were counted as days off. Fighting went on all around, even on working days. 'There was fighting on 10 and 11 August [1985],' writes Yuriev in his diary. 'Many dead and wounded. We open a branch of the Institute for Youth Workers of the Central Committee of the DOMA … Comrade Khanif spoke at the meeting. He said that the branch was being opened in the middle of a war. But that was necessary, because young people needed to learn the theory of revolution, and use it in the course of the revolutionary struggle. In the open, on the street, I hold the first lesson for students of the branch on "The place and role of DOMA in the political system of Afghan society".' [50]

The advisers could go for weeks without hearing a word of Russian spoken. Not everyone was able to stand the nervous tension. 'How can one describe the conditions in which we lived?' asked Alexander Gavrya, who was in Afghanistan from October 1982 to October 1985, and again from April to November 1988. 'Well, take for example Chagcharan, in the province of Ghor. It was deep in the mountains, and helicopters flying there were shot down, so that you had to get there in an armed column, which might have to fight its way through. I was there once, and called in on Sasha Babchenko, one of our advisers. Suddenly I heard someone wailing on the other side of the wall, loudly, terribly, like an animal. I jumped for my gun. "Don't worry," said Sasha, "that's an adviser from another department. He gets drunk and wails every evening. The boys will soon calm him down."' [51]

The rebels controlled the countryside by night, even if they did not do so by day. There was little opportunity to work effectively with the peasants. And there was of course no proletariat to work with since there was almost no industry in the country anyway. So the advisers concentrated on building up the local party and youth organisations, on helping the schools, and setting up children's summer camps. One visitor from the Soviet Union tactlessly gave a talk to a local school on how Soviet children helped their elders fight the Germans by putting sand in their machine guns and tanks. The listeners naturally pricked up their ears. The divisional commander was duly furious: 'Don't ever let a loudmouth like that get within range of my pistol again.' [52]

Yusuf Abdullaev, another youth adviser, reported on a trip round the provinces in June 1981: 'The situation is very difficult. Only the regional centres are in the hands of the people's power [the Kabul regime] ... Everyone's efforts are directed to the struggle against the rebels. After an attempt to open a school they broke the arms and the legs of four of the children. There are strong feelings of hostility towards the Soviets, and towards the Russian soldiers, for which the soldiers themselves are often to blame. The rebels have burned a column of eighteen vehicles carrying food, which they commandeered in order to sell. There is no sign of the Afghan army and Tsarandoi. The people who are doing the fighting are our own military units and some of the *malishi* [militia detachments for the defence of the revolution] from among the local population. The rebels terrorise the locals – they fine the families of those who are collaborating with the authorities twenty or forty thousand *afgani* [the Afghan currency].'[53]

By February 1982 Abdullaev was even more gloomy. There were over a hundred schools in Farakh province: perhaps no more than ten were open. Only four thousand out of more than twenty-one thousand children of school age were studying. Not one of the fifty-one cooperatives was working. The local Communist youth organisation was totally disorganised, and probably had no more than two hundred members. There were more than forty rebel bands operating in the area; their average age was under thirty. Abdullaev nevertheless believed that most of the population accepted that government terror and violence had declined with the installation of the Babrak regime, and that the bands were discrediting themselves by their behaviour. But people remained very cautious. A few months later Abdullaev reported from Khost that no one mentioned Babrak Karmal, apart from an Afghan officer who had shouted out, 'Death to Karmal!' at a political meeting in his artillery regiment.

Herat, where it had all started, was contested territory throughout the war. The mujahedin controlled the old city, while the government and the Russians controlled the suburbs and the essential main road which skirted them. The Soviet advisers lived in the Hotel Herat, which had been built a few years earlier on the edge of the city on the road to the airport, and had been popular with tourists. By now it had been transformed into a small fortress: sandbags on the balconies, a BTR and a mortar team at the entrance, and instead of a liveried doorman a heavily armed soldier in a flak jacket. The inhabitants were advised to travel with an armoured escort even inside the city.

In June 1981 one of the Komsomol advisers, Gena Kulazhenko, set off to drive the short distance from the airport to the hotel. There was no escort available, so he took a Toyota taxi. He never arrived.

His colleagues from Kabul got no help from the Soviet military or civilian authorities, and went themselves to Herat to find out what had happened. They managed to find the Toyota, riddled with bullets; a local mullah said he knew where Kulazhenko's grave was. They set off escorted by a tank and two BTRs, which promptly got stuck in the narrow street of the local *kishlak*. The mullah led them on foot to a grave, but the corpse they dug up was badly decomposed and was not that of Kulazhenko. They then fell into an ambush. Later one of the local rebel bands put out a leaflet saying that Kulazhenko had been executed and buried in secret.[54]

This was the first of four fatal casualties suffered by the Komsomol advisers. Nikolai Serov then died in 1984 of cancer of the blood, Ator Abdukadyrov was killed in a bombardment, and Alexander Babchenko died in 1987 just before he was due to go home.

Nikolai Komissarov was a Komsomol official from Kazan. He was sent to Faisabad in 1982. There were eighteen other advisers there, four military, the rest civilians, living in rented accommodation in the town. Komissarov was responsible for eleven *kishlaks*, which he and his Tajik interpreter visited regularly, unarmed, to do youth work; one of their triumphs was to persuade the local girls' school to abandon the veil. They had other tasks as well: to acquire intelligence and to help set up local self-defence organisations.[55]

When Komissarov heard that the whole of the senior class in one of his schools had been persuaded to go over to the rebels he took a military driver and drove off to see what was happening. The *kishlak* was deep in the countryside and to go there without an armoured escort was an exceptionally dangerous thing to do. Two armoured vehicles were sent to rescue him if they could. It turned out to be unnecessary. 'When we were halfway there,' Captain Igor Morozov recounted, 'we found his car. The soldier, white-faced from what he had been through, was gripping the steering wheel convulsively. Komissarov was sitting beside him without batting an eyelid, and even tried to make a joke of it, the bastard. What he had said to those schoolboys no one knows. But it's a fact that none of them joined the rebels. Komissarov was reprimanded for his breach of discipline – quite rightly.'[56]

Vyacheslav Nekrasov came from Sverdlovsk (Yekaterinburg),

where he worked as a lathe operator and foreman in a defence factory, served in the army, and studied at the Higher Komsomol School. He was twenty-eight years old and working as First Secretary of a local Komsomol committee when he was chosen in 1982 to go to Afghanistan to advise on youth affairs. Like others, he told his family he was being sent to Mongolia. He would work there for a year, he said, and would then bring them out to join him. He bought a Mongolian dictionary to back up his story.

Nekrasov and his interpreter, Dodikhudo Saimetdinov, flew to Kabul in October 1982, which they found far more sophisticated and Westernised than they had been led to believe. In November they were sent to work in Faryab province in northern Afghanistan.

Here Nekrasov was given a good deal of freedom by his bosses to act as he thought best. One project was to send a group of young leaders to see how Muslims lived in the Soviet Union. Nekrasov and Saimetdinov managed, with considerable difficulty, to persuade a local mullah to go with them. It was worth it: shortly after the mullah returned, Nekrasov heard him describe the visit in glowing terms over the muezzin loudspeakers.

On a visit to Kabul, Nekrasov laid hands on a mobile cinema, complete with a library of Indian, Soviet, and Afghan films and three Afghan operators. He cadged an aeroplane to fly the team to Fariab and took it around the province. The films were popular even in otherwise hostile *kishlaks*. Nekrasov's team did not charge for tickets and there were only two conditions: there should have been no shooting in the *kishlak* for a week before the performance and weapons had to be left outside. Ironically, one film popular among the Afghans was the comedy thriller *White Sun of the Desert* (*Beloe Solntse Pustynya*), among the most successful of all Soviet films, about the war in the 1920s against the rebels in Central Asia – rebels who were ethnically similar to the Afghans themselves.

Like the other civilian political advisers, Nekrasov did get mixed up in military operations from time to time. But his contacts also occasionally enabled him to negotiate ceasefire arrangements with the local guerrilla leaders, saving civilian lives as well as those of the fighters on both sides.[57]

The number of specialists and advisers was run down from 1986 onwards as the aim of modernising Afghanistan's society and its political and economic system came to seem more and more unattainable. It was a bitter disappointment for those who had risked their lives and health in what they believed was a good cause.

And yet when people back in the Soviet Union asked them how they managed to survive the horrors, many of them discovered that they had fallen in love with Afghanistan. 'We did not survive – we lived. We lived life to the full. Everything was interesting, every day was packed,' wrote Vyacheslav Nekrasov. 'Of course we were young, carefree, quick to make new friends. Even though more than ten years have passed, we are still like a single family of brothers.'[58]

– EIGHT –
SOLDIERING

Even when they are on campaign, the soldiers in most armies spend little time fighting. Instead they hang around, grumble about their officers, their sergeants, and the stupidity of the military machine in general, avoid extra duties, scrounge for food, try to get drunk, think and talk incessantly about women (though not in battle, when they have other things on their minds), boast disgracefully, and engage in laddish horseplay which sometimes degenerates into bullying and physical violence. All this apparently pointless activity, which the British call 'soldiering', has one invaluable by-product. It reinforces the sense of comradeship which is essential to the soldiers' survival in a fight.[1]

The soldiers of the 40th Army were little different. They lived in primitive and unhealthy surroundings, freezing in winter, boiling in summer, with few amenities and practically no female company. They ate bad and sometimes insufficient food. They succumbed to epidemic disease. They were often bullied by their officers, by their sergeants, and by the senior soldiers. They got no leave, except perhaps to attend the funeral of an immediate family member. But they endured hardship with the stoicism of the Russian soldier throughout the ages, and they were willing to go on fighting for their comrades even when the war itself seemed to have lost any purpose.

The Conscripts

However reluctantly, most young men in the Soviet Union accepted service in the army as an inescapable staging post on the road to adulthood. The ideals of patriotism, duty, the leading role of an omniscient Communist Party, and the superiority of the Soviet way of life were drilled into them from their earliest days. Some of these ideals stuck.

Conscripts served for two years. The annual batch of recruits was called up in two massive levies, in spring and autumn, and their heads were shaved, a tradition from Tsarist times. After one month's basic training, those destined for Afghanistan were usually sent for three months into 'Quarantine' – training camps in the Central Asian republics – where the physical conditions were similar to those in Afghanistan. So those who were called up in the spring might not actually get to Afghanistan itself until August. They would then serve there for some twenty months, though commanders could and did hold back soldiers due for demobilisation until the next bunch of new recruits had arrived.[2]

Conscripts who already had a speciality – higher education, medical or other relevant qualifications – would serve in an appropriate capacity; or they might be selected for six months' training as sergeant-drivers or gunners before going to Afghanistan, and would then serve there only eighteen months. Able soldiers could be promoted to sergeant after a year or eighteen months in the field. The power lay with their commanders, who could also reduce a sergeant to the ranks again if he failed to perform.[3]

Despite the surrounding secrecy, parents quickly realised what was going on. Those with money or influence – parents from Moscow or Leningrad or the Baltic States – had regularly bribed the recruiting office or pulled strings to keep their sons out of the army.[4] They did so with even greater determination once the war began. And so the boys who fought were mostly from the rural and working classes. A survey of fifteen hundred soldiers taken in 1986 showed that more than two-thirds were from the countryside or from working-class families with no secondary education, at a time when nearly two-thirds of the population already lived in cities. Nearly a quarter came from broken families. Not one came from a family with a background in the

Party, bureaucratic, institutional, or military elite.[5] Colonel General Krivosheev, the military historian, remarked sarcastically that they might as well restore 'the old romantic name of the armed forces – The Workers' and Peasants' Red Army'.[6]

Sometimes the authorities did not bother to tell the conscripts where they were going, but simply bundled them off with a round of vodka to ease the transition.[7] Even when they knew their destination, they were supposed to tell their families only that they would be serving abroad. The prohibition was eroded with time, but many soldiers – like the youth adviser Vyacheslav Nekrasov – still tried to ease their families' anxiety by saying they were going to Mongolia. Most parents were not fooled: Vladislav Tamarov's father replied to his first soothing letter home that he shouldn't think his parents were stupid: they knew perfectly well where he was.[8]

On the eve of his departure Andrei Ponomarev was paraded with his fellow conscripts and told that anyone not wishing to go to Afghanistan should take three paces forward: he would then serve in the Soviet Union. Much as they might have liked to, neither Ponomarev nor anyone else did so out of a sense of shame and a fear that they would be ostracised. Ponomarev later served in the 860th Independent Motor-rifle Regiment in Badakhshan in north-east Afghanistan.[9]

In May 1985 Vitali Krivenko and his fellow conscripts were taken by train and plane more than twelve hundred miles from his home in Kazakhstan to a training camp outside Leningrad. There they were sent to the bathhouse, given two hours to get their new uniforms in order, and started their training straight away. The standard infantry training – route marches, field exercises, shooting, drill, political classes, and PT – was very harsh. So were the drill sergeants. But when it came to the test of battle, Krivenko found that the training had served him well and that he had become a good general-purpose soldier.

Problems

There had always been a great deal of bullying in the Soviet army, and in the Tsarist army before it. But a more established ritual of bullying, *dedovshchina*, the 'grandfather system', emerged in the late 1960s.

Russian commentators give various reasons for the rise of

dedovshchina. The conscript army was demoralised. It was too large and the soldiers were underemployed. Many conscripts fell below the standards needed by a technically sophisticated force. Some were recruited from the prisons and brought with them the bullying rituals of the criminal world.

Under this system, a soldier in his last six months was known as a 'grandfather' (*ded*). New recruits were made to clean the barracks, look after the grandfathers' kit, get them cigarettes from the shop and food from the canteen. They were ritually humiliated, and beaten sometimes to the point of serious injury. Most endured, and consoled themselves with the thought that they too would be grandfathers one day. Some broke under the strain: they deserted, mutilated themselves, or committed suicide.

Some, of unusual physical as well as moral strength, stood up for themselves and were eventually left alone. Krivenko was older than the other conscripts because he had spent time in prison. His age and experience gave him authority among the other soldiers, and the grandfathers dealt with him cautiously.[10] Sergei Nikiforov was a judo expert and fought his tormentors to a standstill. Soldiers from the same republic or region stuck together in self-defence. The grandfathers in one unit were warned that if anything happened to the only two Chechen soldiers there, their countrymen would take a merciless revenge.[11]

It depended, too, on where you were. The army could not afford to employ substandard soldiers in the elite strategic rocket forces, where the grandfather system was much less brutal. It was the same in the KGB's frontier forces, who had a real job to do; and in the elite special forces and parachute units, where morale was usually high. Sergei Morozov, a sergeant in the 56th Guards Independent Airborne Assault Brigade, claimed that there was no *dedovshchina* in his unit: people were always too busy or too tired. When they were not on operations, all they wanted to do was eat and sleep.[12]

In Afghanistan the system was less oppressive even in the motor-rifle units, because there too the soldiers had real work to do. The grandfathers still gave their juniors the run-around, but it was hard to preserve the distinctions in battle. And a bully risked being cut down by a bullet from his own side, as well as from the enemy: in the heat of the fight no one would bother to investigate.[13] Even so, 33 per cent of the military crimes dealt with in the 40th Army in 1987 were 'military bullying'. More than two hundred soldiers suffered in one year: some had been killed and others severely wounded.[14]

Some Afgantsy maintained that despite its obvious negative features *dedovshchina* helped to maintain order and discipline.[15] In front-line units, they said, the seasoned soldiers taught the new arrivals to keep themselves clean, obey orders, and care for their equipment. As a recruit, Andrei Ponomarev found the bullying very difficult to bear, and though he did not break, he often crept away after a ritual beating to weep in a corner. He and his colleagues vowed that when they became senior soldiers in their turn they would not use the methods that had been applied to them. But they found this did not work. The new recruits ceased to respect them and would not do what they were told. So Ponomarev too started to use his fists: it was, he said, the only reliable way of getting your point across.[16] He and those who thought like him knew well enough that in other armies the positive aspects they claimed for *dedovshchina* were the responsibility of experienced professional NCOs. Alexander Gergel, a conscript sergeant in the 860th Independent Motor-rifle Regiment, accepted that *dedovshchina* had eaten away at the military system. That would not change, he thought, until the Russian army too was given the corps of long-service professional NCOs it lacked.

In one serious way the 40th Army in Afghanistan differed from its predecessors: it had a massive health problem, of a kind the Soviet army had never experienced before. The Russians built seven military hospitals in Afghanistan, but chronic lack of funds meant that they were badly equipped, undermanned, and barely able to cope.[17] The near collapse of the 40th Army's medical services was one of the worst consequences of the improvisation and lack of funding which accompanied its deployment. One doctor in a brigade casualty clearing station expressed himself with particular bitterness: 'One has to stick it out and look as if one is saving people. But how can you save people, when there are no medicines, no bandages, and no doctors? People die of infections, of disease, because they weren't helped in time. Our superiors think that you can save people by giving them one injection against shock. But you can't, and when the effect of the injection wears off, the patient gives up the ghost and there's nothing we can do to help him. The only thing we have is alcohol, and even that doesn't always help. If we had what we needed, we could save three-quarters of them, but as it is ...' [18]

He may have been exaggerating. But what is clear is that the medical services almost lost the battle not against war wounds, but against infectious disease. The figures speak for themselves. More than three-quarters of those who served in Afghanistan spent time in hospital. Some 11 per cent were wounded or injured. The rest – 69 per cent of all those who served during the war – suffered from serious sickness: 28 per cent from infectious hepatitis, 7.5 per cent from typhoid fever, and the rest from infectious dysentery, malaria, and other diseases. [19]

Units were often far below strength because so many of the soldiers were sick. The main scourge was hepatitis. The joke among the soldiers was that soldiers got jaundice, officers got Botkin's disease, and generals were treated for hepatitis. There were stories that some soldiers evaded duty by getting medical orderlies in the hospitals to give them urine from infected patients: if you drank it, you got the disease. [20]

By the end of 1981 every fourth soldier in the 5th Guards Motor-rifle Division in Shindand had been laid low. The commander, Boris Gromov, his deputies, and all the regimental commanders were down at the same time. The division was effectively unfit for battle. [21] At any given moment up to a quarter, perhaps even a third, of the 40th Army might be incapacitated by disease. At the height of the epidemic, there was only one nurse for every three hundred patients. [22]

Hepatitis was not the only problem. In the summer of 1985 a patrol from the 66th Independent Motor-rifle Brigade in Jalalabad drank the water from a roadside spring as they were returning from patrol. A few days later three of them collapsed on parade with cholera. More than half the brigade fell sick. A rumour circulated that the water had been deliberately infected by 'two Europeans dressed in local clothes'. To prevent further infection, people said, the bodies were being cremated – something almost unheard of in what was still at heart an Orthodox country. [23] The sick were isolated behind barbed wire, the doctors and nurses were isolated with them, and additional medical staff had to be flown in from Moscow as reinforcements.[24]

The situation of the 40th Army thus resembled that of the British and French armies in the Crimean War, and for much the same reasons: dirty water, appalling sanitation, dirty cooks, dirty canteens, dirty clothes, poor diet. The Soviets prided themselves on the number of hospitals and orphanages they built in Afghanistan. But they filled more hospitals and orphanages than they constructed, and the bigger the hospital, the worse the sanitary conditions: the rate of hepatitis was highest not in the small outposts, but in the base camps, where it should have been easiest to prevent. The Soviet medical services in the Second World War were much better at controlling disease than their successors.

But the successors were better off in one important way: they could evacuate casualties from the battlefield by helicopter. One sanguine account claimed that nine out of ten wounded soldiers received first aid in thirty minutes and got to a doctor in six hours.[25] It was a matter of pride to evacuate the wounded and the bodies of the dead, even under fire and even at the risk of further casualties. The collapse of this tradition, said one officer who had served in both wars, marked for him the degradation which distinguished the Soviet army in Afghanistan from the Russian army in Chechnya.[26]

Everyday Life

The 40th Army was deployed in four main bases, each housing a division and other units. The 5th Guards Motor-rifle Division was in Shindand near Helmand, where there was also a major airbase. The 201st Motor-rifle Division was in Kunduz in the north. The 108th Motor-rifle Division was in Kabul, and later at the airbase in Bagram. The 103rd Guards Air Assault Division was at Kabul airport. Lesser forces were based around the country – brigades detached from their parent divisions, independent regiments, isolated battalions, special forces units, and in the numerous *zastavas*. These were concentrated particularly in the south and east, facing the vulnerable thirteen hundred-mile frontier with Pakistan around Kandahar, Gardez, and Jalalabad. All these bases, even in Kabul, were defended against terrorist attack by rings of mines, barbed wire, and guard posts.

In the larger bases the officers, the medical section, and the shop were eventually accommodated in 'modules', single-storey prefabricated plywood huts, painted green, with tiled washrooms, though the staff of the 108th Motor-rifle Division on the edge of Kabul continued to live in scruffy huts on the back of lorries.[27] The rest – unlucky junior officers, the soldiers, the canteen, the kitchen, the stores, the armouries – were usually accommodated in tents. Women usually had separate modules, though occasionally they had to share them with the officers, separated by a partition from the men, though this did not always present an absolute barrier to the enterprising.

Each base had a military hospital or casualty clearing station to deal with battle casualties and the far larger number of soldiers suffering from diseases, and a morgue where the dead were prepared for their journey home. Even the smallest bases had a 'Lenin Room', in which the soldiers could relax, with a portrait of Lenin and the current Soviet leader on the wall, a noticeboard with the latest political slogans, a few books and magazines, and somewhere to sit and write letters.

Sometimes units were accommodated in existing buildings. The 3rd Battalion of the 56th Independent Air Assault Brigade was based in a former Anglican church mission near the Pakistan border. The handful of buildings and the wall around them were built of mud bricks mixed with cement. Outside the wall was a large refuse dump, where the garrison got rid of unwanted munitions along with household rubbish. Once the dump caught fire, and going to the nearby latrine became a dangerous business as shells and rockets exploded. The base was surrounded by minefields laid by the motor-rifle unit which had been there earlier. They had not had the sense to leave maps behind and so two or three times a year someone – usually one of the locals – blew himself up on an anti-personnel mine. By day the government controlled the surrounding villages; by night they were controlled by the rebels. A major operation was mounted against the rebels every year, but even if the authority of the government could be reasserted, it was never for long.[28]

The 860th Independent Red Banner Pskov Motor-Rifle Regiment occupied a typical medium-sized base in Faisabad in Badakhshan province in north-east Afghanistan. The regiment arrived there in late

January 1980 from its home in Kyrgyzstan, after marching for a month through the snow-covered mountains and over passes up to sixteen thousand feet high, a march which went down in army legend. The regiment soon suffered its first casualties: one soldier was captured and his mutilated body was found two days later. His murderer had foolishly held on to the man's rifle. He was found and shot on the spot.[29]

The regiment's task was to block the caravan route from Pakistan and China through the Wakhan Corridor, a thin sliver of land carved out by the British eight decades earlier as a barrier between themselves and the Russians, and to prevent the lucrative export of lapis lazuli, which the insurgents mined in the high mountains. Its nominal strength was 2,198, but in practice it could usually muster no more than some fifteen hundred men because of casualties, sickness, and detachment.[30] The base was about three miles outside Faisabad itself, in a broad valley surrounded by hills and mountains. It had a hospital, a shop, a bakery, a library, and a laundry. You could bathe in the fast-flowing River Kochka nearby, a dangerous business: thirty soldiers drowned in the course of five years. Such accidental deaths were normally written off for the record as battle casualties.

The officers lived in modules. The soldiers lived in tents, each with room for sixty men, heated by two wood stoves in the winter. The better tents were made in three layers: the outside layer consisted of waterproof canvas, the next was made of thick material to provide insulation, and the inside layer was of light cloth to brighten the tent up.[31] The inhabitants often covered the inside of their tent with wood from ammunition boxes. This made it more homely, kept out the draughts in the winter, and stopped it blowing about so much in the wind. The soldiers had no proper boxes in which to keep their possessions, so they used the space between the walls of the tents to hide letters, photos, presents for their families, home-brewed beer, drugs, and other contraband.

The 1st Battalion was lucky enough to live in more permanent accommodation at Bakharak, some twenty-five miles from Faisabad, in a valley surrounded by high mountains and fed by three rivers, whose banks were thick with cherry trees. Villages lay on the broad mountain terraces, surrounded by orchards and small cultivated fields. Irrigation canals watered the whole valley. The battalion consisted of three rifle companies, mortar, rocket, and howitzer batteries, a reconnaissance platoon, a signals platoon, and an administrative platoon – nominally about five hundred men, though at times the number might fall to half that.

The road from Bakharak to Faisabad was open at first. Supplies got through without trouble and the battalion commander could go to regimental meetings in Faisabad by jeep. But by the end of 1980 the battalion was cut off from the rest of the regiment by the insurgents. Attempts were made each summer to send through a supply column. Each summer the column got bogged down under fire and needed to turn back. So the battalion had to be supplied by helicopter: twice a day, except on Sundays, weather permitting. The helicopters would arrive in pairs, two Mi-8s, flying at a great height until they were over the landing strip, firing flares as protection against the mujahedin's anti-aircraft rockets. The soldiers would rush to greet them as they landed, to unload the cargo and to collect their letters from home.

The battalion lived in an old Afghan fort, about seventy-five yards square, with a watchtower on each corner. The men were on duty from five in the morning to ten at night, and slept in rooms built into three of the mud walls. The fourth wall was more than three feet thick and twelve feet high. The roofs were flat, made of wood branches and earth which had bonded together and kept the place cool in summer and warm in winter. The windows were covered with plastic and looked out on a gallery surrounding the internal courtyard. The soldiers built another low wall around the territory. It contained the elements of a garden, with shady trees, roses, and grass. A huge apricot tree stood in the middle and a thick mulberry tree in one corner. There were irrigation ditches with running water even inside the perimeter of the fort. Outside the wall were a small helicopter pad and a park for the battalion's armoured vehicles. The generator sometimes worked for only two hours a night and the soldiers had to make do with kerosene lamps.[32]

Improvements were added gradually. In the first year there was no bathhouse: the soldiers remained dirty throughout the winter until the ice broke on the river and they could wash themselves.[33] The quarters were given wooden ceilings so that bits of wood and earth no longer fell on the sleepers' heads. The walls were whitewashed. Brick stoves were built to keep the place warm. A line of concrete blocks was set up to commemorate the battalion's dead. It was called the Alley of Glory, and the soldiers goose-stepped past it when they mounted the guard. The 'Lenin Room' acquired a television set: you could just about get two Soviet programmes when the generator was working. Sometimes a cinema operator brought a film from Faisabad. But for the most part the soldiers of the 1st Battalion had to amuse themselves as best they could. There were of course no women at Bakharak. From the vantage of their watchtowers, the soldiers would unscrew the sniperscopes from their rifles to look at the local women in their courtyards.[34]

There was a straggling *kishlak* of about fifteen hundred inhabitants a few hundred yards from the fort. In 1982 the mujahedin shelled the fort a couple of times with mortars. Towards the end of the war a sentry was killed by a sniper. Otherwise the relationship between the inhabitants of the fort and the inhabitants of the *kishlak* was not particularly hostile. The soldiers were not supposed to go there on their own lest they were attacked or kidnapped. But they were occasionally allowed to visit the bazaar in armed groups with an officer, sometimes accompanied by armoured vehicles, to buy cigarettes and matches, sweets as a substitute for the sugar that they used to brew their own beer, *braga*, lamb and rice to make *plov* (pilaf) to celebrate someone's birthday, jeans and tape recorders to take home, and fresh fruit, which cost next to nothing in season. The drugs were cheap too, or you could get them in exchange for a bar of soap.[35]

Despite the hardships, the morale of the soldiers held up, for the most part, well enough. They did their duty on the battlefield and they endured stoically until the longed-for day of demobilisation arrived. Everything depended on the quality of their officers. The Soviet officers had been thoroughly trained in the principles of leadership: how to look after their men and how to manage them in battle.[36] But when they arrived in Afghanistan most of them had no practical experience. And – as in other armies – not all of them were up to the job.

The soldiers knew well enough what they wanted from their officers: competence and fairness, personal courage, tactical skill, and a sense that their lives would not be sacrificed unnecessarily. What they did not want, but felt they got too often, were commanders more concerned with promoting their military careers than caring for their soldiers' lives. These are the concerns of soldiers throughout the ages: Private Warren Olney, who fought for the Union in one of the first battles of the American Civil War, expressed himself in almost the same terms.[37]

Long after they had served together in Bakharak, Alexander Gergel called on his company commander, Captain Yevgeni Konovalov, in retirement. 'With his Cossack moustaches he was dashing in appearance, lively, full of joie de vivre in every word and movement ... When I now look back over those past events, I am horrified to think what a difficult position the company commander found himself in: on the one hand, the oppressive commands of his superiors and on the other, the commands of his conscience, which prevented him from sacrificing his eighteen-year-old soldiers to promote the interests of a few careerists, who looked on the war as a way of getting on in the service more quickly. I greatly respected my commander when I was serving with him. But later I respected him even more when I understood how much he had really done to protect us, and to ensure that we got back safe and sound to our parents. Under Konovalov, our company was one of the best. But I think that he soon understood the pointlessness of the war, and was determined not to expose his people unnecessarily to hostile fire, or carry out stupid orders with too much zeal.'[38]

'The main thing,' said Alexander Kartsev about his time as an infantry lieutenant, 'was to keep the men occupied with real work. After I ... was sent to command a platoon at a guard post, I found that the senior soldiers (and the cronies of the deputy platoon commander) had got into the habit of making the new arrivals do sentry duty at the worst times: at night and before dawn. Since I had to sign the roster, it was not difficult to see what was going on. And if instead of sleeping you go round the sentries twice a night, you see and learn a great deal. We sorted out the problem within a week.

'Then we made sure that the men were always busy, so that they did not have too much free time. In addition to the necessary business of strengthening our fortifications, I organised daily PT sessions. We had no radio or television, the newspapers arrived irregularly, and we were seriously short of information. So in the evening I got each soldier to talk about his home and his family, and those who could play the guitar or the harmonium would put on concerts.

'And the platoon commander needed to know his men: not only his deputy, but the four sergeants, the Komsomol secretary, the medical orderly, the drivers, the gunners. That was already half of the platoon; and you got to know the rest by inspecting the sentries at night.

'Of course, I was lucky. I didn't go to Afghanistan immediately I had finished officer school, but did specialist training for another whole year. It could be difficult for the young lieutenants who went out to Afghanistan straight from their basic training. The sergeants were often more experienced than they were and they found it hard to establish their authority. Many of them were too arrogant to sleep in the same tents as the men, as I did; others became too familiar with the soldiers, and their authority was undermined. The trick was to find the golden mean.'[39]

Russians and Afghans

Russians later claimed that, despite all the brutalities of the war, on a human level they got on with the Afghan population rather well – better than the NATO soldiers who succeeded them.

It is a large claim, but it may be justified. Because many Soviet soldiers came from poor rural backgrounds, they could relate to the Afghan peasants and the lives they lived. Andrei Ponomarev, who served in Bakharak, came from a village in the Kaluga province south of Moscow. For a while he was stationed at a *zastava* guarding a bridge across the river which was manned by Afghans as well as Soviet soldiers. The Afghans lived in dugouts interspersed with the Russian ones. Ponomarev got on well with the Afghan conscript soldiers, who were on the whole better fed than the Russians. In civilian life they were peasants like him: only the land they had to cultivate was much poorer than that in Kaluga. They were anxious to learn Russian, and he did what he could to teach them.[40]

Ponomarev's comrade Alexander Gergel put it like this: 'I can't answer for all of my fellow soldiers, but I myself never felt any hatred towards the Afghan people. Every now and again, when the conditions in which I was living became particularly unbearable, it seemed to me that it was the locals who were to blame for everything. I was irritated to the point when I wanted to mow down each and every one of them. But then I saw the people working in their barren fields and I felt sympathy for them all over again. Fury and hatred broke through only when I was in battle. When we fought we were often outnumbered by the enemy. And we rarely got air support. So one could say that we fought as equals: we had the better weapons, but they were better at tactics, fighting as they were in surroundings with which they were familiar.' [41]

Quite junior Soviet commanders worked out their own deals with the local villages and mujahedin commanders, and especially of course with those who represented the regime – soldiers, policemen, the head of the village defence force. The relationship was a complex one. Fighting alternated with cooperation and compromise: an informal ceasefire, a willingness to turn a blind eye to smuggling provided weapons were not involved. The tiny detachments in the *zastavas* had little choice but to get on with the local villagers: they could not otherwise have survived. For that purpose they were supplied with goods for barter and bribe: canned food, sugar, cigarettes, soap, kerosene, matches, used clothing and shoes, and so on.

The 2nd Battalion of the 345th Guards Independent Parachute Assault Regiment kept an eye on the lower reaches of the Pandsher Valley. Their headquarters was in a little fort in Anava. Their doctors would help with simple medicine where they could. They showed films to the villagers and exchanged visits with the local authorities. They tried to mediate in incomprehensible local conflicts. They provided the poorest families with flour, tinned food, vegetable oil, salt, sugar, and condensed milk. Their officers would be invited to dinner by the KhAD representative in Anava to meet the local worthies: the secretary of the party committee, the head of the local administration, the local doctor and teacher. There would be portraits of Lenin and Gorbachev on the wall, generous food, sweets from Pakistan served on delicate porcelain, meat, rice, potatoes, onions, against a background of popular Afghan music from a tape recorder. The mujahedin bombarded the fort in a desultory manner, usually on Sundays, and the Russians responded by shelling the local mountains. The mujahedin did try once to storm one of the battalion's *zastavas*, but that was an exception: they were getting their own back because they had recently lost a caravan.[42]

Much depended on the personality of the local commanders, both of the Soviet soldiers and of the mujahedin bands. Alexander Kartsev was on good terms with the locals. But the commander of the neighbouring *zastava* was not. His *zastava* was regularly attacked, while Kartsev and his people were on the whole left alone.

Kartsev used his limited medical skills to improve his relationship with the villagers. Because they had had no contact with modern medicines they reacted well to aspirins, standard antibiotics, and so on. Kartsev's reputation grew. On one occasion he was kidnapped while he was tending his patients in the local village. He feared the worst, but it turned out that the brother of the local mujahedin commander, Anwar, had accidentally shot himself and Kartsev was needed to cure him. Luckily for him, he succeeded in doing so.

Some months later, two Afghan government BMPs arrived at his *zastava* carrying several local officials. They had come to negotiate a deal with Anwar. It was a trap: Anwar took them prisoner and threatened to kill them. Colonel Wahid, commanding the local KhAD, asked Kartsev to negotiate the release of the men and the vehicles. Kartsev was escorted to see Anwar, who told him that he would release the BMPs, but the prisoners would be executed, because they were allies of the enemies of Islam. As a gesture to Kartsev, they would not be tortured. Kartsev argued that it was wrong to kill envoys and that reprisals would certainly be taken against the village and the crops. Many of the faithful would die. Anwar thought it over, consulted his colleagues, and let both the prisoners and the BMPs go.[43]

The relationships worked in other complicated ways. In August 1984 an Afghan tank regiment was involved in a joint operation in Paktia province. One of the regiment's tanks was blown up by a remote-controlled mine, rolled over and crushed a KhAD officer. A week later an old man and his four sons turned up in the office of the regiment's Soviet adviser. The brothers were tall and powerful, festooned with weapons like a Christmas tree. They told the adviser that the dead KhAD officer was their brother. He had studied in the Soviet Union, but they were with the mujahedin. The adviser gave them tea, talked about the weather, then showed them on the map where the mine had gone off and gave them the name of the local rebel commander. They thanked him and went off to revenge themselves on the man who had placed the mine which killed their brother.[44]

The Lion of Pandsher

The most elaborate of these ambiguous relationships between the Russians and their enemies was that with Ahmad Shah Masud, who caught the imagination of Afghans and Russians alike with his gallant defence of the Pandsher Valley. Masud, whose name meant 'the lucky one', was an authentic and charismatic hero, the most competent and statesmanlike of all the rebel leaders. 'Pandsher' was supposed to mean 'the Five Lions' and Masud was widely called the 'Lion of Pandsher'. General Ter-Grigoriants, who fought against him, called him 'a very worthy opponent and a highly competent organiser of military operations. His opportunities for securing weapons and ammunition were extremely limited, and his equipment was distinctly inferior to that of the Soviet and government forces. But he was nevertheless able to organise the defence of the Pandsher in a way which made it very difficult for us to break through and to take control of the valley.'[45]

Masud came from the *kishlak* of Jangalak in the Pandsher Valley. His father was a professional army officer from an influential local family. He studied engineering at the Polytechnic Institute in Kabul, where he was drawn towards the Islamic ideas of the fundamentalist Gulbeddin Hekmatyar and the more moderate Burhanuddin Rabbani, and joined the Muslim Youth organisation, which drew much of its inspiration from the Muslim Brothers in the Middle East. The Muslim Youth was not merely a study group. Its members attacked women they considered improperly dressed and brawled with their Maoist and Communist opponents. In the spring of 1973 the Muslim Youth split into the Islamic Party of Afghanistan (Hezbi-I Islami) under Hekmatyar and the Islamic Society of Afghanistan (Jamiat-I Islami) under Rabbani. Masud allied himself with the more moderate Rabbani; but when Hekmatyar bungled an army coup against Daud, he fled with the leading Islamists to Pakistan.

He soon returned to the Pandsher to organise a rising against Daud. His men captured the main administrative centre at Rukha and other key villages. But he mishandled the politics: he failed to secure the support of the local inhabitants, and the criminals he released from the local prison went on the rampage. Once again he sought refuge in Pakistan. But he had learned an important lesson: success in guerrilla warfare depends on having the people on your side.

Masud applied this lesson very carefully during the war against the Russians. He ensured that his people had a minimum of food and shelter, and during the Russian incursions he moved them away from the bombs and the soldiers into the side valleys or up into the high mountains. He stuck closely to the fundamental maxim that irregular fighters should always avoid direct confrontation with their enemies. Until the war against the Russians was over, he did his best to keep clear of the vicious internecine fighting which so often erupted between rival mujahedin forces. He systematically built up institutions of local government and administration, financed with taxes imposed on precious stones mined in the area, land, goods, and on Panshiris living in Kabul. It was always his eventual ambition to win power in Kabul itself and in 1984 he began military operations outside the valley. None of the other mujahedin commanders had the same broad ambitions and the same interest in institution building.[46]

The vicious fighting in the Pandsher Valley in the first years of the war gave the Russians a healthy respect for Masud's military skills and in January 1983 they negotiated a ceasefire with him which was more or less scrupulously observed by both sides until April 1984. The negotiator was a colonel in the GRU, Anatoli Tkachev, who had been unimpressed with the failure of successive operations in the Pandsher Valley. He spoke first to General Akhromeev, at that time still a member of the Ministry of Defence's Operational Group in Kabul. 'I told him that we ought to try to reach an agreement with Ahmad Shah on a ceasefire, since the peaceful population was being killed by artillery and air strikes, and soldiers were being killed by the mujahedin. He answered that all those old men, women, and children were relatives of the rebels, and as for the deaths of our soldiers, they were only doing their duty. If one was killed, ten more could be sent to take his place.

Ahmad Shah should be brought to his knees and made to lay down his weapons.'

Tkachev's idea was, however, supported by the head of the GRU in Afghanistan, and by Akhromeev's superior, Marshal Sokolov. In reply to a proposal for a meeting which Tkachev sent through agents among the Pansheri refugees in Kabul, Masud laid down the conditions. The meeting was to take place on New Year's Eve 1983, in the Pandsher Valley on territory controlled by his men. Tkachev was to go to the meeting by night, unarmed, and without an escort.

At nightfall on New Year's Eve Tkachev set out with his interpreter for the meeting place. As soon as he got there he fired a rocket, the agreed signal, and a group of rebels emerged from the frozen darkness, led by the head of Masud's counter-intelligence, Tajmudin. Tajmudin asked Tkachev if he would like to rest. 'No,' said Tkachev, 'let's get a move on. The business is the main thing.' They marched through the night for about four hours until they reached Bazarak, the place where Tkachev was to meet Masud.

'The attitude of the mujahedin was quite friendly. They put us up in a well-heated room. There was no electricity, but there was a kerosene lamp and a Soviet stove. The mujahedin looked at us carefully as we began to get undressed, in case we had explosives hidden under our clothes. Then they offered us tea, and brought in mattresses and clean bed linen – all army stuff, with official stamps on it. We went to bed at about four in the morning and slept in the same room as the mujahedin.

'At breakfast the following morning, we were given all the traditional honours: we were the first to wash our hands and to dry them with a fresh towel, the first to break the bread, and the first to begin eating *plov* from the common bowl. We were consumed by curiosity as we waited to see Masud: after all, no Soviet officer had seen him before, even in photographs.

'Exactly at the time laid down, three or four armed men came into the room. These were Masud's bodyguards. Immediately behind them appeared a young and not very tall man. He was dark-haired, dressed in traditional Afghan costume, and the expression on his face was of concentration and openness: quite unlike the picture painted by our propaganda.

'After a second's confusion we exchanged traditional greetings and general conversation in the best Afghan style for about half an hour. Then we were left in the room alone. Masud suggested we get down to business. We began by discussing the history of friendly and traditionally good neighbourly relations between Afghanistan and the Soviet Union. Masud said sadly, "What a great pity that your forces invaded Afghanistan. The leaders of both countries made the greatest possible mistake. You could call it a crime against the Afghan and Soviet peoples." But as for the Kabul regime, he was and would remain their implacable opponent: once the Soviet forces had left, they would have no future.

'When we made the points which had been laid down by our superiors, he was a bit surprised that there were no ultimatums, no demands for capitulation. Our central proposal was for a mutual ceasefire in Pandsher and common measures to enable the local population to lead a normal life. We debated for most of the day and the end result was a genuine ceasefire. The civilian population returned to the Pandsher, the situation on the road between Salang and Kabul became very much more quiet, and there was no major military operation in the Pandsher Valley until April 1984.

'However, this did not suit the Kabul regime, which continually insisted that the Soviet military should take offensive action against Masud. For this reason the ceasefire was broken by us more than once. For example, during one of my subsequent meetings with Masud we heard the sound of helicopters approaching. I said to Masud that as there was a ceasefire we need not worry about the helicopters, but he said that we should go to the shelter just in case. We had barely done that when the helicopters struck the house and half of it was destroyed. Masud pointed to the ruins and said, "International assistance in action."

'The next day I was shown an Afghan government intelligence report which said that there had been a strike the previous day, at one o'clock in the afternoon, on a *kishlak* where Masud and a number of other rebel leaders had been meeting. All had been killed. Masud's arms had been torn off and his skull split. I said that I had been drinking tea with Masud six hours after the alleged strike: so I must have been drinking with a corpse.'[47]

The Soldiers Off Duty

Even on the larger posts the soldiers' day was so filled with physical training, compulsory sports, weapons drill, guard duties, and domestic chores that many yearned to go out on operations to relieve the boredom. But some provision was made for them to relax. The bigger bases had, in addition to the 'Lenin Room', a library where the soldiers could borrow books and chat up the woman librarian. In the Voentorg military shop, the soldiers could use their exiguous pay to buy cigarettes, confectionery, and occasionally Japanese-made electronic gadgets. For Sergeant Fedorov the shop in the base of the 860th Independent Motor-rifle Regiment in Faisabad was a treasure house: 'There were things in it that we could never have imagined in the Soviet Union ... Eau-de-Cologne, lotion, and other products containing alcohol ... were sold under strict control, because some people simply diluted them with water before they drank them; others were clever enough to distil them into proper drinks. Some goods, such as briefcases and sports clothes, were distributed by the political officers to the politically correct or to those who had distinguished themselves in battle. Electrical goods such as tape recorders were held back for the officers. The shortages, real or artificially created, simply led to corruption within the garrison. If you had cheques [military currency] you could get everything, even vodka and champagne.'[48]

But the real treasures were to be found in the bazaars, which bulged with Japanese electronics, fashionable Western clothes, sneakers and jeans, cassette recordings of Western and even Soviet music banned back home. For the shopkeepers at least, the invasion was a business opportunity. For the soldiers, it was their first contact with a market economy, 'a ticket to another life'.[49]

The problem was that neither the soldiers nor the officers had the wherewithal to satisfy their desires. The officers were paid reasonably well by Soviet standards: a lieutenant would get a lump sum of 250 roubles on finishing his training; his pay thereafter would be 200 roubles a month. By way of comparison, at that time an engineer designing rocket-guidance systems got 250 roubles a month.[50] But conscripts did very much worse. Some of their salary was paid into Sberbank, the national savings back, which they could draw when they finished their service. They would get small lump-sum payments for injuries. But in the field sergeants only got twelve to eighteen roubles a month. A specialist – a sniper or a machine-gunner – would get nine roubles. Ordinary soldiers were paid a miserable seven roubles. At that time the average (minimum) wage in the Soviet Union was one hundred roubles a month.

So both officers and men turned to various forms of corruption. The 40th Army was not unique: the victorious Allied armies had done much the same in Europe after 1945. But the corruption in the 40th Army was on a heroic scale. Vladimir Snegirev, the correspondent from *Komsomolskaya Pravda*, called it the *grabarmy* where everyone grabbed what he could (by a useful coincidence, the Russian word *grabarmia* combines the noun *armia* with the verb *grabit,* to steal or loot).[51] The detachments guarding the Salang Highway would shake down passing Afghan vehicles. Storekeepers and lorry drivers would conspire to take their cut from the cargoes they were transporting. 'One enterprising soldier,' wrote Snegirev, 'detached the spare wheel of my car during the brief half-hour that I was talking to the political officer of a helicopter regiment. The theft took place in broad daylight on the territory of an elite unit, right next to the staff building, practically under the eyes of the sentry. Oho! I thought. If the "internationalist warriors" could so cheerfully pinch anything that was not nailed down even from their own people, I could imagine how they behaved with the Afghans.

'The quartermasters of military units stationed throughout the country secretly gave the shopkeepers condensed milk, flour, fat, butter, sugar; and with the money they made they would enthusiastically acquire goods which previously they had seen only on the television. The civilian specialists were not far behind them. For a crate of vodka you could get three fur jackets; back in the Soviet Union you could sell the jackets for enough money to buy a second-hand car.'

The soldiers necessarily operated on a more modest scale. 'If you were cunning you could put together enough money to drink Coca-Cola or Fanta, drinks still unknown in the Soviet Union; or take souvenirs home for your family – a folding umbrella, local jewellery, or (the pinnacle of their dreams) "Montana" jeans.'[52]

'Some of the guys brought porcelain, precious stones, jewellery, carpets,' one private soldier said. 'They picked them up in battle when they went into the villages, or bought them. For example, the magazine of a Kalashnikov bought you a make-up set for your girlfriend, including mascara, eyeshadow and powder. Of course the cartridges were "cooked", because a cooked bullet can't fly, it just kind of spits out the barrel and can't kill. We'd fill a bucket or a bowl with water, throw in the cartridges, boil them for a couple of hours and sell them the same evening. Everyone traded, officers as well as the rest of us, heroes as well as cowards. Knives, bowls, spoons, forks, mugs, stools, hammers, they all got nicked from the canteen and the barracks. Bayonets disappeared from guns, mirrors from cars, spare parts, medals ... You could sell anything, even the rubbish collected from the garrison, full of cans, old newspapers, rusty nails, bits of plywood, and plastic bags. They sold it by the truckload, with the price depending on the amount of scrap metal.'[53]

Much of this thieving went unpunished. From time to time the authorities would send in a team of military prosecutors and a few exemplary punishments would be handed out. Then things would go on as before – not least because senior officers were also on the take.

In the absence of other opportunities for entertainment, there was, of course, a great deal of drinking in the 40th Army. The officers mostly drank vodka and other spirits, which some consumed in vast quantities.[54] The soldiers could not normally afford vodka. But they were philosophical: officers were permitted to drink and it was quite natural that they should. After all, they were long-term professionals, whereas the soldiers only had to put up with the army for two years. Anyway, they could make themselves a moderately alcoholic beer called *braga*, which brewed quickly in the Afghan heat.[55] They hid it between the wooden lining and the canvas wall of their tents, or in the external fuel and water tanks of their armoured vehicles. And they had their drugs, mostly marijuana, which they called *chars*. A particular and rather rare delicacy was tea laced with hashish. They would trade drugs and drink with soldiers from other units, or buy them off the Afghans for cash, or in exchange for military goods of various kinds. They would share a joint or quench their thirst with *braga* on the way to battle, though most had the sense to shake off the influence before the fighting actually began.

There are no reliable statistics about the extent of the drug-taking. Some veterans deny that it was widespread, at least in the elite units, and one has to aim off for the boasting of young men anxious to show how tough they were. Some soldiers became addicts, but most abandoned the habit when they were eventually demobilised. Two who did not were rescued from Pakistan in 1983 by the journalist Masha Slonim at the behest of the *Daily Mail* newspaper. Oleg and Igor both came from Ukraine. Oleg was a simple peasant and not at all bright. Igor was a Russian: he was comparatively sophisticated and wrote poetry. They had deserted because Oleg had accidentally killed a comrade and was under investigation, while Igor had heard that his girlfriend was going out with another man. They broke into the armoury of their unit near Kandahar, stole some weapons, and set out to walk to Pakistan. They had no map, hardly any water, and were soon captured by the mujahedin. They were taken to Peshawar, installed in a villa, and treated reasonably well. But they needed to shoot up, their captors gave them no syringes, and they ran away to get back to Afghanistan to find some. When they were recaptured, their captors chained them to a bed, and there they were kept, thin and unhealthy, until they were released to Masha Slonim. By then they were both in a dreadful state.

On the plane to London they suffered serious withdrawal symptoms and Masha barely managed to keep them under control. They were then taken to a villa in Surrey, where they were to be interviewed for TV. They were in too bad a state and had to go to a London clinic, where their addiction was successfully brought under control. They were placed with a Ukrainian family in London, where they frequented a Russian restaurant in London, the Balalaika. A constant visitor there was a nice man from the Soviet Embassy, who regularly bought them drinks. One fine day Igor and Oleg disappeared. They turned up at a press conference in the embassy, saying they wanted to go home and denouncing everyone they had met in Britain as intelligence agents – except Masha. After the two went back to the Soviet Union the *Daily Mail* reported that they had been shot. It was not so. Ivan wrote to say he was alive and well, though Oleg never surfaced again.[56]

Guitar and Kalashnikov

The soldiers took their guitars to Afghanistan, and they wrote and improvised a great deal of music and poetry, some of permanent value. These songs and poems reflect the history of the war: from a confident belief in the rightness of the cause, through the sounds of battle and the loss of comrades, to the disillusion and bitterness of failure.

Some popular songs were written by established artists who visited the bigger bases from time to time. Alexander Rozenbaum's song 'The Black Tulip', about the planes which flew the coffins of dead soldiers back to the Soviet Union, and 'We Will Return', about Soviet prisoners of war, remained popular long after the war was over. Enterprising Afghan traders imported from the West recordings of songs that were frowned upon in the Soviet Union: the music of the Beatles and ABBA, and the songs of the immensely popular Soviet singer Bulat Okudzhava (1924–97), whose pieces hovered just this side of dissent and were not much appreciated by the authorities.

But the soldiers' attitude towards the professional singers was ambivalent. However eloquently these people sang, they had not seen battle themselves. Their music was artificial, constructed for effect, and over it, some thought, hung an atmosphere of commercial exploitation. For the real thing the soldiers made their own music on the guitars they had taken with them to the war. Or they listened to the songs of the soldier-bards, the people who had shared their trials, songs which became very popular, to the consternation of the authorities. The songs were banned by the political censorship, and the customs officers on the frontier cracked down heavily on attempts to bring taped versions into the Soviet Union. None of this stopped the songs from circulating throughout the 40th Army.

The Afgantsy were acutely aware that their fathers and grandfathers had fought gloriously in the war against Hitler and there are self-conscious overtones almost of rivalry between the generations in the earlier songs. They were influenced by the songs of Vladimir Vysotski (1938–80), who had not fought in that war but had caught its spirit in many songs. They fastened on the poems of Kipling and his picture of Afghanistan, its people, and the fighting there. The authorities were less enthusiastic because Kipling was, they considered, an apologist for

British imperialism in Afghanistan. Around the middle of the war a new theme emerged: nostalgia and sympathy for the White Guards, the soldiers who fought on the losing side of the civil war after the revolution in 1917 and who had upheld the heroism and discipline of Russian arms even as their country fell apart around them. The bards picked up the romances of those days about love and war and honour even in defeat. '[W]hy in the years of my youth did nobody publicly speak of the self-sacrifice of the White generals?' wondered Alexander Karpenko, a bard and military interpreter. 'And at this point my thoughts about the White Army's role in the fate of Russia came to mingle with what was happening in Afghanistan. The prohibitions and silence which surrounded the White idea also stimulated the creative energies of the Afgantsy, including my own.'[57] Towards the end, the mood of the songs began to change. Nostalgia was replaced by bitter songs about the sense of futility and defeat which settled on the 40th Army as the country in whose name it had been fighting began to fall apart.

Most of the soldier-bards were officers, many from the special forces. Sergei Klimov wrote one of the first songs, about the explosion in the Afghan government communication centre which triggered off the attacks in Kabul in December 1979.[58] But Yuri Kirsanov is often regarded as the dean of the bards. He served with a special forces group called *Karpaty*, an offshoot of *Kaskad*. He joined the KGB in 1976 and when he was posted to Afghanistan in 1980 he took his guitar with him. He was stationed in Shindand. He found – bizarrely – that travelling on operations in a BTR stimulated his creative ingenuity. He and a colleague systematically recorded the sounds of Afghanistan on a small tape recorder – the call of the muezzin, the rattle of armoured vehicles, the noise of battle and the cry of the jackal – and he used them as the introduction to his own songs. These he recorded in 'studio' conditions – in the regimental bathhouse, where he worked at night, when the electric current was more or less stable and the noise of war had died away. He composed to express the emotions of war and the soldiers' hopes for a safe return. 'Kirsanov's songs succeeded in doing what the professional artists were unable to do,' remarked one journalist. 'They preserved the real and genuine truth of the Afghan war.'[59]

Igor Morozov studied in the prestigious Bauman Technical University and then worked for a while as an engineer in the defence industry, where he helped to develop the improved model of the infantry warhorse, the BMP-2 infantry fighting vehicle. But then his father, who had been in military intelligence during the Second World War, persuaded him to go into the First Directorate of the KGB, the foreign intelligence department, which he joined in August 1977. He was sent to Afghanistan in 1981 after two months' special training, served for a while in Kunduz, and was then posted to command the detachment of *Kaskad* in Faisabad in 1982. The team consisted of three officers and a handful of soldiers. They lived in a villa on the edge of the town guarded by KhAD. They had three BTRs, of which only one worked, three GAZ jeeps, two machine guns, two mortars, and three tons of ammunition. Neither the team commander nor his deputy spoke the local languages, and for three months they were without an interpreter. No one knew what the situation was in the province. The soldiers were members of the KGB's frontier force (*pogranichniki*), and they were on the books of the 40th Army for pay and rations. But the three officers depended on headquarters in Moscow, who simply forgot about them. Their pay was six months in arrears and they had to scrounge their rations from the soldiers. They had to get their experience from the soldiers as well: the soldiers had been in Afghanistan for six months, they could speak a few words of the language, and had some idea of the situation.[60]

By then Morozov was already a committed songwriter: ironically, 'Batalionnaya Razvedka' (Battalion Reconnaissance), which he wrote in honour of his father in 1975, later became one of his most popular 'Afghan' songs. He had quickly concluded that 'the patriotic songs and music recommended by the authorities were not understood or accepted by the soldiers, because they absolutely failed to reflect either the spirit or the character of the war. The first signs of moral and spiritual decay were already beginning to appear in the Limited Contingent.' He believed that 'A country's songs tell you what is ailing it.' He began by playing Kirsanov's songs to his soldiers, but soon began to compose for himself. When the fierce sandstorms whipped up by the wind which the soldiers called the 'Afganets' blew for days at a time, operations would be called off and Morozov would use the break to write. Soon his songs, too, were circulating throughout the 40th Army: 'The Return' and 'We're Leaving', about the final departure of the 40th Army; 'The Convoy from Tulukan to Faisabad', 'Rain in the Mountains of Afghanistan', 'The Song of the Bullet', about the fighting; 'Guitar and Kalashnikov', about the relationship between art and war; songs from an earlier age such as the 1930s hit 'The Blue Balloon'.

Morozov finally left Afghanistan over the Salang Pass with the parachutists of the Vitebsk Division in 1989. Valeri Vostrotin's 345th Guards Independent Parachute Assault Regiment, which was guarding the pass, is said to have started every day with Morozov's bitter song 'We're Leaving'. Morozov and his friends, by now elderly colonels in retirement, were still performing their songs two decades after the war was over.[61]

Most of the soldiers of the 40th Army were, of course, only too anxious to get away from the monotony and the fighting, to return home as soon as they could, to resume the lives which had been disrupted when they were issued with their call-up papers. Some – Lieutenant Kartsev and Sergeant Sergei Morozov – were to remember the years in Afghanistan as the best of their lives. More than one felt a pang as they left for the Soviet Union. 'Suddenly they understood with blinding clarity that over there, in the future, there was nothing. All was dark, impenetrable, a vacuum. If you shouted, there would be no echo; if you hurled a stone, you would not hear it land. Life was carrying them into that emptiness, unmapped, unstoppable. From now on, everything lay in the past.'[62]

- NINE -

FIGHTING

Fighting, like soldiering, differs little from time to time or place to place. It is something that cannot be properly understood by those who have not been there. Even among the soldiers themselves, there is 'a gulf between men just returned from action, and those who have not been in the show, as unbridgeable as that between the sober and the drunk'. The Soviet soldiers in Afghanistan fought for the same reasons as the British soldiers on the Somme, the Russians on the Eastern Front, the French in Indo-China and Algeria, and the Americans in Vietnam and Iraq: to do a job, for the sake of their fellow soldiers, to kill rather than be killed. Sometimes they broke. Sometimes they preferred a firefight to the frustration and boredom of soldiering. They rarely cared about the wider political implications of their war – their horizons were bounded by their platoon, their company, or their battalion. They counted the days until they could go home; and when they got home, some missed the comradeship and the rush of adrenalin. Life in battle had a meaning which civilian life could not match. An American soldier who fought in Afghanistan two decades later said, 'People back home think we drink because of the bad stuff, but that's not true … we drink because we miss the good stuff.'[1]

Most of the fighting in Afghanistan was on a comparatively small scale: minor operations commanded by lieutenants, captains, and majors. The nearest the 40th Army got to real old-fashioned war was when it conducted large-scale operations to clear out a rebel stronghold, relieve rebel pressure on a town, or close the border with Pakistan. This was where the colonels and the generals had their chance to exercise their skill in the art of war. These sledgehammer blows involved thousands of troops, hundreds of armoured vehicles and helicopters, massive air and artillery strikes. They continued for weeks at a time and had few lasting results.

The Weapons

The men of the 40th Army were generously equipped with sophisticated weapons. Some achieved the status of icons – the Kalashnikov automatic rifle, the infantry fighting vehicle, the BMP (Boyevaya Mashina Pekhoty), and the battle helicopter, the Mi-24. But the weapons, like the men, had been intended for use against the armies of NATO. They now had to be adapted to a quite different kind of war. Determined attempts were made to improve the weapons systems. Designers and engineers regularly visited Afghanistan to listen to complaints and suggestions from the soldiers.[2] Some of the weapons the Russians brought with them turned out to be irrelevant – heavy anti-aircraft weapons, for example, useful for fighting an enemy air force, but not much use against partisans – and were sent back to the Soviet Union.

The backbone of the Soviet army was the motor-rifle unit, motorised infantry which travelled across the battlefield in armoured personnel carriers, BTRs (Bronetransportyor), which had a crew of three and carried seven soldiers; and in the ubiquitous BMP, which also had a crew of three and could carry eight soldiers. The BMP was an advanced vehicle for its time, but its cannon could not be elevated sufficiently to engage rebels shooting from the mountains above: this defect was rectified in a later model, the BMP-2. It was designed to resist small-arms fire, but it was very vulnerable to mines and anti-tank rockets. If a large mine went off under a BMP, it would drive the floor up against the deck, crushing those inside. The soldiers often preferred to ride on the outside: you were exposed to the bullets, but if the vehicle hit a mine you had some chance of being thrown off and surviving. The driver, of course, had no choice.

The Mi-24 attack helicopter, which the soldiers called the 'Crocodile', stars in most films about the Afghan war. It carried a crew of three and eight passengers or four stretchers. A sinister-looking beast, it could mount a variety of formidable weapons to use against people, buildings, and armoured vehicles. The Mi-8 transport helicopter, the 'Bee', was the workhorse of the 40th Army. It came into service in 1967: more were said to have been produced than any other helicopter in the world. With a crew of three, it could carry twenty-four passengers, or twelve stretchers, or a load of three thousand kilograms. Little more than a decade after the Soviet war was over, the Americans hired Mi-8s to supply their special forces because they were particularly well adapted to operate in the high mountains of eastern Afghanistan. The aircraft were flown by Russians – sometimes by the same men who had flown them during the Soviet war. But this time they were flown not by military crews but – because Russia was now a capitalist country – by the employees of a commercial company called, appropriately enough, Vertical-T. When one of these helicopters was shot down in 2008, the Russian Ambassador in Kabul contacted the Taliban for the return of the bodies. 'You mean they were Russians?' said the Taliban. 'We thought they were Americans. Of course you can have them.'[3]

The soldiers' personal weapons were good, and they too were steadily improved throughout the war. Their other equipment was less suitable. They were issued at first with uncomfortable uniforms in the wrong camouflage pattern, a clumsy flak jacket which weighed twenty kilograms until a newer model got it down to twelve, a skimpy cotton sleeping bag that let the water in, a heavy rucksack, and boots ill-adapted to marching across mountains. They had no proper identity discs, but kept their personal details in an empty cartridge case hung round their necks, just as their fathers and grandfathers had done in the Great Patriotic War.[4]

So they improvised. At headquarters in Kabul the dress code was rigidly enforced. But out in the field the soldiers wore whatever worked. They sewed their own 'brassieres', *lifchiki*, to carry spare magazines, grenades, signal rockets, and other paraphernalia. Instead of heavy army boots, officers and sometimes even soldiers wore light trainers of Soviet manufacture, or foreign ones bought or looted from the Afghan *dukany* (shops) or captured from the enemy.[5] A great prize was a light-weight sleeping bag, acquired in the same way.

The elite forces were much more colourful. They celebrated fearsome drinking rituals before they went out on operations and wore the most picturesque rig even on parade: 'We were wearing the clothes we fought in. A few were wearing SpetsNaz overalls. Some were wearing the "afganka" jacket. Most were dressed in a canvas windcheater [*shtor-movka*], tank crew overalls, long Afghan shirts and baggy trousers [*shalvary*]. Our equipment was just as varied. Some had captured Kalashnikovs of Arab or Chinese manufacture. Some had Soviet automatics, with a sniperscope or night sight attached and a silencer. Some had modernised versions of the Kalashnikov sub-machine gun [PKMP] or self-loading carbines [SKS], instead of our Dragunov sniper rifles. The sergeant major had a silenced Stechkin pistol as well as his PKMP. We looked like the crew of a pirate ship.'[6]

The soldiers operated as beasts of burden, as soldiers have done throughout history. Even on raids they were supposed to carry their weapons, helmets, a flak jacket, a sleeping bag, a tent, dry rations for three days, bottles of water, up to six hundred rounds for their automatic rifles, two shrapnel and two attack grenades, signal rockets and smoke flares, and one or two 82mm mortar rounds. The whole lot weighed more than forty kilograms. The signallers carried radios, while the mortar and machine-gun crews carried the ponderous and awkward parts of their heavy weapons.[7] When he first joined the signal platoon of the 1st Battalion of the 860th Independent Motor-rifle Regiment in Bakharak, Andrei Ponomarev remembered, he was neither strong nor fit enough for the job. Carrying the radio in addition to his personal kit, weapons, and ammunition was a nightmare. But you could never admit that you weren't up to it: you would be despised and probably beaten by the other soldiers. During his first operation he gritted his teeth, on the edge of tears, and struggled on. Some of the others eventually gave him a hand, carrying the radio in turns while he continued to operate it.[8]

Not surprisingly, even the soldiers of the motor-rifle units, when they went on raids, especially at night, often left their helmets and flak jackets behind, and took the lighter weapons and no more than ten magazines of ammunition.[9] Their senior officers never cottoned on to that: they were still saying long after the war that man for man the Soviet soldier could not match the Afghan fighter because of his lack of training and his clumsy equipment.[10]

The Enemy

The mujahedin against whom the soldiers of the 40th Army and their Afghan allies fought for nine years were formidable warriors, highly motivated, brave, determined, skilled in guerrilla warfare. Some were professionals – army officers who had turned against the government. Others were driven by religious passion, the desire for revenge, an ingrained unwillingness to do what the government told them to do. Some fought for money. Some who had been driven out of their homes by war had little alternative. Since for the most part they were drawn from the ordinary people of the villages, it was hard for the Russian soldiers to distinguish between friend and foe. A man working in his field might shoot at you as you drove past. The apparently friendly people in a village might direct you along a road which they knew led to an ambush. Faced with these lethal uncertainties, soldiers often shot first and asked questions afterwards, and their commanders would call in an air or artillery strike on a village if they encountered opposition without worrying too much about collateral damage.

But the insurgents, like the Kabul government itself, suffered from 'the fundamental characteristic of Afghan society – its incoherence'.[11] For much of the war there were seven main mujahedin parties, based in Pakistan, with representatives inside Afghanistan itself, who organised the supply of money and arms to the fighters. In May 1985 these parties formed themselves into a loosely organised Alliance of Seven. But they remained rivals rather than partners, and after the Russians left Afghanistan in 1989 the tensions between them broke into open civil war. Like the Afghan Communist Party these groupings had their origins in the university politics of the 1970s, where their leaders, such as Rabbani, the leader of the moderate Islamist Jamiat-i Islami, and Hekmatyar, the leader of the radical Islamist Hezb-i Islami, had already made a mark.

All were Sunnis, and all were Pushtun, except for Rabbani's Jamiat-i Islami, who were Tajiks and were led inside Afghanistan by Ahmad Shah Masud. (See Annex 3, 'The Alliance of Seven and Its Leaders', p.346.)

Field commanders, nominally answering to their party leaders in Pakistan, recruited and organised their fighters in Afghanistan and in the refugee camps. Individual warlords raised fighting bands for the glory of God or for their own glory, for local power or for loot. Their loyalties were uncertain and they would change sides in pursuit of personal advantage. Some individuals happily sold their services to the highest bidder. Internecine warfare between the fighting bands inside Afghanistan resulted in thousands, maybe tens of thousands, of deaths among the guerrillas and the civilian population.[12]

Figures for the number of guerrilla fighters can only be estimates. The total number in 1980–82 might have reached 250,000. In the last full year of the war, between 35,000 and 175,000 might have been operating on any given day. The group led by Gulbuddin Hekmatyar is said to have consisted of 40,570 men, one-third of the total.[13] Such figures give an idea of the order of magnitude, but are not backed by hard evidence.

The Pakistani military intelligence organisation, the Directorate for Inter-Services Intelligence (ISI) did what they could to monopolise outside support for the resistance. They set up training camps on the Afghan border, and insisted that weapons and money provided by the CIA and others should pass through their hands. Their aim was to secure a regime in Kabul that was not only friendly to Pakistan, but also to their own belief in Islamist government. So they helped those commanders, such as the Pushtun Hekmatyar, who shared their religious and political views, and gave scant support to those who did not, such as the Tajik Masud. The French and British recognised Masud's importance and did what they could to help him. It was not all that much, because their resources could not begin to match those of the Americans.

The successes of the mujahedin grew from the start. The chief of Soviet army intelligence in Afghanistan reported in the middle of 1980 that 'If in April this year there were 38 terrorist acts, and 63 people killed, then in May there were 112 terrorist attacks, killing 201 people. In a directive of the Islamic Party of Afghanistan ... the rebels are instructed to continue to avoid direct armed confrontation with regular forces, and to camouflage themselves among the civilian population'.[14] The mujahedin regularly launched rocket attacks on Kabul itself, infiltrating the outer line of defences despite the best efforts of the Soviet and Afghan forces. One of their greatest successes occurred in August 1986, when rockets fired by a time fuse hit a major ammunition dump outside Kabul, destroying forty thousand tons of ammunition at a cost to the Soviets estimated by the Pakistanis at $250 million. Two years later, in April 1988, another large dump exploded, this time outside Rawalpindi, in Pakistan. Ten thousand tons of ammunition, plastic explosive, rockets, and other ordnance blew up, killing a hundred people and injuring another thousand. The timing seemed significant, just as the Geneva Agreements were about to be signed and the Russians were preparing for the first phase of their withdrawal. The KGB had considerable respect for the ability of their colleagues in the KhAD to conduct special operations and believed they were responsible. Pakistani intelligence officers blamed the Russians. The more paranoid even suspected the Americans. The most likely explanation is that it was an accident.[15]

At first the insurgents were not as well armed as they later became. The professional soldiers among them knew how to operate armoured vehicles and aircraft, but did not acquire such sophisticated weapons until after the Soviets had left; then they used them against one another. But very soon, with the assistance of the Americans, the Pakistanis and others, they began to get mortars, mines, heavy machine guns, and radios, many of them of Soviet design imported from China, Egypt, and elsewhere. And even the old British Lee-Enfield rifles, which they used from the start, and which the Soviet soldiers called 'Boers' from some vague notion that they had been used during the Boer War, were more accurate than the Soviet automatic rifle and far outranged it. Soldiers began to die at the hands of distant snipers, and panic spread among them which their officers had difficulty in countering.[16]

The Russians and their Afghan allies used helicopters and fighter bombers to destroy villages suspected of harbouring rebels, to supply isolated garrisons, and to place their troops in ambush. But the mujahedin were not defenceless against aerial attack. In skilful hands, their Soviet-designed heavy machine guns could bring down even the armoured assault helicopters. Two or three years into the war they obtained – with CIA assistance – the very effective but too cumbersome Swiss Oerlikon light anti-aircraft gun. They made some spectacular attacks on Soviet and Afghan airbases, destroying a number of aircraft on the ground. From 1984 they began to use Chinese and Soviet anti-aircraft missiles and the dubiously effective British Blowpipe. The Blowpipes found their way to Afghanistan through a variety of covert sources so that their provenance could not be proved. The missile was used by both sides in the Falklands War, where one British officer remarked that it was like 'trying to shoot pheasants with a drainpipe'. Senior Soviet officers such as General Varennikov and helicopter pilots such as Boris Zhelezin nevertheless regarded the weapon with a certain respect.[17]

But what the mujahedin really wanted was the American Stinger, a sophisticated portable rocket launcher which could seek out and hit an aircraft at a range of three miles, at altitudes between six hundred and twelve thousand five hundred feet.[18] The US military opposed supplying Stingers to the mujahedin since they feared – correctly, as it turned out – that the weapons would leak to the Russians and others. It was not until February 1986 that the Americans finally decided to supply some two hundred and forty launchers and a thousand missiles.[19]

The first Stingers were fired on 26 September 1986, when a Soviet-trained engineer called Ghaffur shot down three Mi-24 helicopters that were coming in to land at Jalalabad.[20] The initial impact on Soviet tactics and morale was considerable. Alla Smolina had just arrived in Jalalabad to work in the office of the military procurator when the three helicopters were shot down. 'The old hands said that previously there had been nothing frightening about flying around Afghanistan,' she wrote later. 'Soviet and Afghan planes travelled for all sorts of reasons all over the country at all hours of the day and at all altitudes. Jalalabad was one of the few places where roses grew in the winter. So the Kabul garrison sent planes there at the end of every year to collect roses for their New Year parties.'

Smolina's flight into Jalalabad was the last to land in the old carefree way. Thereafter planes flew at night if possible, approached the airfield at a safe height of several thousand feet, and landed in a tight, quick spiral. You felt, she said, as if you were in a spacecraft, leaving your insides behind you. Parachutes became obligatory, though it was hard to see how they could be used if your plane was hit by a rocket. And anyway most of them were too big if you were a woman. People cut their air travel to a minimum. But if you travelled by land you risked being ambushed. Some people gave up travelling altogether. Others still flew to the base, either on business or to enjoy its various attractions: a shop, a club, a hairdresser, even a discotheque run by a paratroop lieutenant.[21]

The Soviets were now forced to refine the tactics they had developed against anti-aircraft missiles and heavy machine guns. Their aircraft fired infrared flares to confuse the Stingers' guidance systems. Fixed-wing aircraft flew above sixteen thousand five hundred feet – beyond the range of the Stinger. Soviet bombing became even more inaccurate, and even more destructive of civilian lives and property.[22] Helicopters flew very low among the mountains, because the Stinger was unreliable except against a background of sky. Most transport flights took place at night. These measures successfully reduced losses. But they were not infallible. One aircraft was hit over Khost at a height of thirty thousand feet, though it managed to land with a large hole in the tailplane.[23]

The Soviet Minister of Defence promised that the first person to get hold of a Stinger would be made a Hero of the Soviet Union. There are two versions of what then happened. One is that, acting on intelligence, a special forces detachment under Major Sergeev, flying in four battle helicopters, successfully intercepted a motorcycle caravan on 5 January 1987. The mujahedin fired two Stingers at them, which missed, and another was captured intact.[24] A more colourful version is that the successful commander was called Major Belov and that he was given the lesser Order of the Military Red Banner when it was discovered at the last minute that 'he had a drink problem and was brusque in his attitude to his superiors'.[25]

The Russians also set out to buy Stingers from the rebels: the going price was $3,000.[26] The Iranians did the same, and displayed several Stingers during a military parade in September 1987 which were allegedly sold to them by two mujahedin commanders for $1 million.[27] After the war was over, the CIA were still sufficiently worried to try to buy back unused Stingers at twice their original cost. But few were recovered, and between two hundred and four hundred remained at large.[28]

Large claims have been made about the military and political significance of the Stingers.[29] According to official Russian figures, the 40th Army lost 113 fixed-wing aircraft and 333 helicopters during the course of the war; by comparison, the Americans lost 5,086 helicopters during the Vietnam War.[30] After the initial panic, the Soviet countermeasures reduced the loss rate to much what it had been before the Stingers arrived. No convincing evidence has appeared from Russian sources that the Stingers affected the political decision-making process in Moscow, or that they had much beyond an immediate tactical effect on the Soviet conduct of military operations. Gorbachev took the decision to withdraw from Afghanistan a full year before the first Stinger was fired.[31]

The Salang Highway

The one battle the Soviets could never afford to lose was the battle to keep open the Salang Highway. It was along this road that three-quarters of the 40th Army's supplies were brought from the Soviet Union. Huge supply columns, as many as eight hundred vehicles, moved from the great logistics base in Khairaton, just on the Afghan side of the Amu Darya River, for more than 280 miles over the Hindu Kush to Kabul.[32]

The road starts in the fertile plains of the north, and then winds its way up increasingly bleak mountains to Pul-i Khumri, which is about the halfway point. It then continues south until it passes through the Salang Tunnel, built by the Soviets in the 1960s about seventy-five miles north of Kabul to provide an all-weather route through the Hindu Kush. The tunnel is three miles long and when it was built it was, at eleven thousand feet above sea level, the highest tunnel in the world. Even today it is an intimidating place, narrow, unlined, ill-lit and ill-ventilated, just wide enough for two lorries to pass, with the raw rock seemingly pressing down upon your head. In the course of the war, the 40th Army moved 8 million tons of supplies through this tunnel.

It normally took about fifteen minutes to negotiate the tunnel, though the big convoys took much longer. In November 1982 an Afghan government convoy broke down inside the tunnel, blocking the way for the Soviet column following behind it. It was very cold and the drivers left their engines running. Sixty-four Soviet soldiers and 112 Afghan soldiers died of carbon monoxide poisoning. This was not the first such case: twelve soldiers died in the tunnel in December 1979 and two more in spring of the following year. Indeed, people were still dying in the tunnel even after it had been rebuilt and reopened in 2002. After the disaster of 1982 a much stricter traffic control was instituted and there were no more incidents on that scale.[33] But it could still be a very dangerous place, even in peacetime: in the winter of 2010 over 160 people were killed when the Salang was struck by a series of avalanches.

On the southern side of the tunnel the road descends in broad serpentines, dominated by bleak cliffs and mountains on one side and falling steeply away on the other: ambush country. After passing through scattered villages, the road comes to the first major town, Charikar, known for its grapes and its pottery, where Captain Codrington and his Gurkhas were massacred during the First Anglo-Afghan War. Lesser roads branch out from Charikar, westwards to Bamyan and eastwards to Bagram, Afghanistan's main airbase, and the Pandsher Valley, the base for Ahmad Shah Masud's formidable guerrilla fighters. The fertile Shomali Plain begins here, a green zone of walled villages, tangled vineyards, small fields, and intricate irrigation ditches running close to the road for about sixty miles all the way to Kabul and to the outskirts of the great airbase at Bagram. It is an ideal place for snipers, the laying of ambushes, and the planting of roadside bombs and mines. Soviet troops went into the villages of the Shomali Plain at their peril. In one incident, a *praporshchik* (warrant officer) took the short cut from Kabul to Bagram through the green zone. The mujahedin waited until he and his column were well inside, then shot them to pieces. The vehicles were destroyed and only one wounded man managed to get back to the main road. When the Russians went to retrieve the bodies and wreak their revenge, they lost a helicopter.

A pipeline ran alongside the Salang Highway, carrying fuel oil from the Soviet Union, and followed the road as far as the airbase at Bagram. A similar pipeline ran along the western highway to Shindand.[34] Small detachments from the Pipeline Brigade – seven men under a conscript sergeant – guarded and maintained the pumping stations along the route. If there were an incident or a mechanical failure, day or night, they would go out to investigate. It was not a glamorous service. But it was dangerous, and in 1986 nearly a third of one Pipeline Battalion was decorated.[35]

The Russians cut down trees and destroyed villages along their main supply routes to deny cover to potential ambushers. They placed their *zastavas* close enough together to give mutual support or on heights overlooking the road. They positioned larger garrisons at intervals of about twelve miles, with a mobile reserve of motor-rifle troops, armour, and artillery. Before a convoy set out along a particularly vulnerable route, special forces and paratroopers travelled by forced march or by helicopter to occupy the heights before the mujahedin could get there and to block off their line of retreat. One column, which was sent to supply the garrison at Chagcharan in the mountains midway between Herat and Kabul, consisted of 250 army lorries and several hundred civilian vehicles with goods for the civilian population. It was supported by four motor-rifle battalions, five reconnaissance companies, two troops of tanks, a battery of artillery, and thirty-two helicopters.[36]

A typical skirmish occurred on the Salang Pass on 16 October 1986, shortly after midday, when a column of oil tankers, more than a mile long, was attacked by several hundred of Masud's fighters from the Pandsher Valley, accompanied, it is said, by a Western TV crew out for some spectacular footage. A BTR escorting the column was put out of action in the first salvo of mortar shells. A number of tankers were set on fire and the drivers bailed out to take cover.

Ruslan Aushev (1954–) was just descending towards Charikar with a small armoured task force (*bronegruppa*) of seven armoured vehicles and two tanks when he heard the firing. He had already been made a Hero of the Soviet Union for action in Afghanistan. Now he reversed his column to go to the aid of the stricken convoy. They passed the wrecked BTR and a few tankers which had escaped from the ambush. On a narrow stretch, two burning oil tankers had slewed across the road and had blocked it entirely. Aushev tried to push them off the road with his tank. When the tank itself risked catching fire, he blew the two vehicles away with a couple of shells fired at point-blank range.

What was left of the convoy was trapped higher up. The young lieutenant commanding the next *zastava*, Nikolai Kiselev, radioed that he was sending his small force to help. Between them Aushev's *bron-egruppa* and Kiselev's little force rescued the survivors. But Kiselev was killed and Aushev severely wounded.[37]

Though not as important as the Salang route, the western highway which led from Kushka in Uzbekistan to Herat, Shindand, and Kandahar also had to be kept open. It was less vulnerable than the Salang, since much of it lay across open desert with little cover for ambushes. But it was never safe. Major Vyacheslav Izmailov commanded a transport battalion based in Shindand which ran columns between Herat and Kandahar. The journey usually took three days. Major Izmailov's columns might consist of up to two hundred lorries, escorted by three or four BTRs and occasionally tanks. They hardly ever had air cover.

Perhaps because he came from Muslim Dagestan and understood the local customs better, Major Izmailov never had any serious trouble. You needed to treat the Afghans with respect, he said: you drove through their villages at two or three miles an hour, you didn't drive away from accidents, you talked to the village elders. If there were some incident, the Afghans would take payment in cash or kind in compensation, even for a death. But if the Russians refused to accept responsibility or give compensation, then the Afghans would exact their compensation in blood, mining the routes and ambushing the convoys. Through their agents, the mujahedin always knew who was in command of a convoy. They did not attack those who played the game.

Compensation could include sacks of rice or money for the funerals. When Izmailov's men once casually shot up and destroyed a couple of disabled Afghan trucks by the roadside the local leaders told him that the truck owners risked losing their livelihoods. They would be left with nothing to do but to join the mujahedin. Izmailov arranged a complicated deal which involved siphoning fuel out of his tankers, passing it through a third party to the local leaders, and so on to the truck owners.

Another transport battalion followed a different policy and suffered a different fate. Colonel Kretenin always led his columns at great speed through populated areas as well as open countryside, raising clouds of dust, not stopping for accidents. The Afghans decided to teach him a lesson. In February 1987 he set out with a column from Kandahar to Shindand. Izmailov followed more slowly. Ninety miles out from Kandahar, he heard on his radio that Kretenin was under fire. By the time he got to the scene most of the convoy had been destroyed and Kretenin was dead.

The Soviet supply lines were never seriously threatened. But the convoys inevitably suffered heavy losses from time to time. One column destined for Faisabad in the north-east started out from the Soviet Union with twelve hundred vehicles, but only seven hundred reached their destination. Another column took eleven days to cover twenty-five miles.[38] Many of the columns were organised by a joint Afghan-Soviet company, Afsotr, which was still in existence in 2008. The lorry drivers were civilians and many of them died: more than nine thousand received Soviet or Afghan awards during the war. More than eleven thousand lorries and fuel tankers were lost, and the mountain passes and valleys of Afghanistan were still littered with their carcasses twenty years after the war had ended.[39]

Operations

The Russians did not of course stay perpetually on the defensive; they took the war to the enemy as well. In September 1983 Colonel Rokhlin, the commander the 860th Independent Motor-rifle Regiment in Faisabad, was sacked for mismanaging a major operation against a concentration of mujahedin which cost fifteen killed and seventy-eight wounded, and went down in regimental legend as the 'Bakharak Massacre'. He was replaced by Colonel Valeri Sidorov, a well-connected officer whose father taught in the General Staff College and whose mother was a member of the Supreme Soviet. Sidorov was not popular. He was courageous and led from the front, but his soldiers found him hard-driving and ambitious, careless of their lives as he devised ever more ingenious and dangerous operations to enhance his career. The shadow under which the regiment was living after the 'Bakharak Massacre' spurred his ambition still further: he would, by his deeds, restore its reputation.

His first big operation, in January 1984, was aimed at rooting out the guerrillas around the village of Karamugul, a few miles along a gorge from Faisabad. The whole regiment would be involved, including the cooks and drivers. The grandfathers who were expecting to go home in a matter of weeks were particularly unhappy at the news: it was a rule of thumb among the soldiers that courage begins to run out as the prospect of survival draws closer.

After a rousing speech by the colonel, they moved out early in the morning. An hour later they were clambering up on to the plateau on the western side of the gorge. The temperature was just above zero, it was raining, and by two o'clock they were soaked. Because of the weather they had no air cover.

By five o'clock in the morning Karamagul was effectively blockaded. The temperature had fallen to between minus fifteen and minus twenty degrees, and officers and men were huddling together for warmth. The soldiers from the reconnaissance company – the *razvedchiki* – went into Karamugul at six. The village was empty by then, though the stoves were still warm: both the villagers and the insurgents had got out in good time. There was no point in hanging about and at eight o'clock the troops began to withdraw. They were immediately set upon by mujahedin. Only the *razvedchiki* managed to get to their BMPs and pull out.

The third platoon covered the retreat on the plateau. They were more heavily armed than the mujahedin, but the latter had the advantage of numbers and mobility. The cooks and the drivers, together with some wounded and men from the mortar battery, were ordered straight back to the regimental base under a *praporshchik*, Sandirescu. They started off across the plateau, but after they were caught in crossfire Sandirescu took them down into the gorge which led to the base, hoping that would be the quickest way home. The rest of the battalion managed to disengage at the cost of a few lightly wounded, but when they reached the edge of the plateau overlooking their base, they once again came under fire. They slid down the snow-covered slopes on their behinds and eventually worked their way home.

When the roll call was taken, it was discovered that Sandirescu and his party had still not returned. The *razvedchiki*, who were still comparatively fresh, set off in their BMPs to find them. They returned at five o'clock in the evening, with the body of one of the cooks. They had picked up six more soldiers stumbling back to base. Sandirescu was one of them, but he was too shocked to say what had happened. Two others turned up during the night: a cook who had lost his boots and whose feet were cut to pieces; and one of the drivers, nicknamed the 'Moldovan', whose weapon had to be taken by force from his frozen hands. All he could say was that the rest were dead, except for one soldier, Pashanin, who had been taken prisoner.

Colonel Sidorov realised he was in trouble. He would be castigated for not waiting for better weather and a helicopter escort; the village was known to be well defended; his force was too small for the job; the cooks and drivers had been hopelessly unsuitable for battle. How was he to explain to his superiors that no one knew what had happened to the missing men? The exhausted soldiers were asked to volunteer to go out to find them. During the night – something unprecedented in army life – a grandfather and five new recruits stayed up to clean their weapons, get them dry clothing from the store, and dry their boots. The next day, swearing mightily, the volunteers set off into a cold clear dawn, a light snow falling, escorted this time by helicopters.

While half the soldiers climbed back on to the plateau to cover them, Ponomarev and his men were sent to the gorge along which Sandirescu had tried to withdraw. They found some landmines and some piles of spent cartridges. The river was frozen and they systematically broke the ice in case there was something beneath it. Almost at the end of their strength, they eventually found the frozen, mutilated, and emasculated remains of seven soldiers.

It was clear what had happened. Under fire, the wretched cooks had rushed as fast as they could towards their base, instead of taking up a defensive position and calling for help. The Moldovan and Pashanin, the two oldest soldiers in the group, had covered their retreat as best they could. The mujahedin had attacked the little detachment from both ends of the gorge. A third group had mowed them down from above. After running out of ammunition, the Moldovan had saved himself by jumping into the frozen river. Pashanin had refused to follow and was captured. The regiment later heard through their Afghan agents that he had been castrated and a ring put through his nose. He had been dragged naked through the villages and finished off a month later.

Six months later a scruffy small boy came to the base and offered to show them where Pashanin's body was buried – for a price. The corpse was unrecognisable. The soldiers buried the body and for good measure slapped the small boy about a bit. In the absence of positive identification, Pashanin was recorded as missing in action.

Undismayed, Sidorov decided to mount another major operation. The direct route from Kishim to Faisabad – the Old Kishim Road – ran for about twenty miles. But it went over the Argu Pass, which was firmly controlled by the mujahedin. The only other available route was the New Kishim Road, which wound by a roundabout way for over sixty miles. The journey normally took three to four days, since the convoys, escorted by armoured vehicles, sappers, and the reconnaissance company, moved at a walking pace: quite literally, because the sappers had to go ahead on foot, looking for mines and roadside bombs. Even so, there were usually two or three explosions each time a convoy went out. If a column was fired upon, it would destroy the nearest village to deter further attacks. By the end of 1983 the New Kishim Road was lined with ruins.

Sidorov decided to reopen the Old Kishim Road and thus free for offensive operations the two battalions now immobilised by guard and escort duties. The whole regiment would take part in the operation, leaving only small garrisons to guard the regimental and battalion bases.

The operation took place at the end of May 1984. The evening before it began Sidorov gave another fiery speech to his men, calling on them to be worthy of their fathers and to fight to the last in the pursuit of victory. This time the temperature was forty degrees in the shade and several men fainted before he had finished.

The task force moved off the following morning in a cloud of black smoke, its engines roaring. At first things went well enough. But after the operation had been under way for several days it was decisively brought to an end by an avoidable accident.

Sidorov's command vehicle got stuck in a river crossing. His driver was unable to get it going again. Sidorov hauled him out of the driver's hatch, sent him on his way with a few well-placed blows, and slid into his place. As he did so, a grenade he was carrying snagged. The fuse ignited and in the few seconds remaining before the grenade went off Sidorov was unable to get rid of it. In the last second, he tried to shield the other men in the vehicle from the blast. He himself was killed.

The operation was immediately called off. That evening all the officers of the regiment got drunk. They fired off their guns and signal flares, and for good measure four tanks let off a salvo at the nearest *kishlak* so that the locals too should also have something to remember Sidorov by. The soldiers got no vodka, but they were given extra helpings of meat and fried potatoes. The new recruits were detailed off to mount the guard for the night.

The mutilated body was put back together in the regimental morgue and dressed in Sidorov's parade uniform. The next day the regiment paraded to honour his coffin. The guard of honour was mounted by the regimental officers, all with hangovers. The regimental band played as the coffin, loaded with Sidorov's medals, was carried to the helicopter to begin the long journey back to a grave in Moscow's Kuzminskoe Cemetery.[40]

The Sledgehammer

Most of the 40th Army's large-scale operations took place in the imposing mountains on the border with Pakistan, across which lay the mujahedin's main supply routes, or in the fertile Pandsher Valley, from which bands could threaten the Russians' own supply lines across the Salang Pass.

The city of Khost is only ten miles from the eastern border with Pakistan, about ninety miles south of Kabul and sixty miles from Gardez, to which it is linked by a strategic road, open to ambush and rising to ten thousand feet where it crosses the Satykandav Pass. During the Soviet war the guerrilla force in these parts was led by Jalaluddin

Haqqani (*c.* 1950–). Twenty years later the same force was led by his son, Sirajuddin. By then the Russian base in Khost was being used by the Americans: it was here that seven CIA employees were killed by a suicide bomber in December 2009.

Jalaluddin's base at Zhawar consisted of a complex of tunnels whose entrances faced towards Pakistan, only a couple of miles away. Inside were arms depots and repair shops, a garage, a medical station, a radio centre, a kitchen, a mosque, and a hotel. Five hundred mujahedin defended the base, armed with a howitzer, rocket launchers, heavy anti-aircraft machine guns, and two T-55 tanks they had captured from the Afghan army in 1983. From this base Jalaluddin was able to keep Khost under constant threat.[41]

In late 1985 the Afghan army, supported by Soviet units, launched a major operation to smash the Zhawar base.[42] The initial attacks were unsuccessful. An airborne assault by the Afghan 38th Commando Brigade got lost in the darkness and landed on the wrong side of the frontier. They were surrounded and taken prisoner. By now the government troops had lost some two-thirds of their strength through death, wounds, and desertion, and were no longer effective.

Varennikov flew to Khost to sort things out. This time the Soviets provided three battalions from the 56th Guards Independent Airborne Assault Brigade and two from the 345th Guards Independent Parachute Assault Regiment to support the Afghans. The Afghans succeeded in capturing Zhawar – only to find that it had been abandoned. Soviet engineers were given a little time – too little – to destroy the tunnels. The troops were then withdrawn. A victory parade was held back in Kabul. The mujahedin reoccupied the Zhawar complex in a matter of days. For good measure, they executed seventy-eight captured Afghan army officers, including the commander of the 38th Commando Brigade.

The following autumn it had to be done all over again. The operation was code-named *Magistral* (Highway), and the commanders were General Gromov and the Afghan Minister of Defence, Colonel General Tanai, he who had helped evacuate the advisers from Herat in March 1979. About ten thousand Soviet and eight thousand Afghan troops were involved. Because of its size and political significance, *Magistral* would be one of the most substantial operations of the whole war.[43] Once again the blockade was raised and on 30 December the first supply columns started to reach Khost. Once again the Soviet forces withdrew and the mujahedin returned. Varennikov was made a Hero of the Soviet Union. Those who believed that it was others who had done the actual fighting were not best pleased.[44]

One of the most famous incidents of the whole war occurred in the aftermath of Operation *Magistral*. This was the defence of Hill 3234 by the 9th Company of the 345th Guards Independent Parachute Assault Regiment – the same company which Vostrotin had led in the storming of the Taj Bek Palace in December 1979. The hill – over ten thousand feet above sea level – commanded a significant sector of the road to Gardez, which the Soviet commanders were determined to keep open. The 9th Company, thirty-nine men in all, were landed on the hilltop on 7 January 1988, and were attacked almost immediately by a mujahedin force estimated at between two hundred and four hundred men. The attacks continued until the following morning, by which time the defenders were almost out of ammunition and had lost six dead and twenty-eight wounded. Two of the dead, a sergeant and a corporal, were made Heroes of the Soviet Union. In 2005 a big-budget film, *9th Company*, was made about the incident. It had considerable commercial success in Russia and abroad, but most Afghan veterans thought it bombastic and historically inaccurate, not at all like the war that they had experienced.

Jalaluddin resumed the blockade around Khost. Charlie Wilson, the US Congressman who was one of the most effective supporters of the mujahedin, visited Jalaluddin and pronounced him 'goodness personified'.[45] He finally captured Khost in April 1991, two years after the Soviets had left Afghanistan. He later joined the Taliban and remained with them after 9/11. Charlie Wilson's hero became number three on the Americans' 'wanted' list.[46]

The Pandsher

It was the operations of the 40th Army in the Pandsher Valley that caught the imagination of Russians and foreigners alike. There were nine major operations in the valley, according to most calculations, though there are arguments about definition. The pattern of all these operations was similar. The 40th Army swept into the valley and took the ground, but was unable to inflict a decisive defeat on Masud because of his evasive tactics. The Russians would then pull out, leaving Afghan military units and civilian representatives of the Kabul regime to hold the territory. This they regularly failed to do: Masud reoccupied the valley, killed, seduced, or expelled the regime's representatives, and the whole thing had to be done all over again. Even so the Russians always maintained a toehold in the valley. In addition to its fort in Anava, the second battalion of the 345th Guards Independent Parachute Assault Regiment had twenty *zastavas* spread through the lower reaches, each manned by up to a dozen men under a lieutenant. They were usually supplied by helicopters, a dangerous business: though Masud's men did not have Stingers, they used their heavy machine guns to good effect, and nearly a third of the local helicopter squadron was lost. There was a regular trickle of casualties: soldiers stepped on mines or were hit by snipers. If there were no helicopters available, a small armoured group would be put together to evacuate the wounded by road to Bagram, putting other soldiers at risk.

The Pandsher Valley is a place of spectacular beauty. Its people are Tajiks, devout but not fanatical Sunni Muslims, often at odds with the Pushtuns to the south. Alexander the Great went this way in an epic winter march in pursuit of Bessus, the last claimant to the imperial Persian throne. Later the locals made a living by extracting tribute from the rich caravans from China which passed through the valley, until the twentieth century one of the main trade routes northwards from Kabul. The painters of the European Renaissance used lapis lazuli mined around the upper valley for making the blue paint for the robes of their Madonnas. The mines generated an income of more than $5 million a year even during the war; they were carefully camouflaged, heavily protected against air attack, and exploited with the help of Japanese and West German engineers. Because of their economic importance to the resistance, the mines were attacked – unsuccessfully – in June 1981 by long-range bombers from bases in the Soviet Union.[47]

After the road over the Salang Pass was built, the valley lost its significance as a trade route. But despite its diminished importance, its position – dangerously close to Bagram, the main Soviet airbase, to the main Soviet supply line across the Hindu Kush through the Salang Tunnel, and to Kabul itself – meant that guerrilla forces operating out of the valley were a thorn in the Russians' side from the first day of the Soviet occupation to the last (see Map 4).

The entrance to the valley from the Shomali Plain, about fifty-five miles north of Kabul, is forbidding. From the town of Charikar you pass through a narrow gorge, the Dalang Sang. The Pandsher River foams along, up to sixty feet below you, and the road clings to the sheer rock face on your left. It was along this narrow road that the Russians had to funnel their soldiers, their guns, and their armour as they stormed the valley time and again in the first five years of the war.

Once you are through the gorge, the valley opens out. In its lower reaches there are vineyards, orchards of mulberries and apricots, and irrigated fields of wheat and maize. The river itself is rich with fish. *Kishlaks* are spread out along the river and up the sides of the hills, many with no more than a single street with shops or a market. They are often guarded by a small fort, and the houses themselves are walled and capable of defence.

From Charikar to the upper end of the valley is more than a hundred miles.[48] During the Russian time the road petered out after fifty-three miles. After that you had to proceed on foot or on horseback, over increasingly rugged country, until you were up among the glaciers of the Hindu Kush, between ten and twenty thousand feet high and very close to the border with Pakistan and China.[49] Two passes lead out of these high mountains and mark the end of the valley: the Khawak Pass (12,624 feet) to the northern plains and the Anjoman Pass (14,534 feet) to Badakhshan, the most north-easterly province of Afghanistan. Passable with difficulty in summer, in the winter they are closed for most purposes. It was over these passes that determined men brought goods, arms, and ammunition to feed the rebellion.

The first Soviet operation in the Pandsher Valley took place in April 1980, only four months after the invasion. Three Soviet battalions participated, including the 4th Battalion of the 56th Guards Independent Airborne Assault Brigade under the command of Captain Leonid Khabarov. About a thousand Afghan soldiers and security police went with them. The plan was that the Soviet troops would block the *kishlaks* as they advanced and the Afghans would search them. To oppose this force Masud had little more than a thousand men. They were armed mainly with old-fashioned rifles and they had not yet constructed much in the way of defensive works. They mined the only road in the valley, destroyed the bridges, and planned to ambush the invaders.

At first the operation went smoothly. The Russians cleared the mines, rebuilt the bridges, and advanced with reasonable speed. Where the ruined road made it impossible to move forward, they drove along the bed of the river. They quickly reached Masud's headquarters at the *kishlak* of Pasishah-Mardan. It had been abandoned in a hurry: the prison was empty and files of documents, lists and identity documents lay scattered all around.

Sergei Morozov, a sergeant in the 56th Guards Independent Airborne Assault Brigade, said, 'This was the first operation where we met major resistance. There were ambushes, the roads were blown up. Of course I did not know exactly what was going on because I was only a sergeant. We drove as far as we could and then dismounted. After leaving the *kishlak* which had housed Masud's headquarters, we marched right to the end of the Pandsher Valley. It was the furthest anyone got during the whole war, and very close to the Pakistan frontier.

'On the way back along the mountain path, my battalion was ambushed. Thirteen men were killed in the leading platoon. My own platoon had been in the lead on the way out and so we were in the rearguard on the way back. We stopped for the night and had to beat off a number of mujahedin attacks. Their weapons in those days were simple, many of them home-made. They didn't get mortars until later. The numbers opposing us were very small – perhaps only a few dozen. We had helicopter cover throughout, though not of course at night. During the long march most of the radios failed because the batteries ran out. But I was familiar with radios from before the war and I had turned off my radio when it was out of range or blocked by the mountains. So I had enough power to call in helicopter support when it became necessary … It took us some time to get away from the inflex- ible tactics we had learned for war in Europe. Although our brigade had been formed for operations in the desert and the mountains, there was a difference between theory and practice. After the first Pandsher operation, I asked my company commander, Captain Khabarov, whether it made sense to advance in clumsy columns, which could get stuck, and often could not turn round. Would it not be better to leapfrog troops forward with helicopters? And of course we did in time learn to do those things.'[50]

The Russians called it a victory. But the rebels considered that the victory was theirs. An Afghan historian has claimed that there were only two hundred armed rebels in the valley at the time, and their only anti-tank weapons were three rocket launchers. They deliberately offered no resistance to the initial Russian advance, but fell on the Russians as they withdrew down the mountains. The rebel newspaper *The Call of the Jihad* claimed that a hundred Soviet and Afghan soldiers were killed, ten guns were captured, and eight tanks and other vehicles damaged. The rebels lost four dead. Twenty-five civilians were also killed.[51]

Naturally enough, Masud used the ceasefire of 1983–4 to enlarge and re-equip his forces. Soviet intelligence calculated that by then he had three thousand five hundred men. Five hundred were defending the entrance to the valley. Another two thousand were operating against the Afghan and Soviet garrisons. The remainder were in the north-east part of the valley, and their task was to ward off airborne landings.[52]

Under pressure from the Afghan leadership, Moscow decided in the spring of 1984 to deal with Masud once and for all. This time they would use a total of 11,000 Soviet and 2,600 Afghan troops, together with 200 aircraft and 190 helicopters.

Special forces troops went in first. They discovered that the rebel positions were empty. The Russians decided not to call off the operation, since the bombers, carrying cluster as well as high explosive bombs, the largest weighing nine tons, had already taken off from their bases inside the Soviet Union.[53] The air strike lasted about two hours.

The main force moved in at four o'clock on 19 April, preceded by sappers. On 30 April the second battalion of the 682nd Motor-rifle Regiment was particularly badly hit, thanks to the carelessness of the regimental commander, who had ordered it to advance into a ravine leading off the valley without first securing the commanding heights. At first the battalion met no resistance. They lowered their guard and were promptly ambushed from three sides. In the resulting fight, the battalion lost fifty-three dead, including twelve officers, and fifty-eight wounded. Private Nikolai Knyazev described the aftermath.

'My platoon was guarding the regimental command post when we heard a sudden commotion, and the regimental commander told us that one of our battalions had been attacked, and that there were wounded and dead.

'We loaded stretchers on to our armoured vehicles and started up the ravine. After waiting for darkness, we continued on foot. There were about ten of us together with the platoon commander. It was not easy to make our way along the mountain paths and it took us a long time, since there were boulders and terraces everywhere, which made it difficult to work out the distance we had covered. We seemed to be marching for eternity.

'After a while we saw a strange light shining in the darkness and the platoon commander ordered us to lie down; but we soon worked out that it was light shining through the periscopes of a BMP. We had barely moved any distance further when we were fired on by a Kalashnikov. Our platoon commander, Lieutenant Arutiunov, fired a rocket, we shouted out, and the firing stopped. We came up close. It was one of our own BMPs, which had been blown up by a mine. The driver and the deputy political officer of the battalion, Major Kononenko, had remained with the vehicle, both suffering from concussion. We moved forward. After a little while we met the *razvedchiki* who had been sent ahead of us. They were carrying some dead bodies, including the body of the battalion commander, Captain Korolev. Everybody sobered up in a moment.

'It was already getting light … as we arrived at a *kishlak*. As we went down the main street, we heard the sound of motors. Two of the battalion's BMPs were moving towards us. They were loaded down with the bodies of dead soldiers. Arms and legs stuck out of the pile in different directions. Smashed-up radios and rocket launchers were piled up as well. A group of soldiers who had survived the battle were walking behind the armoured vehicles. It was terrible to look at their faces. They were finished, they expressed no emotion, they were like zombies.

'We brought the survivors back to the main body of the regiment. A helicopter landed nearby and some generals emerged. One of them ordered the surviving soldiers to form up. They had not yet pulled themselves together and still smelled of corpses – they had been lying among the dead for days (I can't even imagine what had gone on in their heads). One of the visitors came up to them and shouted, 'Bastards! Wankers! You're standing here, you bastards, and your comrades are lying out there! Why are you here?!' – that's how he addressed them. Then he read them the riot act and left with the feeling that he had done his duty. The lads stood silent and unfeeling – perhaps they did not even hear him.

'That evening we were ordered to return to the scene of the action and bring back the remaining bodies. Imagine an open area about a hundred metres square. The river runs through the middle. On the right-hand side there is a level place, a few terraces and a hill about two or three hundred metres high. To the left of the river there is a path, an overhanging wall of rock on one side and on the other a sheer drop into the river.

'It was immediately clear that we were in the right place. There was a heavy smell of corpses – the boys had been lying there for nearly two days, and at that time of year it is already getting hot. We were very much afraid that the rebels were waiting for someone to come to collect the bodies and that we too would end up lying there. We made our way to the foot of the hill, to the terraces. First we came across the body of a sergeant who was due to be demobilised: he had lost his legs either from an explosion or a burst of heavy machine-gun fire. Five or six of the lads were lying piled up in a natural cave on the terrace. They had been cut down either by a machine-gun burst or when the rebels had started to throw hand grenades. So there they lay together where death had caught up with them. We took the bodies across the river mechanically, as if we were asleep. The sight of the bodies was terrible.

'There were rags of something hanging on a tree and below it a mess. Evidently a bullet had hit a mine that one of the soldiers had been carrying.

'Suddenly we heard a weak groan some distance off from the hollow, by the rocks. We carefully went towards the noise and came across a soldier who was still alive. His shin had been shot off and was hanging by rags of tendon. He was weakened by loss of blood, but he had managed to put a tourniquet round his leg and stem the flow. We gave him first aid and took him to the vehicles. He survived. There were no weapons left – they had all been collected by the rebels.

'On the morning of 2 May we returned to the regimental armoured group. The bodies were lying on a stony beach in rows. There were about fifty of them. We were told that some had already been taken away. Our company commander, Lieutenant Kurdiuk, was lying on his back with his elbows bent and his fists clenched, and across his chest you could see a line of bullet holes. It was said that he had been shot by the Afghan soldiers who were marching with the battalion when they started to desert to the rebels, but he had time to order the lads to fire on them.' [54]

This operation too was described by the Soviets as a victory. After it was over, Marshal Sokolov flew to Rukha, the chief town in the valley, to see things for himself. There was nothing to see. Soviet tanks were standing around in the wheat fields. But there was little damage and no sign of the locals. Sokolov called a meeting in the house which was being used by the staff. There were three Afghans there – the *orgyadro*, or organisational cell which was to restore the authority of the Kabul government to the valley. The three men sat despondent and unnoticed among the gathering of generals and colonels.

The generals reported to Sokolov that three thousand rebels had opposed the incursion. Seventeen hundred had been killed, and the survivors had retreated into the mountains, carrying the bodies of their dead comrades with them. That was why there was so little to be seen.

Leonid Shebarshin, the Deputy Chief of the Analytical Department of the KGB's Foreign Intelligence Headquarters in Moscow, was also present. He was not impressed by the figures being bandied around. How many casualties had there been on the Soviet side? How could thirteen hundred rebel survivors have carried seventeen hundred corpses? How could the corpses have been counted, since they were nowhere to be seen? He discovered the answer. Enemy casualties were estimated according to a formula based on the amount of ammunition expended. This charmingly precise formula had enabled the Soviets to claim that the rebels had lost thirty thousand men every year since 1982.[55]

Sokolov reported to Ustinov that 2,800 rebels had been killed and thirty captured. He told Karmal that the way had now been cleared for the Afghan authorities to set up a civilian administration and launch programmes of social and economic reform for the benefit of the peasantry in the valley.[56] Only later did it become clear that Masud, forewarned by his agents in Kabul, had again withdrawn most of his forces to safety before the attack. That was why the Soviet troops had met with so little serious opposition. Their losses came chiefly from mines and ambushes as they were combing through villages. The long-range bombers had had little effect on a dispersed enemy and a rural countryside: as the wretched infantrymen said, 'They didn't earn their chocolate.'[57] Masud's prestige among his own people increased still further. He was able to extend his control in the northern provinces of the country and grew from being an ordinary field commander to being a major political figure, well known inside and outside Afghanistan.

Tactics without Strategy

Sergeant Morozov's commander, Captain Khabarov, never got over his bitterness at the way these operations were conducted. 'Why,' he asked, 'did we leave the Pandsher so quickly? What was the point of the operation? … Throughout the whole of that war practically every operation ended in the same way. Military operations began, soldiers and officers died, Afghan soldiers died, the mujahedin and the peaceful population died, and when the operation was over our forces would leave, and everything would return to what it had been before. I still feel guilty and bitter about the Afghan government forces … whom we betrayed and sold down the river when we left Afghanistan, leaving them and their families to the mercy of the victors.'[58]

The sledgehammer blows were incapable of cracking the nut of an elusive, uncoordinated guerrilla enemy. These operations usually succeeded in their immediate objectives. The garrison would be relieved, the base would be destroyed, the valley occupied. But the Russians never had sufficient troops to hold the ground they took. After a successful operation they would withdraw to their bases and hand responsibility to their Afghan allies. But the government's military and civilian representatives found it impossible to operate amid a hostile population. Too often, under moral and military pressure from the mujahedin, they abandoned their posts, deserted, or went over to the enemy.

And so the Russians discovered, as other armies have discovered in Afghanistan before and since, that once you have taken the ground you need troops to hold it. They might dominate the towns and the villages by day. But the mujahedin would rule them by night. They never broke the rebels' grip on the countryside or closed the frontier through which the rebels received their supplies.

In the end the Russians had good tactics but no workable strategy. They could win their fights, but they could not convincingly win the war. Their best efforts, military and political, went for nothing. They eventually had no choice but to disentangle themselves as best they could.

- TEN -

DEVASTATION AND
DISILLUSION

Armies are institutions for organising and channelling violence in the pursuit of some concept of the national interest. They help to focus the emotions of patriotism, self-sacrifice, and solidarity which states need for their coherence and sometimes for their survival.

Violence is not easy to control, and armies have to cope with violence within their own ranks as well as atrocities against the enemy and the civilian population. Otherwise they risk a breakdown of discipline and a loss of function. Wellington was notoriously severe in his determination to keep his army – 'the scum of the earth enlisted for drink' – under control. Even he did not always succeed.

But commanders also have to preserve the morale of their men and the principle – itself important for effective cohesion – of the 'honour of the uniform'. Time and again, and in all armies, this leads to evasion and cover-up to prevent the stories of military crimes emerging or to limit their consequences: because of the pressure of military and public opinion the US authorities found it impossible to bring to account all those responsible for the massacre at My Lai in Vietnam in 1968. Commanders in the 40th Army were no different. They were blamed by their generals for not exercising a more effective discipline. Fearing for their careers, they often responded by writing off suicides and murders as battle casualties. Some crimes could not be concealed. But there were plenty of other cases where officers managed to avoid formal inquiry into the actions of themselves or their men. And things such as the destruction of villages suspected of harbouring insurgents or firing on the troops were regarded as a legitimate, or at least an unavoidable, act of war.

The 40th Army made it clear enough to its soldiers what would happen if they misbehaved. In 1985 they produced a little booklet 'The Life, Habits and Customs of the Peoples of Afghanistan: Rules and Norms of Behaviour for Military Personnel Serving outside their Own Country'.[1] This described the country and its people, their religion, their fierce sense of independence, their housing, clothing and food, their customs of mutual hospitality and vendetta, the rituals surrounding birth, marriage, and death. It continued with some simple rules of behaviour: remember that you are a representative of the army and be worthy of your historical mission; know and respect the customs of the local people, even if they do not correspond with your own; be very careful to respect Afghan women; do not interfere with a Muslim at prayer and do not go into a mosque without a very good reason; beware of enemy spies; do not drink water from irrigation canals; do not leave camp or accept hospitality without permission. There were strict injunctions against trading, especially in narcotics. The booklet concluded: 'Soldier, remember! … you are criminally responsible for military crimes under the Criminal Code, whether committed negligently, carelessly, or deliberately.' Deliberate killing could be punished by up to ten years; the death penalty could be imposed if there were aggravating circumstances, which included being drunk. Robbery with violence and smuggling into the Soviet Union could both be punished by up to ten years in prison.

Military Crime
These were not idle threats. The Soviet military prosecutors in Afghanistan had to deal with the whole range of military crimes: murder, looting, rape, drug addiction, desertion, self-mutilation, theft, and random violence against the population. Those they found guilty were given harsh sentences of imprisonment, sent to disciplinary battalions

back in the Soviet Union, and occasionally shot. At one time the notorious prison in Pul-i Charkhi outside Kabul held two hundred Russian soldiers accused of a variety of offences against the Afghan population, including murder. By the end of the war over two thousand five hundred Soviet soldiers were serving prison sentences, more than two hundred for crimes of premeditated murder.[2]

Until the files of the Military Prosecutor's office are opened it is not possible to arrive at any reliable overall figures. Those that are available are very patchy. A senior general speaking to the commanders of the 40th Army in 1988 claimed that in 1987 the number of crimes went down to 543 compared with 745 the previous year. He named several units whose record was particularly poor: reconnaissance units, which were notoriously free and easy about discipline, the air force, the 108th and 201st Motor-rifle Divisions, the 66th and 70th Independent Motor-rifle Brigades, the 860th Independent Motor-rifle Regiment. Altogether, according to another source, 6,412 criminal charges were preferred against soldiers in Afghanistan, including 714 cases of murder, 2,840 cases of weapons sales to Afghans, and 534 drug-trafficking offences.[3]

Despite the sanctions, soldiers committed many brutal acts individually or in groups. The excuse often was, 'They did it to us, so we have a right to do it to them.' Soviet commanders made a point of telling their men the stories of Russian prisoners being executed or tortured by the mujahedin, the mutilated bodies left for their comrades to find. The stories were not untrue: they belonged, after all, to an old tradition in Afghanistan, to which Kipling bore witness. One minor mujahedin leader boasted that he had made a practice of half-skinning Russian prisoners after a successful ambush, and leaving them alive, surrounded by booby traps, to catch the Soviet rescue teams.[4] Varennikov described what happened when a raid by a company of the 22nd Special Forces Brigade ended in disaster in April 1985 in the eastern mountains of the Kunar province, scene of some of the Americans' most vicious fighting twenty years later. The company had not expected opposition. They were ambushed and thirty-one were killed. In recovering their bodies, the Soviet forces lost three more men. It was clear that seven of the soldiers had killed themselves rather than surrender.

The others had been mutilated or burned alive. Varennikov went to see the survivor, a sergeant who had lost his mind.[5]

The soldiers committed their crimes sometimes in cold blood, more often in the heat or aftermath of battle. 'The thirst for blood … is a terrible desire,' wrote one of them. 'It is so strong that you cannot resist it. I saw for myself how the battalion opened a hail of fire on a group that was descending towards our column. And they were OUR soldiers, a detachment from the reconnaissance company who had been guarding us on the flank. They were only two hundred metres away and we were 90 per cent sure they were our people. And nevertheless – the thirst for blood, the desire to kill at all costs. Dozens of times I saw with my own eyes how the new recruits would shout and cry with joy after killing their first Afghan, pointing in the direction of the dead man, clapping one another on the back, and firing off a whole magazine into the corpse "just to make sure" … Not everyone can master this feeling, this instinct, and stifle the monster in his soul.'

Vanya Kosogovski, a soldier from Odessa in the 860th Independent Motor-rifle Regiment, was a cheerful fellow, liked by everyone. His company was sent out by helicopter to follow up an intelligence report about a village some fifteen miles away from the regimental base. On the way the gunners amused themselves by machine-gunning a herd of oxen and sheep: their excuse was that they were denying the mujahedin their supplies. After shooting up the village itself, the soldiers landed to comb through it. In one house Kosogovski noticed a small door and heard people breathing behind it. Above the door was a small aperture. He took a grenade, pulled out the pin, shoved it through the hole, and followed the explosion with a burst from his gun. When he kicked down the door, he saw the results of his handiwork. An old woman lay dead, a younger woman was still breathing, seven children aged between one and five lay beside them, some still moving. Kosogovski emptied his magazine into the heaving mass and followed it up with another grenade.

'I don't know why I did it,' he said later. 'I was beside myself. Perhaps I didn't want them to suffer. Anyway, I would have had the military police on my back.' And indeed, he might well have ended up in a disciplinary battalion, had his officers not covered up the affair.[6]

On 14 February 1981 a reconnaissance patrol of eleven soldiers from the 66th Independent Motor-rifle Brigade led by a senior lieutenant broke into a house in a village near Jalalabad. There they found two old men, three young women, and five or six children. They raped and shot the women and then shot the rest, except for one small boy, who hid himself and survived to be a witness. General Maiorov, the Chief Soviet Military Adviser in Kabul from June 1980 to November 1981, immediately ordered an investigation. The perpetrators confessed and were arrested. Fearing that the mujahedin leadership would use the incident as an excuse to launch a countrywide jihad, Maiorov strengthened the security regime in the major cities. And he apologised for the incident to the Afghan Prime Minister, Ali Sultan Keshtmand.

He immediately came under pressure to change the story from the Soviet Ambassador, from the KGB representative in Kabul, and from the Ministry of Defence and the KGB in Moscow. The KGB claimed to have information that the atrocity had been carried out as a deliberate provocation by mujahedin dressed in Soviet uniforms. Why, demanded Ogarkov, the Chief of Staff, was Maiorov trying to blacken the good name of the Soviet army? Ustinov, the Minister of Defence, hinted that if Maiorov did not change his tune he would not be re-elected to the Central Committee at the forthcoming meeting of the XXVIth Congress of the Communist Party of the Soviet Union.

Maiorov held out. He was not re-elected to the Central Committee. But Karmal complained directly to Brezhnev, who gave orders for condign punishment. The perpetrators of the crime were sentenced to death or to long terms of imprisonment. The brigade commander, Colonel Valeri Smirnov, was severely reprimanded. The brigade itself was on the verge of being disbanded, saved only by its glorious record in the Second World War.[7]

Even senior officers could be punished for allowing their troops to commit excesses. After the fifth Pandsher operation in May–June 1982, the commander of the 191st Independent Motor-rifle Regiment, Lieutenant Colonel Kravchenko, was court-martialled and sentenced to ten years for shooting prisoners. The commander of the 860th Independent Motor-rifle Regiment, Colonel Alexander Shebeda, was dismissed in April 1986 after he had been in the job only six months. Twenty prisoners had been captured on a raid and brought back to the base at Faisabad. Shebeda put them into the overnight custody of the reconnaissance company. The company had recently suffered losses and was still smarting. The men killed the prisoners and threw the bodies into the River Kochka. There was a scandal and Shebeda was relieved of his command.[8]

Collateral Damage

These were individual crimes, which the 40th Army could try to prevent or punish more or less effectively. Others were inherent in the nature of the war against a determined but elusive enemy who could merge almost at will with the civilian population. For the soldiers, this war without fronts was particularly terrifying and confusing. You could be blown up by a mine at any moment. The bearded peasant cultivating his field could next minute be firing at you from ambush or laying a bomb; or you might be shot in the back by a woman or even a child. And so the soldiers learned to shoot first regardless of the consequences. They reacted or overreacted savagely, either to defend themselves or to revenge their losses, calling in an air strike or a bombardment by artillery or tanks against villages they suspected of harbouring mujahedin or of firing on their troops, and leaving them in a pile of smoking rubble.

Alexander Rutskoi, an air-force colonel and Hero of the Soviet Union, told the Russian parliament after the war was over, 'A *kishlak* fires at us and kills someone. I send up a couple of planes and there is nothing left of the *kishlak*. After I've burned a couple of *kishlaks* they stop shooting.'[9] Vitali Krivenko tells how his company of the 12th Guards Motor-rifle Regiment was manning a roadblock outside Herat. There were two *kishlaks* nearby. One was deserted, but there were thought to be mujahedin lurking there. The population of the other was friendly. Helicopters were brought in, but they attacked the wrong village. By the time the mistake had been sorted out, the friendly village had been destroyed. 'So what?' Krivenko commented. 'How many other villages got wiped out, for good reason or simply for fun?'[10]

Even when soldiers and their commanders had the best intentions, things could go wrong. It is a fundamental weakness of any counter-insurgency campaign that, too often, there comes a moment when a commander's duty to preserve the lives of his soldiers overrides any wish he may have to spare the lives of civilians. Valeri Shiryaev was involved in just such a case. He was travelling with a convoy of tankers and supply lorries which was half a mile long and moved very slowly. It was preceded by sappers and a few BMPs. The rearguard consisted of more BMPs and four tanks. The convoy came under fire as it was passing through a village. Several tankers were hit and had to be pushed off the road. By the time the shooting had lasted for thirty minutes, four soldiers had been killed and others wounded. In the end the commander of the column ordered the tanks to open fire on the village, even though he knew there must be women and children in it. Each tank fired five salvoes and the village was destroyed. The commander was later reprimanded for not having ordered his tanks to fire sooner.[11]

The result was devastation. 'The aircraft flew over the "green zone",' wrote Alexander Prokhanov in one of his short stories, 'dropped bombs, flattened the gardens and the walls around them, reached down to destroy the roots of the plants, diverted and blocked up the underground arteries of the irrigation system, smashed the *kishlaks* to dust, burned up the very oxygen with the heat of their explosions, and turned the valley into a lunar landscape, grey, friable, where the insects, the seeds, the bacteria, the pollen of the flowers were dying in agony. Sterile and dry, like an overheated crucible, the plain lay bathed in sunshine.'[12]

Several attempts were made by outside observers to chronicle the abuses of human rights committed by all sides in the fighting between 1978 and 2001. In 1984 the United Nations appointed Felix Ermacora, an Austrian human rights lawyer, to investigate, and his reports came out regularly over the next ten years.[13] The Afghanistan Justice Project (AJP) issued another report covering the period 1978–2001, from the Communist coup in April 1978 until the first year of the US/NATO intervention.

The Afghan and Soviet governments initially refused to cooperate with Ermacora, though he was able to visit Afghanistan several times towards the end of the war and thereafter.[14] His earlier reports were therefore largely based on interviews with refugees. Some four hundred thousand people had already fled to Pakistan before the Russians invaded. By the time Ermacora started his studies, the number had risen to 4 million. By the end of the war, he estimated, there were 5 million Afghan refugees in Iran and Pakistan out of a population of 19.5 million.[15]

These people provided many credible accounts of specific abuses by Soviet and government forces: arbitrary arrest, detention without trial, torture, execution, the killing of prisoners, individual and collective rape, the killing of women and children, the bombardment of villages, and the massacre of civilians. Not surprisingly, the witnesses were unable to give details of the units involved or their commanders. It was usually unclear whether the crimes were committed by Afghan or Soviet soldiers, though there is little doubt that Afghan soldiers were as brutal as the Russians in their treatment of Afghan civilians.[16] The AJP report, which accepted that the Soviets had ended the mass slaughter which took place under Taraki and Amin, nevertheless concluded that they bore a general responsibility even for abuses committed by their allies because of their entrenched position in the Afghan government and military.[17]

The insurgents were also guilty of major abuses. The Pakistan-based groups threatened women who failed to conform to their strict ideas of Islamic propriety, assassinated opponents, and maintained prisons in Pakistan where they held, tortured, and in some cases executed Afghan refugees they suspected of opposing them.[18] They systematically, and often indiscriminately, wiped out 'collaborators' and 'spies' inside Afghanistan, sometimes with their families, sometimes whole villages.[19] In one incident in the Pandsher Valley, Masud's men are said to have taken prisoner a thousand men from the 14th Afghan Brigade and shot the lot, so that the river ran red with blood.[20]

The atrocities committed by the mujahedin were in part a reaction to the brutality of the invaders and the Afghan government forces; but they were also a reflection of traditional Afghan methods of warfare. In autumn 1989 Andrei Greshnov interviewed Mohamed Hamid, a highly intelligent rebel prisoner, in the Kabul interrogation prison. Greshnov asked him about the popular attitude to Soviet soldiers. 'It varied. In general nobody was happy with the arrival of foreign forces, or with the government which they had put in place. I personally saw what the *shuravi* (Soviets) got up to in the provinces: they would wipe out whole villages in retaliation for one rifle shot. You yourself travel round the country and have seen for yourself how poorly people live there. People live comparatively well only in the cities. I thought a great deal about what was going on in my country and wrote to my brother, who was studying in the USSR. He and I have taken a different path in life. Part of the population of course supports the present regime. But those who do that are already infidels and they will have to pay for the blood of Muslims that they have shed.'

Greshnov asked whether Hamid had ever had to kill Soviet soldiers, or to take part in the torture of prisoners. He answered, 'I had to fight, not with my tongue but with a machine gun. People who wanted to cut off heads went ahead and did it. People who didn't want to didn't do it. Incidentally, torture and the cutting off of heads are not some kind of special regime thought up especially for Soviet soldiers. Any infidel can end up without his head, including an Afghan. Everybody has his own view of the world. Some people cut off heads, others don't. I prefer to sell my enemy for cash to people who are willing to buy, rather than to torture him. I saw that in the province of Logar. In the region of Sorkhab we destroyed a column and took several Soviet prisoners. They cut off the heads of the soldiers but they sold the officers. Prisoners were mostly sold to Germany, where they were bought by various human rights bodies who paid good money for them.'[21]

The mujahedin were willing to bargain with the Soviets as well. A Soviet officer of Tajik origin based in Shindand, Feliks Rakhmonov, was responsible for relations with the local population. He was liked both by the soldiers and by the Afghans, with whom he maintained contact. The locals would bring back soldiers who carelessly allowed themselves to be taken prisoner. On one occasion the Afghans brought Rakhmonov three soldiers in a donkey cart. The prisoners' hands were tied with their own belts. Rakhmonov exchanged the prisoners for some flour and several canisters of diesel oil. After that – not surprisingly – the number of Soviet soldiers who were taken for profit began to rise.[22]

The AJP report was highly critical of the Russians and the Afghan government. But it was equally clear about the abuses committed by the mujahedin. It gave names of commanders and their bands for the period of the Soviet war. It went on to document in considerable detail the crimes committed by all sides during the civil war, including the forces commanded by Masud and Hekmatyar – the bombardment by rockets and aircraft, the massacre and rape, which laid waste much of Kabul in 1993 and 1994 and resulted in an estimated twenty-five thousand dead between January and June 1994; the murderous regime of the Taliban which followed; and the atrocities on both sides which accompanied the American-backed campaign to expel the Taliban in 2001.[23] These equalled, if not exceeded, the horrors that occurred between 1979 and 1989.

It is not easy to get these stories into a proper perspective. Atrocity stories spread like wildfire in all wars. Some are true. Some are exaggerated in the telling. Some are invented for purposes of propaganda. The revolt of the Netherlands in the sixteenth century, the Thirty Years War in Germany, the French occupation in Spain during the Napoleonic Wars, the Indian Rising in 1857, were all rich in such stories. Even the comparatively clean fighting on the Western Front in the First World War produced the stories, or rather the myths, of the Belgian nuns raped and murdered by German soldiers and the Canadian sergeant crucified with bayonets.

Atrocities are especially prevalent, and especially horrific, in civil wars, and in wars of intervention by a technologically superior force against a determined national insurgency. The figures can never be reliably established, and the facts are too easily twisted for the purposes of controversy. Western propaganda successfully portrayed the 40th Army as particularly brutal in its conduct of the war in Afghanistan. Accusations that the Russians used chemical weapons were common at the beginning of the war. They seem to have used some kind of tear gas at some time: but reports of the systematic use of lethal gases were never verified and eventually faded. There were stories that both sides used booby traps and explosive devices disguised to look like everyday objects such as watches and pens. Much play was made with the story, which figured in a UN report of 1985 as well as in Western propaganda, that the KGB deliberately designed mines to look like children's toys, in order to sow a particularly vicious kind of terror among ordinary Afghans. The Russians countered with stories that this was a tactic of the mujahedin and published photographs to back their claim. The story may have had its origin in the tiny 'butterfly' mines made of brightly coloured plastic, which were scattered from helicopters along rebel trails and supply routes. They were supposed to deactivate themselves after a given period, but often the deactivation mechanism did not work. But these devices were not the product of the twisted imagination of the KGB's engineers. They were directly copied from the American Dragontooth BLU-43/B and BLU-44/B mines, used in very large numbers in Indo-China. They were intended to maim rather than to kill, since a wounded soldier is more trouble to his comrades than a dead one. The official name of the Soviet version was PFM-1, but the soldiers called them *lepestki* (petals). It is not surprising that children should have found them attractive, and that they and their parents should have reported them to journalists as disguised toys. But the experts in the Mine Action Coordination Centre of Afghanistan, whose job it was to know about these things, believed that the story 'gained a life for obvious journalist reasons – but it has we think no basis in widespread fact'.[24]

Disillusion

Whatever overall judgement one comes to about the nature of the war in Afghanistan, one thing is clear. As the war progressed and devastation spread throughout the country, the politicians and generals who had looked for a quick resolution to their problem, and the enthusiasts who had hoped to contribute something to the future of Afghanistan, all began to despair.

The war in Afghanistan was supposed to be secret, and for the first few years the Politburo took drastic measures to ensure that it remained so. Soldiers posted to Afghanistan were told to keep quiet about it. Soldiers returning to the Soviet Union were not allowed into Moscow at the time of the Olympic Games in 1980, for fear that they would talk to the foreign visitors.[25] The local Voenkomats sternly ordered the families of soldiers killed in Afghanistan not to tell anyone of the circumstances of their death.[26] In the first few years of the war, the government made it as hard as it could for ordinary people to discover what was going on.

The official line was that Soviet soldiers were performing their 'international duty' in Afghanistan, but that this involved no fighting. The television carried endless programmes showing Soviet and Afghan soldiers locked in warm embraces, Soviet doctors treating Afghan children, military propaganda units winning hearts and minds, Soviet women meeting the women of Afghanistan, soldiers handing out food and medicine, smiles everywhere.

This led to many absurdities. In 1980, according to the writer Vladimir Voinovich, the censor objected to a passage in a film about Sherlock Holmes in which Holmes deduces that Watson has returned disillusioned from the Second Anglo-Afghan War: instead he was said to have returned from a war 'in some Eastern country'.[27]

As late as 1985, the year Gorbachev came to power, strict rules were still being formulated about what journalists could and could not publish about the war. A list drawn up by the Ministry of Defence and the Foreign Ministry, signed by Kryuchkov and Varennikov, said that the media could report the death or wounding of Soviet military personnel in the execution of their military duty, the repulse of rebels' attacks, and the execution of tasks connected with giving international help to the Afghan people. There was to be no reporting of military actions by units larger than a company, nor about battlefield experience. There was to be no direct television reporting from the battlefield. Journalists could report the heroism of soldiers who had been made Heroes of the Soviet Union, but not the details of the units in which they served.[28] Similar rules were applied by the British army in Afghanistan two decades later: journalists embedded with the military could be forbidden from reporting the composition of forces, details of military movements, operational orders, casualties, place names, tactics, names or number of ships, unit or aircraft and names of individual servicemen. The difference was that the later war was also covered by journalists operating independently of the British military, who could report as they liked if they were prepared to take the considerable risks involved.

Of course, once the coffins started coming home, it became practically impossible to maintain the fiction, despite the best efforts of the Politburo. The decision which they took on 30 July 1981 is a measure of how far out of touch these old men were with political reality, and how little they understood the real limits of their authoritarian power. It had been proposed that each bereaved family should be given a thousand roubles for a headstone on the grave. But Mikhail Suslov, the Politburo's ideologist, asked, '[Is it] politically desirable at this point to raise memorials and write the whole story on the headstones? After all in some cemeteries there will be several such graves.' Andropov agreed that, though of course the soldiers must be buried with honour, it was a bit too early to put up headstones, and the others concurred. Suslov concluded, 'We must work out what to say in answer to parents whose children have died in Afghanistan. There should be no improvisation. The answers should be laconic and standardised.'[29]

For years there were indeed no proper memorials. The fallen were not greeted on their return with military honour and municipal ceremony as – one soldier, Andrei Blinushov, bitterly noted at the time – they would have been in America. Instead they were returned to their families by night, buried in hugger-mugger, in a miasma of threats of retribution if the shroud of secrecy was broken. Official edict was tempered by individual acts of humanity, as it often is in Russia. But few government decisions were so bitterly resented as this one.

The government's attempts to impose secrecy were futile from the start and began to fray almost at once. In July 1980 Andrei Sakharov reinforced his early call for the withdrawal of Soviet troops in an interview with American television from his place of exile in the Volga city of Gorki (after the collapse of the Soviet Union once again called Nizhni Novgorod). He backed the interview with an open letter to the Soviet leadership. 'I am addressing you on a matter of the highest importance,' he began. 'The war in Afghanistan has already been going on for seven months. Thousands of Soviet people have been killed and tens of thousands of Afghans – not only partisans, but above all peaceful citizens, old men, women, children, peasants, and townspeople. More than a million Afghans have become refugees. There are particularly ominous reports of the bombing of villages suspected of helping the partisans, of the mining of mountain roads which threatens whole regions with starvation.'

Ordinary people may not have been as well informed or as courageous as Sakharov, and in later years many of them claimed that they had not realised what was going on in Afghanistan until Gorbachev opened things up with glasnost after 1985. It was not as simple as that. People were inhibited by the official news blackout and by a kind of self-censorship which was very widespread at the time. It was hard to break away from the conventions and conformities of Soviet life, especially for those who had originally supported the war. Many of those who knew what was going on – diplomats, politicians, scholars, advisers – were appalled by what they knew, but kept their mouths shut. 'I'm ashamed to say that, until I learned better, I too divided everything into black and white, friends and enemies, revolution and counter-revolution. Now I remember that bitterly. But perhaps I didn't want to think? Perhaps I was afraid to ask myself the difficult questions? Wasn't it just easier to live that way? My consciousness had become set in concrete, and it was a lengthy journey from being imprisoned by dogma to understanding,' the journalist Vladimir Snegirev wrote later. 'One can hardly demand civic courage from people who lived in the [Brezhnev] era of stagnation and mouthed the standard phrases expected from them. Let everyone look into himself and, if he can, let him remember where, when, how, on what occasions he hid behind a falsehood, failed to stand up for the truth, didn't oppose injustice. No doubt all of us can draw up our own secret list.'[30]

Nevertheless the news seeped through even this veil of self-censorship. Within little more than a month from the invasion, stories were circulating in Moscow that the hospitals in Tashkent were full of wounded soldiers, that aircraft were flying home with coffins, that mourning portraits were being displayed in several Moscow institutions that had sent their specialists to Afghanistan. Soldiers, journalists, nurses, and civilian officials were already returning; and they were gossiping despite the ban. Soldiers told their mothers, the mothers told their neighbours. The rumours spread like wildfire and were often exaggerated in the telling.[31] Alexander Kartsev, the young intelligence officer who was then still a military cadet, heard at his sister's wedding in January 1980 from a soldier who had taken part in the storming of Amin's palace only a few weeks earlier. There was a relentless torrent of news about Afghanistan on foreign radio stations broadcasting to the Soviet Union. And once the zinc coffins started to turn up in small villages and towns throughout Russia, the cat was out of the bag. As one reader wrote to *Komsomolskaya Pravda* a couple of years into the war, 'Don't try to hush things up: a soldier writes home, and the whole village knows; a coffin comes home, and the whole region knows.' [32]

The Critics Speak Out

Some brave spirits discreetly tried to bring their superiors to a sense of what was really going on. A *Pravda* correspondent called Shchedrov wrote to the Central Committee as early as November 1981 to say that the Afghan government was failing completely to take back the countryside from the rebels. People were willing to cooperate with the authorities, but on one condition – that they were adequately protected against retaliation by the government forces. This condition could not be met even in the vicinity of major Soviet bases: the authorities might control the territory by day, but the rebels controlled it by night. Even successful military operations, apparently, could not alter this basic fact.[33]

A persistent critic was Colonel Leonid Shershnev. He made a habit of going into the villages, listening to what the inhabitants had to say and trying to understand their needs. It was he who had helped to write the pamphlet on Afghan traditions and culture which was handed out to officers and men of the 40th Army. In 1981 he was involved with the 190th Military Agitation Propaganda Detachment (BAPO), one of a number of units formed to win the hearts and minds of the Afghan people.[34] The detachment contained a Soviet doctor, a cinema operator, a youth adviser, two or three political officers, a group of young Afghan artists, Party propagandists, and a mullah. The plan was for the group to go into the villages north of Kabul to hand out food, cure the sick, and show films to the peasantry. Some shine was taken off the enterprise because it had to be escorted by a couple of armoured personnel carriers and a flail tank to clear mines. The simple view of the cheerful tank commander was that the only good Afghan was a dead Afghan.

Shershnev concluded that the war was bound to escalate unless the army was involved not only in fighting, but in helping the local people. He wrote in a report to his superiors, 'Since the end of March 1981 the military and political situation almost everywhere in Afghanistan has ground to a halt. The position in the country is now worse than it was in the same period last year. It is striking that the situation has become extremely serious even in regions where there were no large rebel bands, and where the geographical conditions are not conducive to their activities (the north, the plains, the areas bordering on the USSR). That means that part of the population which consists of national minorities related to peoples in the USSR (Uzbeks, Turkmens, Tajiks), who had previously adopted a wait and see attitude, have now joined in the fight against the people's power [the Communist government] and the Soviet forces.

'The enemy are striking in the most sensitive places: they are killing Party activists, patriots (including village elders), they are getting astride all the strategic lines of communication and interrupting transport, they are destroying important economic objects (they have blown up two drilling rigs at the Ainaksk copper mine each worth 200,000 roubles), schools (they have destroyed 1,400 already), hospitals, administrative buildings. Agriculture is suffering serious losses: the number of cattle is falling irreversibly ... The rebels have succeeded in driving the people's power out of a number of districts and regions which were liberated last winter, and have imposed counter-revolutionary organs of power (the so-called "Islamic committees").' He went on to criticise the Afghan political leadership and army. He praised the military skill of the rebels, and warned that they would not only be able to resist the weak Kabul regime for a long time, but would also be able to show a determined opposition to the Soviet forces.

When he put these ideas to his superiors, the deputy commander of the 40th Army told him that his job was to think of his soldiers, not the Afghans. He appealed to Akhromeev, who listened to him attentively, but then told him, 'The army exists to fight. It's not its job to get mixed up in politics.'[35]

Shershnev was not alone. Even so senior a figure as General Alexander Maiorov, the Chief Soviet Military Adviser in the early part of the war, soon came to the view that the war in Afghanistan was unwinnable. He never abandoned the belief that the Soviet Union had followed its legitimate interests by intervening in Afghanistan: the intervention was a consequence of the Cold War logic which led each of the superpowers to try to steal a march on the other wherever it could. But Afghans he respected, some of them serving officers in the Afghan army, told him that Afghanistan could not be conquered; it could perhaps be bought, but the Soviet Union was not rich enough for that. Babrak Karmal, he could see for himself, was weak, and often drunk. He concluded that Karmal should be replaced and that the Soviet Union should withdraw its forces as soon as it could.[36]

In 1984 Shershnev went further, and wrote a long and critical report directly to the General Secretary of the Party, Konstantin Chernenko. He said that military operations in Afghanistan had taken on the character of punitive campaigns, the civilian population was treated with systematic and massive brutality, weapons were used casually and without justification, homes were destroyed, mosques defiled, and looting was widespread. 'We have got ourselves into a war against the people, which is without prospects.'

Surprisingly, Shershnev got away with it. Chernenko scribbled on his report, 'Shershnev is not to be touched.' Shershnev was not sidelined or expelled from the armed forces, partly because he was protected by like-minded senior officers such as General Dmitri Volkogonov, who at that time was head of the Main Political Directorate of the Armed Forces. But his promotion was delayed, and in the end his career came up against the buffers and he resigned from the army in 1991.

Another military critic, Colonel Tsagolov, was less lucky. In August 1987 he wrote a personal and highly critical letter to Yazov, the Minister of Defence. He said in round terms that the Soviet military effort in Afghanistan had produced no results: 'Huge material resource and considerable casualties did not produce a positive end result.' Najibullah's Policy of National Reconciliation would not lead to a breakthrough in the military or political situation, since the regime was rejected in the villages, where most Afghans lived. The PDPA was a broken reed and past saving and the idea of a coalition between the PDPA and any of the seven party leaders in Pakistan was an illusion. Tsagolov recommended 'radical measures' to help progressive forces preserve democracy in Afghan society, and rebuild friendship between the Soviet Union and Afghanistan. These thoughts were too abstract to be of any use. After Yazov failed to respond, Tsagolov took them to *Ogonek*, the campaigning newspaper, and was sacked from the army.[37]

There was dissatisfaction lower down the army as well. Rastem Makhmutov was a professional soldier, a *praporshchik*. He arrived in Afghanistan with the 86oth Independent Motor-rifle Regiment. Six months after he returned to the Soviet Union in the autumn of 1982, he resigned from the army in protest. Other officers who did the same had to apply several times to get out; there would be warnings and harassment, and some had to face a Court of Honour. Makhmutov was comparatively lucky. He got out of the army unscathed and was employed for a while as a test engineer in a factory building rocket engines, where he regularly gave talks about the war to his fellow workers, illustrated with the photographs he had taken in Afghanistan, much to the irritation of the authorities. Then for a while he lived an alternative lifestyle as a bearded goatherd on the Volga. Finally he settled down to run a small business in Moscow.[38]

The main priority of the ordinary soldiers, as with most soldiers in most wars, was not to worry about the politics, or to change the course of events, but to fight as best they could, support their comrades in a scrimmage, and get home safe and sound. 'The propaganda in the Soviet Union was very strong,' said Alexander Gergel, the sergeant gunner from the 86oth Independent Motor-rifle Regiment. 'However bizarre it may seem today and even though I and my comrades knew that our country had got itself into a dead end, we never doubted the final objective – liberty, fraternity, and equality for everyone on the planet. Even the cynics believed in their hearts in the justice of their mission as "warrior-internationalists" in Afghanistan.'[39]

For most soldiers, indeed, doubt and criticism were not an option. People have blamed the army and its leadership for going along with the criminal policies of the political leadership, wrote General Lyakhovski. 'But when an army begins to choose which orders it will carry out and which it will not, it ceases to be an army. It is an old truth that an army does not act in accordance with anything except its orders. It bows neither to common sense nor to necessity nor to anything else. That is what distinguishes it from any other institution. That is what makes it vulnerable.'[40]

People Turn against the War – and the Army
In 1982 a newsreader on the Soviet overseas broadcasting service called Danchev started inserting phrases into his English-language broadcasts such as 'The people of Afghanistan are playing an important role in the struggle to defend their country against the Soviet occupiers' and 'The tribes living in Kandahar and Paktia provinces have joined the struggle against the Soviet invaders.' Danchev's words were played back into the Soviet Union by the foreign broadcasters. Surprisingly, he kept out of trouble for a year. But in May 1983 he overreached himself and attacked the Soviet invasion in three separate bulletins, one after the other. He was expelled from the Party, sacked from his job, and put into a psychiatric hospital.

By then, however, public opinion in the Soviet Union was also turning against the war, and criticism was becoming more vocal and widespread among ordinary people. Letters were coming into Soviet Party bodies and newspapers from all over the country, especially from those who had relatives fighting in Afghanistan or who had lost them there. Shershnev did an analysis of the letters reaching *Komsomolskaya Pravda* which was passed on to Marshal Sokolov, the head of the Ministry of Defence's Operational Group in Afghanistan. The analysis showed how much ordinary people knew about the war even in the first years, and how little they believed in the official propaganda about the soldiers doing their 'international duty', defending the April 1978 Revolution, and helping the Afghan people.

Most of the letters were from mothers whose sons had been killed, or were serving in Afghanistan or due to be called up. Others came from soldiers' sisters and fiancées, or from boys of military age. The letters touched on a variety of themes. There was grief for sons and contemporaries who had died in the war, and fear for those who might be sent there. Parents with only one son suffered in particular. Some correspondents roundly asserted that there was no justification for what was going on in Afghanistan: 'The blood of our sons is being spilled in a foreign land for the interests of foreigners'; 'He died without honour or glory in a foreign land'; 'What right does our government have to keep our forces in Afghanistan?' Service in Afghanistan carried no prestige: one writer compared it with being sent to forced labour in exile. Feeling against the war was growing: the Afghan Communist regime was supported by Soviet bayonets. 'It's their revolution, let them defend it.' People complained about the indifference and callousness of the authorities' attitude and the bureaucratic way they dealt with the relatives of those who had died. They made requests and suggestions for commemorating them. They complained about the inadequacy of official information: 'How revolting it is to read the articles about Afghanistan in the newspapers, nothing but soothing rubbish!'[41]

Opinion turned not only against the war, but against the soldiers who had fought in it, even though most of them had been unwilling conscripts. Stories of the brutality of the war, the massive destruction of villages, livelihoods, and civilian lives, were now becoming widespread. Few seemed to pause to think that it was unjust to blame the individuals who had been sent to fight by their political leaders in a war of intervention which by its nature was likely to be particularly atrocious. One young woman from a middle-class background first heard about the involvement of Soviet troops in Afghanistan right at the beginning, when she was in a Komsomol camp in the winter of 1980. She was fourteen at the time. She and her friends knew that they were not meant to talk about what they had heard and they did not criticise what had happened. But nobody tried to defend it either. Two years later she feared her boyfriend might get drafted and told his father, who was in the military, that the war was a crime.

By the time she got to Moscow University in 1983 rumours were beginning to circulate about the terrible atrocities committed by Soviet soldiers. She was shocked by the story she was told by one of her fellow students, who had served in Afghanistan. A couple of shots came from a village his unit thought it had secured. By then it was dark, and instead of going into the village to find the sniper, the commander ordered it to be destroyed by artillery. The students were told that the mujahedin were using butterfly bombs supplied by the Americans to maim children, and blame the Soviet soldiers. But then in 1988 she heard on the radio that it was the Russians themselves who were using the butterfly bombs and she was sick at the thought of what was happening to the children.

She believed that the veterans who had been through such experiences could not have remained healthy and normal people, that they all took drugs, that all they knew about was killing, that they would all end up in the Mafia or the protection business, that they would never be able to integrate back into society. At that time she felt no sympathy for them: her impression of the Afgantsy was of a dark menacing force that was beyond help and needed to be managed.

By the late 1980s the Soviet press was full of stories about the war. For people of her education and age, who were in Moscow in good schools at that time, Afghanistan was a terrible crime, the invasion was inexcusable, and the war had to be stopped by all means. They compared it with the American war in Vietnam and the atrocities committed there. They looked for parallels in the American movies *The Deer Hunter* and *Platoon*. They were never impressed by the argument that the soldiers were only obeying orders. They found the entire concept of that war repulsive.

In the 1990s her attitude began to change. The only two Afghan veterans she knew well were very happy and friendly and normal. One was legendary for his happy and sunny outlook and his love for life. Another chose to interrupt his studies in MGIMO, the elite Moscow State Institute for International Relations, in order to serve in a special forces unit in Afghanistan. He too was an extremely happy person, very extroverted and artistic. She understood that the soldiers in Afghanistan were ordinary boys who had had no choice but to serve when and where they did.[42]

The criticism of the army's performance in Afghanistan grew manyfold once it became possible to publish such things openly after Gorbachev introduced a measure of freedom in the Soviet press. The contrast between the feeling that they had suffered much, but done their duty, and the attitudes of indifference or even hostility that they encountered among their own people was one of the hardest things the soldiers had to bear when they eventually got home.

The bitterness was forcefully expressed by Vladimir Plastun and Vladimir Andrianov, both of whom were in Afghanistan during the war: 'We have to try to get at [the fundamental reasons why our policy got into a dead end in Afghanistan], even though it is painful. It is not pleasant to look at the evil you have done, *even though you may have convinced yourself that you were proceeding from the best motives.* But it is essential to do that, because the word "Afghanistan" will be associated for many years in the consciousness of honest Soviet citizens with the shame of the Russian people, a stain on the Communist Party of the Soviet Union, the blood of our boys, and the incomprehensible tasks that were given to them (if indeed any such tasks existed), and with the hatred of those who sent us into the "Afghan quagmire" and raised up so much hatred towards us.'[43]

These emotions did not swell into open anti-government protests, as feeling against the Vietnam War had done a decade earlier in America. The massive public demonstrations in the great cities of the Soviet Union still lay in the future and were directed not against the war, which by then was over, but against the fundamental tenets and pillars of the Soviet regime, the Communist Party, the secret police, the injustice, and the economic mismanagement. But they provided a political background which the country's leaders were increasingly unable to ignore as they struggled to find a way out of the mess they had got themselves into in Afghanistan.

PART III

THE LONG GOODBYE

Down from the heights which once we commanded,
With burning feet we descend to the ground.
Bombarded with calumny, slander and lies,
We're leaving, we're leaving, we're leaving.

Farewell, you mountains, you know best
What men we were in that far land;
Now judge us fairly for what we did,
You chair-bound critics who stayed at home.

Farewell, you mountains, you know best
The price we paid while we were here,
What foes unconquered still survive;
What friends we had to leave behind.

Farewell, bright world, Afghanistan,
Perhaps we should forget you now.
But sadness grips us as we go:
We're leaving, we're leaving, we're leaving.

Igor Morozov, May 1988[1]

ELEVEN

GOING HOME

The system in the 40th Army for bringing in new recruits and demobilising the veterans was shot through with its own rituals and conducted with that mixture of inefficiency, brutality, and creative flexibility characteristic of the Soviet system as a whole.

As professionals, officers could usually count on getting home leave at least once during their time of service in Afghanistan. Leave was not always a satisfactory experience, even for those who could get it. Wives and other female relatives expected presents from the exotic markets of Afghanistan, which you could not always get through the customs. And the men would ask you how many people you had killed. The contrast between the reality of the fighting and the almost total inability of the civilians to understand what was really going on was sometimes too much to bear. Like British officers who came home from the trenches in France during the First World War, Soviet officers would sometimes cut short their leave in order to return to the raw but familiar simplicities of the fighting.[1]

Demobilisation

The conscript soldiers were not entitled to go home on leave, though they would be sent to the Soviet Union if they were sufficiently badly wounded, and could sometimes get back for compassionate reasons, such as the death of a very close family member. Their lives were subject to a different rhythm. Twice a year – usually on 27 March and 27 September – the Soviet press would carry a *Prikaz*, an order signed by the Minister of Defence, setting the date for the demobilisation of soldiers called up two years previously. The *Prikaz* for March 1985 read:

> In accordance with the Law of the USSR 'On universal military service', I order:
>
> 1. Personnel who have completed the period of active military service laid down are to be released from the ranks of the Soviet army, the navy, the frontier and internal forces into the reserve in April–June 1985.
>
> 2. In connection with the release into the reserve of military personnel, as indicated in point 1 of the present order, male citizens who have reached the age of 18 before the call-up date are to be called up for active service in the Soviet army, the navy, the frontier and internal forces, as are older citizens of military age who no longer have the right to deferment.
>
> 3. This order is to be promulgated in all companies, batteries, squadrons, and ships.
>
> Minister of Defence of the USSR,
Marshal of the Soviet Union S. Sokolov

The long-awaited publication of this order set off a flurry of activity among those due for demobilisation. These soldiers were known in army jargon as *dembels*, and the process of military bureaucracy and traditional ritual which accompanied them on their departure was obscurely named the *dembelski akkord*, which covered the period – perhaps three months, the *stodnevka*, or 'hundred days' – from the publication of the *Prikaz* to the date on which the soldier actually left Afghanistan.

There was an understanding that the *dembels* should not be sent on dangerous operations during this period. Vitali Krivenko refers to an order to this effect by the Ministry of Defence, which he believed was a response to the letters the Ministry was receiving from the parents of soldiers who were killed on the eve of their return.[2] The understanding was often breached in practice. One group due for demobilisation in February 1987 spent the two previous months on an operation, and arrived back in camp at night, unshaven and dirty, hours before they were due to leave for the Soviet Union. They managed to scrub themselves down and shave, their comrades cut their hair for them, and by the morning they were on parade by the regimental headquarters, smartened up and ready to leave.

The rituals of departure varied. The *dembel's* comrades would have a whip-round so that he could buy presents for the people back home. But there was an official rule that only goods which had been bought in the army shops could be taken back to the Soviet Union. Things bought in the Afghan shops – Japanese tape recorders, cameras, designer clothing, trainers, everything that the soldiers most wanted – risked being confiscated by the Soviet customs officials, who, the soldiers suspected, simply took them for themselves. This was true even of the modest things that were all most ordinary soldiers could afford: a scarf for one's mother, cosmetics for one's girlfriend, a Japanese watch, condoms, musical picture postcards, to say nothing of the pornography with which Afghanistan was by then awash. Some soldiers decided it would be simpler to buy their presents back in Tashkent. But there was a problem here too: the soldiers got hold of Afghan notes and Soviet military currency by a variety of means, most of them illegal. Rates of exchange varied and some notes had magnetic stripes which meant that their provenance could be identified. So there was a real risk that the customs officials would relieve them of their money as well.[3]

Then the *dembel* would have to prepare his dress uniform. The less fortunate would dig out their old parade uniform, crumpled and dirty as it was, and soak it for a week in engine oil to restore the dark colour, clean it in petrol, and hang it out for a month to air. The belt would be brought to a brilliant white, its buckle to a dazzling shine, and an aiguillette braided out of parachute cord.[4] Luckier soldiers might have been issued with the *eksperimentalka*, a new kind of uniform which was being tried out in Afghanistan from about 1985 and looked better than the standard outfit.

The departing soldier would also put together a *dembelski albom*, a scrapbook covering his time in Afghanistan, full of photographs, stories, drawings, diaries, and other material. This was frowned on by the military authorities, who feared that the photographs in particular might breach security. But their attempts to suppress the practice were unsuccessful.

On leaving their unit the departing soldiers would be addressed by the political officer, who would tell them what they could and could not talk about when they got home. The line was that the 40th Army was 'great, powerful and morally healthy'. There was to be no mention of casualties or the brutal nature of the fighting. All photographs and films were to be destroyed. Needless to say, many soldiers ignored all these injunctions: luckily, because a great many of their photographs have survived.[5]

Vitali Krivenko's *dembelski akkord* lasted from May until August 1987. The convention that *dembels* should not go on dangerous operations was waived in his case too. He had prepared all his kit ready for departure, when his regiment was sent off in July on an operation to clear the mujahedin out of Herat. For the first time in his service, he and his company of the 12th Guards Motor-rifle Regiment were landed by helicopter in the mountains in an attempt to cut off the rebels' line of retreat. Six men in his company were wounded and a fully loaded ambulance helicopter was shot down. Krivenko got a small piece of shrapnel in his foot: a nearby parachute captain cut it out and he was little the worse. The mujahedin withdrew in good order; so did the Russians, licking their wounds and carrying their dead. On their way back, Krivenko and his company were sent off on an unsuccessful attempt to intercept a caravan, shot up a couple of villages where the caravan might have been hiding, and got back to base on 1 August.[6]

He and the four other soldiers who were due to leave were up until midnight shaving, packing, sorting out their uniform, and scurrying round the base trying to raise money. He hid his money among some sweets at the bottom of his bag, and a couple of cakes of cannabis in a box of Indian tea, and was ready for the journey.

Next morning their officers thanked them for their service, wished them well, and sent them off by road to Shindand, and thence by air to Tashkent. There Krivenko was pleasantly surprised that the customs officials merely asked if they had any weapons or drugs; when they said, 'No,' they were allowed to go on their way. They were lucky. They met another group of returning soldiers who were so incensed by the behaviour of the customs officials that they refused to hand over their presents and started to smash them up instead. An ugly scene was averted only when an officer intervened and ordered the customs officials to let the goods through.

Tashkent was seething with returning soldiers, but Krivenko and his comrades were mystified that there was no vodka to be had: they had not appreciated the impact of Gorbachev's ban on alcohol. They made do with cannabis instead. The police and the military patrols ignored them.

On the train, it turned out that the conductor did have vodka to sell. The soldiers settled down to drink, play their guitars, and tell their tales. The passengers at first seemed afraid of them, but then decided that they were not bloodthirsty murderers after all. There was only one unfortunate incident. As the bottles were emptied, the conductor put the price up outrageously. The soldiers went to his cabin, had a firm word with him, and relieved him of his remaining bottles. They heard no more from him and finished their journey in peace.

Black Tulips

The majority of those who served in Afghanistan returned home, safe, sick, wounded, or disabled. But many of them did not. The return of the dead was an altogether grimmer affair. The ultimate symbol of the war for many Russians was the Black Tulip, the big AN-12 four-engined cargo plane – the equivalent of the American Hercules – that brought the bodies of the fallen back from Afghanistan. For decades after the war Alexander Rozenbaum's song 'The Black Tulip' could still bring a Russian audience to its feet in silent homage to the dead. There were several stories about how the planes got their romantic name, none of them authenticated.

The nightmare started back in Afghanistan, where the bodies were prepared in the regimental or divisional morgues for their journey home. The morgues were usually in tents or small huts, sometimes with a few more tents attached, on the edge of the garrison territory, under the command of a lieutenant. Inside the morgue there would be a metal table, where the corpse was be cleaned, repaired as far as possible, and dressed in its uniform. It was then placed in a zinc coffin and the lid soldered down. Marked 'Not to be opened', the coffin was placed in a crude wooden box, on which the name of the deceased was stencilled. The box was now ready to be loaded on to the Black Tulip.

The temperature, the humidity, and the stench inside the morgue made the work unbearable for the young conscripts sweltering in their rubber aprons and gloves, although it had the advantage that you did not have to risk your life out on an operation. The men were perpetually drunk and lived in a world of their own. It was bad luck to cross their path if you were going out on a mission and the other soldiers avoided them. They ate at their own separate table in the canteen, glad not to get on friendly terms with men whose torn bodies they might later find themselves piecing together in the morgue.

Indeed it was often difficult to identify the bodies, or to be sure that the right coffin had been given the right name. On his arrival in Afghanistan, Sergei Nikiforov was put in charge of a little medical unit on the strength of a half-completed medical training before the war. He was taken by the doctor, a major, to see the regimental morgue. It was a small hut surrounded by tents. The smell hit him even before he entered. Inside, two soldiers, completely drunk, were picking through a pile of body parts. Another soldier wheeled in a trolley on which there was a long tin box. The two soldiers filled the box with a collection of human bits and pieces which seemed to bear some resemblance to one another, then the box was sent off for the lid to be welded on.

'How many so far?' the major asked.

'That was the twentieth. Five more to go.'

Once outside, the major poured so much alcohol into Nikiforov that his eyes nearly popped out. 'Don't worry,' said the major. 'You'll see worse than that before you're finished. Try not to drink yourself to death, though you'll find it difficult. What you've just seen doesn't happen all that often. A reconnaissance patrol was ambushed, the mujahedin chopped them to pieces, put them in sacks, commandeered a lorry, and sent them back to us as a present.'[7]

For the journey back to the Soviet Union, the boxes were given the neutral code name 'Cargo 200'. Andrei Blinushov, a soldier from

Ryazan in central Russia, who in later life became a writer and human rights activist, was called up in the spring of 1983 and sent off to serve in the headquarters platoon of the garrison in Izhevsk in the Urals. Late one night, some of the grandfathers were called out to pick up a 'Cargo 200'. They barely looked up from their television sets, but delegated the task immediately to their juniors. And that was how Blinushov first came across the Black Tulip.

He and his comrades were taken by the political officer of the HQ platoon, an apparently self-confident lieutenant, straight to the local airport and right up to a large cargo plane standing in the darkness. The hold of the Black Tulip was packed with large boxes, crudely knocked together in wood, piled three high, each with a name scribbled on it. Inside was a *praporshchik*, blind drunk, who ordered them to load the boxes on to their truck and take them to the city morgue.

It was a small building and it was already full of corpses. So the boxes – by now Blinushov had gathered that they contained the bodies of soldiers who had died in Afghanistan – were piled in the corridor. No proper death certificates had been filled out before the bodies had been sealed in their zinc coffins and then cased in wood. So – without any means of checking whether the contents of the coffins matched the names on the boxes – the morgue officials solemnly wrote out the documentation without which the coffins could not be delivered for burial to the relatives of the dead.

Even in 1983 the government was still trying to maintain the fiction that the Soviet troops were not engaged in combat, but merely fulfilling their 'international duty' to help the Afghan people. So the coffins were delivered to the families at dead of night. It was a futile precaution. On almost every occasion the word got out in advance, and the relatives, neighbours, and friends were already waiting when the lorry drove up, the wooden box was broken open, and the zinc coffin delivered to the family.

That first night, Blinushov and his comrades carried the coffin – it contained the body of a helicopter pilot – up seven flights of stairs to the apartment where the man's wife lived, white-faced, unable to cry, clutching her new baby. A neighbour came in to help find somewhere for the coffin to rest. And then the young woman started to scream.

The soldiers somehow slid away, hurtled down the stairs, and rejoined their officer. He had been unable to face the scene and had remained in the lorry.

As time passed, commanders in Afghanistan would sometimes allow an officer or a *praporshchik* to escort the body: usually it was the body of a soldier who been awarded a posthumous medal for gallantry. Cross-examining the escort was, among other things, a good way for the people back home to find out what was going on in Afghanistan.

One young captain, a helicopter pilot, came to deliver the body of a comrade from the same squadron. He showed Blinushov photos – taken illegally, of course – of life in the field: soldiers dressed in an odd mixture of uniform and civilian clothes, and Afghan villages reduced to ruins. The young officer said that the helicopters sometimes had to attack villages when they were operating against the mujahedin. Of course women and children got killed too: he tried unconvincingly to maintain that they had been killed by the mujahedin. He was so nervous about how he would be received by his comrades' family that he asked Blinushov – a private soldier – how he should behave.

He was right to be worried. When he arrived at the house of the dead man with his escort – several soldiers and a *praporshchik* – they found an angry crowd round the house. Someone punched the *praporshchik* in the jaw, his lip was split, and his cap fell into a puddle. The women screamed, 'Murderers! Who've you brought with you! What have you done with our boy?' The men started to attack the soldiers as well, until the women shouted, 'Leave them alone. They're just as unhappy as we are. It's not their fault!'

The soldiers unpacked the wooden box and slowly took the coffin up into the apartment. It was crowded with relatives and neighbours, the mirrors were veiled in black, the women were wailing and the men were drunk. The captain stood awkwardly in the entrance, kneading his cap in his hands. When Blinushov told one of the women that the man had come all the way from Afghanistan to accompany his comrade, she rushed forward, saying, 'Please, forgive us: he was our only son.' Nervous at the prospect of being left alone, the captain tried to persuade Blinushov – they were by now on first-name terms, despite the difference in rank – to stay behind while everyone drank tea. But it was time to return to base and the soldiers left.[8]

It was not only men, of course, who returned to their homes in the zinc coffins. Alla Smolina's friend Vera Chechetova was making the short fifteen-minute flight by helicopter from her outlying base into Jalalabad when her helicopter was shot down on 14 January 1987. She had refused to wear a parachute because it wouldn't fit and because it would have spoiled her dress. It was only by the fragments of the dress that they were able to identify her body. At least, observed Smolina, that meant that her family got the right body when the coffin was delivered to them – something that by no means always happened.[9]

The Missing

If a soldier went missing in action, his family was entitled to no support until his fate had been established. A *praporshchik* from the 345th Guards Independent Parachute Assault Regiment went missing with his BTR and a driver. The BTR was found abandoned and the driver dead, but there was no trace of the *praporshchik*. His wife and two children were condemned to live in poverty.[10]

On the final day of the war, 15 February 1989, the Soviet military authorities had still not fully accounted for 333 soldiers who had gone missing in Afghanistan. Thirty-eight were definitely identified as having been taken prisoner. Forty-four had joined the mujahedin: seventeen of these had subsequently returned to the Soviet Union. To judge by their names, about a quarter of the missing and a quarter of those who served with the mujahedin were Muslims. Nineteen of the missing soldiers had managed to get abroad, to Canada, Switzerland, and the United States. Twenty-four were believed to be dead.[11]

These figures were refined in subsequent years as the authorities continued to try to discover what had happened to their soldiers. A 'Presidential Committee for Soldier-Internationalist Affairs' was set up just after the attempted coup against Gorbachev in August 1991. Following the collapse of the Soviet Union, it was jointly sponsored by all the newly independent former Soviet republics. Ruslan Aushev, who himself served in Afghanistan for four and a half years with distinction, was the first chairman of the committee, a post he still held in 2010. The committee was responsible for defending the interests of veterans of the Soviet Union's (and later Russia's) local wars. But one of its main priorities was to establish the fates of those who had gone missing in the Afghan war, to bring home those who had survived, and to find and return the remains of those who had perished.

In November 1991 the journalist Vladimir Snegirev with two British colleagues, Rory Peck and Peter Joulwan, travelled from Tajikistan over the mountains to make contact with Ahmad Shah Masud, and through him with Soviet soldiers living in Afghanistan. In the course of fourteen days Snegirev managed to meet with six former Soviet soldiers. Four of them had deserted voluntarily to the mujahedin because of the treatment they had received in the army. Two had been taken prisoner. Most had converted to Islam and several had borne arms against their compatriots. Most refused to return home.[12]

At the end of 1991 Andrei Kozyrev, Yeltsin's Foreign Minister, visited Pakistan to discuss the release of prisoners.[13] In March 1992 President Yeltsin (1931–2007) and President Bush established a 'Joint Commission on POWs and MIAs [missing in action]', partly as a result of domestic pressure inside the United States to investigate stories that US servicemen captured during the Vietnam War or even during the Second World War had been held in the Soviet Union. This commission was also given the task of establishing the fates of Soviet servicemen who had gone missing in Afghanistan. The Americans provided kits for the identification of human remains which were used, among other places, in the military morgue in Rostov-on-Don, which still contained the unidentified bodies of Russian soldiers who had died in Chechnya. After the Americans entered Afghanistan in 2001 US forces were put under standing orders to pass on any relevant information they picked up.[14]

In 1998 Ruslan Aushev held talks with Masud, and his committee organised several expeditions to Pakistan and Afghanistan. The remains of four soldiers were recovered in 2003. Six more bodies were found in 2006.[15] In May 2008 a further expedition made contact with five former soldiers who were still living in Afghanistan. One was Gennadi Tsevma from the Donetsk region, who was captured in 1983 and served with the mujahedin in the province of Kunduz. Two earlier attempts to persuade him to return home with his Afghan family and children had failed because he feared what might await him.[16]

By the twentieth anniversary of the Soviet withdrawal, in February 2009, Aushev was able to announce that the broad figures of those still missing had been whittled down to a total of 270, of whom fifty-eight, or about one-fifth, were Muslims. Twenty-two former soldiers had been found alive and most of these had returned home to Russia or to other former Soviet republics.[17]

Few Russian soldiers surrendered to the mujahedin voluntarily: their officers told them that surrender was equivalent to treason, and that they would be routinely subjected to torture if they fell into the hands of the enemy. Many preferred to destroy themselves first. But prisoners did fall into enemy hands from time to time, often because they had been wounded or otherwise incapacitated. Sometimes they were indeed killed in horrible ways. But often the mujahedin either exchanged them for men of their own in Russian or Afghan government hands, ransomed them, or used them as slaves. A number opted to go to Western countries, and their fates were naturally exploited by Western agencies as another stick with which to beat the Soviet adventure in Afghanistan. Those who did return to the Soviet Union were treated with various degrees of severity. Some were sentenced by court martial to various terms of imprisonment, though there is no record of any being shot, the punishment routinely predicted by Western propaganda. One soldier who went over to the mujahedin was exchanged for a prisoner in Soviet hands. He returned in local Afghan costume. He had not fought against his countrymen, but was sentenced to six years' hard labour.[18] Others who returned home suffered more lightly or not at all.

Aleksei Olenin, who was serving in a transport battalion, was kidnapped as he was relieving himself by the Salang Pass. He was beaten up, tried to escape, tried to hang himself, and was finally incorporated into a mujahedin detachment led by a greybeard called Sufi Puainda Mokhmad. After two months in the mountains, Olenin converted to Islam: 'No one made me do it. I simply realised that since I was still alive I must have been preserved by some power ... I would have adopted any faith that was available: after all, up to then I had been a Young Pioneer, a Komsomol, and was preparing to join the Party.' He was given the Muslim name Rakhmatula.

In the course of the next six years four other Russian soldiers were brought into the detachment. One of them was Yuri Stepanov, who was renamed Mukhibullo. He too had been captured on the Salang Pass when his *zastava* was attacked.[19]

Then the news came through that the 40th Army was leaving Afghanistan. The members of the detachment returned to their farms, and Olenin went with them: 'In those days we grew wheat. The poppies only came with the Taliban.' Sufi Puainda, who still regarded the Russians as his property, decided that they should all take wives. The Afghan fathers were reluctant to surrender their daughters, because the Russians could not afford the bride price, and because they feared that the girls would be dishonoured when the Russians eventually abandoned them and went home. But one poor man was willing to give Olenin his daughter Nargez. By now Olenin thought that his chances of returning home were in any case at an end.

He was wrong. Before the marriage could take place, the Russian government had successfully negotiated for the return of prisoners. General Dostum (1954–), the Uzbek commander in the north of the country, was anxious to strengthen his relations with the Russians and arranged for Olenin and Stepanov to travel home. He first brought their mothers to meet them in his stronghold of Mazar-i Sharif. Olenin's mother fainted when she saw him. The prisoners then left via Pakistan, where they were received by Benazir Bhutto (1953–2007): one story was that she had provided the money for their ransom. Olenin arrived back in Otradnoe in May 1994, to find a country transformed beyond his recognition by the collapse of the Soviet Union. His mother paraded the local girls before him in the hope that he would marry one of them and settle down. But his conscience weighed on him and after six months he went back to Afghanistan to find and marry Nargez. He intended to take her back to Russia. But the arrival of the Taliban in power meant that he was once again trapped in Afghanistan. His small business profited, his wife bore him a daughter, and it was not until 2004 that he finally returned again to Otradnoe, this time with his family. He remained a Muslim and the women of the village noticed that he worked harder and drank less than the other men in the village.[20] *Musulmanin* (The Muslim), a film made in 1995, explores just such a theme: the contrast between the orderly piety of a Russian Muslim convert from Afghanistan and the disorderly and dysfunctional life of the family and village he left behind him.

Nikolai Bystrov also served with the mujahedin. He was called up in spring 1982 and posted to Bagram to patrol the airport. In the middle of 1983 he and two others went – contrary to the regulations – to a *kishlak* about a mile away to buy food. One of the villagers told them that their route home would be ambushed and advised them to go a different way. That was the trap: the ambush was waiting for them there. In the resulting firefight, one soldier was killed immediately. Bystrov and the other were wounded, the latter so severely that the Afghans finished him off. One or two of the Afghans were killed as well; the others took the bodies away.

At first Bystrov was put by his captors in a house in the *kishlak* where he had been captured. When he tried to escape by climbing through a window, he got as far only as the next courtyard before he was caught and beaten, some of his teeth were knocked out, and some ribs were broken. There were two different mujahedin groups involved in his capture and they fought over who should keep him. Several were killed in the process. He was then taken off and marched after dark for two or three days with a gun stuck in his back. When he made another attempt to escape, they threatened to hang him; they showed him an Afghan soldier they had already hanged as an example.

Bystrov was then taken to the small house at Badarak, in the Pandsher Valley, which was Masud's headquarters. Everyone crowded round to look at him. Only one could speak Russian – an engineer. When Bystrov went up to greet him, Masud shook him by the hand, an unusual gesture. Masud, who knew a bit of Russian and could understand more, ate with his men and Bystrov joined them.

The next night Bystrov was taken deep into the Pandsher Valley. There were two or three Russian prisoners already there: one was called Samin and another Fedorov. They made a further attempt to escape, and were put in a cell for a month. They were properly fed and treated, and began to learn the local language. A Turkmen prisoner was brought in to join them. His name was Balashin Abdullah. There was something odd about him: they were not allowed cigarettes, but he smelled of tobacco. One day they woke up and he was no longer there. He was clearly a spy. Two or three more prisoners were brought in. Later the Russian prisoners were taken to Chayavu, where Masud's own prison was. Apparently without his knowledge they were thrown into a pit, where they spent six months. One of the Russians escaped into the mountains and was rescued by a patrol of paratroopers. When Masud turned up later, the others were moved to more decent accommodation in a stone house.

Masud offered them a choice. They could be exchanged for mujahedin prisoners in the hands of the Russians; or they could go abroad to Pakistan and on to Switzerland, Canada, or America. Twelve prisoners left for Pakistan, but Bystrov and one other remained. All of them were afraid of what might await them if they returned to the Soviet Union; but Bystrov himself thought that going to Pakistan might be equally risky.

Bystrov therefore accompanied Masud and his men into the mountains. While they were resting near the top of one of the mountain passes, Bystrov was given a Chinese automatic rifle and a flak jacket, and told that henceforth he would be one of Masud's bodyguards. Bystrov could not understand why he was being shown so much trust. He checked the weapon: it was in full working order, and there was a full supply of ammunition. He could have killed Masud and the rest of the bodyguard, and taken himself off. But he decided that, since Masud had trusted him, he should stick with him. Masud was a good judge of people.

In 1986 Bystrov married a woman from the same tribe as Masud. He remained in Masud's bodyguard until 1995, when, on Masud's advice, he returned to Russia with his wife to avoid the Taliban. Once the Taliban had been ejected, he began to visit Afghanistan again, to see his wife's relatives and to search for the remains of Soviet soldiers. His method was simple: he would go to a village where there had been a fight and ask the inhabitants where they had buried the bodies. They would tell him, then he would exhume the remains and arrange for them to be returned to Russia. He became a minor celebrity in his own country, but remained a good if somewhat melancholy Muslim.[21]

The Mothers

Because no one else seemed willing to take much responsibility for the welfare of the conscript soldiers, the mothers of the soldiers in Afghanistan took matters into their own hands. Since comparatively few of the sons of the better-off and influential served there, it was the mothers of soldiers from poorer families in the towns and the country, with no experience of political life, who became an increasingly powerful force throughout the war.

These women had to contend with a sentimental image of the soldier's mother which had an echo in the emotions of ordinary people, but was also cultivated by the authorities because it helped to minimise trouble. On the twentieth anniversary of the withdrawal from Afghanistan one semi-official organisation offered the mothers of soldiers the following advice: 'What can a Mother do for her soldier son? What? … Only one thing – she must wait … It is You,' the announcement continued, 'who bear the lofty title of "Mother of the Defenders of the Motherland" and it is You who bear the responsibility of passing on to new generations the genetic code of love for the Fatherland … It is You who feel the bitter truth and the proud memory of your sons. We congratulate You, Mothers of this great country, who wait day and night for their sons to come home. They will come back!' [22]

Many mothers had little choice but to heed such condescending stuff. But others were unwilling to remain passive. They badgered the bureaucrats, protested individually, and attempted – sometimes successfully – to get to Afghanistan to see for themselves what was going on. They had four main concerns. The first was to try to prevent their sons from going there at all. The second was to protest against the abuses of *dedovshchina* and to minimise them where they could. The third was to discover the fate of those who had perished in Afghanistan, especially those who had gone missing in action. The fourth was to secure the return of those who had been taken prisoner. The mothers' movement was one of the first effective civil rights movements to be organised in the Soviet Union, and gathered strength as the Soviet political system began to loosen up under Gorbachev. And after the war was over, the mothers formed themselves into more formal bodies, standing up for soldiers' rights and helping the conscripts sent to Chechnya.

Alla Smolina worked in the office of the military procurator in Jalalabad for nearly three years from the autumn of 1985. Her task was to manage the archives and documentation which passed through the office, and it was for the most part a depressing business. She dealt not with the records of the heroic officers and men fighting in the nearby mountains, but with the files of murderers, looters, rapists, drug addicts, deserters, self-mutilators, bullies, and thieves, complete with photographs of suicides, mutilated bodies, and mass graves. She had been present at one exhumation where among the remains there was a child's tiny foot still in the rubber boot which had prevented it from decomposing. After a while, such things became routine, and Smolina – with some assistance from tobacco and alcohol – no longer reacted to them.

From time to time the procurator's office received letters from the mothers of soldiers who had fallen foul of military law. It was a strict rule that these letters should be filed away unanswered: the correct channel for enquiries about individual soldiers was through their immediate commanders. But one letter attracted Smolina's particular attention. It was from a Ukrainian woman who had become a single mother at seventeen. She had brought up her son, Viktor, her letter said, to be a good boy, more interested in literature than in drinking and fighting with his mates. Now he had stopped writing home and his mother was determined to know what had happened to him.

Smolina got down the file. Alas, Viktor, in despair at the bullying to which he had been subjected by the 'grandfathers', was under arrest for shooting himself in the legs. Military commanders usually tried to cover up such incidents by reporting them as accidents or the result of military action. But the doctors treating the victims could usually tell whether wounds had been self-inflicted or not. Once they had cured Viktor, they reported their medical findings to his commander, who placed him under arrest pending investigation.

Then it all went wrong. A Tajik soldier threw a grenade into the sleeping tent of the soldiers who had been bullying him, took a gun from the armoury, and made off. He was soon caught and locked up in the same guardroom as Viktor. There he persuaded Viktor to escape and get to America on one of the programmes for helping Soviet deserters.

They broke out successfully, were picked up by the mujahedin, and were lucky enough to survive. Viktor converted to Islam.

At that point Smolina got another letter from Viktor's mother. She had tried to get a job with the 40th Army. But she had failed. Now she had sold her possessions to buy an air ticket to Tashkent. From there she would wangle a lift into Afghanistan. Smolina did not tell her that Viktor was no longer in the country. She wrote urging Viktor's mother not to move until the investigation was over.

That was the end of the correspondence. But it was not the end of the story. Smolina picked up a rumour from some helicopter pilots that a crazy young Ukrainian woman had tried to cross the frontier to see her soldier son who was in trouble. She had smuggled herself aboard a column of vehicles preparing to leave for the south but was caught. She had cadged lifts on helicopters. She had in the end been locked up by the local military police in Termez.

The woman in question was indeed Viktor's mother. After the war Smolina tried but failed to track her down through official channels. Then, more than two decades later, she succeeded in reconstructing the story from scraps of information on the Internet. Viktor never got to America. He trained with the mujahedin in Pakistan, went back to Afghanistan, but did not actually fight against Soviet troops. He then made his way to Iran, contacted the Soviet Embassy there, and eventually returned to the Soviet Union.

The Rising in Badaber

Stories about Soviet defectors and former prisoners of war continued to surface for many years. An officer from the GRU is said to have deserted to the mujahedin, taking with him the names of Soviet and Afghan government agents. The mujahedin rounded up the agents and the officer helped to execute them. He then led a band of fighters against his former comrades before making his way to the West. A group of GRU officers swore to punish him. They eventually tracked him down and killed him in Poland, more than a decade after the war had ended.[23] At the end of 2009 eight Soviet soldiers who had remained in Afghanistan were said to be fighting with the Taliban against the forces of the US-led coalition.[24] One incident was hushed up at the time, but later became a legend: the rising on 26 and 27 April 1985 of Soviet and Afghan army prisoners of war held in the prison-fortress of Badaber, just south of Peshawar in Pakistan.

Badaber had been home from 1958 to 1970 to a US Air Force secret intelligence listening post, the 6937th Communications Group. It was from there that secret missions were flown by U2 reconnaissance aircraft into the Soviet Union, whose frontier was only two hundred miles away. Gary Powers took off from Badaber on the ill-fated flight which ended when he was shot down on 1 May 1961 over Sverdlovsk, deep inside the Soviet Union, thus triggering off a major East–West crisis.

During the war the fortress at Badaber was used for the storage of arms and ammunition, and as a training base for the fighters from Burhanuddin Rabbani's Jamiat-i Islami. According to Rabbani, the base was entirely under his control: the Pakistan government did not attempt to interfere with what went on there. From 1983 Soviet and Afghan government prisoners were taken there to work in the ammunition stores and in the nearby quarries. They were kept in underground prison buildings – *zindands*. In 1985 there were about twelve Soviet prisoners there – most of whom had been captured by Masud's men in the Pandsher Valley – and forty Afghan government soldiers and policemen. The men were worked very hard and the non-Muslims among them were given Muslim names as a preliminary to their conversion. It was by these names that their guards addressed them and by which they were expected to address one another.

At about six o'clock on the afternoon of Friday 26 April, so the story goes, most of the mujahedin guards were at prayer on the drill square. Only two were left to guard the prisoners. They were overpowered by a particularly powerful Ukrainian named Viktor Dukhovchenko (whose Muslim name was Yunos) and placed in the custody of one of the Afghan prisoners and a Soviet prisoner called Mohamed Islam. The other prisoners then broke into the armoury and seized the weapons. Their original plan was to make a break for freedom. But at this point the remaining guards were alerted by Mohamed Islam. They surrounded the compound and prevented the captives from escaping. The prisoners then barricaded themselves into the armoury, setting up heavy machine guns and mortars on the roof. Detachments of mujahedin and Pakistani army units including tanks and artillery were brought up, but their initial attempts to recapture the fortress were repelled.

Rabbani arrived at the base in the late evening to negotiate with the insurgents, promising them their lives if they surrendered. They demanded instead that they should be allowed to see the ambassadors of the Soviet Union and Afghanistan, and representatives of the Red Cross. They threatened to blow up the armoury if their demands were not met.

Rabbani rejected these demands. He narrowly missed being killed by a rocket fired by the insurgents and some of his bodyguards were seriously hurt. The following morning he ordered an all-out attack on the fort, supported by rocket artillery, tanks, and helicopters. The outcome was never in doubt, but it was determined when the armoury blew up and the prison was practically destroyed. Some say the building exploded when it was struck by an incoming shell; others that the insurgents blew it up themselves. Three of the insurgents survived, badly wounded. They were finished off with grenades. The explosion destroyed many of the attackers as well: some Russian accounts claim that 120 mujahedin were killed, along with up to ninety Pakistani regular soldiers and six American instructors.[25] The story later circulated that Soviet special forces were preparing to free the captives when the tragedy occurred.

The following day Gulbeddin Hekmatyar, the most extreme of the mujahedin leaders, issued an order to his men that in future no Russians were to be taken prisoner.

Neither the Soviet nor the Pakistani government had any interest in publicising these events. The Soviets were still maintaining that the 'Limited Contingent of Soviet Forces in Afghanistan' was not engaged in war; the presence of Soviet prisoners of war in far-distant Pakistan could not be reconciled with that bland line. The Pakistanis were equally maintaining the fiction that they were giving no assistance to the mujahedin: they sealed off the area of the prison and neither journalists nor foreigners were allowed near the place. An issue of the Peshawar newspaper *Safir*, which had carried a report of the incident, was destroyed.

Despite the official reticence, the news did seep out, but the details remained fragmentary and disputed. Some of the Afghan prisoners escaped in the confusion, eventually made their way home, and were able to provide the only direct accounts of what had happened. An American satellite is said to have transmitted a photograph on 28 April showing that the training camp had been destroyed by an explosion which had left a crater eighty yards across. The American radio station Voice of America reported on 4 May that twelve Soviet and twelve Afghan prisoners had been killed in the blast. The electronic intelligence branch of the 40th Army picked up exchanges between the Pakistani helicopters and their base. On 9 May an official of the International Red Cross informed the Soviet Embassy in Islamabad that there had been a rising in the camp. On 27 May the Soviet news agency *Novosti* reported, 'Kabul. Popular meetings are continuing across the country in protest against the death in an uneven fight with the counter-revolutionaries and regular units of the Pakistan army of Soviet and Afghan soldiers kidnapped by the rebels on the territory of the DRA [Democratic Republic of Afghanistan] and secretly transferred to Pakistan. Peasants, workers, and representatives of the tribes are angrily condemning the barbaric action of Islamabad, which is crudely distorting the facts in a clumsy attempt to evade responsibility.'

The records of the prison camp were destroyed in the explosion, and so there was no reliable list of names of those prisoners who had died. Confusion was compounded because such lists as existed gave only the Muslim names of the prisoners, and their original names could only be reconstructed on the basis of fragmentary evidence. After the war was over the Russian Ministry of Foreign Affairs, the Foreign Intelligence Service (SVR), the GRU and the Veterans Committee of the Commonwealth of Independent States all made it their business to piece the story together. The first breakthrough did not come until December 1991, when a delegation led by Rabbani visited Moscow to persuade the new Russian government to cut off aid to the Communist government of President Najibullah. The mujahedin refused to negotiate on prisoners until they had received satisfaction on the main issue. They insisted that, in so far as there were any Soviet prisoners in their hands, they were guests and free to return home or go elsewhere as they pleased. But a Pakistani Deputy Foreign Minister with the delegation gave the names of five of the Soviet soldiers believed to have perished at Badaber.[26]

Badaber was visited in 1992 by Zamir Kabulov from the Russian Embassy in Islamabad, who subsequently became Russian Ambassador in Kabul. The search was given a renewed impulse in 2003, thanks to the efforts of the Veterans Committee under General Aushev. Over the years seven names were established fairly securely: several were awarded posthumous medals for valour. Applications for awards on behalf of three others, Igor Vaskov, Nikolai Didkin, and Sergei Levchishin, were turned down by the Russian Ministry of Defence in 2002 because the evidence was insufficient.

One mother continued to hope that her son would return, long after all reasonable grounds for hope were gone. Alexander Zverkovich was an apprentice welder in Minsk in Belorussia when he was called up in 1983. In March 1984 his mother, Sofia, heard from his commander that he had gone 'missing in action while carrying out his military duties'. Even before the Soviet Union collapsed, she went with other mothers of missing soldiers to Moscow to ask the authorities to help find their sons and bring home those who had survived as prisoners of war; but without result. In the mid-1990s she appealed to the courts to rule that her son was dead, so that she could receive the benefits to which she was entitled. But in 2006 her hopes were revived when she learned that her son had participated in the rising in Badaber. 'They say a monument has been put up in Moscow to those who took part in the rising,' she told her local newspaper. 'The radio said that some of them survived. Some people in the village even said that they had seen Sashenka [Alexander] on the television … I've even been to fortune-tellers. Some say he died; others maintain that he is alive and living beyond the ocean. I'd give anything to know the truth, however bitter it was.' Alexander Zverkovich's name is one of the seven on the list of those who died at Badaber.

The whole truth – even the names of those who died – may never be known for sure. The Pakistani intelligence authorities refused to release whatever documents they may have had, and other accounts of the tragedy were based on circumstance, hearsay, and wishful thinking.[27]

TWELVE

THE ROAD TO THE BRIDGE

Within weeks of sending the troops into Afghanistan, the Politburo was already talking about how to get them out again. After visiting Kabul in February 1980, Andropov reported that the situation was becoming more stable, although the Afghan government needed to overcome their domestic dissensions, improve the fighting capacity of their army, and strengthen their links with the people. Ustinov was cautious: it would be a year, or even two, before the troops could be withdrawn. Brezhnev agreed; and suggested that it might even be necessary to increase the numbers somewhat. Gromyko thought it would be prudent first to seek guarantees of Afghanistan's security from China, Pakistan, and others.[1]

The caution was entirely justified. The massive popular demonstrations in Kabul in late February, and the action which the 40th Army took to bring them under control, demonstrated beyond a doubt that the situation in Afghanistan was not stable at all. Major military operations started almost immediately in the Kunar Valley and in the Pandsher.

Brezhnev Looks for a Way Out
It took some time before the Soviet leaders were willing to recognise

that their hope for a quick exit was vain. Brezhnev told the French President, Giscard d'Estaing, in May 1980 that he knew that the troops would have to leave: 'I will make it my personal business to impose a political solution. You can count on me.' A month later he ordered the withdrawal of units which were no longer needed in Afghanistan and told Andropov to discuss the details with Karmal.[2] In the winter of 1980–81 the Soviet Ambassador in Islamabad talked with the Pakistani President, Zia ul-Haq (1924–88), about the possibility of talks under the auspices of the United Nations. Ustinov, once a hawk, began to have serious doubts, and wrote to the Politburo saying that no military solution to the war was possible, and it was necessary to find a political and diplomatic way out.[3] Andropov, too, had lost his appetite for foreign adventures: when the Polish crisis blew up later in 1980, he said, 'The quota of interventions abroad has been exhausted.'[4] In the autumn of 1981 he and Ustinov sponsored a paper by the Foreign Ministry proposing proximity talks between Afghanistan and Pakistan.

Andropov succeeded Brezhnev in November 1982. At Brezhnev's funeral he assured Zia ul-Haq of the 'Soviet side's new flexible policy and its willingness to bring an early solution to the crisis.'[5] The only condition was that Pakistan stop its aid to the mujahedin. By then Gromyko had already chaired an interdepartmental meeting on plans for a Soviet withdrawal.

In February 1983 Andropov told the Secretary General of the UN with considerable force that the Soviet Union had no intention of keeping its troops in Afghanistan indefinitely. The operation was expensive; the Soviet Union had plenty of domestic problems; and the war had complicated the Soviet Union's relationships with the United States, the Third World, and the Islamic world. Speaking very slowly and emphasising each word, he added that he sincerely wanted 'to put an end to this situation'. The argument, commonly bandied about in the West, that Soviet troops had never withdrawn from any country where they had once been stationed was disproved by history. But others were interfering in Afghanistan's affairs. 'Soviet troops would have to stay for as long as necessary because this is a matter which concerns the security of the Soviet Union's southern border.'[6]

Andropov's good intentions were undermined by his own failing health and by the shooting down by Soviet fighters of a Korean airliner on 1 September 1983, which led immediately to further worldwide condemnation of the Soviet Union for what President Reagan called a 'massacre'. His efforts ran out of steam even before he died in January 1984.

His successor, Konstantin Chernenko, was also seriously ill and barely able to take a grip on policy. He died on 10 March 1985. By now it was obvious to the senior Soviet politicians that the Soviet system was not working as it should. Within hours of Chernenko's death they elected Mikhail Gorbachev as his successor, because he was young, energetic, imaginative, and – they believed – orthodox.

Gorbachev Moves

Gorbachev came to power determined to press ahead for a solution in Afghanistan. As a first step he requested a policy review from the Committee on Afghanistan, which was told to look into 'the consequences, pluses, and minuses of a withdrawal'. Later he decided that this committee of old men was a brake on progress and abolished it.[7]

Some Western accounts said that Gorbachev gave the generals a year to finish the job by military means, and that in 1985–6 the pace of the fighting was increased to the highest level of the war. Kryuchkov, always a hostile witness, claimed that Gorbachev first criticised the Ministry of Defence for not prosecuting the war more energetically, but soon swung to the other extreme.[8] There were of course some major military operations in 1985, notably the Kunar offensive in May–June. The Special Forces Brigade was introduced in the same year, as the Russians moved away from massive ground operations towards more flexible actions in support of the Afghan army, backed where necessary by long-range bombers from Soviet territory. But Soviet casualties peaked in the period before Gorbachev came to power and began to fall from May 1985 onwards. That is hardly compatible with a 'Gorbachev surge'.[9]

Whatever the truth of the story, Gorbachev made up his mind well before the year had expired. In October 1985 he summoned Babrak Karmal to Moscow and raised the prospect of Soviet withdrawal. Karmal was shocked to realise that the Russians needed him less than he needed them. He went white and said, 'If you withdraw the troops now, next time you will have to send in a million.'[10] Gorbachev told him that Afghanistan would have to be able to defend itself by the summer of 1986. The Soviet Union would no longer help with troops, though it would continue to supply military equipment. Karmal should forget about socialism, share power with others, including the mujahedin leaders and others who were now his enemies, and restore the rights of religion and the religious leaders.

Anatoli Chernyaev, the former Party official whom Gorbachev had appointed as his diplomatic adviser earlier in the year, commented in his diary, 'Ten of our boys are dying every day. The people are disenchanted and ask: How long are our troops going to remain there? And when will the Afghans learn to defend themselves? The main thing is that there is no popular base, and without that no revolution can defend itself. What's recommended is a sharp U-turn, back to free capitalism, to Afghan and Islamic values, to a real division of power with the opposition and even with the enemy ... I advised that a compromise should be sought even with the leaders of the mujahedin, and of course with the emigration. Will Karmal go that far? Above all, is he capable, is he sufficiently in command of the situation, for his present enemies to go to meet him?'[11]

Gorbachev now made clear to the Politburo that he was determined to grasp the nettle. Deliberately playing on his listeners' emotions, he read out letters received in the Central Committee from the parents of those who had died.[12] Many were signed. Women spoke of the moral as well as the physical damage being done to their sons. Officers, and even one general, said that they were no longer able to explain to their men what the war was about. Soldiers complained that, because of the press restrictions, the newspapers were reporting that all the fighting was being done by the Afghan army, which was the opposite of the truth. 'In whose name are we in Afghanistan? Do the Afghans themselves want us to do our "international duty" in their country? Is it worth the lives of our boys, who don't understand what they are fighting for? What are you doing, throwing young recruits against professional killers and gangsters? You people in the Politburo made a mistake, and it is up to you to put it right – the sooner the better, while every day sees more casualties.' The Politburo agreed with Gorbachev's conclusion that the object of Soviet policy should now be to build up the Afghan state and leave.[13]

Gorbachev went public in February 1986, when he told the delegates to the XXVIIth Party Congress in Moscow that the Soviet troops would leave once a political solution had been negotiated which left Afghanistan as a friendly, independent, and non-aligned state, with guarantees against external interference in its affairs.

Although the war was by now increasingly unpopular among the people and the military, it was not of course enough for Gorbachev simply to take the decision to leave. He had also to face up to a difficult problem of domestic politics which has puzzled other nations finding themselves in similar circumstances. How could the Russians withdraw their army safely, with honour, without looking as if they were simply cutting and running, and without appearing to betray their Afghan allies or their own soldiers who had died? The 40th Army had not been defeated on the battlefield; but how was the obvious blow to the prestige of the Soviet Union and its army to be avoided?

Moreover, Gorbachev had to persuade the other parties to the war – the mujahedin, eternally warring among themselves but determined to get rid of the godless Communists in Kabul; the Pakistanis, who wanted to see a friendly Islamist government there; and the Americans, many of whom wished to wipe out the memory of defeat in Vietnam by making the Russians pay the highest possible price in blood and humiliation, at whatever cost in Russian, or indeed Afghan, lives. It is not surprising that the negotiations went on much longer than Gorbachev had envisaged.

The first need was to beef up the Afghan government. The Russians had lost faith in Babrak Karmal: they found him weak, indecisive, and increasingly addicted to drink. In April 1986 they decided that he must go. Gorbachev called on him in a Kremlin hospital where he was being treated for kidney trouble, but failed to get him to leave quietly. Karmal returned to Kabul in a huff and on 1 May Kryuchkov was sent to have another go at him. Their first meeting was interrupted by a noisy street demonstration of support for Karmal. Kryuchkov said coldly that he knew perfectly well how such demonstrations were organised and within five minutes the demonstrators had dispersed. On that visit Kryuchkov got nowhere. But he returned to Kabul a few days later and, after twenty solid hours of persuasion, Karmal finally agreed to resign.[14] The reason given publicly was that he was suffering from ill-health, a line which was somewhat dented when the Soviet doctors, who had not been properly briefed, reported that his health was fine.[15] He was replaced by the younger and more effective Najibullah, the head of the secret police, the KhAD. Karmal hung on as President, without effective power, until Najibullah was elected to the post in November 1986. He then went to Moscow – ostensibly for medical treatment, but actually into permanent exile – and died there a decade later.

Najibullah was not without his critics. A GRU analysis of April 1986 showed, once again, the divergence of views between parts of the Soviet military, who favoured the Khalq faction and their officers in the army, and the KGB, who favoured the Parcham faction represented by Karmal and Najibullah. Speculating on rumours that Najibullah might succeed Karmal, the GRU analysts said that Afghan politicians regarded him as a strong personality. But they feared the power he had exercised through the KhAD, which he had exploited for his own purposes, and whose brutalities he had done nothing to mitigate. Under his regime, the Pul-i Charkhi prison had filled up with Khalqists. He was notoriously a Pushtun nationalist. He was regularly accused of allowing theft, bribery, and corruption on a scale previously unknown. The GRU were not at all sure of his loyalty to the Soviet Union: he had not studied there and, unlike many other Afghan Communist leaders, he had no military experience. The GRU concluded, 'He will not be able to unite the party, the army, and the people to bring about peace.'[16]

These views were not shared by General Varennikov, the most senior soldier in Afghanistan at the time. Najibullah's candidature was also favoured by Kryuchkov. His Pushtun nationalism undermined his ability to persuade the Tajiks and others of the virtues of his Policy of National Reconciliation – an inability which was to prove fatal in the civil war which followed the Soviet withdrawal. But there were no other obvious candidates. And whatever Najibullah's weaknesses, most observers, then and since, agreed that he had many of the qualities of an effective leader: he was able, energetic, willing to try new ideas, and a good public speaker. Kryuchkov and Shevardnadze, the Soviet Foreign Minister, became his particular advocates in Moscow, and were strongly critical of the way he was eventually abandoned by the Soviet and later the Russian regime. Their commitment to Najibullah led to many conflicts within the Politburo in the last year of the war.

But however able Najibullah was as a leader, the real power had still not shifted sufficiently. The bloated body of Soviet advisers in Afghanistan – two and a half thousand of them in 1986 – continued to get in Najibullah's way. 'We're still doing everything ourselves,' complained Gorbachev. 'That's all our people know how to do. They've tied Najibullah hand and foot.' Gorbachev grumbled that Tabeev, the Soviet Ambassador, was acting like a governor general, telling Najibullah that it was he who had made him General Secretary.[17] Tabeev was recalled in July 1986. But despite his determination that the Afghans should take responsibility for their own fate, even Gorbachev could not resist trying to micromanage Afghan politics. And the Russians soon began to have doubts about Najibullah too. 'It's difficult to build a new building out of old material,' Gorbachev remarked to the Politburo. 'I hope to God that we haven't made a mistake with Najibullah.'

The problem was that Najibullah's aims were almost diametrically opposed to those of the Russians. It was in his interest, by fair means or foul, to get the Soviet soldiers to remain. For how else were he and his government to survive once they left, as the rebels got stronger and his own forces teetered on the brink of dissolution? He accepted that some negotiation and compromise with the opposition side was unavoidable: his Policy of National Reconciliation was designed to bring moderate representatives of the political opposition and the mullahs into government. But Najibullah was determined that the PDPA should keep the key political and administrative posts, including the ministries of Defence, Internal Affairs and Security; and he was unwilling to cooperate with non-Pushtun politicians. This was not all that different from the policy which Karmal had attempted to pursue. Najibullah pursued it with greater energy and was more willing to try to win over the mujahedin commanders. But the rebels were as suspicious of him as of his predecessor, and his olive branch found few takers.

Many Russians no longer cared much about the composition of the government in Kabul anyway. For them the most important thing was to create a respectable cover for withdrawal, in the meanwhile cutting down the scope of military operations and reducing casualties to a minimum.[18] The Soviet generals were not too happy about that. They had a war to fight and the restrictions which were now placed on them went against their instincts. For the most part they gritted their teeth and did what they were told. But the old conflicts of interest between the main Soviet institutions in Moscow – the army, the KGB, the Party, and the government – and their representatives in Kabul continued to dog the course of the Soviet withdrawal, at times raising serious doubts over its timing and manner. Najibullah exploited the differences with skill.

In July 1986 Gorbachev withdrew six regiments from Afghanistan. That showed, he told the Politburo, that the USSR did not intend to stay in Afghanistan or to 'break through to the warm ocean'. The Soviet Union was matching deeds to words. Najibullah needed to understand that and to take matters into his own hands. This was a genuine reduction of fifteen thousand in the 40th Army's strength. It brought the Russians no credit in the outside world, where it was dismissed as a propaganda stunt.[19]

In November 1986 Gorbachev spelled out the issues to the Politburo yet again. 'We've been fighting for six years already! Some people are saying that if we go on like this, the war could last for twenty or thirty years … People are beginning to ask, Are we going to sit there for ever? Or should we finish off this war? If we don't, we will cover ourselves with shame in every respect. The strategic objective is to finish off the war in one or at the most two years and withdraw our forces.' Shevardnadze added that the Soviets needed to decide who was in charge on their own side: was it the army or was it the KGB?

The military situation was clearly still unsatisfactory. The Russians had failed to close the Afghan frontier. The rebels had changed tactics and gone underground. Akhromeev, by now the Chief of the General

Staff, said what many of his soldiers had been telling him for some time: 'In the past seven years Soviet soldiers have had their boots on the ground in every square kilometre of the country. But as soon as they left, the enemy returned and restored everything the way it was before. We have lost this war. The majority of the Afghan people support the counter-revolution. We have lost the peasantry, who have got nothing from the revolution. Eighty per cent of the country is in the hands of the counter-revolution. And the position of the peasants there is better than it is in the territory controlled by the government.'

The Politburo agreed that the aim was no longer to build socialism in Afghanistan, but to withdraw half of the Soviet troops in one year and the remainder in two; to broaden the political and social base of the regime; and then leave them to get on with it. Gorbachev proposed direct negotiations with Pakistan.[20]

The Politburo's next discussion in January 1987 was a gloomy occasion. The difficulty of withdrawing with honour had become increasingly apparent. As Gorbachev said, 'We could leave quickly, without worrying about the consequences, and blame everything on our predecessors. But that we cannot do. We have not given an account of ourselves to the people. A million of our soldiers have passed through Afghanistan. [He was badly briefed: it was about six hundred thousand.] And it looks as if they did so in vain. So why did those people die?'

Shevardnadze had just visited Kabul. He reported that the traditional goodwill towards the Soviet Union had gone. Too many people had died. '[W]e went in without knowing anything at all about the psychology of the people, and that's a fact. And everything we have done and are doing in Afghanistan is incompatible with the moral basis of our country.' Najibullah made a good impression, but his support was crumbling. The military situation was getting worse. It was impossible to close the border with Pakistan. The war could not be won by military means. Summing up, Gorbachev pointed out that in Poland, despite ideological misgivings, the Soviet Union had accepted the position of the Church, private agriculture, political pluralism. One had to face reality. It was better to pay with treasure than with blood.

In January a Deputy Foreign Minister, Anatoli Kovalev, went to

Pakistan to talk to President Zia ul-Haq. In February Gorbachev re-emphasised the importance of involving the Americans and suggested that he might invite Zia ul-Haq for talks to Tashkent. When Gromyko argued that there was no alternative to a military withdrawal, Gorbachev replied sharply, 'There is an alternative. We could bring in two hundred thousand more troops. But that would lead to the collapse of our whole cause.'[21]

The Politburo met again in May 1987, with senior officials from Kabul in attendance, including Varennikov. By now, they lamented, the Afghan army was falling apart; the Americans and the Pakistanis were doing all they could to undermine the Policy of National Reconciliation; and Najibullah was failing to get a grip. Akhromeev argued that making Najibullah the centrepiece of a new political line-up would simply lead to endless fighting. Gorbachev said that there was no one else. The Russians would be accused of treachery if they simply abandoned him: 'We won't be able to explain that to our own people. And in Afghanistan the supporters of the mujahedin will remember for a long time how we destroyed them, and the supporters of Najibullah will remember how we left them in the same boat as their enemies. We will be left with an unfriendly Afghanistan. But at the same time we can't go on with this war for ever.'

Summing up a somewhat despairing discussion, Gorbachev concluded that the UN and the Americans needed to be more fully involved. The UN could provide a neutral framework for negotiation. The Americans were by far the largest suppliers of arms to the mujahedin, and no guarantee of non-interference would hold without them.[22] Najibullah should be given more economic aid, but be firmly told that the Russians intended to finish with the Afghan question in eighteen months. Ways should be found of associating with the government, the mujahedin, the exiled king, Zahir Shah, and moderates such as Rabbani.[23]

The Diplomatic Manoeuvring
The next ten months were taken up with diplomatic manoeuvring in Geneva, Islamabad, Moscow, New York, and Washington, against the background of the UN negotiations, which had sputtered on since

1982. The Americans had in fact been involved from the earliest days of the Reagan presidency. Jack Matlock, the US Chargé d'Affaires in Moscow in 1981, was instructed to tell the Russians that the Americans would 'discuss ways to ensure the security of the Soviet Union's southern border and also make a commitment not to use the territory of Afghanistan against the Soviet Union'. The message received no response. After the Geneva Summit, Reagan wrote to Gorbachev on 28 November 1985 saying, 'I want you to know that I am prepared to cooperate in any reasonable way to facilitate [a Soviet withdrawal from Afghanistan] in a manner which does not damage Soviet security.' [24] This letter too received no response.

Now, in 1987, Moscow stepped up the tempo. In September Shevardnadze told US Secretary of State George Shultz (1920–) that 'we will leave Afghanistan. It may be in five months or a year.' [25] Shultz was struck with this news, but believed that it would fall foul of the right-wingers in Reagan's cabinet. He kept it to himself for weeks, for fear he would be accused of going soft on Moscow. [26]

Three months later Gorbachev told Reagan that he agreed that Afghanistan should be neutral, independent, and pluralistic. Afghanistan was not a socialist state. How it developed was a matter for the Afghans themselves. The Soviet Union needed a friendly Afghanistan, but was not seeking bases there. Both the Americans and the Russians should back the process of National Reconciliation. The Americans should cease their support for the mujahedin. Once there was an agreed date for the withdrawal of Soviet forces, they would no longer participate in military operations. But the two men did not settle on any matter of substance. Reagan even suggested – bizarrely – that the Kabul government should disband its army. [27] Gorbachev left Washington with the impression that the Americans were happy to leave the Russians to flounder and even to hamper the departure of their troops.

The Russians and the Americans later disagreed on what had passed at this meeting, each believing that the other had failed to take the opportunity to make a positive move. The Russians believed that Reagan had indicated that he was willing to cut off supplies to the mujahedin. Shevardnadze so informed Najibullah – and, rather incautiously, the Afghan press – in January 1988. Shultz issued a furious denial.

The Soviet Foreign Ministry asked Jack Matlock, by then ambassador in Moscow, for a clarification. After consulting Washington, he replied that the Americans would refrain from supplying the mujahedin if the Soviets cut off military supplies to the Kabul government. This was not of course a deal that the Russians could easily accept, and in the event both sides continued to supply their protégés. The Russians retained an obscure feeling that they had been somehow double-crossed.

Matlock believed in later years that agreement on an orderly withdrawal, including a provision for the Americans to cease aid to the mujahedin without the Soviets having to cut off support for Kabul, could have been reached in 1986 or 1987 if Gorbachev had been willing to engage Reagan earlier. Whether the domestic politics of either side would have permitted that is a very open question.[28]

On 1 April 1988 the Politburo met to consider the outcome of the Geneva negotiations. The Americans were now ready to sign, provided that there was no mention of military aid to the mujahedin. Chernyaev thought that the issue was now moot: the mujahedin would get their aid whatever the final agreement said, and the Russians were preparing to withdraw their troops whether or not the agreement was signed. Gorbachev asked for views. Everyone agreed that the Soviet Union should sign. Gorbachev gave the news to Najibullah in Tashkent ten days later; he took it with apparent equanimity.[29]

The agreements were finally signed in Geneva on 14 April 1988 under the aegis of the United Nations. A bilateral agreement between the Kabul government and Pakistan provided for non-interference and non-intervention. The Russians and the Americans signed a declaration on international guarantees. And there were provisions for the Soviet troops to withdraw in two stages by 15 February 1989. The mujahedin were not a party and refused to accept the terms. This opened the way to the fall of the Najibullah regime and the subsequent murderous civil war: the nightmare that Gorbachev had feared when he confided to Chernyaev in September 1987 that the Soviet withdrawal might be followed by a bloodbath 'for which we would not be forgiven, either by the Third World, or by the shabby Western liberals who have spent the last ten years lambasting us for occupying the place'.[30]

Shevardnadze signed in Geneva with a heavy heart. 'One would have thought I would have been happy: no more coffins were coming home. We'll close the account: both of the deaths and of the drain on our resources, which had reached 60 billion roubles ... It was hard for me to realise that I was the Foreign Minister who had signed what was certainly not an agreement about a victory. There aren't many examples of that in Russian or Soviet history. And I couldn't stop thinking about the people we had trained up, pushed into a revolution, and were now abandoning to face a mortal foe alone.' [31] Such sentiments were to affect the policy advice he gave over the next two years.

'We will leave the country in a deplorable situation,' he told the Politburo on his return, 'ruined cities and villages, a paralysed economy. Hundreds of thousands of people have died. Our withdrawal will be regarded as a major political and military defeat. Within the Party and among the people the attitude to our departure is ambiguous. We must at least announce that the introduction of our troops was a gross error, that even then the experts and the public were against that adventure ... We may not be able to distance ourselves easily from the past by arguing that we do not bear responsibility for our predecessors.' He suggested that ten to fifteen thousand Soviet troops should be left behind to support the regime, a proposal clearly at odds with the agreement he had just signed. Kryuchkov supported him. Gorbachev reacted strongly to what he called 'Shevardnadze's hawkish scream'. It did not matter, he said, whether Najibullah survived or not. The legal basis for the Soviet withdrawal meant that it could not be compared with the way the Americans had bolted from Vietnam. Everything possible had been done to limit the negative consequences of the war.[32]

Disagreements about how far the Russians should assist Najibullah – if necessary by using military force – continued to bedevil Soviet policymaking until well after the withdrawal was completed. Shevardnadze and Kryuchkov continued their hawkish stance, opposed for the most part by the military.

The First Phase of the Withdrawal: Summer 1988
The Defence Minister, General Yazov, had already issued plans for the

withdrawal. The total Soviet force now numbered about a hundred thousand. Half would leave by 15 August 1988, the remainder by 15 February 1989. The routes would be the same as those for the original invasion, but in reverse: in the west from Kandahar via Shindand and Herat to Kushka; in the east over the Salang Pass to Khairaton and across the Friendship Bridge to Termez.

The first move was to bring outlying garrisons into their parent regiments. The garrisons on the eastern border with Pakistan – Jalalabad, Gardez, and Ghazni – were withdrawn completely. So were the southward-facing garrisons in Kandahar and Lashkar Gar. The Russians also pulled out of their positions in the north-east in Kunduz and Faisabad. By the end of the first phase, the Soviet forces were concentrated between Shindand and Kushka in the west, and between Kabul and the great supply base of Khairaton in the east.

The garrison from Jalalabad was the first to leave. A tribunal was hastily erected on the parade ground for the benefit of the senior Soviet officers and Afghan local politicians. A group of uncommunicative UN military observers was there to ensure that the Geneva Agreements were properly carried out. Behind the tribunal was a buffet loaded with ham, sausage, cheese – things the garrison never normally saw. At dawn the armoured vehicles were drawn up on the square, their crews beside them. Their faces were grim, unsmiling, exhausted, as they listened to the endless speeches. Their officers congratulated them on having fulfilled their 'international duty'. Crowds of Afghans gathered to wave them goodbye. They threw bouquets of flowers at the departing troops. Among the flowers were other small gifts: stones and pieces of camel dung.[33] Then the orchestra played the traditional march, 'The Slav Girl's Farewell', and the column started on the hundred mile journey to Kabul, through the passes where the British Army of the Indus had been wiped out in January 1842. The battle helicopters clattered overhead to protect it from attack, turning aside to investigate when little puffs of gun smoke from the mountainsides revealed the presence of snipers.

'All along the way,' wrote David Gai, a Soviet journalist who accompanied the column, 'was what remained of the roadside *kishlaks*. Not one was undamaged: the walls were overturned, the houses were smashed, the trees were twisted. The fields were bare and uncultivated, the irrigation systems had been turned into marsh. And who had gained from the way everything had been reduced to useless collapse? How much effort would have to be put into restoring life to that dead space? The futility of those 3,200 (or however many it was) days of war made one's eyes burn with shame ... The only good thing was that the boys were going home.' [34]

Soviet long-range bombers continued to strike mujahedin positions around Kandahar and Jalalabad after the troops had left. [35]

The 860th Independent Motor-rifle Regiment also left Afghanistan as part of the first wave. By then Alexander Gergel had long returned home. He got the story of his battalion's last days in Bakharak from Anastas Lizauskas, whom he tracked down on the Internet in 2005.

The fighting went on to the last. The rumour spread among the soldiers that a foreign film maker, who had made one film about the Russians destroying peaceful villages, now wanted to make another about the destruction of a Soviet battalion. He encouraged the mujahedin to attack. The Russians and the mujahedin bombarded one another inconclusively for a week. As an Afghan general came to take over the fort the soldiers, furious at leaving with their tails between their legs after nine years of war, erupted in an orgy of destruction. They put shells down the lavatories, destroyed the sports facilities, set fire to the sleeping quarters, knocked down the memorials in the Alley of Glory, and destroyed the vehicles while the Afghan soldiers looked on in silent rage. As a final gesture, someone fired a signal rocket into the canteen. Then the soldiers, each with his personal weapon and as much loot as he could squeeze into a sack, hurried to the helicopters. The mujahedin were already closing in from the mountains. A week later the Afghan soldiers handed the fort over to the mujahedin. It was destroyed in subsequent months by a series of strikes by Soviet and Afghan government aircraft. [36]

The Second Phase of the Withdrawal: Winter 1988–9
The second phase of the withdrawal was supposed to begin in November, before the heavy snows settled. This timetable was disrupted by the

mujahedin, by Najibullah's government, and by conflicts within the Soviet administration both in Kabul and in Moscow.

The mujahedin were still receiving arms and other supplies from the Pakistanis and the Americans. According to Soviet figures, 172 large caravans arrived in September and October alone.[37] By now Najibullah was deeply worried that his interests and those of the Soviet Union were rapidly diverging. In early September he told Varennikov with remarkable frankness that he was doing everything he could to slow the departure of the Soviet forces so as to offset American and Pakistani violations of the Geneva Agreements. Varennikov told Najibullah firmly that both Soviet and international opinion would be incensed if the Soviet troops did not leave on time.[38] Najibullah returned to the charge in October, when he met the senior Soviet representatives in Kabul. Masud was the main problem, he said, and would have to be dealt with by military means if negotiation failed. He claimed for good measure that Masud was plotting with the CIA to let in the Americans.[39]

There was sympathy for Najibullah both in Moscow and among the senior Russians in Kabul: they had put him in place and they could not with honour abandon him. For them, too, the main problem was Masud; but they disagreed among themselves on what should be done. Once it was clear that the Soviets were indeed going to withdraw, Masud's men had been careful to avoid provocation, especially along the Salang Highway. But government forces were continuing to fire upon the neighbouring villages, and Masud warned that if this did not stop, he would take counter-measures. Varennikov helped negotiate a temporary ceasefire: by now it had become normal for Soviet commanders of all levels to make such arrangements with the elders of nearby *kishlaks* and the commanders of rebel groupings as a way of reducing losses.[40] But the practice was not appreciated or understood by the Afghan government leaders, who believed that the Russians were intriguing with the opposition because they did not want to fight.

Varennikov believed that the Russians had an interest in remaining on reasonable terms with Masud. Masud was highly effective militarily, he commanded unequalled authority among the people, he had ordered his men not to attack the Soviet forces, and he was being obeyed. Although he remained a determined opponent of the government, in accordance with the Policy of National Reconciliation his forces fired only if they were fired on. Varennikov pointed out to Moscow that if the Russians did what Najibullah wanted, and resumed military action against Masud, the 40th Army would suffer heavy losses, the withdrawal timetable would be disrupted, the Soviet Union would be in breach of the Geneva Agreements, and domestic opinion would be outraged. Masud was of course the main threat to the Kabul regime, and would probably step up his military activity once the Soviets had left. But in the long run he could become a major political figure in post-war Afghanistan, someone with whom the Soviet Union could cooperate. It was better to have him as an ally than an enemy. The Soviets should get into direct contact with him through intelligence channels.[41]

At this point a new player arrived on the scene: Yuli Vorontsov, Yegorychev's replacement as ambassador in Kabul, and one of the Soviet Union's most experienced diplomats. Vorontsov had already had some direct dealings with the mujahedin. On 6 December he met Rabbani and other representatives of the Alliance of Seven in Saudi Arabia.[42] The meeting got off to an awkward start until Rabbani decided that he could after all shake hands with the representative of the enemy. Vorontsov said that the Soviets would leave as they had promised. Rabbani clearly thought he was lying and said, 'What do you mean, you're leaving? You have put so much into Afghanistan. So many of your people have died there. You're not going to leave. Stop talking rubbish!' Vorontsov replied that from now on Afghans like Rabbani were going to have to be responsible for their own country. Once the Soviets left, Afghanistan could expect no more assistance from them. He repeated the message when he met the mujahedin again in Islamabad. The Russians did not want to leave in a welter of blood, said Vorontsov, and appealed to them to respond in kind. They replied, 'If you really leave, then we won't shoot at you.' They more or less kept their promise.[43]

On 18 December Varennikov wrote to Masud direct. He suggested that representatives from both sides should meet within a week. He made concrete proposals for managing the highway from Kabul to Khairaton to ensure that food and other goods continued to flow. If Masud was willing to guard the highway, the necessary agreements should be signed with the local authorities along the road. If not, the

Soviet and Afghan forces would set up their own posts; and would take appropriate measures if Masud's men fired on them.

Lyakhovski drew up a list of political propositions to be discussed with Masud. These included the creation of an autonomous Tajik region in the north, with its own armed forces operating under the general authority of the Afghan military; a centrally backed plan for economic development; representation in the organs of central government; direct trade and economic and cultural links between the autonomous Tajik region and their cousins in Soviet Tajikistan. These ideas were approved by Varennikov, Vorontsov, and, rather surprisingly, the Afghan leadership.

They did not, however, survive the strong pressure for military action against Masud which had now developed in Moscow. Yazov, Kryuchkov, and Shevardnadze all favoured it, and accused Varennikov of conspiring behind the backs of his superiors and refusing to carry out their orders and the requests of the Afghan government.[44] Yazov rang Gromov direct to ask why Masud had not yet been dealt with. When Gromov objected that the operation would be bloody and pointless, Yazov said, 'Get on with it, and smash him.'

The military caved, and launched air strikes against Masud's men deployed around the lapis lazuli mines outside the Pandsher itself. Masud was told that the strikes were a deliberate warning. Inevitably he regarded them as a serious breach of faith by the Russians. His reply was swift and conclusive. He wrote on 26 December: 'I was already wanting to go to meet the Soviet representatives when I got your last letter. I will speak quite plainly. We have already had to bear this war and your invasion for ten years. God willing, we will manage to stick it out for a few more days. But if you take military action, we will resist appropriately. That is all I have to say! From today we will put our detachments and groups on full military alert.'

That was the last attempt by the Soviet military to negotiate with Masud. But there was to be one more military action against him. In the middle of January Shevardnadze visited Kabul. Najibullah asked that Soviet troops should remain – temporarily – to guard the Salang Highway; and that Soviet bombers should be on permanent alert at bases close to Afghanistan to strike the rebels if necessary. He complained that no major operation had been mounted against Masud for four whole years. As long as Masud survived, it would be impossible to get supplies through to the capital. That was the key to whether the present regime lived or died. Shevardnadze pointed out the international implications: Najibullah's proposal would bring the Soviet Union into conflict with the USA and Pakistan. But he promised to look into the matter and told the senior Soviet representatives in Kabul that, to prevent a blockade of the capital, Soviet forces should remain, perhaps indefinitely, to guard Kabul airport and the road across the Salang. He instructed the embassy to work out a plan to leave twelve thousand soldiers behind, either under UN auspices or as 'volunteers'.

Varennikov and his colleagues were furious at what they saw as yet another betrayal of the military by Shevardnadze and the other politicians to serve Najibullah's political ambitions. Gritting their teeth, they put the withdrawal on hold while they planned for what they called, perhaps with deliberate irony, Operation *Typhoon*, the code name which the Germans had given to their offensive against Moscow in 1941. The operation was due to begin on 24 January. Najibullah appealed to the population along the road to move out for the time being. Heavy artillery and rocket launchers were put in place.

Meanwhile Shevardnadze forwarded to Moscow another proposal from Najibullah that the Soviets should send a brigade to lift the blockade of Kandahar and protect arms convoys to the city. When he heard of it, Chernyaev exploded. 'Has he gone off his head? Doesn't he see Najibullah is laying a trap to ensure we don't leave, and to embroil us with the Americans and the whole of the rest of the world? Or hasn't he got the guts to produce the counter-arguments?' Najibullah's regime was finished anyway: all the Soviets could now do was save his skin. Chernyaev listened in as Gorbachev phoned Shevardnadze. Shevardnadze started to blame the military. Chernyaev interrupted: 'All the military have done is to work out the technicalities of the political plan which you've agreed with Najibullah. But that plan is clean contrary to our whole policy, and to plain common sense, without mentioning the losses to which you will be exposing our boys.'

'You've not been there,' replied Shevardnadze angrily. 'You've no idea all the things we have done there in the past ten years!'

'But why should we compound our crimes! What's the logic in that? We're not going to be able to save Najibullah anyway …'

'But he says that if he can hold out for a year after we leave, he will be able to survive indefinitely …'

'And you believe that? And for that you're ready to sacrifice our boys and break the engagement we gave in Geneva?'[45]

The Politburo met on 24 January. Shevardnadze insisted that the Soviet Union could not be indifferent to the fate of Najibullah's regime. Ten to fifteen thousand Soviet troops should be left behind, not least because they would be guarding the roads along which the army would withdraw. Once again he was supported by Kryuchkov. But Gorbachev summed up against him. The Soviet Union had a moral obligation towards Najibullah: everything should be done to help him survive as long as he could. But there were only twenty days left and the withdrawal was to be completed on time.

Operation Typhoon

The Politburo decision came too late to halt *Typhoon*. Yazov had already ordered Varennikov to begin the operation a day early, on 23 January. It lasted for two days.[46] The morale of the troops was by now at rock bottom. Why, the soldiers wondered, should they risk their lives yet again, on the eve of departure for a homeland where, they knew, the war was seen as unjust, no better than the American performance in Vietnam. One young officer asked his superior on the eve of the operation, 'Why does there have to be more bloodshed? … I will try to encourage the men in my battalion. But I tell you frankly, that if I am ordered to shoot, I will carry out the order, but I will hate myself.'[47]

Fighter bombers and heavy bombers from bases inside the Soviet Union launched more than a thousand sorties against the rebel bases. More than four hundred strikes were carried out by rocket and conventional artillery. At times the bombardment resembled the massive storm of artillery which preceded the Red Army's great offensives in the Second World War.[48] After it was over, the staff of the 40th Army reported that six hundred rebels had been killed. The survivors were demoralised, and continued air and artillery strikes were preventing them from regrouping and bringing up reinforcements. A tented camp had been put up for the civilian refugees, and army political officers were busy explaining to them that what had happened was the consequence of Masud's 'criminal position'. The Soviets lost three dead and five wounded. They did not try to count the civilian dead.

Masud's reaction was swift and bitter. Nothing, he wrote to Vorontsov, had been changed by the 'cruel and shameful actions' of the Russians. Ten years of a horrible war should have taught the Soviets that the Afghan people could not be brought to their knees by force and threats. Instead the Russians were continuing to support 'a handful of hirelings, who have betrayed themselves and for whom there is no place in the future of the country'. He hoped that the new Soviet leadership would understand that they could not impose a dying regime on a Muslim people, and that they would gather the courage to act in accordance with reality and with their own convictions.[49]

The judgement of the Soviet military was just as bitter. General Sotskov, who was the Chief Soviet Military Adviser in Kabul in 1988 and 1989, wrote of Operation *Typhoon*, 'Almost ten years of the war were reflected as if in a mirror in three days and three nights: political cynicism and military cruelty, the absolute defencelessness of some and the pathological need to kill and destroy of others. Three awful days absorbed in themselves ten years of bloodletting.'[50]

Once Operation *Typhoon* was over, the Soviet withdrawal resumed on 27 January. Civilians and soldiers had been pulling out since the New Year – the families had left earlier. The weather conditions were exceptionally difficult, with snow, fog, and icy roads especially on the Salang Pass. Avalanches formed obstacles of snow and stone for many miles which had to be cleared by the engineers. But the work was done, and the long columns of armoured vehicles and lorries continued to move north according to the timetable set by the generals and the Geneva Agreements.[51]

The Soviet aircraft based in Bagram flew out between 30 January and 3 February. By 4 February the last troops had left Kabul. As they moved north the guard battalions placed to secure their passage folded seamlessly in behind them. In these two last weeks of the war the Russians lost thirty-nine more men. One of them was Igor Lakhovich, of the 345th Guards Independent Parachute Assault Regiment, who

Kabul – Babur's tomb

abur's garden and tomb in 2008. Built around 1528, both were very badly damaged
uring the civil war which followed the Soviet departure in 1989. They were recon-
ructed after the expulsion of the Taliban with funds given by the Aga Khan.

10. Kabul – two palaces

Top: The Arg, renamed by the Communists the House of the People, was built b Abdur Rahman in the centre of Kabul. Two presidents were murdered here: Presider Daud in 1978 and President Taraki in 1979.

Bottom: Amin moved to the Taj Bek on the outskirts of town hoping to avoid a simila fate. He was killed there by Soviet special forces on 27 December 1979. This pictur gives a good idea of the difficult ground over which the Russians had to attack. Th 40th Army then used it as their headquarters. The palace and the surrounding garder were reduced to their present ruinous state after they left.

Top: Ahmad Shah Masud – the Lion of Pandsher.

Bottom: Sher Ahmad Maladani (*left*) from Herat, who fought the Russians for nine years and the Taliban until they captured him, and who thought that the Russians were better foes than the Americans. On the right is an unknown man by the Salang Tunnel.

Top: These soldiers have bailed out of their BTR (armoured personnel carrier) and are fighting off an ambush.

Bottom: These soldiers are relaxing on their BMP (infantry fighting vehicle) outside a *kishlak*, an Afghan village.

Top: Mi-24 battle helicopters, called Crocodiles by the soldiers. They were heavily armoured and carried a variety of formidable weapons. They were vulnerable to the heavy machine guns and missiles of the mujahedin, but operated effectively until the end of the war.

Bottom: Mi-8 helicopters, Bees, delivering supplies to a mountain *zastava*. These machines, flown by Russian crews, were hired by the Americans to perform the same role during their war in Afghanistan.

The Russians called it a 'war of mines'. Both sides used mines extensively and indi criminately to block their enemies' communications and defend their own position The mujahedin were highly skilled in laying mines provided from Western sources, ar constructing roadside bombs. The Russians produced a variety of mechanical devic to deal with the mines. But it was the sappers and their dogs who bore the brunt. Th said: A sapper only ever makes one mistake.

hree-quarters of the 40th Army's supplies were brought from the Soviet Union. Huge
pply columns, as many as 800 vehicles, travelled for more than 280 miles over the
indu Kush to Kabul. The columns were often ambushed, but the mujahedin never
anaged to close the road.

The valley in September 2008. The picture is taken looking down from the road whic winds its way up the valley. The derelict tank is halfway down the hillside. The Russia successfully stormed the valley many times. But they never had enough troops to ho it.

was shot by a sniper and left Afghanistan wrapped in a groundsheet and bound to the deck of a BMP, according to legend the last Soviet soldier to be killed in the war.

General Sebrov, who had entered Afghanistan with the 103rd Division in 1979, was not impressed by the official speeches, the crowds, and the flowers. He summed it up bitterly: 'The country we had been helping in every possible way for ten years now lay in ruins. Everyone had contributed to the destruction … but a significant part of the blame lay on us. It was impossible not to be struck by the change in people's attitude to our army and our soldiers. We were greeted with sympathy and friendship when we came in. Now the ordinary Afghans threatened and insulted us as we departed.'[52]

Crossing the Bridge

General Gromov, the commander of the 40th Army, woke up as usual, and in a good mood, at half past six on 14 February 1989 in Tashkurgan, about an hour's drive from the frontier. Once upon a time Tashkurgan boasted an ancient and famously beautiful market, but that was destroyed in the fighting. For much of the war it was the base of a motor-rifle regiment, and since January it had been the last headquarters of the 40th Army. Now the Afghans were wandering around the place as if they owned it, working out the value of the buildings of which they were soon to take possession. At ten o'clock Gromov's small column, the Reconnaissance Battalion of the 201st Division, set out for Khairaton, the transit base on the Afghan side of the river.

Here, as Gromov and his colleagues set down once again to check that no one from the 40th Army had been left behind, there was a panicky call from Yazov. The Foreign Ministry lawyers had pointed out that the Geneva Agreements stated that the Soviet forces should be out of Afghanistan by 15 February. In other words, they should have got back to the Soviet Union by 14th February. Gromov replied that he had already spoken to the United Nations representatives, who had decided to turn a blind eye. Then Yazov asked, 'Why are you intending to leave last, and not lead the troops out, as a commander should?' Gromov said that he thought he had earned the right after serving more than five years in Afghanistan. Yazov was obstinately silent.

All day the soldiers and officers checked their vehicles and cleaned up their best uniforms, while Gromov went to look at the transit base. It was so huge that he would have needed a week to explore it all. There were great stores of tractors, agricultural vehicles, roofing material, cement, sugar, flour. His Afghan guide showed him one container that had been sealed since it had arrived in 1979 until a few days earlier, when it had been opened. It was full of cakes and confectionery, which had all quietly rotted away.

On returning to his soldiers, Gromov paraded them to make sure they were fully prepared for the next day's event. He had his own vehicle – BTR No. 305 – inspected and checked and then inspected again. The last thing he wanted was for it to break down in the middle of the bridge.

He did not sleep well that last night. He felt emptied of emotion: the exhilaration of the previous days had evaporated. He dozed off at four o'clock, but woke up even before his alarm clock rang. By five o'clock the base was already coming alive. Soldiers were moving about and laughing, and the first vehicles were warming up their engines. Someone started to sing.

At nine o'clock Gromov called in his adjutant to check that his uniform was in order and at nine thirty he gave the order to move. The battalion's armoured personnel carriers passed before him on to the bridge. Some of the soldiers were weeping. At nine forty-five Gromov followed them in his command vehicle, carrying the banner of the 40th Army. It was the last vehicle across. The withdrawal was complete.[53]

The other side of the river was crowded with local Party and government officials, hundreds of Soviet and foreign journalists, and the relatives of soldiers who had not returned, hoping against hope to get news that they had perhaps been found safe and well at the last minute. Among the crowd was Alexander Rozenbaum, a young journalist from *Severny Komsomolets*, the Archangel youth newspaper. Fifty-nine boys from Archangel had been killed in Afghanistan and Rozenbaum's moving report of the ceremony at the bridge ended with the questions which everyone was now asking: Why did we go in? Who are the guilty men?[54]

People embraced the soldiers, kissed them, threw flowers under the tracks of their vehicles. Gromov's son Maksim was there, and ran to embrace him. Then there were speeches, a meal in a nearby café for the officers. Gromov phoned Yazov, who congratulated him unenthusiastically. And then, apart for the administrative chores, it was all over.

Even now the official press was still peddling the old myths. In those very last days *Pravda* wrote, 'An orchestra played as the Nation welcomed the return of her sons. Our boys were coming home after fulfilling their international obligations. For 10 years Soviet soldiers in Afghanistan repaired, rebuilt, and constructed hundreds of schools, technical colleges, over 30 hospitals and a similar number of nursery schools, some 400 blocks of flats and 35 mosques. They sank dozens of wells and dug nearly 150 km of irrigation ditches and canals. They were also engaged in guarding military and civilian installations in trouble.'[55]

But there was no one from Moscow to greet the soldiers at the bridge – no one from the Party, no one from the government, no one from the Ministry of Defence, no one from the Kremlin. Years later their excuse was that it had been a dirty war, that to have made the journey to Termez would have been in effect to endorse a crime.[56] It was an extraordinary omission – very bad politics, as well as very bad behaviour. The soldiers never forgot or forgave the insult.

THIRTEEN

THE WAR CONTINUES

The men of the 40th Army who crossed the bridge were not the last Russian soldiers to leave Afghanistan, nor the last to see action there. Parachutists were stationed in the embassy grounds to guard the ambassador and his much diminished staff, who were now brought in from their outlying apartments in the *microrayons* and elsewhere. Soviet military specialists remained to assist the Afghan army to operate the more sophisticated equipment. And Soviet special forces and reconnaissance troops continued to operate in the outlying provinces, especially on the borders of the Soviet Union.[1]

And some people were moving in the opposite direction, back to Kabul on planes that were by now half empty. When he returned at the beginning of January, Andrei Greshnov had more than 250 kilograms of hand baggage. Luckily there were no Afghan customs officers on duty as he arrived, so he did not have to explain that the jam jars and rubber-topped bottles he was carrying were full of alcohol. He and the other Soviet correspondents, who for the most part were hanging around with nothing to do, remained in their villas, but installed backup teletype machines in case something went wrong in their offices in town.

The austerity had its compensations. The embassy shop was

stuffed with goodies, a rich and unfamiliar choice of food products and consumer goods: everything left in the army shops had been moved to the embassy. The spirit ration was raised to four bottles of Moldovan cognac and four bottles of white wine. The limit on beer was lifted entirely.

Before they left, the departing soldiers had sold everything that could possibly be sold: ammunition, food, blankets, sheets, consumer goods, corned beef, Greek juices, Dutch fizzy drinks, Polish and Hungarian ham, green peas, sunflower oil, tinned meats, tea, and cigarettes. So surfeited was the market that Soviet goodies remained on sale in Afghan shops for years afterwards.

One particularly imaginative racket was dreamed up by a group of warrant officers. The air force was abandoning boxes of plastic nose cones – *nursiki* – for their rockets. You could drink from them, but apart from that they were not much good for anything. The racketeers started by going round the shops and asking the traders if they had any *nursiki* for sale. The traders had never heard of *nursiki* and asked what they were for. 'You wouldn't understand,' said the racketeers. 'They are very useful, very scarce, and very expensive.' After they had launched a few boxes of nose cones on to the market, the racketeers bought them back at inflated prices. The cupidity of the traders pushed the price sky high, and when demand seemed to be at its height, the racketeers sold off two lorry-loads and pulled out. When the traders complained to the Soviet Embassy, they were told, 'If you can't stand the heat, don't go into the kitchen.' Years later the traders were still wondering how they could have let themselves be so comprehensively fooled.

One thing in particular caught Greshnov's eye in the Kabul of those last days. There was a T-62 tank on a pedestal as a monument outside the Central Committee of the National People's Army in Kabul. It had been there for ten years at least: Greshnov had seen it at the time of the coup against Amin. He wondered whether it was still in working order. Three years later the tank was removed from its pedestal by the forces of Ahmad Shah Masud as they retreated from the capital. They filled it up with diesel, put in a new battery, and drove it off to the Pandsher Valley.[2]

The Civil War Continues

The 40th Army had gone, but the Afghan civil war continued with horrifying force. The morale of the mujahedin was high. Arms continued to reach them from Pakistan in contravention of the Geneva Agreements. These the Pakistanis had never had any intention of observing: President Zia ul-Haq told President Reagan that they had been denying their activities in Afghanistan for eight years, and that Muslims had the right to lie in a good cause.[3] Most people predicted that the Najibullah government would soon be replaced by an Islamic, possibly fundamentalist, government which 'at best', the CIA observed gloomily, 'will be ambivalent, and at worst ... may be actively hostile, especially toward the United States.'[4]

For their part the Russians continued to supply Kabul with massive quantities of food, fuel, ammunition, and military equipment. A Soviet military delegation led by Varennikov visited Afghanistan at the beginning of May 1989 to discuss ways and means.[5] By 1990 Soviet aid to the Kabul government had reached a value of $3 billion a year. The Afghan army and air force were entirely dependent on these supplies, and fought well against the mujahedin as long as the supplies continued.

A major battle erupted around the city of Jalalabad almost immediately after the 40th Army had left. The fall of this city would, the Pakistanis believed, be followed by the fall of Kabul and enable their protégé Hekmatyar to seize power.[6] The mujahedin began their offensive at the beginning of March 1989, capturing an outlying post by bribing the officer in charge.[7] They then attempted to take the airport, but were repulsed with heavy losses, compounded by the failure of individual mujahedin commanders to agree on a common plan. Early in the battle the mujahedin executed a number of prisoners, which reinforced the determination of the government soldiers to resist.

Once again Najibullah asked for Soviet air support. Gorbachev called an emergency meeting on 10 March to consider the request. It was rejected.[8] But further attacks were broken up by the government's own aircraft and by April the government troops were on the offensive. They bombarded the mujahedin with over four hundred Scud missiles developed from the Germans' wartime V2 rockets and fired by the Soviet crews who had remained behind. Like the V2, you got no warning of the Scud's arrival until it had exploded. 'The mujahedin, who, one would have thought, were already inured to the use in their homeland of every kind of weapon,' wrote Greshnov, who visited Jalalabad at the time, '…were psychologically unable to cope when these rockets were employed against them … Losses among the civilian population could be counted in thousands, and the battle itself acquired such a massive and brutal character that it could be compared in military terms perhaps only with the battle for Stalingrad.'[9] The soldiers cleared the road from Kabul – the old 'English' road, along which the Army of the Indus had retreated in 1842 – and relieved the city. By the time the battle was over, in July 1989, the mujahedin had lost more than three thousand killed and wounded. One mujahedin field commander lamented that 'the battle of Jalalabad lost us the credit won in ten years of fighting'. In the eyes of Brigadier Mohamed Yousaf, the ISI officer responsible for supplying the mujahedin with arms for much of the war, 'The Jehad has never recovered from Jalalabad.' He was writing just after the war was over and predicted that the ragged end to the war would 'not bring peace or stability to Afghanistan or the border areas of Pakistan'.[10] His words turned out to be prophetic.

Kandahar had always been a dangerous city for foreigners, full of sullen Pushtun bazaars, where people assumed that if you spoke their language it was because you were a spy. Greshnov visited it with a party of foreign journalists in the summer of 1989, a year after the Soviet garrison had left in the first phase of the withdrawal.

The city looked very different from his previous visit in 1983. 'We drove through the green belt and past the first roadside shops. Everywhere the same hostile, cautious looks. A city of enemies, soaked in hatred for the Soviets. What has changed here? Well, almost nothing, if you ignore the fact that Kandahar has been largely destroyed. I had not seen the consequences of the Soviet air raid which took place on 8 December 1986. Now I saw for the first time how Kandahar looked without the Soviet forces.

'We stopped opposite the place where there used to be a coffee shop under a sign saying "Toyota". It was a part of the town I knew well. But the coffee shop was no longer there … Everything was recognisable, but everything was now different. Children clung to the BTRs. "*Ingrizi? Feransavi? Amrikai?*" … I calmly said that I was a *shuravi*, a Soviet. They didn't believe me until I let out a stream of good Russian swearwords. They were overwhelmed by a childish delight which had not been driven out of them by the experience of war: perhaps they're the only people in Kandahar who did not remember us with hatred. Shoving their dirty fingers into their mouths to show they were hungry, they cried in Russian, "Soviet, Soviet, fuck your mother, good, give us baksheesh, give us a cigarette!"[11]

Kandahar was still under government control, but it was being regularly bombarded by the forces of Hekmatyar. It had endured two massive attacks in the past few months. Eighty per cent of the shopkeepers in the bazaar, the city governor told Greshnov, were mujahedin taking a rest from fighting. They used to come in for two to three days a month. Now they were coming in for fifteen to twenty days at a time. The number of mujahedin in the region had grown four- or fivefold since the departure of the Soviet forces. They were honest fellows, said the governor. They had no interest in destroying the city; they merely wanted to liberate it. The governor himself was in discreet touch with their leaders.

What were things coming to, wondered Greshnov, when the official governor of a major city started talking about 'honest mujahedin'?[12]

The Fall of Kabul

In 1989 and 1990 Najibullah's government had some success in strengthening the armed forces at its disposal. The KhAD had financed the creation of militia forces drawn from the former mujahedin: 100,000 former insurgents are said to have joined the government militias. The 17th Division in Herat – whose mutiny in March 1979 had helped launch the resistance to the Communists – now consisted of 3,400 regular troops and 14,000 militiamen. According to one calculation, the total numbers of security forces available to the government from all sources in 1988 was almost 300,000.[13]

The respite was shortlived. The rebels had not yet learned how to conduct conventional warfare and throughout 1989 the government forces were mostly successful at beating off their attacks.[14] But by the end of the summer of 1990, Afghan government forces were everywhere on the defensive. Masud by now commanded a force of twenty thousand men with tanks and artillery. By the first half of 1991, the government controlled only 10 per cent of Afghanistan, the city of Khost had finally fallen to the rebels, the morale of the army had collapsed, and desertion was rife. Shevardnadze and Kryuchkov had continued to oppose moves to cut off supplies to Najibullah. But Shevardnadze had resigned from the Soviet government in December 1990 and Kryuchkov was arrested after the abortive coup in August 1991. Najibullah no longer had a senior advocate in the Soviet government. The Soviet Union itself was on the verge of economic and political collapse. An Afghan official visiting Moscow at the time remarked, 'We saw all these empty stores in Moscow and long queues for a loaf of bread and we thought: what can the Russians give us?'[15]

Yeltsin, the coming power in Russian politics, had no interest in spending Russian money to ameliorate the consequences of a Soviet disaster. His officials began to talk openly of getting rid of Najibullah in favour of an Islamic government. That autumn Najibullah wrote bitterly to Shevardnadze, 'I didn't want to be president, you talked me into it, insisted on it, and promised support. Now you are throwing me and the Republic of Afghanistan to its fate.'[16] In December 1991 the representatives of the KGB finally abandoned Kabul and their long ambition to control Afghan affairs.[17] Even before the collapse of the Soviet Union, Yeltsin and his people had begun to deal directly with mujahedin leaders as part of their overall aim of wresting control of foreign policy from Gorbachev's government.[18] In January 1992 Yeltsin's new Russian government cut off military supplies and fuel to Najibullah.

The rot spread very fast. Najibullah's air force, his most effective weapon against the mujahedin, was grounded for lack of fuel. The rebels continued to receive supplies from Pakistan. They began to capture major cities and terrorist acts started to multiply in Kabul itself. In January 1992, on the fifth anniversary of the launching of his Policy of National Reconciliation, Najibullah publicly blamed the Soviet Union for the disasters that had overtaken Afghanistan and called the day of the Soviet withdrawal 'the Day of National Salvation'. But his government was now beyond any salvation.

The Russians hung on in Kabul for as long as they could. By now the embassy had been turned into a fortress. It was surrounded by a double concrete wall with steel gates. Before they left in February 1989, Soviet military engineers had spent the whole year building an immense air-raid shelter just by the administrative block. The shelter had its own supply of water and electricity, an air-filter system, a substantial stock of food, and everything else that was necessary for the whole staff of the embassy to hold out there for some time. A large refrigerator was designated as a morgue. A separate secure apartment was set aside for Najibullah in case he should seek political asylum.[19] There was an atmosphere of hectic but suppressed tension inside the embassy in these last days. Fighting continued to grow in the western part of the city and one day the staff were ordered to the shelter, where they spent much time as the embassy and the area around it were increasingly subjected to deliberate rocket and artillery bombardment.[20]

Galina Ivanov and the other embassy wives lived in the shelter while their men went to their offices to work. There were two or three dozen men there as well. Several of them behaved badly: they let themselves go, did not bother to shave, quarrelled over the ration of food and water, and complained when Galina put a little food aside for the embassy dog. It got so unpleasant that she and the other women took to sleeping in the polyclinic until her husband, Valeri, acting on a hunch, rang to say that an attack was expected any minute: they were to get out of the polyclinic and seek proper shelter in the cellar of the embassy shop. The polyclinic was blown to pieces just as they were leaving and they barely escaped.[21]

The ambassador did what he could to build a workable relationship with such Afghan government as there still was. Soviet trading organisations continued to operate in Kabul under the overall direction of Valeri Ivanov. Yuri Muratkhanian was the director of Afsotr, the joint Soviet-Afghan transport company. On 12 August 1992 he was drinking tea with his wife, Nina, in their flat with Yevgeni Konovalov, the bookkeeper at the Russian trade office, when the building was hit by a shell from a tank. Nina and Konovalov were both mortally wounded, and died a few days later. Their bodies were sealed in zinc coffins and stored in the refrigerator which had been set aside as a morgue. The electricity kept failing and the freon in the refrigerator began to run out. Some Afghan friends braved the bombardment to bring in more.[22]

That same evening Najibullah called in the senior Russian military adviser, General Lagoshin, and told him that he and his colleagues – there were by now only seven military advisers left in Kabul – must leave Afghanistan urgently. The rebels would soon take power and he himself could survive in the post of president for only five more days. Najibullah added that, although the Soviets had betrayed him, he felt it was his duty to send the military advisers home safe and sound. And indeed, when the airport authorities put up various obstacles to their departure the next day, Najibullah came personally to the airport to help get them off to Tashkent.[23]

The following day Najibullah appealed to the UN to fly him into exile as his government finally fell to pieces. His party was stopped at the airport, which was now controlled by General Dostum, and he sought asylum in what he hoped would be the safe haven of the UN headquarters in Kabul.[24]

By now it made no sense to keep people in Kabul and the Russians decided to evacuate the embassy. The operation began at four o'clock on the morning of 28 August, when three aircraft left Termez for Kabul. The new ambassador, Yevgeni Ostrovenko, who had only been in Kabul for a few months, drove to the airport with his staff, picking up diplomats from Mongolia, China, Indonesia, and India on the way.

Both what was left of the Afghan government and the mujahedin had guaranteed that the Russian aircraft would land and leave Kabul safely. The three Il-76s flew in, firing flares to decoy rockets. Valeri Ivanov and his wife, Galina, the coffins containing the bodies of Nina Muratkhanian and Yevgeni Konovalov, and a number of other people and goods were loaded on to the first plane. It took off safely, climbing steeply to thirteen thousand feet to avoid the rockets before setting course for home. But then the mujahedin started to bombard the airport. The second aircraft also took off successfully, though several tyres on the undercarriage had been shredded by splinters. But the third aircraft was set on fire, and the ambassador's wife, who had already gone on board, barely escaped. The paratroopers and aircrew were able to save some documents but no baggage as they jumped out of the aircraft just before it blew up.

The commander of the first aircraft refused to return to pick up those left behind, explaining to Ivanov that he had run out of flares. 'You would have to pay a very great deal to get me to change my mind,' he said, presumably as a joke. In Termez – in what was by now independent Uzbekistan – the airport staff refused to refuel the aircraft or supply food and water for the crew and the passengers unless they were given the two KaMAZ lorries the aircraft was carrying as a bribe. That was a measure, Ivanov thought, of how far things had deteriorated since the break-up of the Soviet Union.

The remainder of the embassy staff, including Ambassador Ostrovenko and his wife, had to be ferried out to Mazar-i Sharif in several An-12s provided by General Dostum. From there they were flown home.

One of the soldiers had rescued the bullet-riddled flag from the flagpole on the Russian Embassy. Years later it still hung in his office.[25]

Those who looked for parallels remembered that, two decades earlier, the American Embassy staff had been rescued from Saigon in circumstances even more humiliating.

There was now no coherent authority in the capital. The Uzbek militia commander General Dostum, who had hitherto been one of Najibullah's most effective commanders, had joined Masud and Hekmatyar in a drive on the capital. But their unity was ephemeral. The endemic hostility between the various mujahedin factions now broke out in an even more vicious form. Kabul had suffered little during the nine years of the Soviet war. Now much of it was destroyed by indiscriminate bombardment, and its people were subjected to looting, rape, and murder. Masud's troops were involved in some of the worst atrocities against the Hazara minority. By 1996 some forty thousand of the inhabitants are said to have been killed and two hundred thousand had fled.[26]

The civil war was brought to an end by the Taliban. Many of them had grown up in the refugee camps in Pakistan and had been educated in the orthodox Muslim schools there. They enjoyed their first success in the spring of 1994, when they captured the town of Spin Boldak on the Pakistani frontier. From then on they moved inexorably forward, capturing Kandahar but checked for a while at Kabul, where Masud seemed to be prevailing. Backed by Pakistan, they then turned their attention to the west of the country, taking over the base at Shindand with its aircraft, and capturing Herat without a fight in September 1995. The fighting around Mazar-i Sharif was marked by massacres on both sides, but the Taliban finally established themselves there in August 1996. Jalalabad and Kabul fell in September.[27]

For most of the inhabitants of Kabul the victory of the Taliban was, at least at first, a return to a kind of security and some sense of order, even if it was enforced by a brutal version of sharia law. But for Najibullah it was the end. The Taliban forcibly seized him and his brother in the UN headquarters, tortured them, castrated them, and hanged their bodies in the centre of the city.

Masud's Assassination

At first Masud's political and military career continued to flourish after the Russians had left. But the changing fortunes and shifting alliances of the civil war, and above all the rise of the Taliban, saw him increasingly on the defensive, under air attack, pushed back from Kabul. He fought with all his old skill, supported by Iran, Uzbekistan, and Russia. But he was eventually driven back into his old base in the Pandsher Valley. There he became leader of the United Islamic Front for the Salvation of Afghanistan, the Northern Alliance, which grouped together the leaders of the small proportion – one-tenth – of the country which was still free of the Taliban.

Despite these setbacks, the Russians continued to build up their links with Masud and the Northern Alliance. He corresponded with President Yeltsin and Yevgeni Primakov (1929–), who at that time was heading the Russian Foreign Intelligence Service.[28] In February 1994 Russian representatives came for secret talks with him in Afghanistan. In 1998 Masud sent his Foreign Minister, Abdullah Abdullah, to Moscow for talks about military-technical cooperation and the provision of military assistance. His representatives met with the Russian Chief of

Staff, General Kvashnin, Yeltsin's assistant Sevostyanov, and Deputy Foreign Minister Pastukhov. In 2000 serious fighting flared up again. The Taliban used tanks and aircraft against Masud, who despite being increasingly short of equipment and supplies was able to beat them off. In the spring of that year the Taliban declared a jihad against Russia. In October Masud met the Russian Minister of Defence, Marshal Sergeev, in Dushanbe and the Russians agreed to supply him with weapons and ammunition. The Taliban promptly issued a warning: 'Russia should cease interfering in the internal affairs of Afghanistan, otherwise it may create for itself many dangerous problems and grave consequences.' In December 2000, on the proposal of Russia and the United States, the United Nations Security Council agreed on further sanctions against the Taliban. In April 2001 Masud visited the European Parliament in Brussels and asked for help in the fight against the Taliban, whose associates Al Qaeda, he warned, would next turn their attention to the US and Europe.[29]

At the beginning of September 2001 Arkadi Dubnov, a journalist from *Novoe Vremya*, was staying in a guest house in the Pandsher Valley, waiting for an interview with Masud, whom he had got to know well since he first started working in Afghanistan in 1993. He shared a room with two Arab journalists who also wanted to interview Masud. The Arabs got their interview on 9 September and killed Masud with a bomb concealed in their TV camera. They were said to be Moroccans from a news agency in London. Scotland Yard therefore investigated the affair and Dubnov was interviewed by them. But the investigation was apparently abandoned for lack of sufficient evidence.[30]

President Putin (1952–) immediately telephoned President Bush (1946–). 'I said that Masud, the leader of the Northern Alliance, had just been killed. I told my American colleague: "I'm very worried. Something big is going to happen. They're planning something."'[31] The Twin Towers in New York were bombed two days later. Putin was the first foreign leader to express his condolences to Bush, and immediately took practical steps to support the forthcoming American campaign to destroy the Taliban and Al Qaeda. His people handed over a good deal of intelligence, including minefield maps – many of them inevitably inaccurate after the passage of time. He opened Russian air space to American military flights and persuaded the leaders of the Central Asian states to do the same. He met the leaders of the Northern Alliance, stepped up Russian military support for them, and convinced them to cooperate with the Americans. This collaboration did not flag. The northern supply route through Russia became increasingly important, as the Americans got into trouble with their supply route from Pakistan. The flow of intelligence continued. In October 2010 Russians provided support and advice for a US-led raid on four major narcotics factories, the first joint operation of its kind. Many Russians felt that the Americans were insufficiently grateful for what Putin had done to help them.[32]

Once the Americans' initial campaign was over and a new regime was installed in Kabul, the Russians continued to strengthen their links with the new Afghan regime, travelling to Afghanistan on open and confidential business as officials, journalists, and even tourists, as they had done almost uninterrupted since the end of the Soviet war.

Masud was buried in the Pandsher Valley, on a hill by his native village, Jangalak, and a monument was erected to him immediately. A substantial Russian delegation led by General Varennikov took part in the ceremonies at his grave on the second anniversary of his death. Over the years, as the cult of Masud grew more elaborate, the grave was converted into a massive mausoleum. The Russians continued to pay their annual respects. The Pushtuns looked on with resentment at this glorification of a man who was not one of them and who, they grumbled for years afterwards, had signed ceasefires with the Russians instead of continuing the struggle against them.[33]

The 201st Division Fights On

For one of the divisions of the 40th Army the war never stopped. The 201st Division withdraw from Afghanistan to Tajikistan, and remained there after the country became independent on the collapse of the Soviet Union. Its headquarters were in the capital, Dushanbe, and its two regiments were deployed towards the Afghan frontier in Kulabe and Kurgan-Tobe. When civil war broke out in 1992 between the central government and Islamic rebels, the local Tajik conscripts deserted. The Russian officers and warrant officers withdrew to their barracks with their families and refused to surrender to the mob. Yeltsin took the division back under Russian jurisdiction. Its numbers were made up with Russian conscripts and contract soldiers on generous terms, and it formed the core of the peacekeeping force set up by the Commonwealth of Independent States, a grouping of former Soviet republics. The force was disbanded when the civil war ended in 1997, but the division remained in Tajikistan, its status undefined.

The war did not stop for the KGB's frontier forces either. They too had their headquarters in Dushanbe, with detachments on the Afghan frontier. Some had been involved in operations inside Afghanistan, and some were among the 576 members of the KGB who had died there. Now they continued to guard the frontier between Afghanistan and Tajikistan against drug smugglers and the incursions of bands of fundamentalists anxious to support the Islamic rebels inside the country. They too were eventually brought under Russian jurisdiction. In May 1993 Russia and Tajikistan signed an agreement on friendship and cooperation which handed formal responsibility for the defence of the frontier to Russia.

Attacks against the frontier posts had already started. On 13 July a massive attack was launched in the early hours against the 12th *zastava* by about four hundred men, a mixture of mujahedin and soldiers from the 55th Infantry Division of the regular Afghan army. The garrison of the *zastava* consisted of forty-eight frontier force soldiers. Aroused by their watchdog, the garrison made for their battle positions as fire was brought down upon them from the surrounding hills and from the Afghan side of the frontier. The crew of the *zastavas'* one BTR were the first to die, even before they could mount their machine. After the twenty-five-year-old commander was killed, his deputy decided that the survivors would have to make a break for safety. A small force from the 201st Division and the Tajik army, backed by a couple of helicopters, was put together to rescue the beleaguered garrison. It ran into mines and ambushes on the only approach road, and the Tajik troops turned back. When the Russian relief force finally got through, they found that twenty-five of the garrison had been killed and their bodies mutilated.

Six members of the garrison were made 'Heroes of Russia' – four of them posthumously – to join the eighty-six men who had become 'Heroes of the Soviet Union' during the Afghan war.[34]

FOURTEEN

A LAND FIT FOR
HEROES

The soldiers who crossed the Friendship Bridge on 15 February returned to a country which had less than two years to live, a country which in its own way was as shattered as the one they had left behind them. A radical electoral process was under way which would see senior officers losing the parliamentary seats which they believed were theirs by right. The whisperings of discontent in the non-Russian republics of the union were becoming louder. The economy was in rapid decline. The press had always treated the military with respect: it now had free rein to criticise them unmercifully. There was much to resent, but the soldiers particularly resented a poem by the popular poet Yevgeni Yevtushenko, describing the thoughts of an Afghan ant as it crawled on the face of a dead Russian soldier.

The blows that then struck the Soviet army came close to destroying it as an effective military force.

The 40th Army had withdrawn from Afghanistan, in the eyes of its commanders, with its military reputation and its honour intact. It had achieved the limited tasks laid upon it by the politicians: to hold the towns, to keep open the communications, to keep the rebels at bay sufficiently for the government in Kabul to build up its military position and survive, at least for a time. The soldiers had done their duty, and they had not been defeated on the battlefield. The war had been a bitter experience. But from the military point of view at least, it had not been a humiliation. Now, within months, the 40th Army, one of the most powerful in Soviet history, was disbanded, its generals, its divisional commanders, and their deputies transferred or sent off to military academies, its regimental commanders dispersed to units throughout the Soviet Union.

When the Soviet Union fell apart less than two years later, many of these officers found themselves serving in the armed forces of what were now independent countries. They had sworn an oath to the Soviet Union; some of them refused to swear another and gave up their military careers.

The Bitterness of the Officers

In their bitterness and confusion, many of the officers turned to the older traditions of their country. They began to feel a guilty sense of shame towards Russia, towards the land of their fathers, its villages depopulated, its churches in ruins, the village blacksmith silent, a country which had changed almost out of recognition, abandoned and forgotten, as one of them remarked, 'by me and people like me'.[1] They had sympathised with their great-grandfathers, the officers of the old Tsarist army who had been forced to choose sides in the civil war. Now, as civil war seemed to loom once again, they found themselves having to face a similar choice. Should they go with the new regimes of Gorbachev and Yeltsin? Or should they do what they could to preserve what was best in the Soviet regime?

They found themselves drawn willy-nilly into the increasingly confused and violent politics within the Soviet Union itself. The 345th Guards Independent Parachute Assault Regiment had been one of the first to enter Afghanistan and one of the last to leave. Now it was sent to Kirovabad in Azerbaijan, where there were no barracks, no motor park, no accommodation, and no money. In early April 1989, a mere two months after leaving Afghanistan, the regiment was sent urgently to Tbilisi to take part in the brutal suppression of an anti-government demonstration. Nineteen civilian demonstrators were killed by soldiers using a noxious riot-control gas and wielding sharpened entrenching tools. Most of the dead were women and girls. The ultimate responsibility for the action was obscure, but most of the soldiers laid the blame on Gorbachev himself. Moscow, however, blamed the local Georgian politicians and the local military commanders. General Rodionov, the commander of the Caucasus Military District, who had been a distinguished commander of the 40th Army, was sacked and sent off to become principal of the General Staff College.[2] Nine months later, in January 1990, two hundred demonstrators were killed by the army in Baku, the capital of Azerbaijan. Among those involved were a number of senior officers who had served in Afghanistan.

In September 1990 the Soviet government agreed on the reunification of Germany. In the eyes of many officers this was a betrayal of the victory against Hitler and a sell-out by Gorbachev, Shevardnadze, and the other 'liberals' who were now running the Soviet government. By then the withdrawal from Eastern Europe had already begun. In autumn 1989 a British general visited a tank division in the Ukraine which was due to be disbanded. The major general commanding the division said to him in front of his brother officers: 'Some people are beginning to say that the whole army is being thrown on the scrap heap … [pause] I agree with them.'[3] Over the next couple of years nearly 500,000 soldiers and their families were withdrawn from the German Democratic Republic and the countries of Eastern Europe. The soldiers returned to poverty-stricken chaos. Many officers had nowhere to live, and had to survive with their families in tents and packing cases. The muttering among the soldiers was becoming increasingly audible. Senior officers were beginning to advise their sons not to follow them in the profession.

The Party had always been determined to keep the army non-political by sacking (or, under Stalin, by shooting) any general they suspected of 'Bonapartism'; and by allowing them a priority share of the country's economic resources for the design and mass production of weapons to match those of the other superpower, the United States of America. Now things began to take an increasingly sinister turn as the army started to slip from the control of the politicians. By the autumn of 1990 Gorbachev was being noisily attacked in public and in private by the two 'black colonels', Alksnis and Petrushenko, who regularly accused him of outright treachery and got away with it. Party members wrote in to denounce him for betraying Eastern Europe and destroying the Soviet armed forces. In December 1990 fifty-three prominent personalities, including General Varennikov, who after Afghanistan had been appointed Commander of the Ground Forces, General Moiseev, the Chief of Staff, and Admiral Chernavin, the Commander-in-Chief of the Navy, called publicly for a state of emergency and presidential rule in conflict zones if constitutional methods proved ineffective. At the turn of the year twenty senior officers, including Akhromeev, by now a marshal, privately presented Gorbachev with an ultimatum setting out their grievances and demands.[4]

All this was unprecedented: the military had never before intervened so openly in politics. But in January 1991 things moved from words to action. Thirteen people demonstrating in favour of national independence were killed by special forces troops in Vilnius, the capital of the Lithuanian Soviet Socialist Republic. The circumstances remained obscure. It was not clear how much, if anything, Gorbachev knew or approved of the action in advance. But among those who were involved in its planning and execution was General Varennikov.

The Coup against Gorbachev

The methods Gorbachev used to get out of Afghanistan and to pursue a more general reform may well have been the only ones likely to be effective. It was largely thanks to Gorbachev that the collapse of the Soviet Union and the rebirth of Russia were accomplished with comparatively little bloodshed. But the generals never forgave him for what they saw as the treachery which had led to the destruction of a great power. They firmly regarded him and his associates as traitors pure and simple. In his memoirs, Varennikov accuses Gorbachev of cowardice, demagogy, indecisiveness, ignorance of military and economic reality, and hostility towards the armed forces and the defence industry. He and his fellow senior officers came to believe that Gorbachev was an outright traitor.[5] These extreme views may have borne little relation to the facts. But what many officers saw as Gorbachev's lack of understanding or sympathy for the fighting men and his failure to treat them with the respect they believed they had earned in Afghanistan reflected a political reality, which was to dog Gorbachev for the remainder of his time in office.

By now Varennikov and other senior officers had had enough, and became actively involved in the attempted coup against Gorbachev in August 1991.[6] On 17 August, the day before the coup itself, Varennikov attended a meeting called by Kryuchkov, the head of the KGB, to discuss what needed to be done to save the Soviet Union from political and economic collapse. Varennikov and others then flew down to the Crimea to see Gorbachev, who was on holiday there. When Varennikov told Gorbachev that, if he was not capable of running the country, he should draw the appropriate conclusion, the meeting broke up. Varennikov always regretted that no one had the necessary guts to remove Gorbachev on the spot. He himself went on to Kiev, where he tried to persuade the Ukrainian leaders to impose a state of emergency and to issue a warning that military force would be used to put down any attempt by local nationalists to exploit the situation. He failed, and much bloodshed was no doubt averted thereby.

The next day the plotters declared a national state of emergency and moved troops into Moscow. General Lyakhovski helped draw up plans for an assault on the White House, the seat of the Russian government and its defiant president, Boris Yeltsin.[7] But the coup split both the army and the KGB: many officers of both organisations were appalled by the way their former colleagues had taken arms against a legitimate government. Among the defenders of the White House were Colonel Rutskoi, the Afghan veteran decorated after being shot down over Pakistan, and veterans from the special forces in their characteristic blue and white striped T-shirts. The defenders had no more than a handful of weapons, and the assault, if it had come, would have been over very quickly. But the order was never issued and the coup collapsed. It was the Afgantsy who efficiently marshalled the funeral procession for the three young men – one of them himself a decorated Afghan veteran – who were killed in a muddled shoot-out on the second night of the coup.

The generals too were riven by internal disagreements, and during the coup some of them found themselves on opposite sides of the barricades. The most tragic was Marshal Akhromeev. A man of high intelligence and integrity, with an ironic sense of humour, he was caught

between two fires. No longer entirely trusted by his colleagues because
he had done his best to serve Gorbachev as military adviser, sufficiently
appalled by what was happening to his beloved military to sign the
secret protest to Gorbachev at the end of 1990, he hanged himself on
the collapse of the coup. Varennikov himself was arrested for his part
in the coup and charged with treason. Yeltsin amnestied the plotters
in February 1994. Varennikov refused to accept the amnesty, claiming
that he had committed no treason: he had been defending the Soviet
Union, which was the legitimate state at that time. He insisted on a
trial and was acquitted.

The generals did not forgive Gorbachev's successor, Boris Yeltsin,
any more than they forgave Gorbachev. They gritted their teeth and
stormed the White House on his orders during the parliamentary
rebellion of October 1993. The official figures for casualties were 187
dead and 437 wounded. Unofficial sources put the dead as high as two
thousand. It was the deadliest street fighting in Moscow since 1917.
The orgy of political and official corruption and profiteering which
accompanied Yeltsin's economic reforms turned many of the generals
against the whole idea of liberal democracy. It was not very surprising
that many welcomed the more assertive and less democratic Russia
championed by Vladimir Putin when he became President in 2000.

Now, disgusted by these events, many officers left the army altogether. They included some of the most famous soldier-bards: Viktor
Kutsenko, Sergei Klimov, Vadim Dulepov, Vladimir Koshelev. One
worked as a taxi driver, and when the 1991 putsch happened he drove
from his Volga city to fight for Yeltsin on the barricades. Then he tried
to go into commerce. But he did not like the corruption involved
and went to work for the Moscow Metro instead. Another became
a star of the music hall. One wrote philosophy. Another spent two
years in prison for killing someone in a nightclub brawl.[8] Igor Morozov
resigned his commission in 1993, at the age of forty-one. He went to
live in the Ryazan oblast, on the land where his father and ancestors
had come from. By fair means or foul the local authority was trying to
take over the land, systematically driving out people whose families had
lived there for generations. All Morozov's time and energy now went on
fighting to keep his land and his house.[9]

The Fate of the Soldiers

In the aftermath of the war in Afghanistan, the generals were sustained by their sense of military honour, and by the habits of thought of a professional life spent in the sequestered world of the military. But the conscripts who had borne the brunt of the fighting had no military tradition to fall back on. They had neither the time nor the energy to get mixed up in high politics. They were too busy trying to adapt to civilian life and to eke out a living in a country whose political and economic system had fallen apart, and whose citizens were themselves too traumatised by the collapse, and too bound up in their own struggle for everyday existence, to pay much attention to the problems of the returning soldiers.

While a war is still going on, the soldiers are told or convince themselves that everything will be different once it is over, that they will be rewarded with jobs, and homes, and appreciation by a grateful government and people. They are almost always disappointed. Prime Minister Lloyd George campaigned in 1918 on the election promise that he would 'make Britain a fit country for heroes to live in'.[10] It did not happen. Within a couple of years, the country was hit by an economic slump which left many of them without jobs or proper homes. The victory of the Labour Party in the British election of 1945 led many soldiers to believe that this time it would be different. The new government did indeed create full employment, a tax-funded universal National Health Service, and a cradle-to-grave welfare state. But although Labour fulfilled its promises, Britain after the war was a very poor country. Housing was scarce, not least because so much had been destroyed by German bombing. The national finances were in disarray. Food rationing did not finally end until July 1954. The promises to the veterans were largely fulfilled, but at a miserable level.

The soldiers who returned from Afghanistan were just as convinced that their government had promised them jobs, homes, medical care, benefits in kind, and cash. But because the Soviet Union was on the verge of political and economic collapse, many veterans found it hard to get even the things they were entitled to. The financial benefits were inadequate, and homes and jobs were few and far between as factories shut down and workers were laid off. Artificial limbs were crude or non-existent. So were even simple things like wheelchairs. Veterans found it hard to cope with the psychological trauma of battle, or kick the habit of drugs and violence acquired in Afghanistan. Some broke with their wives and girlfriends. Some took to crime. Most did in the end find their way back into civilian life. But all felt some sense of betrayal. 'The boys had lived through so much over there, they'd looked death in the eye, they'd lost their friends … Then they came home to our everyday, not very cheerful life, and their raw nerves … felt all the falsehood, the hypocrisy, the indifference, the gross prosperity of some and the bitter poverty of others. And they were hurt, too, because no one cared about what they had been through, about their physical and spiritual wounds. That's when they began to idealise the past.'[11]

In February 1980, just after the war began, the government increased the wages and improved the pensions of regular soldiers and provided for the families of those who had died. It made no specific provision for conscripts. If the soldier became an invalid, he might qualify for the same benefits as an invalid from the Second World War, but by 1980 these had become quite inadequate. Otherwise he qualified only for the even less generous benefits available to those who had suffered an injury at work.

Another decision followed two years later which specifically covered soldiers and civilians in Afghanistan and their families 'for the successful execution of tasks set by the Government of the USSR'. It did not mention that these 'tasks' were military. It provided pensions, medical services, housing, transport, and so on, similar to those granted to veterans of the Second World War, though more limited in scope. There was less to these improvements than met the eye. In the first place the benefits were not at all generous. They were paid according to rank. An officer got a one-off grant equivalent to three months' pay. A soldier who had served beyond his term got five hundred roubles. A conscript got three hundred roubles. Invalids got half that amount, but they were given a month in a sanatorium after coming out of hospital. Benefits were also set for the families of the dead, whether they were soldiers or civilians. But this was a framework decision only, and had to be supplemented with a whole raft of executive regulations. These were not published, and local authorities were often either ignorant of them or ignored them.[12] So the veterans stumbled into a wall of bureaucratic confusion and obfuscation. Unhelpful officials would say, 'It wasn't me who sent you to Afghanistan,' to justify their refusal to give the veterans the benefits to which they thought they were entitled.

By now the press was weighing in openly. In 1987 *Pravda* wrote of the difficulties veterans faced at the hands of their fellow citizens, who themselves were short of money, proper medical care, and adequate accommodation, and saw little reason why the queues should be jumped by men who had not, after all, been fighting in a real war. An opinion poll of veterans conducted by *Komsomolskaya Pravda* reported that 71 per cent of the veterans thought that the benefits existed only on paper.[13] The veterans still found it hard to discover their rights. And there was no coherent administrative mechanism to administer the benefits properly, no one-stop shop. The veterans had to traipse from one bureaucratic office to the next in order to get what they were entitled to.

In February 1989 the Afgantsy were given the formal status of 'Warrior-Internationalists', a term first applied to the foreign volunteers who fought on the Soviet side during the civil war of 1917–23, and then to the Soviet soldiers who fought in the Spanish and Chinese civil wars, and on the side of 'progressive' regimes in Cuba, Korea, Angola, Ethiopia, Vietnam, and elsewhere. An appropriate campaign medal was issued. It consisted of a five-pointed star on a gold laurel wreath. In the centre was a handshake, and under it a shield, as a symbol of the defensive nature of the operation. None of this satisfied the Afgantsy, who wanted to be given the same status as veterans of the Second World War.[14]

Housing was perhaps the worst nightmare of all. When a veteran killed himself because he had been unable to get anywhere to live, one of the trade union officials involved commented, 'I understand what it was like for him. When the boys were fighting in Afghanistan they were probably promised the earth. But the factory can't just provide an apartment at the drop of a hat. The necessary regulation doesn't exist. And then you have to understand that we have to build the houses ourselves, and with the dreadful new accounting standards we can barely make ends meet. Sasha was the twelfth in the queue. There were veterans from the Second World War ahead of him, and Afghan veterans too, who had arrived in the factory before he got here.'[15]

The Soviet Union had always been a very poor country. There had never been enough wealth to support the general promise of the country's state welfare system to its citizens. With the best will in the world, the promise of special privileges for returning veterans could rarely be fully met in practice. One returning officer recognised the problem: 'The country's level of economic development set the level of social help that the state can give to the various levels of society. If we did not have a housing problem, we would not have a problem finding accommodation for the Afgantsy... It's not a result of a lack of warmth, it's not a result of a lack of attention, it's the result of the problems which exist in the country.'[16]

Not surprisingly, however, few veterans saw it that way. They felt that society had failed to award them even the moral recognition to which they were entitled. The promises that had been made to them were not fulfilled. They had to struggle to get the meagre benefits to which they were entitled. And some civilians grudged them even these.[17]

But one way in which the treatment of the Afgantsy differed from that of the veterans of earlier wars was a direct result of the loosening of the rigid state control which had marked all public activity in the Soviet system. For the first time it became possible for citizens to found their own independent organisations. Towards the end of the war, a number of official and semi-official organisations were set up to help the veterans directly and to bargain with the authorities from a position of greater strength. The importance of this change should not be exaggerated. Some of the new organisations were not very efficient. Some of them were rather corrupt. It sometimes looked as if they were run not so much to benefit their members, but to bring prestige, position, and wealth to their leaders. They were often very close to the authorities.

In 1986 the Komsomol set up a new Administration for Afghan Questions. In April 1990 the Supreme Soviet set up a Committee for Soldier-Internationalists' Affairs: there were thirteen Afgantsy among its members.[18] The Union of Veterans of Afghanistan (SVA) was set up in 1989 by Alexander Kotenov, the son of a Soviet officer who had spent four years in the Gulag. After being blown up by a mine, and disillusioned by the war, Kotenov became a military historian. By 1991 the SVA claimed to represent more than three hundred thousand Afghan veterans. Kotenov resigned in 1995 in protest against government interference in the organisation's affairs.[19]

The Russian Union of Veterans of Afghanistan (RSFA), was set up as an offshoot of the SVA in November 1990. Those present at the founding congress included General Varennikov, Vice-President Alexander Rutskoi, Metropolitan Pitirim and Chief of Staff General Moiseev. Its first chairman was Yevgeni Lyagin. He was followed at the end of 1991 by Kotenov, and then in 2001 by Frants Klintsevich, a political officer in the 345th Guards Independent Parachute Assault Regiment.

The Russian Fund for Invalids of the War in Afghanistan (RFIVA) was set up in 1991. Its subsequent career was turbulent. Its chairman, Mikhail Likhodei, was assassinated in November 1994. Two years later a subsequent chairman, Sergei Trakhirov, and fourteen others were killed, and twenty-four more wounded, when a bomb exploded as they were laying a wreath at a memorial to the Afgantsy in the Kotlyarovskoe Cemetery in Moscow. The subsequent attempt to bring the perpetrators to justice was murky and only partly successful. One suspect was still standing trial in the summer of 2007.[20] After these excitements the RFIVA was renamed the All Russian Social Organisation for Invalids of the War in Afghanistan (OOOIVA). Such stories were not uncommon in the Yeltsin years, when ambitious and ruthless men were fighting – literally – to the death to get their hands on the spoils of the failed Soviet state.

The Boevoe Bratstvo, the Brotherhood of Arms, was set up under General Gromov in 1997. With close links to the authorities, it became one of the most influential veterans' organisations in the new century. It joined the Internet age with enthusiasm, setting up its own national and regional websites, which it claimed were the largest of their kind in Russia.

Yeltsin gave the veterans' organisations special privileges – tax breaks, commercial privileges, customs exemptions on alcohol, tobacco, and oil products, access to foreign currency, sanatoriums, and commercial enterprises worth millions of roubles – which had become available through his policies of 'privatisation'. Bodies such as the National Sporting Fund were similarly privileged, and the practice was one more sign of the collapse and fragmentation of the state. In effect the state handed over to the private sector its responsibilities for those who had fought in its wars. In the chaotic and corrupt conditions of the early 1990s, all this was a licence to print money. A small number of people at the top of the Afghan veterans' organisations got very rich. Only 24 per cent – and according to some calculations, only 9 per cent – of the money actually reached the disabled ex-servicemen for whom it was intended.[21]

This dubious system began to be rethought even before the explosion in the cemetery. In 1995 a revised Veterans' Law finally awarded the Afgantsy the full status and title of 'veterans'.[22] This law gave veterans of all classes fairly broad social benefits, but unfortunately these were no more adequately funded than the benefits that preceded them. Matters were further confused by the Russian government's decision in 2004 to convert benefits in kind – bus passes, holiday vouchers, and the like – into financial payments of dubious value in an inflating economy. The reform of local government in 2006 reallocated responsibility for the administration of benefits yet again. The rapid growth in the Russian economy after 2000 did, however, significantly improve the state's ability to meet its financial obligations to its citizens.

Because these veterans' organisations saw it as one of their tasks to encourage patriotism and respect for the armed forces, especially among the young, their place in President Putin's more assertive Russia was assured. Some of their leaders, such as Frants Klintsevich, went into national politics; by 2007 he was deputy leader of the pro-Putin United Russia faction in the Duma, and Chairman of the Duma Committee which dealt with the problems of pensioners and veterans. In the autumn of 2007 several of the veterans' organisations supported the electoral campaign of Putin and United Russia without inhibition.[23]

Soldiers returning from any war have to adjust to a world which cannot understand what they have been through, to people who have not been there, and who are not interested or interested only in a legend of heroism, rather than the traumatic reality of battle. The soldiers have seen horrible things and some of them have done horrible things. They suffer nightmares, they quarrel with their wives, they commit violence in the home and on the street, they drop to the ground at the sound of a car backfiring, they are especially haunted by the death of children.[24] A month or a year may separate these reactions from the events that trigger them off. The sufferers may be able to fend off the memories by shutting down their emotions, by becoming emotionally numb. The condition may last for months or even years. Because they have been in the military, with its culture of heroism, discipline and masculine toughness, they find it hard to talk of their experiences or seek help outside their own circle of fellow veterans.[25]

The suffering is not confined to those who have fought and killed. British peacekeepers in Bosnia, who fought only in self-defence if at all, showed many of the same symptoms. So do civilians who have been involved in catastrophic events – in traffic accidents, natural disasters, or as victims of violent crime. Since the 1980s, the phenomenon has been given a name: post-traumatic stress disorder, PTSD.

American studies show that 20–30 per cent of the American soldiers who had fought in the deeply unpopular Vietnam War suffered from PTSD, compared with only 15 per cent of those who fought in the first Gulf War in 1991, which was popularly perceived as just and necessary.[26] American soldiers returning from the second Iraq war after 2003 were statistically at greater risk – from suicide, murder, assault, drunken driving, and drug use – than they were while they were fighting there.[27]

But even when a nation believes it has embarked on a 'just war', the rationale fades as the carnage mounts, and the soldiers no longer fight for a cause, but to survive and to help their comrades do the same. The victorious British soldiers who came home from the Second World War were heroes in theory. In practice they were often resented by civilians who had themselves experienced real privation and the danger of violent death from the air. Jobs were scarce, or incompatible with the skills and positions that the veterans believed their service entitled them to. The divorce rate in Britain soared by fifteen times between 1935 and 1947, as couples separated by war failed to rebuild their shattered lives. Violent crime increased by two and a half times in the ten years to 1948. Sexual offences tripled. The newspapers were full of stories of soldiers murdering their wives. The veterans turned to the familiar warmth of contacts with surviving comrades, rather than family, as the first line of defence against a civilian world they perceived as unwelcoming, even hostile. As time went by, most of them slowly settled back into civilian and domestic life. Comrades drifted apart and comradeship was replaced by nostalgia for a generalised picture of a heroic war. But the symptoms could return years and even decades after peace had come. As late as 2001, one in five of the British veterans of the Second World War still displayed war-related psychological distress.[28]

In Russia it was called the 'Afghan syndrome' and it was still around twenty years after the war had ended; in 2009 a popular song by the Siberian rock group Grazhdanskaya Oborona (Civil Defence) described the symptoms rather well.[29] For the veterans of Afghanistan, the inevitable feeling of 'them and us' was exacerbated because many of their fellow citizens now regarded the war as dirty and unjustified. Like those who fought in Vietnam, they had found themselves fighting against an enemy often invisible and taking many forms. Now they were called baby-killers and murderers, sadists and torturers, or simpletons who had been too stupid to understand the crimes they were committing, by those who had stood aside from the horrors of a war which many of the soldiers themselves had concluded made no sense. One foreigner remembered eating in a restaurant as two perfectly sober and polite young army officers with combat decorations were chased out by the *maître d'hôtel*, who assured him that this was not the sort of establishment where 'that sort' could expect to eat.[30]

These were not only the sophisticated attitudes of the urban intelligentsia in Moscow and Leningrad and the big cities. The veterans faced hostility in the small provincial towns as well. When Vitali Krivenko returned to his hometown in August 1987, people who had known him before treated him as if he was somehow abnormal. He broke with his girlfriend because she assumed he was a drug addict like everyone else who had been in Afghanistan. Drinking companions who had not been in the war would ask him if he was liable to go berserk if he took a bit too much. He learned to keep quiet about the fact that he had been blown up and suffered concussion when he applied for a job: employers did not like to hire Afgantsy, because they were regarded as difficult, always demanding the privileges they had been promised but had not received. He ended up briefly in prison for hitting a policeman.

The statistics are incomplete and hard to interpret. Something can be gained from the anecdotal evidence. In 2008 Alexander Gergel found that among those who had served with him in Bakharak, one had died of drug and alcohol abuse, one had been the victim of an armed robbery, and one had become a contract killer and was serving a ten-year sentence in prison. This was not a large proportion; the remainder had more or less adapted to civilian life. 'But after a drink or two, as the evening wore on, one realised that something had broken in the soul of almost all of us. I think one might express it this way: life had forcibly transformed us after its own pattern, and none of us had become what we would have wanted to become if we had not passed through Afghanistan. Whether we were better or worse is another story.'[31]

Though there was no nationwide study, individual regions, local veterans' organisations, and local newspapers began to set up their own websites about their young men who had served in Afghanistan. The newspaper *Voronezhskaya Gazeta* reported there were 5,200 Afghan veterans in Voronezh. By the summer of 1996 seventy-five had died, half as a result of accidents, one-third had been struck down by illness, and one in seven had committed suicide. Twelve years later, more than five hundred had died – one-tenth of all those who had returned from the war. The paper claimed that the young men died not so much because of what they had been through in Afghanistan, but because no provision had been made for their psychological rehabilitation, because they had been unable to afford proper medical treatment, because many of them had been unable to find work or a decent place to live.[32]

But the amount of psychological rehabilitation available for the soldiers was limited partly by the lack of resources and partly because the concept of trauma was alien. If the soldiers who fought against Hitler could survive without going to the shrink, why should the Afgantsy be different? 'Trauma' was an alien, perhaps an American idea.

Nevertheless, a thin but native Russian tradition did exist. The first work on soldiers suffering from psychological trauma was done in Russia after the Russo-Japanese war in 1904–5 by psychiatrists in the Academy of Military Medicine. The results were largely ignored in the Soviet period and the 40th Army took no psychiatrists with them when they went into Afghanistan. The first specialists went there in the mid-1980s. The symptoms they found among the Afgantsy were much the same as the Americans had identified after Vietnam: a sense of guilt at what they had done, a horror at what they had seen, the same self-reproach that they had survived while their comrades had died. Some specialists reckoned that as many as one in two Afghan veterans needed some sort of help. At first the symptoms were psychological: irritability, aggressiveness, insomnia, nightmares, thoughts of suicide. After five years many would be suffering from physical as well as psychological consequences: heart disease, ulcers, bronchial asthma, neurodermatitis.

The trouble was that, compared with the United States, there were nothing like the facilities available in Russia to treat the traumatised veterans. There were only six specialised rehabilitation centres for the whole of Russia, and these had to deal with people traumatised not only by Afghanistan, but by their experiences of dealing with the nuclear accident in Chernobyl in 1986, and by the fighting in Chechnya, and other places of violent conflict.[33]

One of those who tried to explain the phenomenon scientifically was Professor Mikhail Reshetnikov, the Rector of the East European Institute for Psychoanalysis in St Petersburg. He had himself been a professional military medical officer from 1972 and was posted to Afghanistan in 1986. He sent a paper to the General Staff, based on interviews with two thousand soldiers, which set out the problems from which the 40th Army was suffering: from the inadequacy of the army's supply system to the moral and psychological training of the soldiers. The report had no effect, and he was asked by his superiors why he had deliberately set out to gather facts which brought shame on the Soviet Army. From 1988 to 1993 he directed several programmes for the Ministry of Defence on the behaviour of people affected by local wars, and man-made and natural catastrophes. After retiring from the military he became a member of the Association of Afghan Veterans.

In an article published on the Afghan veterans' website in 2002, Reshetnikov argued that the way Russians surrounded their military past with an aura of heroic myth had a political, a moral, and a psychological function. It helped to compensate for the horrors not only of the Afghan and Chechen wars, but of the Great Patriotic War of 1941–5 itself, the foundation event in all modern Russian patriotic myths. He wrote of some of the dreadful things which had happened in Afghanistan: the rebel sniper captured and burned alive by the soldier whose comrade he had killed, the small boy hurled from a helicopter, the young girl raped by a whole platoon, the scores of peaceful civilians shot, the villages destroyed out of revenge. His conclusions were stark. All wars lead to an 'epidemic of amorality', he argued. Genuine heroism and self-sacrificial comradeship do of course exist. But they are always accompanied, in all wars and in all armies, by murder, torture, cruelty to prisoners, rape, and violent looting, especially when the army is operating outside its own territory. The sense of guilt, the need to atone for what they have done, comes to the soldiers later. It affects all their personal relationships, especially within the family. 'Their memories are poisoned by their criminal and semi-criminal experience, and they become a real threat not only to themselves but to society in general.' Not surprisingly, his article infuriated many of the Afghan veterans who read it. They deeply resented the implication that they had all been criminals to a greater or lesser extent, and they expressed their anger in colourful terms on their website.

The Mood Settles Down

Attempts after 1989 by journalists and liberal politicians to get at the truth of the Afghan war produced a furious reaction not only from the veterans, but from their families as well. When Svetlana Aleksievich published her book in 1990 about the men and women who served in Afghanistan, she was overwhelmed with criticism. 'You wanted to demonstrate the futility and wickedness of war, but you don't realise that in doing so you insult those who took part in it, including a lot of innocent boys.' 'How could you? How dare you cover our boys' graves with such dirt? … They were heroes, heroes, heroes!' 'My only son was killed there. The only comfort I had was that I'd raised a hero, but according to you he wasn't a hero at all, but a murderer and aggressor.' 'How much longer are you going to go on describing us as mentally ill, or rapists, or junkies?'

The veterans were particularly infuriated to be told that the war had been a 'mistake'. 'Why all this talk of mistakes? And do you really think that all these exposés and revelations in the press are a help? You're depriving our youth of their heroic heritage.' 'I don't want to hear about any political mistakes … Give me my legs back if it was all a mistake.' 'We were sent to Afghanistan by a nation which sanctioned the war,' one woman said, 'and returned to find that same nation had rejected it. What offends me is the way we've simply been erased from the public mind. What was only recently described as one's "international duty" is now considered stupidity.' 'They put the blame on a few men who were already dead [Brezhnev, Andropov, Chernenko]. And everyone else was innocent – apart from us! Yes, we used our weapons to kill. That's what they handed them out for. Did you expect us to come home angels?' And more calmly: 'Of course there were criminals, addicts and thugs. Where aren't there? Those who fought in Afghanistan must, absolutely, be seen as victims who need psychological rehabilitation.'[34]

What the veterans had found almost the hardest of all to bear was the contrast between the way they had been treated and the reception – at least as it was preserved in popular memory – which their fathers and grandfathers had received when they returned as heroes from their victory over Hitler. That too began to change. President Putin moved to restore a sense of pride in Russia's history of the twentieth century, the history of the Soviet Union. There was a new emphasis on patriotism and on the glories of Russia's military past. The war in Afghanistan began to be reinvented as a heroic episode in which the soldiers had done their military duty and defended the interests of the Motherland. On Putin's instructions, a memorial was erected to the Warrior-Internationalists in 2004, in an alleyway of the grandiose war memorial complex commissioned by Brezhnev to stand on the Poklonnaya Gora, the shallow hill on the outskirts of Moscow where Napoleon waited in vain for the city fathers to bring him the keys of the city.[35] An infantry fighting vehicle, painted in desert camouflage, was placed beside it as a modest addition to the military hardware from the Great Patriotic War which was spread across the rest of the site.

The mood started to settle as the controversy over its causes and conduct began to die down. Russian commentators moved on from the endless argument about who was guilty for the Soviet debacle. A whole new dimension entered the discussion with the American invasion of Afghanistan at the end of 2001.[36] The veterans saw the Americans mirroring their own experience and their own mistakes. There was sympathy for the soldiers fighting over the same difficult ground. There was some inevitable *Schadenfreude* as the NATO campaign increasingly bogged down, much tempered by the thought that it was certainly not in the Russian interest to see NATO fail and leave an unstable Afghanistan to their vulnerable south.

The Internet

Four or five years into the new century, another important thing happened. The veterans discovered the Internet, which was beginning to penetrate deeply into Russian society and giving a voice to people who had previously been unable to make themselves heard. The Internet enabled the veterans to bypass the official organisations and make direct contact with one another, to seek out their former comrades. They posted their memoirs, their poems, their short stories, their novels on their own site, Art of War. The quality of many of the literary contributions was high and often remarkably objective: there was comparatively little macho boasting. And the messages did not come only from the intellectuals and the educated. Many came from simple people, whose grasp of spelling and syntax was not always entirely secure. Through the Internet, the veterans began to put together lists of those they had served with, to write a first version of their regimental histories, and to organise their own reunions. Among the most active were the men from the 860th Independent Motor-rifle Regiment and the 345th Guards Independent Parachute Assault Regiment. In the summer of 2009 the veterans of the 860th Independent Motor-rifle Regiment, who by now had tracked down over two thousand of their former comrades, held their third national reunion in a sanatorium outside Moscow. It was attended by men of all ranks, some of whom had been looking for one another for two decades and more. Many brought their wives and children. Colonel Antonenko, who had once commanded the regiment, was there. So were Private Kostya Sneyerov and his commander Yuri Vygovski, who had named his son Konstantin after his former subordinate. They drank the 'Third Toast' in memory of those who had not returned. And they vowed to continue their meetings in future years.[37]

The Twentieth Anniversary

The twentieth anniversary of the withdrawal was celebrated all over Russia in February 2009. In Moscow the celebrations began with a vast ceremony organised in the Olympic Stadium by the Moscow branch of the Boevoe Bratstvo. Some five thousand people attended, veterans, wives and girlfriends, many teenagers, and a huge paratrooper, well over six feet tall and chunky to match. There were interminable patriotic speeches, endless noisy sentimental songs, and a dozen cars were given away as prizes to selected veterans – an ostentatious and very expensive display. Some thought the money might have been better spent on the many veterans still living in poverty.

Sunday, 15 February – the day of the anniversary itself – was cold, with wet sleet and snow falling thickly. The official wreath was laid at the tomb of the Unknown Soldier by the Kremlin, to the accompaniment of some fine marching and a spirited rendering of the old Soviet national anthem. Three or four hundred veterans, including Alexander Gergel and his comrades from the 860th Independent Motor-rifle Regiment, then carried the red banners of the 40th Army from the Kremlin through the snow and slush to the monument to the Warrior-Internationalist, the Afganets, on the Poklonnaya Gora. There they were addressed by their generals: Ruslan Aushev, who had fought his way up the Pandsher Valley, and become a Hero of the Soviet Union and Governor of his homeland, the North Caucasian republic of Ingushetia; and Valeri Vostrotin, another Hero of the Soviet Union, who had stormed Amin's palace and led the 354th Guards Independent Parachute Assault Regiment during Operation *Magistral*. The speeches were sober and mercifully short: Aushev joked that if the politicians had been to staff college and planned the thing properly, the withdrawal would have taken place at a more clement season, and the veterans would not now be standing in the snow. The soldiers, the speakers said, had defended the interests of their country and done what the Motherland had asked of them. They had gone to help the Afghans; and when the Afghans had wanted them no longer, they had left. Frants Klintsevich, the former political officer who was now the Chairman of the Russian Union of Veterans of Afghanistan, said that it had been a bad peace; but a bad peace was better than a good war. The mother of a fallen soldier made a restrained and dignified speech: the Afghan war should be the last war in which Russian boys died. She had forgotten Chechnya.

That evening a grand ceremony was held in the Kremlin. The veterans could feel that after two decades their service and their sufferings in Afghanistan were at last receiving some kind of recognition – even if the state for which they had fought no longer existed.

EPILOGUE:
THE RECKONING

In December 1989 the Congress of People's Deputies of the Soviet Union passed a resolution which said that the decision to intervene in Afghanistan was 'deserving of moral and political condemnation'. In subsequent years right-wing politicians and leaders of veterans' organisations such as Frants Klintsevich attempted to get the resolution formally overturned, or argued that it was not intended as an outright condemnation.[1] But however contorted the wording, it goes rather further than many other countries have done towards apologising for a failed war.

The death and destruction which passed over Afghanistan in the years after 1979 were not unprecedented. When a war of intervention is combined with a local civil war, and especially when one side has an overwhelming technical superiority, the disproportion between the casualties of the two sides is very large. The figures for civilian casualties in such wars are impossible to determine with any accuracy, so that the proportions cannot be accurately drawn. By no means all the blame can be laid on the foreigners: very many Afghans and Vietnamese and Algerians were killed by their own countrymen. But however imprecise the figures, one thing is sure. In a war of intervention the local people die at a much greater rate than the soldiers of the invading force; and the chances of winning hearts and mind – the core of all counter-insurgency theory – is much reduced (See Annex 4, 'Indo-China, Vietnam, Algeria, Afghanistan: A Comparison', page 348.)

For the Soviet Union it was nevertheless, by most measures, a comparatively small war; those who later argued that Russia had lost a whole generation of young men were greatly exaggerating.[2] Some 620,000 young men and a few young women served in Afghanistan in the course of nine years. Of these 525,000 were in the armed forces; the remainder were from the KGB's frontier and special forces and the Ministry of the Interior. This was a mere 3.4 per cent of those eligible for military service. Throughout the war in Afghanistan most Soviet soldiers continued to serve in the Far East or, above all, in Europe, where the main threat lay.

The official figure for the dead was 15,051: 2.4 per cent of those who served. The figure includes those from the KGB's frontier forces, those who went missing in action, and those who died of illness or wounds, including those who died after they left the army (about 5.5 per cent of the total) or in accidents (about 12 per cent). Fifty-two of the dead were women, four of them warrant officers in the military, the rest civilians.

Soldiers from all the peoples of the Soviet Union fought in Afghanistan, from the largest group, the Russians, to some of the very smallest. There were Soviet Germans, Poles, Greeks, Romanians, one Gypsy, one Finn, one Hungarian, and one Czech among the dead. The burden of the war was not evenly distributed, but 52.7 people were killed per million of the Soviet population as a whole. The peoples of Central Asia suffered proportionately the most – 65 killed for every million of the population – the story that Central Asians were unwilling to fight their co-religionists in Afghanistan is a myth. For the Slavs as a whole, the figure was 53.5 per million; for the Russians 51.1 dead per million. The peoples of the Caucasus and the Baltic States believed that they were deliberately targeted for service in Afghanistan because the Kremlin thought they were politically unreliable. The figures show that this was another myth: only 25.8 per million Caucasians and 17 per million Balts died in Afghanistan.

Apart from the dead, more than fifty thousand were wounded, and more than ten thousand became invalids. Many others suffered various forms of post-traumatic stress disorder, took to crime or drugs, or were unable to hold down a permanent job. For these victims of the war the available statistics are thin, misleading, or both. No one disputes the huge overall figure of 469,685 – 88 per cent of all those who served – who fell sick or were wounded during the war.[3]

Western intelligence reports at the time produced wild casualty figures extrapolated from anecdotal evidence. One such estimate was that 20–25,000 Soviet soldiers had died by the end of 1981 and 50,000 by the end of 1983.[4] But the Defence Ministry and the Russian regions produced Books of Remembrance with details of each dead soldier. Local websites tracked the fates of local boys who had served and died. Interest in the issue inside Russia eventually died away, and the official figures were more or less accepted as the best that were likely to become available.

Large claims were made, not least by the mujahedin themselves, about the contribution that the war in Afghanistan made to the collapse of the Soviet Union. In spring 2002 Burhanuddin Rabbani said in Mazar-i Sharif, 'We forced the Communists out of our country, we can force all invaders out of holy Afghanistan ... Had it not been for the jihad, the whole world would still be in the Communist grip. The Berlin Wall fell because of the wounds which we inflicted on the Soviet Union, and the inspiration we gave all oppressed people. We broke the Soviet Union up into fifteen parts. We liberated people from Communism. Jihad led to a free world. We saved the world because Communism met its grave here in Afghanistan!'[5]

The reality was more complicated. The war was an economic and military burden on the Soviet Union, but not a particularly large one measured against the country's overall commitments.[6] The failure in Afghanistan did reinforce the lack of confidence of the Soviet people in their government which was growing throughout the 1980s. But that dissatisfaction was also fed by many other factors: the humiliating spectacle of one gerontocrat succeeding another at the head of government which preceded Gorbachev's election in 1985; the revelation of incompetence and government deceit which followed the explosion at Chernobyl nuclear plant in April 1986; the strains of the arms competition with the United States; an economic malaise which turned into an economic catastrophe towards the end of the decade; the uncertainties and upheavals engendered by Gorbachev's own reforms. All these were the symptoms that the Soviet economic and political system was no longer viable. It was collapsing even without the contribution of the war in Afghanistan.

The Soviet Union was thus damaged not so much by the material losses of the war as by the political costs both domestic and foreign. Domestic opposition to the war was never on the scale that it reached in the United States during the war in Vietnam: that would have been inconceivable, given the nature of the Soviet political system. But the early realisation that the invasion had been a mistake, the moral revulsion which began to be felt by some people even inside the government and the army, the anger of ordinary people as they started to realise what was happening – all this increased pressure on the politicians to find a way out of the quagmire.

For the Afghans, of course, it was not a small war at all. For the mujahedin it was a battle for national dignity and national liberation in which they were prepared to fight – literally – to the death. The casualty figures we have are more or less inaccurate guesses, often put into circulation for propaganda reasons. But probably somewhere between 600,000 and 1.5 million Afghans were killed in the Soviet war.[7] Millions more were driven from their home to seek refuge in Pakistan and Iran. The complex relationships which governed the Afghan way of life were overturned almost beyond repair. But the people of Afghanistan, like the people of Vietnam, had one irreducible advantage over the invader: they were going to stay, while the foreigner would eventually leave. As the saying goes, the foreigners had the watches, but the locals had the time.

Russians and Americans drew the illuminating comparison with the American war in Vietnam both during the Soviet war in Afghanistan and afterwards. The Cold War conditioned the decisions of both governments. Both went to war, on a dubious interpretation of international law, in the belief that they were defending their country's vital interests. Their immediate aims were similar: to protect a client and to deny a strategic territory to the other. Both had more grandiose aims:

to build in a distant country a political, social, and economic system similar to their own. Neither understood what they were getting into. Both thought that they would be able to shore up their local ally – the PDPA government in Kabul and the South Vietnamese government in Saigon – so that they could hand over responsibility for the security of the country and then leave. Both believed that their modern military machine should prevail without too much difficulty over the ragtag guerrilla force which faced them.

And indeed the failures were not military. Neither the Soviet army in Afghanistan nor the American army in Vietnam was defeated: they held the ground and eventually withdrew in good order. The failures in both cases were failures of intelligence, of judgement, and of assessment. Both the Americans and the Russians set themselves unattainable strategic goals. Neither were able to achieve their main political objective: a friendly, stable regime which would share their ideological and political goals. Their protégés were overthrown and the peoples of Vietnam and Afghanistan rejected the political models they were offered. Some among the military in both Russia and America believed that the failure to prevail was the result of the spinelessness of the public and the press, and the weakness, even the treachery, of the politicians. But the entry of the mujahedin into Kabul, like the entry of the North Vietnamese into Saigon, marked a decisive outcome to both wars of a kind which Clausewitz, for one, would have recognised instantly.[8]

Western propaganda successfully portrayed Soviet behaviour in Afghanistan as uniquely brutal. But in Vietnam as well as in Afghanistan the armies went in for the casual and indiscriminate destruction of villages, crops, animals, and people. They used massive firepower in an attempt to overwhelm a ruthless and elusive enemy who never presented them with a target worthy of their sophisticated modern weapons. The Russians were accused of using chemical weapons in Afghanistan, but the accusations petered out. The Americans used the chemical Agent Orange to destroy forests and crops but also killed or disabled large numbers of Vietnamese. The Russians used aerial bombing on a large scale, but never on the scale of the massive American B-52 strikes against North Vietnam. More bombs were dropped by the Americans on Laos than were dropped on Germany by the RAF and the US Air Force combined.[9]

Both wars lasted for nine years. But the Vietnam War was on a much larger scale than the war in Afghanistan. More than 2.5 million Americans passed through Vietnam: nearly five times as many as the number of Soviets who served in Afghanistan. Nearly four times as many died. Many more Vietnamese than Afghans died – perhaps between one and a half to six times as many, depending on which among a number of unsatisfactory figures one chooses.[10] Like the war in Afghanistan, the war in Vietnam was accompanied and followed by a brutal civil war in which large numbers also perished.

This kind of moral calculus is not very fruitful. There is little to choose between the way either war was fought. But there was one essential difference between the two wars – the distinction that Zbigniew Brzezinski drew in his advice to President Carter the day after the Soviet invasion began. The victors in Vietnam, the government in Hanoi, were coherent, dedicated, ruthless, and efficient. At great cost they were able to impose order on their country, which in the next thirty years became increasingly prosperous and open to the outside world. The mujahedin never achieved anything like that coherence and discipline, and their entry into Kabul was only the prelude to more decades of war and foreign intervention, which made it almost impossible to repair the physical, social, moral, and political damage which had initially been caused by the Communist regime and the Soviet intervention. The Vietnamese were able to enjoy the fruits of their victory. The Afghans were not.

Perhaps it was because of the horrors that followed that the Afghans did not in the long run seem to nurture a grudge against the Russians. Leonid Shebarshin returned to Herat only nine months after the 40th Army had pulled out, expecting to be met with fear, hatred, and hostility. Not a bit of it, his Afghan interlocutors told him: you lived with one lot of feelings while the fighting was going on, but once the war was over you had to forget the bad things that had happened.[11] By the time the journalist Vladimir Snegirev returned to Afghanistan in 2003, people were already beginning to compare the Russians favourably to the new invaders who had arrived in 2001. 'They seemed to have forgotten our carpet-bombing, the minefields, the manhunts, the looting, in a word everything which, alas, accompanied the presence of the "limited military contingent".'[12]

Not long after that Russian veterans began to return as tourists to the places where they had fought two decades earlier. To accommodate them, the enterprising Sergei Zharov set up his own guidebook on the web, *The Russians are Back*, advising his countrymen on transport, visas, places to visit, and places to avoid.[13] Igor Yamshchikov went with a friend to Kabul in 2006, and then drove along the road to Jalalabad, filming the guard posts where they had served in 1981–2 and posting the results on YouTube.[14] Andrei Kuznetsov and two comrades from the 345th Guards Independent Parachute Assault Regiment also visited Kabul in 2006. They hired a cab for $100, drove on from Bagram to the Salang Pass, and put up a memorial stone there. When they got home they too posted their stories on the Internet.

In the spring of 2009 Dmitri Fedorov, a former senior sergeant with the 860th Independent Motor-rifle Regiment, returned to Afghanistan through Osh and Ishkashim, and along the mountain roads of Bada-khshan to Bakharak and Faisabad – the same route that the regiment had taken when it entered Afghanistan nearly thirty years earlier. Much had changed in the meanwhile. The tracks along which the regiment had struggled with so much difficulty had been replaced with decent roads. The town of Faisabad had nearly tripled in size and now boasted a proper hotel, which belonged to the former mujahedin commander Basir. A suburb now bordered the two or three miles which had separated the town and the regiment's base. The base itself was unrec-ognisable. The barren terrain where the soldiers had vainly attempted to sow trees was now a flourishing oasis with gardens and houses, sur-rounded by Lebanese cedars. Fedorov and his colleagues talked to those who had fought against them. To the men who had been on the same side, men from KhAD and the Tsarandoi, they handed out certificates marking the twentieth anniversary of the Soviet withdrawal. One thing had not changed, said Fedorov. The region was no more under the control of the central government than it had been during the Soviet time. In and around Faisabad, Basir and the other local potentates were in charge, as they had always been.

Afghans told these tales not only to Russians, whom they might have wanted to flatter, but to other visitors, whom they did not. When I visited Afghanistan in September 2008 – a national of one of the foreign countries now fighting there – I was told by almost every Afghan I met that things were better under the Russians. The Russians were not so stand-offish as the Americans, who had no interest in Afghanistan itself, and who looked like Martians with their elaborate equipment, their menacing body armour, and their impenetrable Ray-Bans when they briefly emerged from the high walls behind which they barricaded themselves. The Russians, I was told, had built the elements of industry, whereas now most of the aid money simply ended up in the wrong pockets in the wrong countries. In the Russian time everyone had had work; now things were getting steadily worse. The last Communist president, Najibullah, had been one of the best of Afghanistan's recent rulers: more popular than Daud, the equal of Zahir Shah. Video recordings of Najibullah's speeches were being sold round Kabul, with their warnings – which turned out to be true – that there would be civil war if he were overthrown. People were discreetly dismissive of President Karzai, whom they said was a puppet of the foreigners. Sher Ahmad Maladani, a mujahedin commander in Herat who fought the Communists and the Russians for a decade and the Taliban after them, told me that if Najibullah instead of Karmal had taken over in 1979, the country would not be in its present mess. He too preferred the Russians. The Russians were strong and brave, he said. They fought man to man on the ground, and they used their weapons only when their enemy was armed. They never killed women and children. But the Americans were afraid to fight on the ground and their bombing was indiscriminate.

As history much of this was travesty. But it did seem to indicate that the latest attempt to help the Afghans to help themselves was having little more success than its predecessor.

Leaders take their countries into foreign wars for reasons of ambition, greed, moral or messianic fervour, or on a calculation of national advantage which may or may not be flawed.

The generals manage the wars as well as they can. The best try to husband the lives of their soldiers and to keep them under proper control. When it is all over, they ransack the archives and write their memoirs, to carve out their niche in history, to justify the decisions they took, and sometimes to take a sideswipe at a former colleague.

The soldiers who do the actual fighting come home having seen and done terrible things which return to haunt them. The stories of heroism and comradeship help them to manage their memories and give meaning to what they have been through. Some claim that the war years were the best of their lives. Many more say nothing, and go to their graves without telling even their nearest and dearest what it was really like.

So it is after all wars. So it was after the Soviet war in Afghanistan.

ANNEXES

TIMELINE

1717	Peter the Great sends an expedition to Central Asia. It fails.
1747	Ahmad Shah Abdali elected ruler of what becomes modern Afghan state.
1801	British take Peshawar from Afghans, later give it to Sikhs.
1835	Jan Witkiewicz, first Russian envoy to reach Kabul.
1838–42	First Anglo-Afghan War.
1878–80	Second Anglo-Afghan War.
1880–1901	Abdul Rahman Khan takes power, greatly strengthens state and army.
1901–19	Habibullah succeeds Abdur Rahman. Assassinated.
1919–29	Amanullah succeeds Habibullah. Exiled.
1919	Third Anglo-Afghan War.
1921	Afghan–Soviet Friendship Treaty signed.
1929–33	Nadir Shah, Amanullah's uncle, takes power. Assassinated.
1933–73	Zahir Shah succeeds (dies in exile in 2007).
1959	President Eisenhower visits Afghanistan.
1965	Afghan Communist Party founded.
1973	Daud proclaims himself President.
April 1978	Afghan Communists seize power, kill Daud.
March 1979	Anti-Communist rising in Herat.

September 1979	President Taraki arrested and killed by Prime Minister Amin.
December 1979	Soviets enter Afghanistan. Amin killed, replaced by Babrak Karmal.
January 1980	UN condemns Soviet invasion.
February 1980	Massive demonstrations in Kabul. Soviets begin major operations.
November 1982	Leonid Brezhnev dies, succeeded by Yuri Andropov.
February 1983	UN Secretary General Perez de Cuellar discusses withdrawal with Andropov.
February 1984	Andropov dies, succeeded by Konstantin Chernenko.
March 1985	Chernenko dies, succeeded by Mikhail Gorbachev.
October 1985	Politburo agrees troops should leave Afghanistan within eighteen months.
February 1986	Gorbachev tells Soviet Party Congress that troops will leave Afghanistan.
May 1986	Karmal replaced by Najibullah.
September 1986	First Stingers are fired, down three helicopters.
January 1987	Najibullah announces 'National Reconciliation'.
December 1987	Operation *Magistral* relieves Khost.
December 1987	Gorbachev and Reagan discuss Afghanistan.
14 April 1988	Agreements for Soviet withdrawal signed in Geneva.
May 1988	40th Army begins withdrawal.
15 February 1989	Last Soviet troops leave.
April 1992	President Najibullah overthrown.
August 1992	Russian Embassy evacuated from Kabul.
September 1996	Taliban captures Kabul and kills Najibullah.
9 September 2001	Mujahedin leader Ahmad Shah Masud assassinated by Al Qaeda.
11 September 2001	Twin Towers destroyed in New York.
December 2001	Northern Alliance, backed by US, drives out Taliban.

ORDER OF BATTLE OF THE 40TH ARMY

Formations mentioned in the text are marked *.

Divisions

*5th Guards Motor-rifle Division (Shindand)**
12th Guards Motor-rifle Regiment (Herat)*
101st Motor-rifle Regiment (Herat)*
371st Guards Motor-rifle Regiment (Shindand)
24th Guards Tank Regiment (Shindand)
1060th Artillery Regiment (Shindand)
1122nd (later 1008th) Antiaircraft Rocket Regiment (Shindand)
650th Guards Reconnaissance Battalion (Shindand)
68th Guards Independent Engineer-sapper Battalion (Shindand)

*108th Motor-rifle Division (Kabul, later Bagram)**
177th Motor-rifle Regiment (Jabal-Ussuraj)
180th Motor-rifle Regiment (Kabul)*
181st Motor-rifle Regiment (Kabul)
1074th Artillery Regiment (Kabul)
1415th (later 1049th) Antiaircraft Rocket Regiment (Kabul)
781st Independent Reconnaissance Battalion (Bagram)
271st Independent Engineer-sapper Battalion (Bagram)

*201st Motor-rifle Divison (Kunduz)**
122nd Motor-rifle Regiment (Tashkurgan)
149th Guards Motor-rifle Regiment (Kunduz)
395th Motor-rifle Regiment (Pul-i Khumri)
234th Tank Regiment (Kunduz)
998th Artillery Regiment (Kunduz)
990th Antiaircraft Rocket Regiment (Kunduz)
783rd Independent Reconnaissance Battalion (Kunduz)
541st Independent Engineer-sapper Battalion (Kunduz)

*103rd Guards Air Assault Division (Kabul airport)**
317th Guards Parachute Assault Regiment (Kabul airport)
350th Guards Parachute Assault Regiment (Kabul airport)
357th Guards Parachute Assault Regiment (1980–86: Bala Hissar fortress;
    1986–9: Kabul airport)
1179th Guards Artillery Regiment (Kabul airport)
62nd Guards Independent Self-propelled Artillery Battalion (Kabul airport)
130th Guards Independent Engineer-sapper Battalion (Kabul airport)
105th Independent Antiaircraft Rocket-artillery Battalion (Kabul airport)

Independent Brigades and Regiments
56th Guards Independent Airborne Assault Brigade (Kunduz)*
66th Independent Motor-rifle Brigade/106th Motor-rifle Regiment (Jalalabad)*
70th Guards Independent Motor-rifle Brigade/373rd Guards Motor-rifle
    Regiment (Kandahar)
191st Independent Motor-rifle Regiment (Pul-i Khumri/Ghazni)
345th Guards Independent Parachute Assault Regiment (Bagram)*
860th Independent Motor-rifle Regiment (Faisabad)*

264th Independent Special Forces Regiment (Radio and Radiotechnical
    Intelligence) (Kabul)
15th Special Forces Brigade (Jalalabad)*
22nd Special Forces Brigade (Asadabad)*

58th Automobile Brigade/159th (Engineering) Road-construction Brigade
    (Kabul)
59th Logistics Brigade
276th Pipelaying Brigade (Doshi)*

278th Road-security Brigade (Doshi)
28th Artillery Regiment/Rocket Artillery Regiment (Shindand)
45th Engineering-sapper Regiment (Charikar)
103rd Independent Communications Regiment (Kabul)

Establishment of Motor-rifle Units
The establishment of motor-rifle divisions and their subordinate formations and units varied from time to time and place to place. Formations and units were almost never up to their establishment in Afghanistan. The following information is therefore not definitive.

Motor-rifle Division: 12,000 men – 287 tanks, 150 BMPs (infantry fighting vehicles), 221 BTRs (armoured personnel carriers), 6 rocket launchers, 18 130mm heavy assault guns, 18 anti-tank guns, 126 self-propelled and towed howitzers, 96 mortars and multiple rocket launchers, 46 mobile anti-aircraft missile complexes, 16 self-propelled automatic anti-aircraft guns.
Independent Motor-rifle Regiment: 2,198 officers and men, 132 BMPs, 40 tanks, 18 122mm self-propelled howitzers, 264 vehicles.
Motor-rifle Battalion: 481 men, 41 BMPs.
Motor-rifle Company: 101 men, 11 BMPs.
Motor-rifle Platoon: 30 men, 3 BMPs.

Army Aviation
The 40th Army was unique in having its own integral air force. It consisted of two combat air regiments and one combat squadron, a mixed air regiment, three independent helicopter regiments, a helicopter detachment, and three independent helicopter squadrons, a total of 60 combat aircraft, 19 transport aircraft, and 253 helicopters. The aircraft shared their bases in Kabul, Shindand, Bagram, and Kandahar with Afghan air-force units.

The 40th Army was also supported by long-range bombers flying from bases in the Soviet Union.

Sources: 'Komandiry soedinenii i chastei 40 Armii', compiled by A. Volkov (http://www.rsva-ural.ru/library/mbook.php?cid64); V. Korolev, 'Uroki voiny v Afganistane 1979–1989 godov' (http://www.sdrvdv.org/node/159); 'АВИАЦИЯ' (http://pressa.budet.ru/article/detail.php?ID47643); 'Dalnyaya Aviatsia Rossii' (www.sinopa.ee/davia003/dav03.htm); information kindly provided by Alexander Kartsev.

– ANNEX THREE –

THE ALLIANCE OF SEVEN AND ITS LEADERS

There were more than seventy groups and parties opposing the Kabul government, most of little significance. The seven major parties which operated out of Pakistan made several abortive attempts to unite in order to direct the battle inside Afghanistan and to operate more effectively at the UN and elsewhere. The Pakistan government encouraged these efforts at unification, as did the Americans, Saudis, Chinese, and Muslim clerics both inside and outside Afghanistan. In May 1985 the seven formed themselves into a loosely organised alliance. This did not solve the underlying problem. The seven remained rivals rather than partners, and after the Russians left Afghanistan in 1989 the tensions between them broke out into open civil war. Another alliance, of less importance, operated from Iran.

Most of the seven parties originated in the university politics of the 1970s. They fell into two categories: Islamist and conservative nationalist. The Islamists were Hezb-i Islami (Gulbuddin), Hezb-i Islami (Khalis), Ittihad-i Islami Baraye Azadi Afghanistan, and Jamiat-i Islami Afghanistan. The traditionalists were Mahazi-Melli-Islamiye-Afghanistan, Jahar-i Nejar-i Melli, and Harakat-i Enqelab-i Islami (Islamic Revolution Movement). All were Sunnis and all were Pushtun, except *Jamiat-i Islami*, who were Tajiks. The conservative Islamists in the Pakistani military intelligence organisation, the ISI, favoured the three Pushtun Islamist parties, who got most of the money and weapons coming from the Americans and others.

Jamiat-i Islami and its effective field commander, Ahmad Shah Masud, were not well regarded by the Pakistanis because they were not Pushtuns and were unwilling to submit to Pakistani or Pushtun direction. In consequence they received comparatively little support from Pakistan or the Americans. They were the favourites of the British and French, who had, however, far fewer resources with which to support them.

These organisations fought among themselves during the war, and especially after it was over. In one of the most notorious incidents, in July 1989, after the Soviet war was over, Sayyed Jamal, one of Hekmatyar's commanders, ambushed and murdered thirty of Masud's men in northern Afghanistan.

Source: The information in this annex is based on G. Dorronosoro, *Revolution Unending: Afghanistan, 1979 to the Present* (New York, 2005), p. 152.

INDO-CHINA, VIETNAM, ALGERIA, AFGHANISTAN: A COMPARISON

In Indo-China and Algeria the French fought colonial wars in a vain attempt to preserve their empire. By contrast the American wars in Vietnam and South-East Asia and the Soviet war in Afghanistan were wars of intervention against a background of Cold War rivalry. But despite the differences, all these wars have much in common. They were conducted by sophisticated modern armies against determined guerrilla forces fighting on their own territory against a background of vicious civil war. The outsiders had superior weapons and were able to inflict devastating destruction, destroying towns, villages, crops, and animals, and killing disproportionate numbers of enemy soldiers and civilians. And yet all these wars ended in failure.

The figures for French, American, and Soviet losses in personnel and equipment are reliable: sophisticated armies keep accurate records of their casualties.

The figures for military and civilian losses among the Vietnamese, the Cambodians, the Laotians, the Algerians, and the Afghans are almost wholly unreliable: nobody on either side had the time or the interest to count the dead. In all these wars large numbers of casualties were inflicted by all sides in the civil wars that were being fought in parallel; and large numbers were inflicted in the revenge killings which followed the formal ending of hostilities.

But an extremely rough calculation indicates that the French lost one soldier for every eight Vietnamese who died in the Indo-Chinese war from 1945 to 1954. One French soldier or civilian died for every twenty-two Algerians in the war of

1954–62. Between twenty-seven and sixty-eight Vietnamese may have died for each American between 1959 and 1975. In Afghanistan somewhere between forty and 100 Afghans may have died for each Soviet soldier killed.

French Union military casualties in Indo-China were 75,867: this figure includes French colonial troops. Figures for Vietnamese deaths are estimated at 500–600,000.

The French lost 17,456 soldiers and 2,788 civilians in Algeria; about 141,000 Algerian fighters were killed; estimates of the number of civilians killed during the war range from 30,000 to 300,000; perhaps 150,000 more Algerians died in revenge killings after the war; Algerian sources have claimed that up to a million Algerians died as a result of the wars; the French deny this.

US military casualties in Vietnam were 58,260 killed, and missing. The North Vietnamese suffered 1.1 million combat deaths, the South 266,000; estimates of civilian deaths range from 361,000 to 2 million.

15,051 Soviet soldiers died in Afghanistan. For Afghan civilian casualties, Dr Antonio Giustozzi has suggested a low figure of 600,000; a widely accepted figure is 1–1.5 million; General Lyakhovski gives the highest figure of 2.5 million, but he gives no source.

Sources: 'Secondary Wars and Atrocities of the Twentieth Century' (http://users.erols.com/mwhite28/warstat3.htm) contains tables and bibliographical references for a wide range of estimates of casualties in Indo-China and Algeria, and for the casualties in the civil wars and mass repressions that followed the American departure from Vietnam; http://en.wikipedia.org/wiki/Vietnam_War_casualties) gives figures, with references, for losses on both sides in the US war in Vietnam; see also http://en.wikipedia.org/wiki/Vietnam_War_casualties#United_States_Armed_Forces); for statistical information about casualties of the Vietnam War see the National Archive (http://www.archives.gov/research/vietnam-war/casualty-statistics.html); G. Krivosheev, *Rossia i SSSR v voinakh XX veka: Poteri vooruzhennykh sil* (Moscow, 2001), is reliable on Soviet losses; Dr Antonio Giustozzi, conversation, London, 5 December 2010; A. Lyakhovski, *Tragedia i doblest Afgana* (Moscow, 2009), p. 1018.

NOTES

Prologue

1 Thucydides, Book II, 8.

2 W. Olney, *'Shiloh' as Seen by a Private Soldier: A Paper Read before California Commandery of the Military Order of the Loyal Legion of the United States, May 31, 1889* (Kessinger Publishing, Whitefish, Mont., 2007).

3 V. Krivenko, *Ekipazh mashiny boevoi* (St Petersburg, 2004), p. 380.

4 Unnamed Communist, quoted in R. Sikorski, *Dust of the Saints: A Journey to Herat in Time of War* (New York, 1990), pp.180–83.

5 Sher Ahmad Maladani, interview, Herat, 10 September 2008.

6 Afghanistan Justice Project, *Casting Shadows: War Crimes and Crimes against Humanity, 1978–2001*, The Century Foundation (www.tcf.org), 2005, p. 21 (http://www.afghanistanjusticeproject.org/).

7 Ismail Khan, who was an officer in the Herat garrison, gave an extensive account of the rising to Sikorski (*Dust of the Saints*, pp. 228 et seq.). The casualty figures Khan gives are not credible, and his role in the rising has been exaggerated, though he later became a major mujahedin leader; he fought the Russians, was captured by the Taliban, and served as a minister in the government of President Karzai. For a scholarly account of his career, see A. Giustozzi, 'Genesis of a Prince: The Rise of Ismail Khan in Western Afghanistan, 1979–1992', Crisis States Research Centre, London School of Economics, September 2006, and A. Giustozzi, *Empires of Mud* (London, 2009).

Part I: *The Road to Kabul*

  1 A. Snesarev, *Afganistan* (Moscow, 2002), p. 199. The book was originally published in 1921, but the author was arrested under Stalin and it remained largely unknown until it was republished eighty years later.

1: Paradise Lost

  1 P. Hopkirk, *The Great Game: The Struggle for Empire in Central Asia* (London, 1992), p. 305.

  2 W. Ball, *Monuments of Afghanistan* (London, 2008).

  3 A. Rasanaygam, *Afghanistan: A Modern History* (London, 2005), pp. 42–5; L. Dupree, *Afghanistan* (Oxford, 1997), p. 599.

  4 Kh. Khalfin, *Politika Rossii v Srednei Azii (1857–1868)* (Moscow, 1960), pp. 19–43. This scholarly work contains much well-documented information on Russian official thinking about Central Asia in the nineteenth century. Like Khalfin's other book on British policy in Afghanistan, *Proval britanskoi agressii v Afganistane* (Moscow, 1959), you need to aim off for the Soviet and Marxist bias.

  5 A. Lyakhovski and S. Davitaya, *Igra v Afganistan* (Moscow, 2009), p. 16.

  6 Ibid., p. 20.

  7 Hopkirk, *The Great Game*, p. 22.

  8 There is an account of Orlov's expedition in E. Parnov, 'V Indiyu – Marsh', *Znanie – sila*, No. 10/04 (http://www.znanie-sila.ru/online/issue_2962.html).

  9 Russian officers told the journalist Charles Marvin in the late 1880s that Russia could invade India, but had no intention of doing so: C. Marvin, *The Russian Advance towards India* (originally published 1882; Peshawar, 1984), p. 78; for Bennigsen see D. Lieven, *Russia against Napoleon* (London, 2009), p. 64.

10 Khalfin, *Proval britanskoi agressii v Afganistane*, pp. 33–4.

11 There is a cursory and unconvincing discussion of this episode in Lyakhovski and Davitaya, *Igra v Afganistan*, pp. 25–6.

12 Ibid., p. 32.

13 Khalfin, *Politika Rossii v Srednei Azii (1857–1868)*, pp. 31–2 and 73, quoting documents in the Central State Military Political Archive of the USSR (TsGVIA).

14 Ibid., pp. 89–104.

15 This is the broad conclusion of Alexander Morrison's *Russian Rule in Samarkand, 1868–1910: A Comparison with British India* (Oxford, 2008). The quotation comes from p. 292.

16 Khalfin, *Proval britanskoi agressii v Afganistane*, p. 30. Khalfin is a useful corrective to most British accounts of the Afghan wars; J. Stewart, *Crimson Snow* (Stroud, 2008), pp. 39–42.

17 C. Lamb, *The Sewing Circles of Herat* (London, 2004), pp. 221 et seq.

18 G. Forrest, *Life of Field Marshal Sir Neville Chamberlain, G.C.B., G.C.S.I.* (London, 1909), pp. 142–51.

19 D. Loyn, *Butcher and Bolt* (London, 2008), p. 109.

20 Marvin, *The Russian Advance towards India*, p. 43; W. F. Monypenny and G. Buckle, *The Life of Benjamin Disraeli, Earl of Beaconsfield* (London, 1910–20), Vol. VI, pp. 154–5.

21 Hopkirk, *The Great Game*, p. 175, quoting John W. Kaye, *History of the War in Afghanistan* (London, 1851).

22 Lyakhovski and Davitaya, *Igra v Afganistan*, p. 49.

23 Ibid., p. 64.

24 N. Khrushchev, *Khrushchev Remembers* (London, 1971), p. 508.

25 P. Blood (ed.), *Afghanistan: A Country Study* (Washington, DC, 2001).

26 A. Lyakhovski, *Tragedia i doblest Afgana* (Moscow, 1995) (http://www.rsva. ru/biblio/prose_af/afgan_tragedy_and_glory/index.shtml).

27 Lamb, *The Sewing Circles of Herat*, pp. 221 et seq.

28 N. Dupree (Wolfe), *An Historical Guide to Kabul* (Kabul, 1965), p. 68.

29 A. Abram, MS diary (by kind permission of Mr Abram).

30 Lamb, *The Sewing Circles of Herat*, p. 30.

31 J. Steele, 'Red Kabul Revisited', *Guardian*, 13 November 2003.

32 Lamb, *The Sewing Circles of Herat*, p. 216.

2: The Tragedy Begins

1 Alexander Lyakhovski, conversation, Gelendzhik, 19 September 2007.

2 For example, see V. Snegirev, *Ryzhy* (Moscow, 2000), p. 146.

3 V. Kryuchkov, *Lichnoe delo*, 2 vols. (Moscow, 1996), Vol. 1, p. 188.

4 D. Gai and V. Snegirev, *Vtorzhenie* (Moscow, 1991), p. 10.

5 A. Lyakhovski, *Tragedia i doblest Afgana* (Moscow, 1995) (http://www.rsva. ru/biblio/prose_af/afgan_tragedy_and_glory/index.shtml).

6 'An Appeal to the Leaders of the PDPA Groups "Parcham" and "Khalq"', dated 8 January 1974, Cold War International History Project (www.cwihp.

org), by permission of the Woodrow Wilson International Center for
Scholars.

7 Afghanistan Justice Project, *Casting Shadows: War Crimes and Crimes
against Humanity, 1978–2001*, The Century Foundation (www.tcf.org), 2005,
p. 13 (http://www.afghanistanjusticeproject.org/).

8 Lyakhovski, *Tragedia i doblest Afgana*.

9 Dmitri Ryurikov, interview, Moscow, 23 July 2009.

10 Lyakhovski, *Tragedia i doblest Afgana* (Moscow, 2009), p. 108.

11 Gai and Snegirev, *Vtorzhenie*, pp. 81 and 16.

12 Kryuchkov, *Lichnoe delo*, Vol. 1, p. 192.

13 See notes on Puzanov's report taken by Odd Arne Westad from the original
at the Center for the Storage of Contemporary Documentation (TsKhSD),
fond (f.) 5, opis (op.) 75, delo (d.) 1179, listy (11.) 2–17. Westad's notes are
published by the Cold War International History Project at the Woodrow
Wilson Center, Washington, DC (http://www.wilsoncenter.org/index.
cfm topic_id=1409&fuseaction=va2.document&identifier=5034DB6A-
96B6–175C-91262B384BCC068C&sort=Collection&item=Soviet%20
Invasion%20of%20Afghanistan).

14 G. Dorronosoro, *Revolution Unending: Afghanistan, 1979 to the Present*
(New York, 2005), p. 96.

15 N. Ivanov, *Operatsiu Shtorm nachat ranshe* (Moscow, 1993), Chapter 14
(http://militera.lib.ru/prose/russian/ivanov_nf/index.html); Valeri and
Galina Ivanov, interview, Moscow, 14 March 2010.

16 There are conflicting accounts of the rising in R. Sikorski, *Dust of the
Saints: A Journey to Herat in Time of War* (New York, 1990); A. Hyman,
Afghanistan under Soviet Domination 1964–81 (London, 1982); A. Giustozzi,
*Genesis of a 'Prince': The Rise of Ismail Khan in Western Afghanistan,
1979–1992* (Crisis States Research Centre, London School of Economics,
September 2006); Dorronosoro, *Revolution Unending*, quotes Olivier Roy,
Afghanistan, Islam et modernité politique (Paris, 1985), p. 146, as giving a
wide margin for the total number of casualties, between 5,000 and 25,000
victims; A. Lyakhovski and S. Davitaya, *Igra v Afganistan* (Moscow, 2009),
p. 135, give a low estimate for the number of Soviet victims. Other low
estimates are in G. Zaitsev, *Alpha – My Destiny* (St Petersburg, 2005),
p. 118; V. Zaplatin, 'Do shturma dvortsa Amina', *Zavtra*, No. 51 (316), 21
December 1999 (http://www.zavtra.ru/cgi/veil/data/zavtra/99/316/61.htm);
Gai and Snegirev, *Vtorzhenie*, p. 78; and V. Ablazov, *Afganistan chetvertaya
voina* (Kiev, 2002), p. 53. Even some Russians accepted the higher figure.

D. Cordovez and S. Harrison, *Out of Afghanistan* (Oxford, 1995), p. 36, quote a high estimate given by a senior Soviet official in 1989. The Russian Ambassador, Zamir Kabulov, told me in Kabul on 7 September 2008 that he accepted the figure of 100.

17 The official transcripts of these Politburo meetings, and of the telephone conversations with the Afghan leadership, were published informally in the early 1990s, when the archives were briefly open. Most appear in Lyakhovski's *Tragedia i doblest Afgana*. English translations are on the website of the Woodrow Wilson Center's Cold War International History Project, 'Soviet Invasion of Afghanistan' (http://www.wilsoncenter.org).

18 A full text is in Lyakhovski, *Tragedia i doblest Afgana*, 1995, and comes from TsKhSD, f. 89, per. 25, dok. 1, ss. 28–34; a shorter version is in Lyakhovski, *Tragedia i doblest Afgana*, 2004, pp. 119–22; a translation is on the website of the Woodrow Wilson Center's Cold War International History Project (http://www.wilsoncenter.org).

19 Woodrow Wilson Center Cold War Archive: transcript of CPSU CC Politburo Session on Afghanistan, 22 March 1979, TsKhSD, f. 89, per. 25, dok. 2.

20 Ali Sultan Keshtmand, interview, London, 25 May 2009.

21 A. Hyman, *Afghanistan under Soviet Domination 1964–81* (London, 1982), pp. 126, 149, and 152.

22 D. MacEachin, 'Predicting the Soviet Invasion of Afghanistan', Center for the Study of Intelligence (https://www.cia.gov/library/center-for-the-study-of-intelligence/csi-publications/books-and-monographs/); Dorronosoro, *Revolution Unending*, pp. 103–4.

23 For a list of these requests, see O. Sarin and L. Dvoretsky, *The Afghan Syndrome: The Soviet Union's Vietnam* (Novato, CA, 1993), pp. 79–84; and Lyakhovski, *Tragedia i doblest Afgana*, 1995, passim.

24 Gai and Snegirev, *Vtorzhenie*, p. 90.

25 Zaitsev, *Alpha – My Destiny*, pp. 114–15.

26 I. Tukharinov, *Sekretny komandarm* (http://www.rsva.ru/biblio/prose_af/secret_com/index.shtml).

27 Gai and Snegirev, *Vtorzhenie*, p. 69.

28 Lyakhovski, *Tragedia i doblest Afgana*, 2004, pp. 131 and 133. Pavlovski's final report is on p. 192.

29 Zaitsev, *Alpha – My Destiny*, pp. 126–7.

30 Ablazov, *Afganistan chetvertaya voina*, p. 163; Sarin and Dvoretsky, *The Afghan Syndrome*, pp. 79–84.

31 MacEachin, 'Predicting the Soviet Invasion of Afghanistan'.

3: The Decision to Intervene

1 Much remains obscure about these events. The following account draws heavily on two sources: V. Mitrokhin, *The KGB in Afghanistan*, Woodrow Wilson International Center for Scholars, Washington, DC, February 2002, and M. Slinkin, *Afghanistan, Trevozhnye Leto i Osen 1979 g, Kultura narodov Prichenomorya*, No. 4, 1998, pp. 138–52 (http://www.nbuv.gov. ua/Articles/KultNar/avtory/slinkin/knp/index.htm). Mitrokhin was an archivist in the KGB who kept extensive notes on the documents he handled, which he brought to the West when he defected after the collapse of the Soviet Union. He rarely gives document references or even dates, and his account needs to be approached with caution. I have added material from A. Lyakhovski, *Tragedia i doblest Afgana* (Moscow, 1995) (http://www. rsva.ru/biblio/prose_af/afgan_tragedy_and_glory/index.shtml), passim. But the details are still buried in the archives of the KGB and in Kabul.

2 A. Lyakhovski, *Tragedia i doblest Afgana* (Moscow, 2004), p. 153.

3 A. Maiorov, *Pravda ob afganskoi voine* (Moscow, 1996), p. 74.

4 Lyakhovski, *Tragedia i doblest Afgana*, 2004; A. Borovik, *The Hidden War* (New York, 1990), p. 247.

5 Memorandum by Richard Holbrooke in Washington National Records Center, RG 330, McNamara Vietnam Files: FRC 77–0075, Vietnam – 1966. The text was kindly given to me by Sherard Cowper-Coles.

6 That at least is the opinion of Mitrokhin and Lyakhovski. I have not come across any confirmation from the Afghan side that it was so perceived by Taraki.

7 Lyakhovski, *Tragedia i doblest Afgana*, 2004, p. 155.

8 M. Slinkin, *NDPA u vlasti* (Simferopol, 1999), p. 128.

9 Lyakhovski, *Tragedia i doblest Afgana*, 2004, p. 160.

10 Mitrokhin, *The KGB in Afghanistan*, p. 52. This passage seems to be a continuation of the telegram of 13 September referred to above.

11 Telegram from Puzanov and others to Brezhnev, ibid., p. 53.

12 Ibid., p. 55.

13 Ryurikov kept a diary on behalf of his ambassador, which is at Mitrokhin, *The KGB in Afghanistan*, pp. 59–62. This account of the shoot-out comes from the diary entry for 19 September, supplemented by interview with Ryurikov in Moscow on 24 July 2009 and 9 March 2010. According to

Ryurikov, copies of his diary were sent to a number of departments in Moscow. See also Lyakhovski, *Tragedia i doblest Afgana*, 2004, p. 173.

14 Interview with Taraki's wife in D. Gai and V. Snegirev, *Vtorzhenie* (Moscow, 1991), p. 45.

15 V. Ablazov, *Afganistan chetvertaya voina* (Kiev, 2002), pp. 163–8.

16 Lyakhovski, *Tragedia i doblest Afgana*, 2004, p. 156.

17 Gai and Snegirev, *Vtorzhenie*, p. 44.

18 Ibid., p. 42.

19 Lyakhovski, *Tragedia i doblest Afgana*, 2004, pp. 167–9.

20 Ibid., pp. 176–80. Kurilov's account has been much shortened. General Bogdanov believes that Kurilov was carried away by his imagination. In his book *The Great Gamble: The Soviet War in Afghanistan* (New York, 2009), Gregory Feifer reports Gulabzoi's insistence that he did not leave Kabul in a box.

21 Lyakhovski, *Tragedia i doblest Afgana*, 2004, p. 181.

22 Mitrokhin, *The KGB in Afghanistan*, p. 71.

23 This account is based on the sometimes contradictory depositions of Ekbal, Vadud, and Jandad during the investigation into Taraki's death which was conducted after Amin was overthrown. See Ablazov, *Afganistan chetvertaya voina*, pp. 149–56.

24 Lyakhovski, *Tragedia i doblest Afgana*, 2004, pp. 185–6.

25 Ye. Chazov, *Zdorovie i Vlast* (Moscow, 1992), p. 182. Chazov is reporting what he was told by Andropov.

26 The views of Gorelov, Zaplatin, and Tabeev are recorded in Gai and Snegirev, *Vtorzhenie*, pp. 71–7.

27 G. Dorronosoro, *Revolution Unending: Afghanistan, 1979 to the Present* (New York, 2005), pp. 96–7; Lyakhovski, *Tragedia i doblest Afgana*, 2004, p. 189.

28 A. Volkov, '40-aya Armia: Istoria sozdania, sostav, izmenenie struktury' (www.rsva-ural.ru/library/?id63).

29 Lyakhovski implies as much in *Tragedia i doblest Afgana*, 2004, p. 213, though the facsimile of Chernenko's note which he reproduces on p. 214 indicates that Grishin, Kirilienko, Pelshe, Tikhonov, and Ponomarev were also present.

30 R. Gates, *From the Shadows* (New York, 1996), p. 132.

31 Dorronosoro, *Revolution Unending*, p. 310.

32 S. Coll, *Ghost Wars* (London, 2005), p. 48.

33 This account of Andropov's paper is based on notes taken by A. Dobrynin provided to the Cold War International History Project by Odd Arne Westad.

34 Lyakhovski, *Tragedia i doblest Afgana*, 2004, p. 215; facsimile on p. 214.

35 Quoted in Lyakhovski, *Tragedia i doblest Afgana*, 2004, pp. 218–20.

36 A. Lyakhovski, *Cold War International History Working Paper No. 51: Inside the Soviet Invasion of Afghanistan and the Seizure of Kabul, December 1979*, Woodrow Wilson International Center for Scholars, January 2007, p. 27.

37 Lyakhovski, *Tragedia i doblest Afgana*, 1995, Chapter II.

4: The Storming of the Palace

1 A. Lyakhovski, *Cold War International History Working Paper No. 51: Inside the Soviet Invasion of Afghanistan and the Seizure of Kabul, December 1979*, Woodrow Wilson International Center for Scholars, January 2007, pp. 30 and 32.

2 Yevgeni Kiselev, interview, Moscow, 24 March 2010.

3 Figures from http://ru.wikipedia.org/wiki/Операция_«Дунай».

4 See http://en.wikipedia.org/wiki/Soviet_war_in_Afghanistan.

5 A. Savinkin, *Afganskie uroki: Vyvody dlya budushchego v svete ideinogo nasledia A. E. Snegareva* (Moscow, 2003), p. 755.

6 L. Shebarshin, *Ruka Moskvy: zapiski nachalnika sovetskoi razvadki* (Moscow, 2002), p. 195.

7 Directive No. 312/12/001, signed by Ustinov and Ogarkov and despatched on 24 December. See A. Lyakhovski, *Tragedia i doblest Afgana* (Moscow, 2004), p. 252.

8 Order No. 312/1/030, 25.12.79, is referred to ibid., p 258; it is quoted in full there in Chapter 2.

9 D. Gai and V. Snegirev, *Vtorzhenie* (Moscow, 1991), p. 107.

10 Lyakhovski, *Tragedia i doblest Afgana*, 2009, p. 331; V. Korolev, 'Uroki Voiny v Afganistane 1979–1989' (http://www.sdrvdv.org/node/159).

11 FCO File FSA 020/9: Soviet Intervention in Afghanistan, Folio 2: Kabul telegram to FCO of 27 December 1979.

12 Gai and Snegirev, *Vtorzhenie*, pp. 106–7.

13 Article on the history of the 56th Guards Independent Airborne Assault Brigade (http://www.andjusev.narod.ru/a/56_DSCHB.htm).

14 Sergei Morozov, interview, Moscow, 31 May 2007.

15 B. Gromov, *Ogranichenny kontingent* (Moscow, 1994) (http://www.rsva.ru/biblio/prose_af/limited_contingent/index.shtml).

16 I. Tukharinov, *Sekretny komandarm* (http://www.rsva.ru/biblio/prose_af/ secret_com/index.shtml).

17 Gromov, *Ogranichenny kontingent.*

18 Many accounts wrongly say that Amin moved to the nearby Dar-ul Aman Palace, which was built by Amanullah.

19 Lyakhovski, *Tragedia i doblest Afgana*, 2004, p. 246.

20 L. Grau, *The Take-down of Kabul: An Effective Coup de Main*, Combat Studies Institute, Command and General Staff College, Fort Leavenworth, Kansas, 2 October 2002.

21 Lyakhovski, *Cold War International History Working Paper No. 51*, p. 63.

22 Lyakhovski, *Tragedia i doblest Afgana*, 2004, p. 249.

23 Ibid., pp. 249 and 253.

24 Lyakhovski, *Cold War International History Working Paper No. 51*, pp. 49 and 52.

25 Alexander Lyakhovski, conversation, 18 September 2007.

26 Lyakhovski, *Tragedia i doblest Afgana*, 2004, pp. 242 and 253–382.

27 There is a brief note on Colonel Kuznechkov in T. Popova, *Pomyani nas, Rossia*, Leningrad Committee of Mothers, 1991, which contains photographs and notes on the soldiers from Leningrad who died in the war. Kuznechkov was the first.

28 The story about the KGB cook is repeated in, among other places, V. Kuzichkin, *Inside the KGB: Myth & Reality* (London, 1990), p. 315. Kuzichkin's account of events in Afghanistan is inaccurate, but he claims to have heard the story from Talybov personally. See also V. Kryuchkov, *Lichnoe delo*, 2 vols. (Moscow, 1996), Vol. 1, p. 206.

29 Alexander Shkirando, interview, Moscow, 27 July 2007.

30 Lyakhovski, *Cold War International History Working Paper No. 51*, p. 454.

31 Ibid., p. 67.

32 Lyakhovski, *Tragedia i doblest Afgana*, 2004, p. 288.

33 V. Snegirev, *Ryzhy* (Moscow, 2000), p. 145.

34 Other versions are that he was killed by a grenade splinter, or even by his own guards: Lyakhovski, *Cold War International History Working Paper No. 51*, p. 62.

35 In Lyakhovski's successive accounts, the casualty figures vary. In his *Tragedia i doblest Afgana*, 2004, pp. 285 and 295, he gives slightly higher figures for the Soviet casualties than those in *Cold War International History Working Paper No. 51*, p. 64. I have taken the latter figures.

36 Lyakhovski, *Tragedia i doblest Afgana*, 2004, p. 285.

37 Galina Ivanov, interview, Moscow, 14 March 2010.

38 S. Balenko, *SpetsNaz GRU v Afganistane* (Moscow, 2010), p. 69. Since the early 1990s, when the veil of secrecy on the storming of the palace began to be lifted, there have been a number of more or less coherent reconstructions of these confused events. One of the most lucid is Lester Grau's 2003 article, 'The Takedown of Kabul: An Effective Coup de Main' (http://www.cgsc.edu/carl/download/csipubs/Block/chp9_Block_by.pdf). This is based on the testimony of eyewitnesses and the technical analysis of the Russian general staff. Map 3 is based on the detailed map in Mr Grau's article.

39 The cat features in Lyakhovski, *Tragedia i doblest Afgana*, 1995, and in General Drozdov's account of the storming of the palace in Balenko, *SpetsNaz GRU v Afganistane*, p. 66.

5: Aftermath

1 A. Lyakhovski, *Tragedia i doblest Afgana* (Moscow, 2004), pp. 308–9.

2 Dr Lutfullah Latif, interview, London, 18 July 2008.

3 A. Kalinovsky, 'A Long Goodbye: The Politics and Diplomacy of the Soviet Withdrawal from Afghanistan, 1980–1992', PhD thesis, London School of Economics, 2009, quoting C. Andrew and V. Mitrokhin, *The World Was Going Our Way* (New York, 2006), p. 407.

4 A. Greshnov, *Afganistan: Zalozhniki vremeni* (Moscow, 2006), pp. 44, 134, and 136.

5 There are many accounts of this embarrassing moment. See, for example, *Rasskazy ob operatsiakh – Baikal* (http://antiterror.ru/to_profs/tales/71898035).

6 Greshnov, *Afganistan: Zalozhniki vremeni*, p. 42.

7 A. Sukhoparov, 'Afganski sindrom' (www.russia-today.ru/2009/no_02/02_world_02.html).

8 A. Belofastov and A. Rebrik (eds.), *Mushavery* (Moscow, 2005), p. 44.

9 The Americans lost twenty-four soldiers dead and 325 wounded. The Panamanian military lost about 205 dead. US military estimates of civilian casualties range from 200 to 1,000. Other estimates range from 2,000 to 5,000 (http://en.wikipedia.org/wiki/United_States_invasion_of_Panama).

10 Dmitri Ryurikov, interview, Moscow, 24 July 2009.

11 The Bonner and Sakharov texts are at www.hro.org-editions-karta.

12 M. Galeotti, *Afghanistan: The Soviet Union's Last War* (London, 1995), pp. 139–54.

13 Lyakhovski, *Tragedia i doblest Afgana*, p.19; interview with Oleg Bogomolov, Moscow, May 2007.

14 Information from Dr Galina Yemelyanova, a former scholar from the institute, 6 June 2009.

15 Information from Sir Christopher Mallaby, who was serving in the Foreign Office at the time.

16 A. Chernyaev, *Sovmestny iskhod: Dnevnik dvukh epokh 1972–1991 gody* (Moscow, 2008), diary entries for 30 December 1979, 5 February 1980, and 9 February 1980, pp. 386, 391, and 392.

17 A. Savinkin, *Afganskie uroki: Vyvody dlya budushchego v svete ideinogo nasledia A. E. Snegareva* (Moscow, 2003), p. 728.

18 S. Coll, *Ghost Wars* (London, 2005), pp. 132–3.

19 D. MacEachin, 'Predicting the Soviet Invasion of Afghanistan', Center for the Study of Intelligence (https://www.cia.gov/ library/center-for-the-study-of-intelligence/csi-publications/ books-and-monographs/).

20 Coll, *Ghost Wars*, pp. 132–3.

21 FCO File FSA 020/2, Folio 74e: Howell Minute of 28 November 1979.

22 Alexander Maiorov, who was the Chief Soviet Military Adviser in Afghanistan in 1980–81, says that Ustinov, the Defence Minister, spoke of both objectives. There is no evidence that Ustinov was talking about concrete plans rather than vague aspirations: A. Maiorov, *Pravda ob afganskoi voine* (Moscow, 1996), pp. 50 and 269; R. Gates, *From the Shadows* (New York, 1996), p. 148; FCO File FS 021/6: letter of 28 September from South Asia Department to High Commission in Islamabad.

23 'Grain Becomes a Weapon', *Time*, 21 January 1980.

24 FCO File EN021/1/1980, Folio 103: Washington Tel 137 of 9 January 1980 to FCO.

25 See http://en.wikipedia.org/wiki/Carter_Doctrine.

26 G. Dorronosoro, *Revolution Unending: Afghanistan, 1979 to the Present* (New York, 2005), p. 192, fn.

27 Z. Brzezinski, 'Reflections on Soviet Intervention in Afghanistan', 26 December 1979 (http://www.cnn.com/SPECIALS/cold.war/episodes/20/ documents/brez.carter/).

28 Coll, *Ghost Wars*, p. 44; Brzezinski interview with *Le Nouvel Observateur*, 15–21 January 1998 (http://www.globalresearch.ca/articles/BRZ110A.html).

29 *Daily Telegraph*, 14 January 1985.

30 J. Prados, *Safe for Democracy: The Secret Wars of the CIA* (Chicago, 2006), pp. 488–90.

31 Memorandum of 6 December 1984, quoted in Coll, *Ghost Wars*, p. 102. The point about the politicisation of American support for the mujahedin was made to me by Artemy Kalinovsky.

32 They base themselves primarily on Brzezinski's interview with *Le Nouvel Observateur* in January 1998.

33 A. Lyakhovski, *Cold War International History Working Paper No. 51: Inside the Soviet Invasion of Afghanistan and the Seizure of Kabul, December 1979*, Woodrow Wilson International Center for Scholars, January 2007, p. 64.

34 G. Feifer, *The Great Gamble: The Soviet War in Afghanistan* (New York, 2009), p. 97.

35 V. Kryuchkov, *Lichnoe delo*, 2 vols. (Moscow, 1996), Vol. 1, p. 207.

36 Private information.

Part II: The Disasters of War

1 I. Chernobrovkin, 'Desyat gorkikh let' (http://www.centrasia.ru/newsA.php4?st=1091161680).

6: The 40th Army Goes to War

1 A. Lyakhovski, *Tragedia i doblest Afgana* (Moscow, 2004), p. 251; D. Gai and V. Snegirev, *Vtorzhenie* (Moscow, 1991), p. 91.

2 I. Tukharinov, *Sekretny komandarm* (http://www.rsva.ru/biblio/prose_af/secret_com/index.shtml).

3 A. Kalinovsky, 'A Long Goodbye: The Politics and Diplomacy of the Soviet Withdrawal from Afghanistan, 1980–1992', PhD thesis, London School of Economics, 2009.

4 Some 155 officers died between 1946 and 1950 in the Chinese civil war; 168 during the Korean War; twelve during the fighting in Vietnam between 1965 and 1974; seven from accidents and illness in Cuba in 1962–4; eighteen in the wars between the Arabs and the Israelis in 1967–74; twenty-three in Ethiopia; forty during the fighting along the frontier with China in 1969: G. Krivosheev, *Rossia i SSSR v voinakh XX veka: Poteri vooruzhennykh sil* (Moscow, 2001), pp. 521–34.

5 Ibid., p. 537.

6 Anatoli Yermolin, conversation, Warsaw, September 2006.

7 Alexander Kartsev, interviews, and material from his memoir *Shelkovy put* (privately published, 2004).

8   O. Caroe, *The Pathans* (New York, 1964), p. 320.

9   According to the UN, more than half of Afghanistan's gross domestic product in 2005 came from the production of drugs. In many parts of the country 'opium was the only commercially viable crop', *UNODC Afghanistan Opium Survey 2005* (http://www.unodc.org/newsletter/en/200504/page008.html).

10 A. Prokhanov, *Tretii tost* (Moscow, 2003), p. 61.

11 M. Townsend, 'I Could Feel the Breeze as the Bullets Went By', *Observer*, 5 August 2007.

12 A. Kartsev, *Voenny razvedchik* (Moscow, 2007), p. 47.

13 Yu. Lapshin, *Afganski dnevnik* (Moscow, 2004), p. 62.

14 Gai and Snegirev, *Vtorzhenie*, p. 236; Lapshin, *Afganski dnevnik*, p. 101.

15 L. Grau, 'The Soviet-Afghan War: Superpower Mired in the Mountains' (http://www.smallwars.quantico.usmc.mil/search/LessonsLearned/afghanistan/miredinmount.asp); V. Korolev, 'Uroki voiny v Afganistane 1979–1989 godov' (http://www.sdrvdv.org/node/159).

16 S. Kozlov (ed.), *SpetsNaz GRU: Afganistan* (Moscow, 2009), p. 25; 'Istoria SpetsNaza GRU' (http://bratishka.ru/specnaz/gru/history.php); 'Afganistan' (http://www.agentura.ru/dossier/russia/gru/imperia/specnaz/afgan/).

17 Lecture by General Vadim Kokorin, Chief of Intelligence of the 40th Army 1985–7: copy kindly given to me by Colonel Ruslan Kyryliuk.

18 Igor Morozov, interviews, Moscow, 19 February 2007 and 11 March 2010; http://www.agentura.ru/specnaz/bezopasnost/kaskad/; 'Nezavisimoe Voennoe Obozrenie' (http://nvo.ng.ru/spforces/2000–09–22/7_kaskader. html); R. Kipling, *Stalky & Co.* (London, 1899), p. 257.

19 L. Kucherova, *SpetsNaz KGB v Afganistane* (Moscow, 2009), pp. 321 and 319.

20 V. Kharichev, 'Pogranichniki – v ognennoi voine Afganistana' (http://pv-afghan.ucoz.ru/publ/ctati/1).

21 V. Ogryzko, *Pesni afganskogo pokhoda* (Moscow, 2000), pp. 30–31.

22 Lecture by General Vadim Kokorin.

23 According to Gorelov, the Soviet military adviser in Afghanistan at the beginning of the war, the Afghans had ten divisions, 145,000 men, 650 tanks, eighty-seven infantry fighting vehicles, 780 armoured personnel carriers, 1,919 guns, 150 aircraft, and twenty-five helicopters.

24 M. Galeotti, *Afghanistan: The Soviet Union's Last War* (London, 1995), p. 7.

25 The first figure is from M. Urban, *War in Afghanistan* (London, 1990), p. 106; the second from G. Dorronosoro, *Revolution Unending: Afghanistan, 1979 to the Present* (New York, 2005), p. 188.

26 Valeri Shiryaev, interview, Moscow, 12 March 2010.

27 G. Bobrov, *Soldatskaya saga* (Moscow, 2007), pp. 237–40.

28 Ogryzko, *Pesni afganskogo pokhoda*, p. 49.

29 V. Kryuchkov, *Lichnoe delo*, 2 vols. (Moscow, 1996), Vol. 1, p. 213.

30 Gai and Snegirev, *Vtorzhenie*, p. 137.

31 Ibid., p. 113.

32 Lyakhovski, *Tragedia i doblest Afgana*, 2009, p. 450; M. Kakar, *Afghanistan: The Soviet Invasion and the Afghan Response, 1979–1982* (Berkeley, CA, 1995), pp. 114–19.

33 Tukharinov, *Sekretny komandarm*.

34 Lapshin, *Afganski dnevnik*, p. 101.

35 Lyakhovski, *Tragedia i doblest Afgana*, 1995 (http://www.rsva.ru/biblio/prose_af/afgan_tragedy_and_glory/index.shtml).

36 V. Varennikov, *Nepovtorimoe*, 7 vols. (Moscow, 2001), Vol. 5, pp. 117–29.

37 Tukharinov, *Sekretny komandarm*.

38 J. Prados, *Safe for Democracy: The Secret Wars of the CIA* (Chicago, 2006), pp. 488.

39 M. Yousaf and M. Adkin, *Afghanistan: The Bear Trap* (Barnsley, 1992), p. 208.

40 'Dalnyaya aviatsia Rossii' (www.sinopa.ee/davia003/dav03.htm).

41 Krivosheev, *Rossia i SSSR v voinakh XX veka*, p. 539.

42 Lyakhovski, *Tragedia i doblest Afgana*, 2004, pp. 766–7.

43 See http://www.militaryphotos.net/forums/showthread.php?t=16922.

44 Air Assault Comes to Afghanistan (http://www.militaryphotos.net/forums/showthread.php?16922-(Soviet)-Air-Assault-Comes-to-Afghanistan-1984).

45 B. Gromov, *Ogranichenny kontingent* (Moscow, 1994) (http://www.rsva.ru/biblio/prose_af/limited_contingent/index.shtml).

7: The Nationbuilders

1 Martha Brill Olcott, 'Soviet Islam and World Revolution', *World Politics*, Vol. 23, No. 2, July 1982, p. 488, quoted in A. Kalinovsky, 'Intruder in the "Communal Apartment": The Afghan War, Soviet Muslims, and the Collapse of the USSR', paper prepared for the HY510 seminar, London School of Economics, 11 November 2009.

2 These aid figures come from A. Kalinovsky, 'The Blind Leading the Blind: Soviet Advisors, Counter-insurgency and Nation-Building in Afghanistan', paper prepared for HY510 seminar, London School of Economics, 11 February 2009, and A. Kalinovsky, 'A Long Goodbye: The Politics and Diplomacy of the Soviet Withdrawal from Afghanistan, 1980–1992', PhD thesis, London School of Economics, 2009, p. 120.

3 D. Gai and V. Snegirev, *Vtorzhenie* (Moscow, 1991), p. 322; V. Snegirev, *Ryzhy* (Moscow, 2000), p. 157.

4 Gai and Snegirev, *Vtorzhenie*, p. 323.

5 Ibid., p. 361.

6 V. Kryuchkov, *Lichnoe delo*, 2 vols. (Moscow, 1996), p. 220; B. Padishev, 'Najibullah, president Afghanistana', *International Affairs* (Moscow), January 1990, p. 23, quoted in Kalinovsky, 'A Long Goodbye'.

7 V. Snegirev in A. Belofastov and A. Rebrik (eds.), *Mushavery* (Moscow, 2005), p. 27.

8 A. Maiorov, *Pravda ob afganskoi voine* (Moscow, 1996), p. 117.

9 Gai and Snegirev, *Vtorzhenie*, p. 317.

10 Valeri and Galina Ivanov, interview, Moscow, 14 March 2010.

11 Maiorov, *Pravda ob afganskoi voine*, p. 110; Valeri Shiryaev, interview, Moscow, 12 March 2010.

12 I. Tukharinov, *Sekretny komandarm* (http://www.rsva.ru/biblio/prose_af/secret_com/index.shtml); Valeri Shiryaev, interview, Moscow, 12 March 2010.

13 Kalinovsky, 'The Blind Leading the Blind'.

14 Gai and Snegirev, *Vtorzhenie*, p. 317.

15 G. Kireev, *Kandagarski dnevnik* (http://kireev.info/index.html).

16 Belofastov and Rebrik (eds.), *Mushavery*, p. 13.

17 Ibid., pp. 40 and 41.

18 Yevgeni Kiselev, interview, Moscow, 24 March 2010.

19 A. Greshnov, *Afganistan: Zalozhniki vremeni* (Moscow, 2006), pp. 26 and 27.

20 J. Van Bladel, *The All-Volunteer Force in the Russian Mirror: Transformation without Change* (Groningen, 2004).

21 A. Smolina, 'Larisa-parikmakhersha' (http://artofwar.ru/s/smolina_a/text_0160.shtml).

22 One such case is mentioned in Gai and Snegirev, *Vtorzhenie*, p. 277.

23 A. Smolina, 'Otvet "Afganki" dla avtorshi "Tsinkovykh Malchikov"' (http://artofwar.ru/s/smolina_a/text_0150.shtml).

24 Gai and Snegirev, *Vtorzhenie*, p. 284.
25 G. Krivosheev, *Rossia i SSSR v voinakh XX veka: Poteri vooruzhennykh sil* (Moscow, 2001), p. 537.
26 'Veterany boevykh deistvii NizhneKamsk' (http://www.afgankamsk.ucoz. ru/index/0–4).
27 Smolina, 'Larisa-parikmakhersha'.
28 A. Smolina, 'Medsestra Tatiana Kuzmina (1951–1986)' (http://artofwar.ru/s/ smolina_a/).
29 A. Smolina, 'Otvet "Afganki" dla avtorshi "Tsinkovykh Malchikov"' (http:// artofwar.ru/s/smolina_a/text_0150.shtml).
30 S. Aleksievich, *Zinky Boys* (New York, 1992), p. 114.
31 A. Smolina, 'Iz okoshka devichego modulya, ili vospominania "Afganok"' (http://artofwar.ru/s/smolina_a/text_0200.shtml).
32 Colonel Viktor Antonenko, interview, Moscow, 31 May 2007.
33 Aleksievich, *Zinky Boys*, p. 114.
34 Ibid., pp. 41 and 24.
35 Private information.
36 Alexander Khoroshavin posted his comments in the online 'smoking room' of the regiment on 25 June 2006 (http://artofwar.ru/b/bobrow_g_1 / kurilka860doc.shtml).
37 A tactic also adopted by women working in other circumstances, such as the intimate conditions of a long posting to a scientific research station in the Antarctic, where one or two women may be cooped up with their male colleagues for months at a time: conversation with Meredith Hooper, 17 May 2008.
38 A. Dyshev, *PPZh: Pokhodno-polevaya Zhena* (Moscow, 2007). The book's verisimilitude is vouched for by Colonel Antonenko, Valeri Shiryaev, and Alexander Gergel.
39 Dmitri Fedorov, email to author, 25 July 2007.
40 Vyacheslav Nekrasov, interview, Moscow, 28 July 2009; V. Snegirev, 'Nashi', *Rossiiskaya gazeta* (http://www.rg.ru/peoples/sneg/1.shtm).
41 Maiorov, *Pravda ob afganskoi voine*, pp. 145–8.
42 M. Yousaf and M. Adkin, *Afghanistan: The Bear Trap* (Barnsley, 1992), p. 146.
43 Gai and Snegirev, *Vtorzhenie*, pp. 317–18.
44 A. Smolina, 'Nevezukha, ona i v Afgane – nevezukha' (http://artofwar.ru/s/ smolina_a/).
45 Gai and Snegirev, *Vtorzhenie*, pp. 351–5.

46 Ibid., pp. 335–61.

47 Ibid., p. 320.

48 Belofastov and Rebrik (eds.), *Mushavery*, p. 59.

49 Alexander Yuriev, diary entry for 15–16 June 1985, ibid., p. 198.

50 Alexander Yuriev, diary entry for 10–12 August 1985, ibid., p. 203.

51 Ibid., p. 47.

52 Ibid., p. 19.

53 Ibid., p. 16.

54 Ibid., pp. 17 and 111 et seq.

55 Nikolai Komissarov, interview, Moscow, 26 July 2007.

56 Belofastov and Rebrik (eds.), *Mushavery*, p. 48.

57 Vyacheslav Nekrasov, interviews, Moscow, 2007–10.

58 Belofastov and Rebrik (eds.), *Mushavery*, pp. 130–34.

8: Soldiering

 1 The best literary description of 'soldiering' comes in Frederic Manning's *The Middle Parts of Fortune* (London, 2000), about the fighting on the Somme in 1916.

 2 M. Galeotti, *Afghanistan: The Soviet Union's Last War* (London, 1995), pp. 32–7.

 3 Alexander Gergel, email to author, 28 July 2008.

 4 A point made to me by Artemy Kalinovsky.

 5 M. Reshetnikov, 'Psikhofiziologicheskie osnovy prognozirovania effektivnosti boevoi deatelnosti i boevoi adaptatsii voennosluzhashchikh': article kindly provided by Dr Reshetnikov.

 6 Galeotti, *Afghanistan*, p. 30.

 7 S. Aleksievich, *Zinky Boys* (New York, 1992), p. 27. There were similar stories at the beginning of the war in Chechnya.

 8 V. Tamarov, *Afghanistan: A Russian Soldier's Story* (Berkeley, CA, 2001), p. 138.

 9 Andrei Ponomarev, interview, Moscow, 1 March 2010.

10 Vitali Krivenko gives a semi-fictionalised account of his time in Afghanistan in the first part of *Ekipazh mashiny boevoi* ('The Crew of a Fighting Vehicle') (St Petersburg, 2004), pp. 36–336. The second part of the book (*Kak pozhivaesh, shuravi?*, pp. 336–80) is a memoir, from which these details of Krivenko's career are drawn. On bullying, see p. 346.

11 A. Chernyaev, *Sovmestny iskhod: Dnevnik dvukh epokh 1972–1991 gody* (Moscow, 2008), diary entry for 27 August 1985, p. 643.

12   Sergei Morozov, interview, Moscow, 31 May 2007.

13   Krivenko, *Ekipazh mashiny boevoi*, p. 45; S. Nikiforov, *Bez vsyakikh pravil* (St Petersburg, 2008), p. 113.

14   A. Lyakhovski, *Tragedia i doblest Afgana* (Moscow, 1995) (http://www.rsva. ru/biblio/prose_af/afgan_tragedy_and_glory/index.shtml).

15   The problem of *dedovshchina* and the need for professional NCOs are widely discussed. See, for example, S. Belanovski and S. Marzeeva, *Dedovshchina v sovietskoi armii* (Moscow, 1991) (www.sbelan.ru/content/ дедовщина-в-советской-армии); M. Radov, '*Dedovshchina* – istoki i prichiny' (http://slovo.odessa.ua/366/5_4.html); I. Rodionov i, 'Perestroiku armii nuzhno nachinat s serzhantov' (http://tr.rkrp-rpk.ru/get.php?42); Alexander Gergel, email to author, 24 June 2009.

16   Andrei Ponomarev, interview, Moscow, 1 March 2010.

17   The inadequacies are graphically spelled out by D. Gai and V. Snegirev, *Vtorzhenie* (Moscow, 1991), pp. 258–92.

18   S. Nikiforov, *Bez vsyakikh pravil*, p. 100.

19   G. Krivosheev, *Rossia i SSSR v voinakh XX veka: Poteri vooruzhennykh sil* (Moscow, 2001), p. 538.

20   A. Dyshev, *PPZh: Pokhodno-Polevaya Zhena* (Moscow, 2007), pp. 38–9.

21   B. Gromov, *Ogranichenny kontingent* (Moscow, 1994) (http://www.rsva.ru/ biblio/prose_af/limited_contingent/index.shtml).

22   Gai and Snegirev, *Vtorzhenie*, p. 273.

23   A. Smolina, 'Kholera v Dzelalabade' (http://artofwar.ru/s/smolina_a/ text_0070.shtml).

24   A. Smolina, 'Larisa-parikmakhersha' (http://artofwar.ru/s/smolina_a/ text_0160.shtml).

25   Galeotti, *Afghanistan*, pp. 67–8.

26   Major Vyacheslav Izmailov, interview, Moscow, 29 July 2009.

27   Gromov, *Ogranichenny kontingent*, Part III: 'Pervaya Komandirovka, Tashkent–Kabul'.

28   'Istoria 3-ego bataliona' (serg2331.narod.ru).

29   A. Pochtarev, 'An Afghan Diary', *Novaya gazeta* (Moscow), 4 March 2005; Alexander Gergel, interview, Moscow, 16 February 2009.

30   The establishment of a motor-rifle regiment in Afghanistan was 181 officers, 124 *praporshchiki*, 363 sergeants, 1,530 riflemen, 132 BMPs, forty tanks, eighteen 2SIs, and 264 vehicles: A. Vasiliev, '*O 149 Polku*' (about the 149th Regiment) (http://artofwar.ru/w/wasilxew_a_i/text_0010.shtml); G. Bobrov, *Soldatskaya saga* (Moscow, 2007), p. 11; Alexander Gergel,

interview, Moscow, 1 March 2010. See also Annex 2, 'Order of Battle of the 40th Army', p. 342.

31 Bobrov, *Soldatskaya saga*, pp. 51–2 and 81.

32 Alexander Gergel, interview, Moscow, 1 March 2010; S. Demyashov, interview (http://www.peresvet-lavra.ru/index.php?typereview&area2&par ticles&id104&PHPSESSIDcea44aa4bcbb077087dec923e7ece70); Bobrov, *Soldatskaya saga*, p. 170.

33 Andrei Ponomarev, interview, Moscow, 1 March 2010.

34 Alexander Gergel, interview, Moscow, 28 July 2009.

35 This description of the base at Bakharak is taken from interviews with Alexander Gergel and from his story *Pismo schastlivomu soldatu* ('Letter to a Lucky Soldier') (http://artofwar.ru/g/gergelx_a_n/text_0030.shtml).

36 Colonel Ruslan Kyryliuk, conversation, London, 15 July 2010.

37 W. Olney, *'Shiloh' as Seen by a Private Soldier: A Paper Read before California Commandery of the Military Order of the Loyal Legion of the United States, May 31, 1889* (Kessinger Publishing, Whitefish, Mont., 2007), p. 17.

38 Alexander Gergel, email to author, 24 June 2009.

39 Alexander Kartsev, email to author, 22 June 2009.

40 Andrei Ponomarev, interview, Moscow, 1 March 2010.

41 Alexander Gergel, email to author, 23 September 2008.

42 Yu. Lapshin, *Afganski dnevnik* (Moscow, 2004), pp. 50–59 and 89.

43 A. Kartsev, *Shelkovy put* (privately published, 2004), Chapter 13; interview, Moscow, 3 March 2010.

44 Valeri Shiryaev, email to author, 16 March 2010, containing an eyewitness description of the incident by a Soviet interpreter who was present.

45 The main sources for the description of Masud and the Pandsher Valley are A. Lyakhovski and V. Nekrasov, *Grazhdanin, politik, voin: Pamyati Akhmad Shakha Masuda* (Moscow, 2007), pp. 24 et seq.: Ter-Grigoriants's remarks are on pp. 40–43; P. Clammer, *Afghanistan: Lonely Planet Guide* (London, 2007); E. Newby, *A Short Walk in the Hindu Kush* (London, 1974); 'The Pandsher Valley, the Emerald Mines and the Blue Mountain' (http://www.travelafghanistan.co.uk/pages/panj.html); Lyakhovski, *Tragedia i doblest Afgana*, p. 10; and a visit which the author made there in September 2008.

46 A. Giustozzi, *Empires of Mud* (London, 2009), pp. 282 and 287.

47 Lyakhovski and Nekrasov, *Grazhdanin, politik, voin*, pp. 73 et seq.

48 Dmitri Fedorov, email to author, 25 July 2007.

49 Alexander Golts, interview, Moscow, 6 December 2006.

50 Alexander Gergel, interview, Moscow, 24 July 2007: this was his father's salary at the time.
51 Gai and Snegirev, *Vtorzhenie*, pp. 282 et seq.
52 V. Snegirev in A. Belofastov and A. Rebrik (eds.), *Mushavery* (Moscow, 2005), p. 25.
53 Aleksievich, *Zinky Boys*, p. 18.
54 This is confirmed by Alexander Gergel, interview, Moscow, 16 February 2009.
55 Krivenko, *Ekipazh mashiny boevoi*, p. 352.
56 Masha Slonim, interview, Moscow, 14 March 2010.
57 V. Ogryzko, *Pesni afganskogo pokhoda* (Moscow, 2000), p. 45.
58 Ibid., p. 7.
59 Interviews with Yuri Kirsanov (http://torrents.ru/forum/viewtopic.php?t322885); *Komsomolskaya Pravda Ukrainy*, 25 December 2008 (http://kp.ua/daily/251208/67416/); extract from 'Afganski dnevnik' by Viktor Verstakov (http://kaskad-4.narod.ru/Dnevnik_Verst.html); Igor Morozov, interview, Moscow, 11 March 2010.
60 Ogryzko, *Pesni afganskogo pokhoda*, p. 23.
61 Ibid., p. 147; Igor Morozov, interview, Moscow, 11 March 2010.
62 Dyshev, *PPZh*, p. 379. Valeri Shiryaev said that he felt exactly the same way when he left Afghanistan.

9: Fighting

1 F. Manning, *The Middle Parts of Fortune* (London, 2000), p. 5; S. Junger, *War*, Book Three: *Love* (London, 2010), p. 2. I learned a bit about soldiering and comradeship during my military service, but I never saw any fighting. There are, however, convincing accounts by people who did: Frederick Manning fought on the Somme in 1916; Vasil Bykov (*Ego batalion*, Moscow, 2000) was on the Eastern Front in the Second World War; Nathaniel Fick (*One Bullet Away*, London, 2006) was in Iraq in 2003; Bernard Fall (*Street without Joy: The French Debacle in Indochina*, Barnesley, 2005) was in Indo-China; Jean-Jacques Servan-Schreiber (*Lieutenant en Algérie*, Paris, 1957) was in a 'hearts and minds' unit in Algeria; Sebastian Junger was an embedded journalist in Afghanistan in 2007–8. There is a very large literature about the American experience in Vietnam.
2 M. Nawroz and L. Grau, *The Soviet War in Afghanistan: History and Harbinger of Future War?* Foreign Military Studies Office, Fort Leavenworth, Kansas, June 1996.

3   Personal information. Information on Vertical-T (http://vertical-t.biz/).

4   Yu. Lapshin, *Afganski dnevnik* (Moscow, 2004), p. 81.

5   A. Smolina, 'Desantnik, ili pervoe znakomstvo s Dzhelalbadom' (http://artofwar.ru/s/smolina_a/text_0110.shtml).

6   A. Kartsev, *Voenny razvedchik* (Moscow, 2007).

7   A. Kartsev, *Shelkovy put* (privately published, 2004), Chapter 17.

8   Andrei Ponomarev, interview, Moscow, 1 March 2010.

9   Alexander Gergel, interview, Moscow, 1 March 2010.

10 Colonel Antonenko and Alexander Gergel, interview, Moscow, 31 May 2007. Antonenko maintained that one of the reasons why the guerrillas fought better than the Russians was that they travelled light. Gergel said later that Antonenko was right only in part.

11 A. Lyakhovski, *Tragedia i doblest Afgana* (Moscow, 2004), p. 439.

12 Ibid.

13 M. Urban, *War in Afghanistan* (London, 1990), Appendix IV, p. 332; Lyakhovski, *Tragedia i doblest Afgana*, p. 441.

14 Ibid., p. 370.

15 M. Bearden and J. Risen, *The Main Enemy* (New York, 2003), pp. 227 and 333–6; M. Yousaf and M. Adkin, *Afghanistan: The Bear Trap* (Barnsley, 1992), pp. 155 and 220.

16 I. Tukharinov, *Sekretny komandarm* (http://www.rsva.ru/biblio/prose_af/secret_com/index.shtml).

17 D. Gai and V. Snegirev, *Vtorzhenie* (Moscow, 1991), p. 154; Lyakhovski, *Tragedia i doblest Afgana*, pp. 383–432; V. Varennikov, *Nepovtorimoe*, 7 vols. (Moscow, 2001), Vol. 5, p. 85; Boris Zhelezin, interview, Moscow, 19 February 2007.

18 See http://en.wikipedia.org/wiki/FIM-92_Stinger.

19 D. Cordovez and S. Harrison, *Out of Afghanistan* (Oxford, 1995), pp. 194–7.

20 This is the date given by S. Coll, *Ghost Wars* (London, 2005), p. 149. G. Crile, *Charlie Wilson's War* (New York, 2003) gives the date as 25 September.

21 A. Smolina, 'Vsem devushkam, letavshim v afganskom nebe' (http://artofwar.ru/s/smolina_a/text_0080.shtml).

22 Varennikov, *Nepovtorimoe*, pp. 196–7.

23 Lapshin, *Afganski dnevnik*, p. 94.

24 Gai and Snegirev, *Vtorzhenie*, p. 151.

25 Lyakhovski, *Tragedia i doblest Afgana*, 1995, Chapter VI (http://www.rsva.ru/biblio/prose_af/afgan_tragedy_and_glory/index.shtml). There is a

version of this incident in Prokhanov's story 'The Caravan Hunter' in *Treti tost* (Moscow, 2003), pp. 5–103.

26 M. Gareev, *Moya poslednaya voina*, Chapter 6, p. 102 (http://militera.lib.ru/memo/russian/gareev_ma/index.html).

27 See press cuttings from NTI: 'Working for a Safer World' (http://www.nti.org/e_research/profiles/Iran/Missile/1788_1802.html).

28 Cordovez and Harrison, *Out of Afghanistan*, p.198.

29 General Yousaf, the Pakistani intelligence officer, claims that in the ten months to August 1987 the mujahedin had a 75 per cent success rate with their Stingers (Yousaf and Adkin, *Afghanistan*, p. 186). One American study estimated, on the other hand, that the hit rate was 50 per cent; it concluded that about 100 Soviet and Afghan planes had been destroyed before the Stingers were deployed. During 1987, the first full year in which the Stingers were used, the Soviet and Afghan air forces lost 150–200 aircraft. In 1988 the losses fell to fewer than fifty (Cordovez and Harrison, *Out of Afghanistan*, p. 198).

30 Soviet aircraft losses in Afghanistan are given in G. Krivosheev, *Rossia i SSSR v voinakh XX veka: Poteri vooruzhennykh sil* (Moscow, 2001), p. 540; according to the Vietnam Helicopter Pilots Association, the total number of US helicopters destroyed in the Vietnam War was 5,086 out of 11,827 (http://www.vhpa.org/heliloss.pdf).

31 A. Chernyaev, *Sovmestny iskhod: Dnevnik dvukh epokh 1972–1991 gody* (Moscow, 2008), diary entries for 4 April 1985 and 17 October 1985, pp. 617 and 650. See account of the Soviet decision-making process in Chapter 12: 'The Road to the Bridge'. Mikhail Gorbachev has confirmed that the arrival of the Stingers did not affect his decision-making, though of course the military had to take it into account in their tactical planning of the Soviet withdrawal (conversation, Sofia, 7 October 2010).

32 M. Galeotti, *Afghanistan: The Soviet Union's Last War* (London, 1995), p. 197.

33 Gai and Snegirev, *Vtorzhenie* (Moscow, 1991), p. 162.

34 Yousaf and Adkin, *Afghanistan* (Barnsley, 1992), pp. 73–6; Tukharinov, *Sekretny komandarm*.

35 Sergei Morozov, interview, Moscow, 31 May 2007; Yousaf and Adkin, *Afghanistan*, pp. 73–6; Galeotti, *Afghanistan*, pp. 192–7.

36 Gai and Snegirev, *Vtorzhenie*, p. 262.

37 Ibid., pp. 227–9.

38 Alexander Gergel, interview, Moscow, 1 March 2010.

39 V. Ablazov, *Afganistan chetvertaya voina* (Kiev, 2002), p. 189.

40 G. Bobrov, *Soldatskaya saga* (Moscow, 2007), p. 144.

41 Gai and Snegirev, *Vtorzhenie*, p. 139.

42 Varennikov, *Nepovtorimoe*, p. 226.

43 Urban, *War in Afghanistan*, p. 234.

44 The description of Operation *Magistral* and the operations around Khost draws on B. Gromov, *Ogranichenny kontingent* (Moscow, 1994) (http://www.rsva.ru/biblio/prose_af/limited_contingent/index.shtml); L. Grau and A. Jalali, 'The Campaign for the Caves', *Journal of Slavic Military Studies*, Vol. 14, No. 3, September 2001 (http://www.globalsecurity.org/military/library/report/2001/010900-zhawar.htm); E. Westermann, 'Limits of Soviet Airpower', thesis, Air University, Maxwell Air Force Base, Alabama, 1997; Varennikov, *Nepovtorimoe*, pp. 215–40.

45 Crile, *Charlie Wilson's War*, p. 521.

46 A. Imtiaz, 'The Haqqani Network and Cross-Border Terrorism in Afghanistan', *Terrorism Monitor*, 24 March 2008.

47 Lyakhovsky, *Tragedia i doblest Afgana*, 1995 (http://www.rsva.ru/biblio/prose_af/afgan_tragedy_and_glory/index.shtml), p. 10.

48 According to the British Ministry of Defence: email to author, 19 January 2010.

49 A. Lyakhovsky and V. Nekrasov, *Grazhdanin, politik, voin: Pamyati Akhmad Shakha Masuda* (Moscow, 2007), pp. 24 et seq.

50 Sergei Morozov, interview, Moscow, 31 May 2007.

51 S. Grigoriev, *Pandzher v 1975–1990 gg. glazami afganskogo istorika* (St Petersburg, 1997), p. 41.

52 This account is taken from Lyakhovsky and Nekrasov, *Grazhdanin, politik, voin*, pp. 93–121 passim. The figures for the Soviet and Afghan forces involved are on p. 96. Other sources give different figures.

53 'Dalnyaya Aviatsia Rossii' (www.sinopa.ee/davia003/dav03.htm).

54 Private Knyazev's account is at Lyakhovsky and Nekrasov, *Grazhdanin, politik, voin*, pp. 117–21.

55 L. Shebarshin, *Ruka Moskvy: zapiski nachalnika sovetskoi razvedki* (Moscow, 2002), p. 195.

56 Lyakhovsky and Nekrasov, *Grazhdanin, politik, voin*, p. 128.

57 'Dalnyaya Aviatsia Rossii'.

58 Lyakhovsky and Nekrasov, *Grazhdanin, politik, voin*, p. 33.

10: Devastation and Disillusion

1 'Byt, nravi I obychai narodov Afganistana: Pravila i normy povedenia voennosluzhashchikh za rubezhom rodnoi strany', 1985. I was kindly given a copy by Alexander Kartsev.

2 E. Girardet, *Afghanistan: The Soviet War* (Beckenham, 1985), p. 46.

3 A. Lyakhovski, *Tragedia i doblest Afgana* (Moscow, 1995) (http://www.rsva. ru/biblio/prose_af/afgan_tragedy_and_glory/index.shtml); W. Odom, *The Collapse of the Soviet Military* (New Haven, Conn., 1998), p. 290, quoting *Rabochaya gazeta*, 6 April 1990.

4 Thomas Tugendhat, interview, London, 1 December 2007.

5 V. Varennikov, *Nepovtorimoe*, 7 vols. (Moscow, 2001), Vol. 5, pp. 142–50; Russian Wikipedia (http://ru.wikipedia.org/wiki/Гибель_Мараварской_ роты); for the American fighting, see S. Junger, *War* (London, 2010), passim.

6 G. Bobrov, *Soldatskaya saga* (Moscow, 2007), pp. 202–3.

7 A. Maiorov, *Pravda ob afganskoi voine* (Moscow, 1996), pp. 243–79; Vladimir Snegirev, email to author, 12 April 2010.

8 A. Lyakhovski and V. Nekrasov, *Grazhdanin, politik, voin: Pamyati Akhmad Shakha Masuda* (Moscow, 2007), p. 144; information from Alexander Gergel.

9 Quoted in C. Gall and T. de Waal, *Chechnya: A Small Victorious War* (London, 1997), p. 97.

10 V. Krivenko, *Ekipazh mashiny boevoi* (St Petersburg, 2004), p. 372.

11 Valeri Shiryaev, interview, Moscow, 12 March 2010.

12 A. Prokhanov, *Tretii tost* (Moscow, 2003), p. 61.

13 The first was ECOSOC E/CN.4/1985/21 in 1985; the last was E/ CN.4/1995/64 in 1995.

14 Report on the Situation of Human Rights in Afghanistan, UN General Assembly A/43/742.

15 In 1979, according to a government census which may or may not have been accurate, the population of Afghanistan was 15.5 million, of whom just over 900,000 lived in Kabul.

16 Bobrov, *Soldatskaya saga*, p. 283.

17 Afghanistan Justice Project, *Casting Shadows: War Crimes and Crimes against Humanity, 1978–2001*, The Century Foundation (www.tcf.org), 2005, p. 34 (http://www.afghanistanjusticeproject.org/).

18 Ibid., p. 56.

19 Krivenko, *Ekipazh mashiny boevoi*, p. 351.

20 V. Snegirev, 'Afganski plennik', *Rossiiskaya gazeta*, 12 August 2003; Vyacheslav Nekrasov, interview, Moscow, 13 May 2007.

21 A. Greshnov, *Afganistan: Zalozhniki vremeni* (Moscow, 2006), p. 133.

22 Ibid., p. 148.

23 Afghanistan Justice Project, *Casting Shadows*, p. 63.

24 Alan A. H. Macdonald, Chief of Staff, Mine Action Coordination Centre of Afghanistan, email to author, 4 May 2009.

25 Greshnov, *Afganistan*, p. 56.

26 101st Motor-rifle Regiment website (http:/101.int.ruindex. phpoptioncom_content&taskview&id204&ltemid5).

27 V. Voinovich, 'Glavny tsenzor' (http://www.voinovich.ru/home_reader. jsp?books8.jsp).

28 Lyakhovski A, Tragedia i doblest Afgana, Moscow 1995 (http://www.rsva. ru/biblio/prose_af/afgan_tragedy_and_glory/index.shtml); R. Keeble and J. Mair (eds.), *Afghanistan, War and the Media: Deadlines and Frontlines* (London 2010), p. 87.

29 Varennikov, *Nepovtorimoe*, p. 308. The Politburo record has been widely reproduced – for example, by Alexander Lyakhovski – and in other memoirs and histories of the war.

30 D. Gai and V. Snegirev, *Vtorzhenie* (Moscow, 1991), pp. 192, 190, and 175. Sakharov's 'Open Letter to Brezhnev' is at http://www.uic.unn.ru/ads/ biography/txt1.htm.

31 A. Chernyaev, *Sovmestny iskhod: Dnevnik dvukh epokh 1972–1991 gody* (Moscow, 2008), diary entry for 5 February 1979, p. 391.

32 Gai and Snegirev, *Vtorzhenie*, p. 207.

33 National Security Archive, *Afghanistan: Lessons from the Last War*, Vol. II, Document 15, 12 November 1981, translated by Svetlana Savranskaya (http://www.gwu.edu/~nsarchiv/NSAEBB/NSAEBB57/soviet.html).

34 A. Volkov, '40-aya Armia: Istoria sozdania, sostav, izmenenie struktury' (www.rsva-ural.ru/library/?id63).

35 Gai and Snegirev, *Vtorzhenie*, p. 204.

36 Maiorov, *Pravda ob afganskoi voine*, pp. 5, 154, and passim.

37 National Security Archive, *Afghanistan: Lessons from the Last War*, Vol. II, Document 20, 13 August 1987, translated by Svetlana Savranskaya (http:// www.gwu.edu/~nsarchiv/NSAEBB/NSAEBB57/soviet.html).

38 Rastem Makhmutov, interview, Moscow, 27 May 2007.

39 Alexander Gergel, email to author, 23 September 2009.

40 Lyakhovski and Nekrasov, *Grazhdanin, politik, voin*, pp. 213–14.

41 Gai and Snegirev, *Vtorzhenie*, p. 207.

42 Private information.

43 V. Plastun and V. Andrianov, *Najibulla: Afghanistan v tiskakh geopolitiki* (Moscow, 1998), p. 2.

Part III: The Long Goodbye

1 This much shortened translation of one of Igor Morozov's most famous songs is printed with his kind permission. When it was first published the military censorship insisted on changing 'O mighty land for which we fought/Can you now dry our mothers' tears?' to 'O distant land, Afghanistan,/Can you now dry our mothers' tears?' in an attempt to shift the blame for the war away from the Soviet government.

11: Going Home

1 See A. Dyshev, *PPZh: Pokhodno-polevaya Zhena* (Moscow, 2007).

2 V. Krivenko, *Ekipazh mashiny boevoi* (St Petersburg, 2004), p. 9.

3 Ibid., p. 378.

4 This description of how to clean your uniform is in S. Aleksievich, *Zinky Boys* (New York, 1992), p. 50.

5 Ibid., p. 50.

6 Krivenko, *Ekipazh mashiny boevoi*, p. 372.

7 This description of a typical regimental morgue is based on Dyshev, *PPZh*, pp. 28–38; S. Nikiforov, *Bez vsyakikh pravil* (St Petersburg, 2008), p. 99; G. Koroleva, 'Dvadtsat mesyatsev v adu', *Daryal*, No. 3, 2001 (http://www.darial-online.ru/2001_3/koroleva.shtml).

8 Blinushov kept notes on these incidents, which he wanted to work up into a book. But someone told the KGB, who confiscated all the material he had gathered together: A. Blinushov, 'Cherny Tiulpan' (http://www.reznik.pri.ee/document.php?Id108).

9 A. Smolina, 'Vsem devushkam, letavshim v afganskom nebe' (http://artofwar.ru/s/smolina_a/text_0080.shtml).

10 Yu. Lapshin, *Afganski dnevnik* (Moscow, 2004), p. 95.

11 These figures are taken from Appendix 13 of A. Lyakhovski, *Tragedia i doblest Afgana* (Moscow, 1995) (http://www.rsva.ru/biblio/prose_af/afgan_tragedy_and_glory/index.shtml). Though there are a number of soldiers named Viktor in the list who served with the mujahedin, none is easily identifiable with the young man referred to by Alla Smolina.

12 V. Snegirev, *Ryzhy* (Moscow, 2000), pp. 257–304.

13 *Los Angeles Times*, 17 December 1991; A. Kalinovsky, 'A Long Goodbye: The Politics and Diplomacy of the Soviet Withdrawal from Afghanistan, 1980–1992', PhD thesis, London School of Economics, 2009.

14 Report at www.dtic.mil/dpmo/sovietunion/jcsd.htm; article in UralPress. ru of 17 April 2007 (www.uralpress.ru/art111069); record of 19th Plenum of the US-Russia Commission (http://www.dtic.mil/dpmo/sovietunion/AARVer319thPlenum.pdf).

15 See http://ru.wikipedia.org/wiki/Комитет_по_делам_воинов-интернационалистов; NewsRU.com report of 27 September 2006 (www.newaru,com/russia/27seo2006/afgan.html).

16 See http://www.komitet92.com/index.html; http://www.komitet92.com/12poisk.html.

17 *Komsomolskaya Pravda*, 13 February 2009; *FontankaRu* reported on 13 February 2009 that 417 soldiers had gone missing or been taken prisoner during the war. Of 119 who had been liberated, ninety-seven had returned to the Soviet Union. The remainder had stayed abroad (www.fontanka.ru/2009/02/13/031/).

18 Krivenko, *Ekipazh mashiny boevoi*, p. 345.

19 Stepanov's story is in *TrudRu*, No. 206, 8 November 2006 (www.trud.ru/article/08–11–2006/109556_afgandkij_plennik.html).

20 Article in *Vlast*, No. 6 (809), 16 February 2009 (www.kommersant.ru/doc.aspx?DocsID116089&printtrue).

21 Nikolai Bystrov, interview, Moscow, 31 May 2007.

22 101st Motor-rifle Regiment website (http:/101.int.ruindex. phpoptioncom_content&taskview&id204&ltemid5).

23 Private information.

24 Interfax-AVN, 29 December 2009, quoted in Johnson's List, No. 35, 31 December 2009.

25 S. Pakhmutov, 'Badaber – neizvestny podvig' (www.rustrana.ru/article.php?nid8803).

26 V. Ablazov, *Dolgi put iz Afganskogo plena: Stranitsy iz knigi* (http://www.fond-dobrobut.org.ua/download/1991modzaxedmoccba.doc).

27 This account of the rising is based on the 2009 film *Myatezh v Preispodnei*; S. Golesnik, 'Nadezhda ne umiraet', *Soyuz: Belarus-Rossia*, No. 406, 21 May 2009 (http://www.rg.ru/2009/05/21/propal-soldat.html); Pakhmutov, 'Badaber – neizvestny podvig'; Vladimir Snegirev, interview, Moscow, 3 March 2010. The details are fragmentary and contradictory.

12: The Road to the Bridge

1   Record of Andropov at Politburo meeting on 7 February 1980 from Archive of the President of the Russian Federation, fond 3, opis 82, delo 75, pp. 1–4: kindly provided by Svetlana Savranskaya.

2   Much of what follows is based on A. Kalinovsky, 'A Long Goodbye: The Politics and Diplomacy of the Soviet Withdrawal from Afghanistan, 1980–1992', PhD thesis, London School of Economics, 2009. Kalinovsky's account of the Soviet withdrawal is the most scholarly and lucid so far. See also A. Lyakhovski, *Tragedia i doblest Afgana* (Moscow, 2004).

3   D. Cordovez and S. Harrison, *Out of Afghanistan* (Oxford, 1995), p. 65.

4   Kalinovsky, 'A Long Goodbye', quoting V. Zubok, *A Failed Empire: The Soviet Union in the Cold War from Stalin to Gorbachev* (Chapel Hill, NC, 2007), p. 267.

5   O. Sarin and L. Dvoretsky, *The Afghan Syndrome: The Soviet Union's Vietnam* (Novato, CA, 1993), p. 123.

6   Cordovez and Harrison, *Out of Afghanistan*, p. 123.

7   A. Chernyaev, *Sovmestny iskhod: Dnevnik dvukh epokh 1972–1991 gody* (Moscow, 2008), diary entry for 30 March 1985, p. 614; Kalinovsky, 'A Long Goodbye'.

8   V. Kryuchkov, *Lichnoe delo*, 2 vols. (Moscow, 1996), Vol. 1, p. 223.

9   Among those who promoted the idea of a Gorbachev surge was W. Odom, *The Collapse of the Soviet Military* (New Haven, Conn., 1998), p. 103. The sources Odom quotes are unconvincing. Gorbachev himself denies that he had any such intention (Mikhail Gorbachev, conversation, Moscow, 10 March 2010). A more subtle analysis is in J. Prados, *Safe for Democracy: The Secret Wars of the CIA* (Chicago, 2006), pp. 485–7.

10 The story was told by Najibullah, who was present: D. Gai and V. Snegirev, *Vtorzhenie* (Moscow, 1991), p. 365. Snegirev later added that Karmal subsequently hotly denied that he had said any such thing: V. Snegirev, *Ryzhy* (Moscow, 2000), p. 132.

11 Chernyaev, *Sovmestny iskhod*, diary entry for 16 October 1985, p. 647.

12 Kalinovsky, 'A Long Goodbye'.

13 Chernyaev, *Sovmestny iskhod*, diary entries for 4 April 1985 and 17 October 1985, pp. 617 and 650.

14 Kryuchkov, *Lichnoe delo*, Vol. 1, p. 227.

15 Kalinovsky, 'A Long Goodbye'.

16 Lyakhovski, *Tragedia i doblest Afgana*, 2004, p. 532.

17 A. Chernyaev et al., *V Politburo TsK KPSS* (Moscow, 2006), p. 47: Politburo meeting of 29 May 1986, notes taken by Svetlana Savranskaya, in the Gorbachev Foundation.

18 Kalinovsky, 'A Long Goodbye'.

19 Chernyaev et al., *V Politburo TsK KPSS*, p. 68; Prados, *Safe for Democracy*, p. 488.

20 B. Gromov, *Ogranichenny kontingent* (Moscow, 1994) (http://www.rsva. ru/biblio/prose_af/limited_contingent/index.shtml); Chernyaev et al., *V Politburo TsK KPSS*, p. 108: notes taken by Svetlana Savranskaya, in the Gorbachev Foundation.

21 Notes on Politburo meetings of 21–22 January 1987 and 22 February 1987, Chernyaev et al., *V Politburo TsK KPSS*, pp. 136–8 and 149: notes taken by Svetlana Savranskaya, in the Gorbachev Foundation.

22 Kalinovsky, 'A Long Goodbye'.

23 Chernyaev et al., *V Politburo TsK KPSS*, pp. 190–93.

24 Kalinovsky, 'A Long Goodbye', quoting Matlock; Jack Matlock, emails to author, 27–28 February 2010.

25 Kalinovsky, 'A Long Goodbye'.

26 S. Coll, *Ghost Wars* (London, 2005), p. 168.

27 Kalinovsky, 'A Long Goodbye', quoting from Soviet record of conversation between Reagan and Gorbachev on 9 December 1987 in National Security Archive, READD/RADD collection.

28 Jack Matlock, email to author, 27 February 2010.

29 Chernyaev, *Sovmestny iskhod*, diary entry for 1 April 1988, p. 749.

30 Ibid., diary entry for 20 September 1988, p. 765.

31 *Literaturnaya Gazeta*, 18 April 1990, quoted in Gai and Snegirev, *Vtorzhenie*, p. 307.

32 Chernyaev et al., *V Politburo TsK KPSS*, pp. 336–8.

33 Helen Womack, a British journalist, travelled with the column. This detail is from her account.

34 Gai and Snegirev, *Vtorzhenie*, p. 371.

35 'Dalnyaya Aviatsia Rossii' (www.sinopa.ee/davia003/dav03.htm).

36 A. Gergel and A. Lizauskas, 'Proshchai Bakharak!', August 2009 (http://www.navoine.ru/magazines/12/5).

37 V. Varennikov, *Nepovtorimoe*, 7 vols. (Moscow, 2001), Vol. 5, pp. 351–3.

38 Ibid., p. 389.

39 Chernyaev, *Sovmestny iskhod*, diary entry for 20 October 1988, p. 769.

40 A. Lyakhovski and V. Nekrasov, *Grazhdanin, politik, voin: Pamyati Akhmad Shakha Masuda* (Moscow, 2007), pp. 179–87.

41 Varennikov, *Nepovtorimoe*, pp. 378 et seq.

42 *Pravda*, 7 December 1988, quoted in Lyakhovski, *Tragedia i doblest Afgana*, 1995 (http://www.rsva.ru/biblio/prose_af/afgan_tragedy_and_glory/index. shtml).

43 Vorontsov interview, *Rossiiskie Vesti*, No. 18, 23–30 May 2007.

44 The description of the generals' opposition to Operation *Typhoon* is from A. Lyakhovski, *Tragedia i doblest Afgana*, 2004, pp. 668–71.

45 Chernyaev, *Sovmestny iskhod*, diary entry for 20 January 1989, p. 781.

46 Lyakhovski and Nekrasov, *Grazhdanin, politik, voin*, pp. 208–9; Varennikov, *Nepovtorimoe*, pp. 390–93.

47 Ibid., p. 212.

48 Gromov, *Ogranichenny kontingent*.

49 Lyakhovski, *Tragedia i doblest Afgana*, 2004, p. 213.

50 M. Sotskov, *Dolg i soviet* (St Petersburg, 2007), p. 531, quoted in Kalinovsky, 'A Long Goodbye'.

51 Lyakhovski, *Tragedia i doblest Afgana*, 2004, p. 675.

52 Lyakhovski and Nekrasov, *Grazhdanin, politik, voin*, p. 212.

53 L. Grau, 'Breaking Contact without Leaving Chaos: The Soviet Withdrawal from Afghanistan', *Journal of Slavic Military Studies*, Vol. 20, No. 2, April 2007, pp. 235–61.

54 Rodric Braithwaite, Moscow diary (unpublished), entry for 3 March 1989.

55 Quoted in S. Aleksievich, *Zinky Boys* (New York, 1992), p. 9.

56 Anatoli Chernyaev, conversation, Moscow, May 2007.

13: The War Continues

1 Private information.

2 A. Greshnov, *Afganistan: Zalozhniki vremeni* (Moscow, 2006), pp. 7–9, 17, 12, 10, and 61.

3 B. Rubin, *The Search for Peace in Afghanistan* (New Haven, Conn., 1995), p. 89, quoted in P. Corwin, *Doomed in Afghanistan* (New Brunswick, NJ, 2003), p. 10.

4 S. Coll, *Ghost Wars* (London, 2005), p. 171.

5 A. Lyakhovski, *Tragedia i doblest Afgana* (Moscow, 2009), p. 928.

6 G. Dorronosoro, *Revolution Unending: Afghanistan, 1979 to the Present* (New York, 2005), pp. 227 and 228.

7   Vladimir Snegirev says there were only 3,000 defenders and that they were outnumbered by ten to one: V. Snegirev, *Ryzhy* (Moscow, 2000), p. 156.

8   A. Chernyaev et al., *V Politburo TsK KPSS* (Moscow, 2006), pp. 454 and 576.

9   Greshnov, *Afganistan*, pp. 71 and 74; description of Jalalabad fighting, M. Urban, *War in Afghanistan* (London, 1990), pp. 274 et seq.

10 M. Yousaf and M. Adkin, *Afghanistan: The Bear Trap* (Barnsley, 1992), pp. 227–33.

11 Greshnov, *Afganistan*, pp. 84, 92, and 150–51.

12 Ibid., p. 99.

13 A. Giustozzi, *Empires of Mud* (London, 2009), pp. 54–7. Minko A. and Smólynee G., '4-D Soviet Style: Defence, Development, Diplomacy and Disengagement in Afghanistan during the Soviet Period, Part 1: State Building,' *Journal of Slavic Military Studies*, 23, 306–27 (2010), p. 324.

14 A. Lyakhovski and V. Nekrasov, *Grazhdanin, politik, voin: Pamyati Akhmad Shakha Masuda* (Moscow, 2007), p. 220.

15 A. Kalinovsky, 'A Long Goodbye: The Politics and Diplomacy of the Soviet Withdrawal from Afghanistan, 1980–1992', PhD thesis, London School of Economics, 2009, quoting 'Gardez Victory: Soviet Message of Support Revives Kabul Regime', Agence France-Presse, 14 October 1991.

16 M. Gareev, *Afganskaya strada* (Moscow, 1999), p. 316.

17 Lyakhovski and Nekrasov, *Grazhdanin, politik, voin*, p. 227.

18 Giustozzi, *Empires of Mud*, p. 210.

19 Snegirev, *Ryzhy*, p. 157.

20 S. Grigoriev, 'Kak eto bylo: Kabul 1992 god' (http://artofwar.ru/s_grig/publ_grig_5.html).

21 Galina Ivanov, interview, Moscow, 14 March 2010; Grigoriev, 'Kak eto bylo: Kabul 1992 god'.

22 Valeri Ivanov, interview, Moscow, 14 March 2010; D. Lysenkov, 'Posledni flag nad Kabulom', *SpetsNaz Rossii* (www.tuad.nsk.ru/~history/Author/Russ/L/LjysenkovD/flag.htm).

23 Lyakhovski, *Tragedia i doblest Afgana*, 2004, p. 702.

24 Corwin, *Doomed in Afghanistan*, p. 93.

25 Valeri Ivanov, interview, Moscow, 14 March 2010; Lyakhovski, *Tragedia i doblest Afgana*, 2004, p. 706. Where there are discrepancies between the two accounts, I have relied on Ivanov.

26 US Committee for Refugees, *World Refugee Survey, 1997*, pp. 124–5 (http://www.unhcr.org/refworld/publisher,USCRI,HKG,3ae6a8b534,0.html); Corwin, *Doomed in Afghanistan*, p. 128.

27 The account of the rise of the Taliban is summarised from Dorronosoro, *Revolution Unending*, pp. 245–56.

28 Lyakhovski and Nekrasov, *Grazhdanin, politik, voin*, pp. 260–61.

29 Lyakhovski, *Tragedia i doblest Afgana*, 2009, pp. 984–90.

30 Arkadi Dubnov, interview, Moscow, 29 May 2007.

31 President Putin in a 2002 interview for Brook Lapping's BBC television series *Iran and the West*, first broadcast in February 2009.

32 Lyakhovski, *Tragedia i doblest Afgana*, 2009, p. 998. Private information.

33 Pir Said Ahmad Gailani, interview, London, 22 July 2008.

34 The last stand of the 12th *zastava* is described at http://wolfschanze.livejournal.com/tag/%D0%93%D0%A0%D0%9F%D0%92%D0%A2 and http://kua1102.1ivejournal.com/38687.html. The links were kindly given to me by Oksana Antonenko.

14: A Land Fit for Heroes
1   V. Ogryzko, *Pesni afganskogo pokhoda* (Moscow, 2000), pp. 146, 20, and 151.

2   W. Odom, *The Collapse of the Soviet Military* (New Haven, Conn., 1998), p. 259.

3   R. Braithwaite, *Across the Moscow River* (New Haven, Conn., 2002), p. 138.

4   G. Murrell, *Russia's Transition to Democracy* (Brighton, 1997), p. 61; Braithwaite, *Across the Moscow River*, p. 146.

5   V. Varennikov, *Nepovtorimoe*, 7 vols. (Moscow, 2001), Vol. 5, p. 230.

6   The following account is taken from ibid., pp. 192 et seq.

7   Alexander Lyakhovski, interview, Gelendzhik, 19 September 2007.

8   Ogryzko, *Pesni afganskogo pokhoda*, p. 161.

9   Igor Morozov, interview, Moscow, 11 March 2010.

10 David Lloyd George, speech at Wolverhampton on 23 November 1918, reported in *The Times*, 25 November 1918.

11 D. Gai and V. Snegirev, *Vtorzhenie* (Moscow, 1991), p. 253.

12 M. Galeotti, *Afghanistan: The Soviet Union's Last War* (London, 1995), p. 74.

13 *Komsomolskaya Pravda*, 21 December 1989, quoted in N. Danilova, *Rasplata za dolg: Politika i kollektivnye deistvia veteranov voiny v Afganistane* (unpublished), Chapter 2.

14 Danilova, *Rasplata za dolg*, Chapter 2.

15 *Komsomolskaya Pravda*, 22 July 1990, quoted ibid.

16 Galeotti, *Afghanistan*, p. 76.

17 V. Znakov, 'Psikhologicheskie prichiny neponimania afgantsev', quoted in Danilova, *Rasplata za dolg*, Chapter 2.

18 Galeotti, *Afghanistan*, pp. 123–5.

19 A. Kotenov, *Neokonchennaya voina* (http://www.rsva.ru/biblio/prose_af/ unfinished_war/index.shtml); http://kotenev.chat.ru/).

20 Gazeta.Ru, 12 June 2007 (http://gzt.ru/incident/2006/11/12/220000.html).

21 N. Danilova, 'Veterans' Policy in Russia: a Puzzle of Creation', *Journal of Power Institutions in Post-Soviet Societies*, No. 6/7, 2007; 'The Social and Political Role of War Veterans' (http://www.pipss.org/document873.html).

22 Federal Law No. 5-ФЗ of 12 January 1995.

23 OOOIVA website (http://www.rfpi.ru/oooiva/index.php).

24 Information from Dr Rod Thornton, Nottingham University. He served as a sergeant in Bosnia and said that the death of children was the hardest of all things to take.

25 Web interview with Dr Matthew Friedman, Executive Director of the US Veteran Administration's National Center for Post-Traumatic Stress Disorder (http://www.pbs.org/wgbh/pages/frontline/shows/heart/ interviews/friedman.html).

26 Web interview with Colonel Thomas Burke, Director of Mental Health Policy for the US Department of Defense (http://www.pbs.org/wgbh/ pages/frontline/shows/heart/interviews/burke.html).

27 'As a Brigade Returns Safe, Some Meet New Enemies', *New York Times*, 14 July 2010.

28 A. Allport, *Demobbed: Coming Home after World War II* (New Haven, Conn., 2009), pp. 87, 109, 164, and 209.

29 Text at http://www.gr-oborona.ru/pub/rock/group.html.

30 Galeotti, *Afghanistan*, p. 152.

31 Alexander Gergel, email to author, 2 July 2009.

32 Special edition of *Voronezhskaya Gazeta*, 11 February 2009.

33 Yu. Zvyagintsev, 'Afganski Izlom', *Vestnik ATN*, August 1999.

34 S. Aleksievich, *Zinky Boys* (New York, 1992), pp. 185–94.

35 Moscow City website (http://mos.ru/wps/portal/!ut/p/c0/).

36 'Afganski Sindrom dla SShA', *InfoRus*, 14 February 2008 (http://www. inforos.ru/?Id20566).

37 Alexander Yeshanu, email, 9 September 2009, posted on Artofwar.ru/.

Epilogue: The Reckoning

1   N. Shilo, 'Afganistan: 30 let spustya' (http://www.mgimo.ru/afghan/132585. phtml); article by Anatoli Kostyrya (http://www.afghanistan.ru/doc/16256. html).

2   Oleg Bogomolov, interview, Moscow, 7 October 2004.

3   G. Krivosheev, *Rossia i SSSR v voinakh XX veka: Poteri vooruzhennykh sil* (Moscow, 2001), pp. 536–9.

4   A. Arnold, *The Fateful Pebble* (Novato, CA, 1993), pp. 188 et seq.

5   A. Seierstad, *The Bookseller of Kabul* (London, 2008), p. 150.

6   A. Kalinovsky, 'A Long Goodbye: The Politics and Diplomacy of the Soviet Withdrawal from Afghanistan, 1980–1992', PhD thesis, London School of Economics, 2009.

7   The documentary evidence is inevitably thin or non-existent. The lower figure was suggested to me by Dr Antonio Giustozzi. General Lyakhovski quotes a figure of 2.5 million, but gives no source; the figure is improbably high: A. Lyakhovski, *Tragedia i doblest Afgana* (Moscow, 2009), p. 1018.

8   For an extreme example of the belief that the United States actually won the Vietnam War, see P. Jennings, *The Politically Incorrect Guide to the Vietnam War* (Washington, DC, 2010).

9   'More bombs were dropped on Laos than by the US Army Air Force in Europe. This is also true for the RAF in Europe. Further, it is also accurate that Laos got more than both air forces dropped on Germany. But for all air forces (including tactical air) in all of Europe (including Med), WWII outdoes Laos by 2.4M tons to slightly over 2.0M tons': John Prados, email to author, 26 April 2010.

10   For a discussion of casualty figures see Annex 4, 'Indo-China, Vietnam, Algeria, Afghanistan: A Comparison', p. 348.

11   L. Shebarshin, *Ruka Moskvy: zapiski nachalnika sovetskoi razvedki* (Moscow, 2002), p. 220.

12   V. Snegirev, 'Nashi', *Rossiiskaya Gazeta*, 2003.

13   See http://www.zharov.com/afghan/index.html.

14   'Yaroslavtsy v Afganskoi voine' (http://www.afghan-yar.msk.ru/page. php?Id104).

SOURCES

This book is based to a large extent on Russian sources. It draws on such documents as have been published, on many secondary sources, on the Internet, and on interviews with people who fought in Afghanistan or were connected with the events there in other ways.

There are no systematic or convenient sources for the Soviet war in Afghanistan to compare with those available for the Stalin period and the Great Patriotic War – the volumes of documents about the NKVD officially published by its successor, the Federal Security Service, for example, or the numerous volumes produced by the late Alexander Yakovlev and his Democracy Foundation.

However, a significant number of documents have seen the light of day, especially about the decision to invade Afghanistan and about the withdrawal nearly a decade later. One reason is that the military, in particular, were anxious to tell their side of the story. The generals immediately set down to write their own version of events in memoirs and histories, at a time when the archives were in a state of chaos, and access to them was much more open than it had been before, than it was to become later, and indeed than it normally is in most countries.

Other documents concerning the period 1985–91 have been published by the Gorbachev Foundation, notably the notes on the Politburo meetings of those years and the parallel diary of Anatoli Chernyaev, Gorbachev's foreign policy adviser. Still more have been published by the Wilson Center in Washington, DC.

But the way the documents were selected means there are large gaps that will not soon be filled. Few KGB documents have appeared, and there is much that cannot be said for certain about the KGB's role in the Afghan Communists' rise to power. Some crucial aspects of the political decisions taken at the beginning of the war, and at its end, are still shrouded in mystery, a mystery deepened because the witnesses are passing from the scene.

Many of these documents have emerged as a result of the tireless activities of the late General Alexander Lyakhovski, who himself served in Afghanistan from 1984 to 1989. His book *Tragedia i doblest Afgana* (The Tragedy and Glory of the Afghan War) contains a remarkable collection of official documents, both political and military. It also contains records of interviews with participants at all levels. It represents the view primarily of the military, and is not easy to work with: it came out in three editions in 1995, in 2004 and, after the author's untimely death, in 2009. These are not consistent with one another, the sources are not always clear, and the indexing is inadequate. But until the official archives are open, it is likely to remain an essential basis for the study of the war.

There is as yet no literature about the war in Afghanistan to compare with that generated by the Great Patriotic War – Vasili Grossman's *Life and Fate*, Vasil Bykov's novellas or the novels of Konstantin Simonov, for example. But in recent years there has been an increasing number of novels by veterans, thinly disguised autobiographical accounts of their experience. The best of these are thoughtful, perceptive, and often critical; a far cry from the laddish and often boastful stuff produced by some of their opposite numbers in the West. Since they are Russians, many of the veterans have written poetry and songs, some of it of value, often a poetry of yearning for the exotic country where they spent a part of their youth and where they saw their comrades die.

Most useful of all, perhaps, is the Internet. Some important Russian books and memoirs are, to all intents and purposes, only available online: they are out of print in Russia and cannot be found in libraries in Britain. I have given the sites where they can be found, but the electronic copies are not always properly paginated, and those who wish to follow up some of my citations will have to do an electronic search on the text.

The Internet is also an invaluable source of relevant articles. From about 2005 onwards the veterans and others have made increasing use of the Web to express their views, amass information, and publish accounts of their experiences. Much of the writing is excellent – intelligent, perceptive, and of genuine literary quality. There is some ranting as well, but it is easy enough to distinguish. All references to articles are in the notes.

The Russians have made several objective documentary films about the war, notably *Posledni Soldat* (The Last Soldier, 2004). *Afganski Kapkan* (Afghan Trap, 2009) is about the rising in Badaber. Aleksei and Tatiana Krol are making a lengthy multipart documentary, *Afganskaya Voina*, which incorporates a lot of exceptionally interesting interviews and archive footage. The best of the feature films, recommended by many veterans, is *Afganski Izlom* (Breaking Point, 1991), set in the last period of the war. *Musulmanin* (The Muslim, 1995) is a fanciful but interesting film about a soldier, converted to Islam, who returns from captivity to his village deep in the Russian countryside. *Devyataya Rota* (Ninth Company, 2005) is spectacular, Russia's answer to *Saving Private Ryan*, just as macho-sentimental, disliked by most Afgantsy. *Osama* (2003) is a first-class Afghan film about Taliban rule in Kabul. The American film *The Beast* (1988) is better than it sounds. *Charlie Wilson's War* (2007) is amusing but has only an intermittent connection with historical reality.

The songs of the soldier-bards can be found on the Internet, in the form they were recorded during the war. Igor Morozov and others have made their own recordings, which are not widely distributed. The accompaniment to many of the modern recordings is not at all authentic.

I have also drawn a good deal on Wikipedia as a source of new facts and a way of checking old ones. This is frowned on in the academic world. However, the articles in Wikipedia can be subjected to the same critical tests as articles in the academic press and indeed documents in the official archives. Some are clearly authoritative, such as technical articles about the characteristics of Soviet and American weapons. Some are self-evidently biased special pleading. Most come somewhere in between. I hope I have managed to distinguish between them.

Translations are mine except where otherwise indicated.

BIBLIOGRAPHY

Abdur Rahman, *The Life of Abdur Rahman*, Vol. 1 (London, 1900)

Ablazov, V., *Afganistan chetvertaya voina* (Kiev, 2002)

Afghanistan Justice Project, *Casting Shadows: War Crimes and Crimes against Humanity, 1978–2001*, 2005 (http://www.afghanistanjusticeproject.org/)

Akhmetova, T., *Russki Mat: Tolkovy Slovar* (Moscow, 1997)

Aleksievich, S., *Zinky Boys* (New York, 1992)

Alexiev, A., *Inside the Soviet Army in Afghanistan* (Santa Monica, CA, 1988)

Appy, C., *Vietnam* (London, 2006)

Armesto, M.-R., *Son Mari a tué Massoud* (Paris, 2002)

Arnold, A., *The Fateful Pebble* (Novato, CA, 1993)

Assotsiatsia Zhurnalistov, *Afganskaya Voina: Kak Eto Bylo* (Moscow, 1994)

Babur, translated by W. Thackson, *The Baburnama* (New York, 2002)

Balenko, S., *SpetsNaz GRU v Afganistane* (Moscow, 2010)

Ball, W., *Monuments of Afghanistan* (London, 2008)

Bearden, M., *The Black Tulip* (New York, 1998)

Bearden, M., and Risen, J., *The Main Enemy* (New York, 2003)

Belofastov, A., and Rebrik, A. (eds.), *Mushavery* (Moscow, 2005)

Blood, P. (ed.), *Afghanistan: A Country Study* (Washington, DC, 2001)

Bobrov, G., *Soldatskaya saga* (Moscow, 2007)

Bocharov, G., *Russian Roulette: Afghanistan through Russian Eyes* (London, 1990)

Bogdanov, V., *Afganskaya Voina 1979–1989* (Moscow, 2005)

Bologov, V., *Kniga Pamyati o sovetskikh voinakh, pogibshikh v Afganistane* (Moscow, 1995) (http://afgan.ru/memoryafgan/)

Boltunov, M., *Alfa – Sverkhsekretny Otryad KGB* (Moscow, 1992)

Borer, D., *Superpowers Defeated: Vietnam and Afghanistan Compared* (London, 1999)

Borovik, A., *The Hidden War* (New York, 1990)

Braithwaite, R., *Across the Moscow River* (New Haven, Conn., 2002)

Bykov, V., *Ego batalion* (Moscow, 2000)

Byron, R., *The Road to Oxiana* (London, 2007)

Caroe, O., *The Pathans* (New York, 1964)

Chayes, S., *The Punishment of Virtue* (London, 2006)

Chazov, Ye., *Zdorovie i Vlast* (Moscow, 1992)

Chernyaev, A., *Moya Zhizn i Moe Vremya* (Moscow, 1995)

— *Shest Let s Gorbachëvym* (Moscow, 1993)

— *Sovmestny iskhod: Dnevnik dvukh epokh 1972–1991 gody* (Moscow, 2008)

Chernyaev, A., Medvedev, V., and Shakhnazov, G., *V Politburo TsK KPSS* (Moscow, 2006)

Chikishev, S., *SpetsNaz v Afganistane* (http://artofwar.ru/c/chikishew_a/ text_0010.shtml)

Clammer, P., *Afghanistan* (Melbourne, 2007)

Coll, S., *Ghost Wars* (London, 2005)

Cordovez, D., and Harrison, S., *Out of Afghanistan* (Oxford, 1995)

Corwin, P., *Doomed in Afghanistan* (New Brunswick, NJ, 2003)

Crile, G., *Charlie Wilson's War* (New York, 2003)

Danilova, N., *Armia i Obshchestvo* (St Petersburg, 2007)

Dorronosoro, G., *Revolution Unending: Afghanistan, 1979 to the Present* (New York, 2005)

Doubleday, V., *Three Women of Herat* (London, 1988)

Dupree, L., *Afghanistan* (Oxford, 1997)

Dupree, N., *An Historical Guide to Afghanistan* (Kabul, 1971)

Dupree (Wolfe), N., *An Historical Guide to Kabul* (Kabul, 1965)

Dyshev, A., *Afganets* (four stories) (Moscow, 2009)

— *Nazad v Afgan* (Moscow, 2009)

— *PPZh: Pokhodno-polevaya Zhena* (Moscow, 2007)

Elliot, J., *An Unexpected Light: Travels in Afghanistan* (London, 1999)

Elphinstone, M., *An Account of the Kingdom of Caubul* (New Delhi, 1998)

Fall, B., *Street without Joy: The French Debacle in Indochina* (Barnsley, 2005)

Feifer, G., *The Great Gamble: The Soviet War in Afghanistan* (New York, 2009)

Fick, N., *One Bullet Away* (London, 2006)

Forrest, G., *Life of Field Marshal Sir Neville Chamberlain, G.C.B., G.C.S.I.* (London, 1909)

Forsyth, F., *The Afghan* (London, 2007)

Gai, D., and Snegirev, V., *Vtorzhenie* (Moscow, 1991)

Galeotti, M., *Afghanistan: The Soviet Union's Last War* (London, 1995)

Gall, C., and de Waal, T., *Chechnya: A Small Victorious War* (London, 1997)

Gall, S., *Afghanistan: Travels with the Mujahedeen* (London, 1989)

— *Behind Russian Lines: An Afghan Journal* (London, 1983)

Gareev, M., *Afganskaya strada* (Moscow, 1999)

— *Moya poslednaya voina* (http://militera.lib.ru/memo/russian/gareev_ma/index.html)

Gates, R., *From the Shadows* (New York, 1996)

Ghaus, A. S., *The Fall of Afghanistan* (London, 1988)

Giustozzi, A., *Empires of Mud* (London, 2009)

— *Koran, Kalashnikov and Laptop* (London, 2007)

Goodson, L., *Afghanistan's Endless War* (Seattle, WA, 1999)

Gorbachev, M., *Zhizn I Reformy* (Moscow, 1995)

Grau, L., *The Bear Went Over the Mountain* (London, 1996)

Greiner, B., *War without Fronts: The USA in Vietnam* (London, 2009)

Greshnov, A., *Afganistan: Zalozhniki vremeni* (Moscow, 2006)

Grigoriev, S., *Pandzhsher v 1975–1990 gg. glazami afganskogo istorika* (St Petersburg, 1997)

Gromov, B., *Ogranichenny kontingent* (Moscow 1994) (http://www.rsva.ru/biblio/prose_af/limited_contingent/index.shtml)

Henty, G., *For Name and Fame: or, Through Afghan Passes* (Mill Hall, PA, 2002)

Hodson, P., *Under a Sickle Moon* (London, 1989)

Hopkirk, P., *The Great Game: The Struggle for Empire in Central Asia* (London, 1992)

Hosseini, K., *A Thousand Splendid Suns* (London, 2007)

— *The Kite Runner* (London, 2004)

Hyman, A., *Afghanistan under Soviet Domination 1964–81* (London, 1982)

Isby, D., *Russia's War in Afghanistan* (Oxford, 1986)

— *War in a Distant County: Afghanistan – Invasion and Resistance* (London, 1989)

Ivanov, N., *Operatsiu Shtorm nachat ranshe* (Moscow, 1993)

Jennings, P., *The Politically Incorrect Guide to the Vietnam War* (Washington, DC, 2010)

Johnson, C., *Afghanistan* (Oxford, 2004)

Junger, S., *War* (London, 2010)

Kakar, M., *Afghanistan: The Soviet Invasion and the Afghan Response, 1979–1982* (Berkeley, CA, 1995)

Kalinovsky, A., 'A Long Goodbye: The Politics and Diplomacy of the Soviet Withdrawal from Afghanistan, 1980–1992', PhD thesis, London School of Economics, 2009

Kartsev, A., *Shelkovy put* (privately published, 2004)

— *Voenny razvedchik* (Moscow, 2007)

Keeble, R. & Mair, J. (eds.), *Afghanistan, War and the Media: Deadlines and Frontlines* (London, 2010).

Khalfin, Kh., *Politika Rossii v Srednei Azii (1857–1868)* (Moscow, 1960)

— *Proval britanskoi agressii v Afganistane* (Moscow, 1959)

Khrushchev, N., *Khrushchev Remembers* (London, 1971)

Kipling, R., *Kim* (London, 1901)

— *Stalky & Co.* (London, 1899)

Kireev, G., *Kandagarski Dnevnik* (http://kireev.info/w-4.html)

Klass, R., *Land of the High Flags: Afghanistan When the Going Was Good* (Hong Kong, 1964)

Konoplyannikov, Yu., *Vse Eto Zhizn* (Moscow, 2005)

Kotenov, A., *Neokonchennaya Voina* (http://www.rsva.ru/biblio/prose_af/unfinished_war/index.shtml)

Kozlov, S. (ed.), *SpetsNaz GRU: Afganistan* (Moscow, 2009)

Krivenko, V., *Ekipazh mashiny boevoi* (St Petersburg, 2004)

Krivosheev, G., *Rossia i SSSR v voinakh XX veka: Poteri vooruzhennykh sil* (Moscow, 2001)

Kryuchkov, V., *Lichnoe delo*, 2 vols. (Moscow, 1996)

Kucherova, L., *SpetsNaz KGB v Afganistane* (Moscow, 2009)

Kuzichkin, V., *Inside the KGB: Myth & Reality* (London, 1990)

Lamb, C., *The Sewing Circles of Herat* (London, 2002)

Lapshin, Yu., *Afganski dnevnik* (Moscow, 2004)

Lieven, D., *Russia against Napoleon* (London, 2009)

Loyn, D., *Butcher and Bolt* (London, 2008)

Lyakhovski, A., *Tragedia i doblest Afgana* (Moscow, 1995) (http://www.rsva.ru/biblio/prose_af/afgan_tragedy_and_glory/index.shtml)

— *Tragedia i doblest Afgana* (Moscow, 2004)

— *Tragedia i doblest Afgana* (Moscow, 2009)

— *Cold War International History Working Paper No. 51: Inside the Soviet Invasion of Afghanistan and the Seizure of Kabul, December 1979*, Woodrow Wilson International Center for Scholars, January 2007

Lyakhovski, A., and Davitaya, S., *Igra v Afganistan* (Moscow, 2009)

Lyakhovski, A., and Nekrasov, V., *Grazhdanin, politik, voin: Pamyati Akhmad Shakha Masuda* (Moscow, 2007)

Maclean, R., *Magic Bus* (London, 2007)

Maiorov, A., *Pravda ob afganskoi voine* (Moscow, 1996)

Manachinski, A., *Afganistan: Kogda Duyut Vetry Voiny* (Kiev, 2006)

Manning, F., *The Middle Parts of Fortune* (London, 2000)

Marvin, C., *The Russian Advance towards India* (originally published 1882; Peshawar, 1984)

Matlock, J., *Reagan and Gorbachev: How the Cold War Ended* (New York, 2004)

Medley, D., and Barrand, J., *Kabul* (Chalfont St Peter, 2003)

Monypenny, W. F., and Buckle, G., *The Life of Benjamin Disraeli, Earl of Beaconsfield*, 6 vols. (London, 1910–20)

Morrison, A., *Russian Rule in Samarkand, 1869–1910: A Comparison with British India* (Oxford, 2008)

Murphy, S., *A Darkness Visible* (London, 2008)

Murrell, G., *Russia's Transition to Democracy* (Brighton 1997)

Neshumov, Yu., *Granitsy Afganistana* (Moscow, 2006)

Newby, E., *A Short Walk in the Hindu Kush* (London, 1974)

Nikiforov, S., *Bez vsyakikh pravil* (St Petersburg, 2008)

Nojumi, N., *The Rise of the Taliban in Afghanistan* (New York, 2002)

Nosatov, V., *Faryabski Dnevnik* (Moscow, 2005)

Odom, W., *The Collapse of the Soviet Military* (New Haven, Conn., 1998)

Ogryzko, V., *Pesni afganskogo pokhoda* (Moscow, 2000)

Olney, W., *'Shiloh' as Seen by a Private Soldier: A Paper Read before California Commandery of the Military Order of the Loyal Legion of the United States, May 31, 1889* (Kessinger Publishing, Whitefish, Mont., 2007)

Osipenko, V., *Privilegia Desanta* (Moscow, 2009)

Plastun, V., and Andrianov, V., *Najibulla. Afghanistan v tiskakh geopolitiki* (Moscow, 1998)

Popova, T., *Pomyani nas, Rossia* (Leningrad Committee of Mothers, Leningrad, 1991)

Prados, J., *Safe for Democracy: The Secret Wars of the CIA* (Chicago, 2006)

Pressfield, S., *The Afghan Campaign* (London, 2007)

Prokhanov, A., *A Tree in the Centre of Kabul* (Moscow, 1983)

— *Afgan* (collected stories) (Moscow, 2008)

— *Tretii tost* (Moscow, 2003)

Rasanaygam, A., *Afghanistan: A Modern History* (London, 2005)

Rashid, A., *Descent into Chaos* (London, 2008)

Robbins, C., *The Ravens: Pilots of the Secret War of Laos* (Bangkok, 2005)

Roy, O., *Islam and Resistance in Afghanistan* (Cambridge, 1986)

Roy, Ya., *Islam in the Soviet Union* (London, 2000)

Rubin, B., *The Fragmentation of Afghanistan* (New Haven, Conn., 2002)

Sakharov, A., *Memoirs* (London, 1990)

Sale, F., *A Journal of the First Afghan War* (Oxford, 2002)

Sanders, V., *The USA and Vietnam 1945–1975* (London, 2002)

Sarin, O., and Dvoretsky, L., *The Afghan Syndrome: The Soviet Union's Vietnam* (Novato, CA, 1993)

Savinkin, A., *Afganskie uroki: Vyvody dlya budushchego v svete ideinogo nasledia A.E. Snesareva* (Moscow, 2003)

Schofield, V., *Afghan Frontier: Feuding and Fighting in Central Asia* (London, 2003)

Sebyakin, L., *Afgan nakanune tragedii* (Moscow, 2009)

— *Afgan v moei Sudbe* (Moscow, 2006)

Seierstad, A., *The Bookseller of Kabul* (London, 2008)

Servan-Schreiber, J.-J., *Lieutenant en Algérie* (Paris, 1957)

Shebarshin, L., *Ruka Moskvy: zapiski nachalnika sovetskoi razvedki* (Moscow, 2002)

Sikorski, R., *Dust of the Saints: A Journey to Herat in Time of War* (New York, 1990)

Slinkin, M., *NDPA u vlasti* (Simferopol, 1999)

— *Voina pered Voinoi* (Moscow, 2008)

Smirnov, O., *Nikto ne sozdan dla voiny* (Moscow, 1990)

Snegirev, V., *Ryzhy* (Moscow, 2000)

Snesarev, A., *Afganistan* (Moscow, 2002)

Snow, J., *Shooting History* (London, 2005)

Stewart, J., *Crimson Snow* (Stroud, 2008)

Stewart, R., *The Places in Between* (London, 2004)

Tamarov, V., *Afghanistan: A Russian Soldier's Story* (Berkeley, CA, 2001)

Tikhonov, Yu., *Afganskaya Voina Stalina* (Moscow, 2008)

Tukharinov, I., *Sekretny komandarm* (http://www.rsva.ru/biblio/prose_af/secret_com/index.shtml)

Urban, M., *War in Afghanistan* (London, 1990)

Van Bladel, J., *The All-Volunteer Force in the Russian Mirror: Transformation without Change* (Groningen, 2004)

Varennikov, V., *Nepovtorimoe*, 7 vols. (Moscow, 2001)

Westad, O., *The Global Cold War* (Cambridge, 2005)

Yermakov, O., *Znak Zverya* (Moscow, 2006)

Yousaf, M., and Adkin, M., *Afghanistan: The Bear Trap* (Barnsley, 1992)

Zaitsev, G., *Alpha – My Destiny* (St Petersburg, 2005)

Zhitnukhin, A., and Lykoshin, S. (compilers), *Zvezda nad gorodom Kabulom* (Moscow, 1990)

ACKNOWLEDGEMENTS

This book could not have been written without the assistance of a great many people who shared their experiences in Afghanistan, put me in touch with knowledgeable friends, gave me books, and read the manuscript in whole or in part.

The late General Alexander Lyakhovski, Vyacheslav Nekrasov, and Alexander Gergel were particularly helpful over several years. Alexander Kartsev regularly commented by email and in our Moscow meetings. He, Alexander Gergel, Artemy Kalinovsky, Svetlana Savranskaya, and Peter Carson read and commented at length on the draft. Svetlana kindly gave permission to use the documents for which she was responsible. Artemy and Svetlana were assiduous in digging out useful documents and giving scholarly advice. Artemy Kalinovsky's doctoral thesis, 'A Long Goodbye: The Politics and Diplomacy of the Soviet Withdrawal from Afghanistan, 1980–1992', is a most distinguished and elegant work of scholarship, which is now being published by Harvard Press as a book. He and I both read Raymond Chandler, and agreed that neither could claim a monopoly of the title. Masha Slonim, Valeri and Galina Ivanov, Valeri Shiryaev, Vladimir Snegirev, Dmitri Ryurikov, and Alexander Gergel corrected passages relating to them.

Rory Stewart generously let me stay in his room in the Turquoise Mountain Foundation during my brief visit to Afghanistan in September 2008. I owe much thanks to him and his colleagues for enabling me to get an indispensable feeling for a remarkable country – especially Hedvig Alexander and Manja Burton, and to Aziz and Zia, who drove me up the Salang Pass and into the Pandsher Valley, where Aziz showed me his home and introduced me to his wife and family.

Many people gave me introductions, interviews, and useful titbits of information: General Viktor Antonenko, General Ruslan Aushev, Yefim Bashan and Natasha Golitsyna, Professor Oleg Bogomolov, Nikolai Bystrov, Anatoli Chernyaev, Marietta Chudakova, Sherard Cowper-Coles, Vladimir Dolgikh, Arkadi Dubnov, Andrei Dyshev, Dmitri Fedorov, Pavel Felgengauer, Pir Said Ahmad Gailani, Antonio Giustozzi, Captain Yuri Gladkevich, Alexander Golts, Mikhail Gorbachev, Andrei Greshnov, Meredith Hooper, Alexandra Ivanova, Major Vyacheslav Izmailov, Peter Joulwan, Ambassador Zamir Kabulov, Sultan Ali Keshtmand, Yevgeni Khrushchev, Yevgeni Kiselev, Frants Klintsevich, Nikolai Komissarov, Alexander Koniev, Viktor Korgun, General Vladimir Kosarev, Aleksei and Tatiana Krol, Colonel Oleg Kulakov, Colonel Ruslan Kyryliuk, Dr Lutfullah Latif, Colonel Mikhail Lavrenenko, Aleksei Makarkin, Rustem Makhmutov, Sher Ahmad Maladani, Jack Matlock, Omid Mojadedi, Igor Morozov, Sergei Morozov, Mohamed Naser Nahez, Boris Pastukhov, Andrei Ponomarev, John Prados, Professor Mikhail Reshetnikov, Natalia Ryurikova, Ismael Saadat, Valeri Shiryaev, Alexander Shkirando, Alla Smolina, Vladimir Snegirev, Thomas Tugendhat, Rustumkhodzha Tursunkulov, Alexander Umnov, the late General Valentin Varennikov, Alexander Vorontsov, Anatoli Yermolin, Boris Zhelezin.

As always, I have relied shamefully on the generous friendship and hospitality of Yuri Senokosov and Lena Nemirovskaya, and the unfailing help of Inna Berezkina.

LIST OF
ILLUSTRATIONS

Black and White

1. (*Top*) Mikhail Gorbachev with Mohamed Najibullah (RIA Novosti)
   (*Bottom*) Eduard Shevardnadze, the Soviet Foreign Minister, signs the Geneva agreements (RIA Novosti)
2. (*Top*) Nur Mohamed Taraki (Itar-TASS)
   (*Bottom*) Leonid Brezhnev greets Babrak Karmal (Itar-TASS)
3. (*Top*) Communist Activists (photograph courtesy of A. Dyshev)
   (*Bottom*) Students at the Kabul Polytechnic (RIA Novosti)
4. Clockwise from top left: Igor Morozov (Author photograph); Sergeant Alexander Gergel (photograph courtesy of A. Gergel); Nikolai Bystrov (Author photograph) and Lieutenant Alexander Kartsev (photograph courtesy of A. Kartsev)
5. (*Top*) The elite troops – parachutists, reconnaissance units and special forces (photograph courtesy of A. Dyshev)
   (*Bottom*) *Dembels* (photograph courtesy of A. Dyshev)
6. (Top) The 860th Regiment medical team (photograph courtesy of A. Smolina)
   (*Bottom*) Two weddings (photograph courtesy of A. Smolina)
7. Action in the mountains (photographs courtesy of A. Dyshev)
8. Summer 1988. Soviet troops withdraw from Jalalabad towards Kabul (photograph by Richard Ellis)

Colour

9. Babur's garden and tomb in 2008 (Author photograph)
10. (*Top*) The Arg (RIA Novosti)
    (*Bottom*) The Taj Bek (Author photograph)
11. (*Top*) Ahmad Shah Masud – the Lion of Pandsher (Sygmus collection, Corbis)
    (*Bottom left*) Sher Ahmad Maladani (Author photograph)
    (Bottom right) Unknown man by the Salang tunnel (Author photograph)
12. (*Top*) Soldiers fighting off an ambush (RIA Novosti)
    (*Bottom*) Soldiers are relaxing on their BMP (RIA Novosti)
13. (*Top*) Mi-24 battle helicopters, called *Crocodiles* (photograph courtesy of Yannick Fournier)
    (*Bottom*) Mi-8 helicopters, called *Bees* (RIA Novosti)
14. Sappers searching for mines (RIA Novosti)
15. A Soviet supply column in the mountains (RIA Novosti)
16. Pandsher Valley, September 2008 (Author photograph)

While every effort has been made to contact copyright-holders of illustrations, the author and publishers would be grateful for information about any illustrations where they have been unable to trace them, and would be glad to make amendments in further editions.

INDEX